THE SOUTH WAS RIGHT!

Free man of color, Henry Brown, from Darlington, South Carolina, sounds the beat for the Confederate army. Like many blacks, Brown willingly served the South during the War for Southern Independence. (Illustration courtesy of Jim Whittington, Shreveport, Louisiana)

THE
SOUTH
WAS
RIGHT!

James Ronald Kennedy
Walter Donald Kennedy

PELICAN PUBLISHING COMPANY
Gretna 1998

Published by Land and Land, 1991
Extensively revised and published by arrangement with the authors by
   Pelican Publishing Company, Inc., 1994

First edition, 1991
Second edition
   First printing, March 1994
   Second printing, July 1994
   Third printing, November 1994
   Fourth printing, June 1995
   Fifth printing, October 1996
   Sixth printing, December 1997
   Seventh printing, August 1998

Library of Congress Cataloging-in-Publication Data

Kennedy, James Ronald
   The South was right! / James Ronald Kennedy, Walter Donald
Kennedy.
      p.   cm.
   Includes bibliographical references (p.) and index.
   ISBN 1-56554-024-7
   1. United States—History—Civil War, 1861-1865—Causes.
2. United States—Politics and government—Civil War, 1861-1865.
3. Secession.   4. Confederate States of America—History.
I. Kennedy, Walter, Donald.   II. Title
E459.K46   1994
973.7'11—dc20   93-30640
                                                         CIP

Manufactured in the United States of America

Published by Pelican Publishing Company, Inc.
P.O. Box 3110, Gretna, Louisiana 70054-3110

Contents

Preface

No other war or event has captivated the imagination of the American public as the events known as the American "Civil War." It is difficult to understand how an event that happened over 130 years ago can still hold such sway over a people. All types of hobbies, including reenacting the actual battles of that war, have grown up around that conflict. Yet when we consider the scope of that war, the numbers killed, the amount of destruction of public and private property, and the fundamental change that the war had on the political, economic, and social condition of America, it is then that we begin to understand why the War for Southern Independence still holds captive the imagination and passions of so many people.

If war is supposed to settle disputes, we can say that the War for Southern Independence was a failure. Today, we cannot even agree on the correct name for that conflict. The cause or causes of the war are still debated with much passion. But the War for Southern Independence did put an end to some disputes, if only for a while. To most Americans schooled in "American" (i.e., New England) history, the war settled the issue of African slavery, but more to the point, it settled the issue of Southern independence, or so we are told.

As children growing up in Mississippi, we would often hear and repeat the old cliche, "The South shall rise again." We never thought that anyone would take that statement seriously, for after all, we were the generation of children whose parents had fought the great patriotic war (World War II) and had positioned America as the foremost world power: And besides, we lived in a world beset by forces of international communism and the threat of nuclear war. The capitalist and the communist empires were competing to see which would rule the world. There was little or no place in that world for secession movements. How could anyone, North or South, ever think that the South would ever rise from the dead?

We who grew up under the threat of a worldwide communist tyranny have lived to see the Berlin Wall come crashing down. We have seen the once mighty and *perpetual* union of the Soviet empire disappear from the world map. We have watched as little nations that were swallowed up by more powerful nations have reappeared on the stage of world events. Nations that had been denied the right of self-determination for generations are now, once again, free and independent states. In reality, secession has broken out worldwide! It looks as if world events have at last caught up with Southern history. For us die-hard Confederates, we feel as if God's vindication is just around the corner.

In view of the events that have shaken our world in the past few years, it is time that we once again look at why the people of the South made the effort to become an independent nation. For after all, if secession is good for Lithuania, Slovenia, and Croatia, why was it not good for Dixie? *The South Was Right!* looks beyond the battles that were fought to discover the answer to the more important questions of why those battles were made necessary, and how the loss of that war has affected not only the South but all of America.

Unless they are without any capacity for reason, the readers of this book can tell by the title that they have fallen into the company of those who believe that the men and women of the South who fought for Southern independence were correct in their efforts. Don't be dismayed. Every cause has its unbreakable defenders. We implore the skeptical to be open-minded enough to investigate the other side of this very unique coin, the War for Southern Independence.

In the spring of 1861, the call to arms went out across the South. The call was answered with enthusiasm. Why did people feel justified to answer that call? Most Americans today are unprepared to answer that question, but how could Southerners, who are possessed with the blood of those who had fought for self-government and independence all across Europe, do otherwise? The answers to those questions will be found in the pages of this book.

You have in your hands a book different from any other book written about the South. The authors demonstrate that the South had legitimate reasons to assert its claim to independence. We demonstrate the legitimacy of the South's claim of our right to recall our delegated powers and to establish a new government based upon the principle of the consent of the governed. We have demonstrated how this right, in addition to having been reserved by the states when they acceded into the Constitutional Union, was based in antiquity and is a part of our common tradition as English-speaking people. We demonstrate how our Southern nation was invaded and conquered by a cruel and ruthless enemy who despised our people. We demonstrate that our Southern history was perverted into a Yankee myth that is now used by our conquerors to justify their cruel oppression of our right to self-determination. This myth is used to brainwash each successive generation of Southern children into believing that we are all better off because we lost our war for Southern independence.

If all this book accomplishes is to bring these historical facts to light, this alone will mark it as most unusual. But it does more; it calls every true Southerner to consider our lot. Is this big, impersonal, overpowering, and dominating government, which demands our obedience to its every decree, the type of government we are happy with? The authors have taken great pains to present to you, the reader, facts about the War for Southern Independence that most Americans have been denied the opportunity to read. This book looks into why the South went to war with such a sense of being right in its beliefs and considers the consequences for the South and for America as a result of the South losing the war.

This book is a call to action to all people who love liberty and truth. It calls upon Southerners to climb down from the "stools of everlasting repentance" and to take pride in their Southern heritage. What we have attempted to do is to awaken in the heart and mind of individual Southerners the repressed desire to once again be the master in their own home! Yes, that is right! We want every Southerner to awaken to the fact that no force on earth can prevent us from reclaiming our lost estate if and when we decide to free ourselves. The South must put aside the illusion that she will one day be accepted as an equal in this Northern-dominated union. The South must put aside the illusion that the current government is the legitimate outgrowth of the original American Constitutional Republic. These illusions are used by our conquerors to bind the South to this unequal union. The South must reject these illusions and then begin its struggle to regain control of its destiny.

So that no one will be mistaken, let us say it once again; as Americans, Southerners have a right to economic equality with the rest of the nation, a right to a government based upon the free and unfettered consent of the governed, a right to control our local schools, a right to order our society according to the desire of the people. In a phrase, we deserve to be *free*! This freedom would be better served by the South as an equal partner within the Union, *but* better out of the Union than not at all!

This book will challenge (and most likely has already done so) many facts that are often accepted as common knowledge. For instance, the Yankee myth that declares that Appomattox settled everything and therefore Southerners must never again attempt to assert our right to a free and constitutional government. While the liberty of the Eastern European people to assert their right to free government is easily approved by the liberal media, this same right is denied the South. What is more important is the fact that as long as Southerners accept this Yankee myth of history, we deny the right of freedom to ourselves, our children, and generations of Southerners yet unborn!

T. E. Lawrence, the famous Lawrence of Arabia, in his book *Seven Pillars of Wisdom*, noted that the effort to free the Arabic people from Turkish rule was accomplished not when the last battle had been won but when the majority of the Arabic people no longer accepted Turkish rule as legitimate. At that point they were free. It only remained for them to stay loyal to their belief in freedom long enough for the struggle to work out the details of when and how the Turks would leave. The same point is true today for us.

This is the message we are sending to our fellow Southerners. You are not free, because you do not believe you can be free. You are not free, because you do not believe in yourself. As the Holy Bible states, "Where there is no vision the people perish." It is time for Southerners to catch that vision of freedom our Confederate forefathers had and to begin the struggle to turn a dream into reality. The rising of the moon will see a return of government as established by the Original Constitution or if we cannot convince our Northern neighbors to reform this current, overgrown, and unresponsive government of their making, then we shall work for the re-establishment of a Constitutional Republic known as the Confederate States of America!

Not since the end of the War for Southern Independence has such a dramatic challenge been issued to the American people. The struggle our Confederate forefathers made in the 1860s is not over. The principles of local self-government and State's Rights are viable and necessary in today's otherwise impersonal world. The South has always been the eternal enemy of big government. This is what motivated Southerners to take up arms in defense of Dixie in 1861. There must be a radical reformation in the current, overgrown, unresponsive, tax-and-spend federal government. If those who are in control of the government in Washington reject the demands of the people for a government more respectful of our rights, then it will be faced with the prospect of the Southern people following the lead of Lithuania as we demand the right of self-determination.

Deo Vindice

THE SOUTH WAS RIGHT!

John J. Sitton, Oregon County, Missouri, served with the Fourth Arkansas Infantry and the Second Infantry Regiment, Seventh Division, Missouri State Guard, C.S.A. Sitton was fifteen years old when he volunteered to defend his country. (Image courtesy of J. Dale West, Longview, Texas)

CHAPTER 1

The Yankee Myth of History

> What passes as standard American history is really Yankee history written by New Englanders or their puppets to glorify Yankee heroes and ideals.
>
> Dr. Grady McWhiney[1]

INTRODUCTORY COMMENTS

There are still those of us who can recall the days when the playing of "Dixie" at football games and at the close of the radio broadcast day was commonplace. We can remember when all of the fans in the stadium would jump to their feet and cheer at the playing of our Southern national anthem. What has happened?

Michael Grissom, author of *Southern by the Grace of God*, points out that it was not only the federal government that outlawed the playing of "Dixie" but also weak, spineless, Southern politicians who contributed to its demise.[2] But more to the point—Southerners who have been subjected to generations of Yankee brainwashing have become too docile to stand up for their own rights!

How has this occurred? How is it that the very descendants of the greatest fighting force ever to march have become too cowardly to stand up for their own rights? The answer is to be found in this chapter. You will see that our leaders, beginning with President Jefferson Davis and continuing with the leaders of subsequent generations, have warned our people of the danger of allowing Yankees to teach their history to our children. The consequence of allowing Southerners to grow up never having been taught the truth about our history leaves the current generation unprepared to assert its rightful claim to constitutional government.

The Yankee Myth of History

All political systems have a myth that justifies their existence. A Marxist system can justify any amount of repression as long as its

15

people believe in the myth of the eventuality of the evolution of the dictatorship of the proletariat. A system's belief in an idea can be used to control the thinking of its subjects. All arguments used to justify the existence of the state are based upon and measured against the prevailing myth which expresses the deep inclinations of the society to which it belongs. Without the myth, the state's subjects would not submit to the system's repressive rule.

Today, there are two primary foundations for myths: science and history. The propagandists (be they newscasters, newspaper editors, educators, ministers, or any other liberal "wordsmiths") use society's myths to ensure that the majority of citizens remain loyal to the established order.

It is a well-known maxim of war that "to the victor go the spoils." The victor in the War for Southern Independence has claimed, as part of his spoils, the right to record and enforce his point of view as the official and accepted history of the war. Regardless of how insidious a particular instance of persecution, destruction, theft of personal property, oppression of civil liberties, or destruction of constitutional safeguards may be, the Yankee invader justifies these measures as necessary to maintain the Union (a myth), to free the slaves (a myth), or to maintain the legitimate national government (a myth). Our acceptance of the Yankee myth relieves him of the necessity of defending his heinous crimes against the Southern people.

Imperialist powers attempt to force the conquered population to accept the imperial myth.[3] Once this has been accomplished, the population becomes pacified within a few short generations. Then the danger of an insurrection or challenge to the empire is reduced to almost zero. In spite of this diminished threat, truth has a mystical power of its own. Though crushed, like the conquered nation, truth still resides in the public memory and will inevitably re-assert itself with a vengeance.

Southern history, as taught in our public and private schools today, is nothing more than a recitation of the North's justification for invasion, conquest, and oppression of the Southern people. A Southerner who is never made aware of any writings other than those accepted histories taught in Southern classrooms will come away convinced of the righteousness of the Northern cause and with a feeling that the South is "better off because we lost the war"! What a masterpiece of effective propaganda—to have the children of the conquered nation call the invaders "blessed"!

President Jefferson Davis predicted that if the South lost the war, the North would write its history.[4] He knew that the Yankee invaders would attempt to crush the truth to hide their many crimes against the Southern people. He was afraid that future generations would never understand the righteousness of the South's call for independence. His prediction has sadly become reality in classrooms all across the South.

Many of the former leaders of the Confederacy warned against the domination of Yankee history. Varina Davis decried the "startling absence of truth and fact in many of the tales that stand forth as history."[5] In 1889, when the Sons of Confederate Veterans was formed, Gen. Stephen D. Lee gave as part of the commission to the Sons, "It is your duty to see that the true history of the South is presented to future generations."[6] Already those remaining and aging gray troopers could see their honor and loyalty to principles of constitutional liberties being sacrificed to the gods of the Yankee empire. For almost thirty years after the war, many of these men dedicated themselves to writing the Southern Apologia. These men wrote with passionate intensity. They did not write for profit. They knew that few in the South could afford the money or the time for leisurely reading. They wrote in the hope that others yet to come would read and understand. They wrote in defiance of their conquerors who were flushed with victory and full of self-righteousness. Admiral Raphael Semmes, CSS *Alabama*, wrote in his book, *Memoirs of Service Afloat*, that he did not anticipate that Northerners would read his book because "men do not willingly read unpalatable truths of themselves. The people . . . like those best who fool them most, by pandering to their vices and flattering their foibles."[7]

In 1894, J. L. M. Curry, an Alabama educator, became so alarmed at the universal portrayal of the South in the role of a criminal in United States history that he wrote *The Southern States of the American Union*. He complained that "History as written if accepted in future years will consign the South to infamy."[8] Again and again the post-war Confederates sounded this alarm concerning the lack of objectivity in the official and gradually accepted history of the Southern people. If the Northern propagandists could maintain their control and wait for these deposed leaders to die, they could stamp out forever the cries of Southern patriots.

Fortunately for us, a few unreconstructed Southerners remained in each succeeding generation. Shortly after World War I, the Sons of Confederate Veterans felt compelled to issue a defense of the Southern cause. It was a bitter shock to these men, after great effort to demonstrate their loyalty to the "reunited nation" (especially by the shedding of Southern blood in the Spanish-American War and World War I), to find themselves compelled yet again to defend the South from Northern slander. In the introduction to *The Gray Book*, A. H. Jennings, chairman of *The Gray Book* committee, complained of the continuing attacks upon the South and described *The Gray Book* as an attempt to defend "the truth of history."[9] Implicit in his statement is the fact that the South was being slandered by the Northern myth of history (i.e., that the accepted national history was neither accurate nor fair in its representation of the South).

Jennings continued his defense of the South by declaring that:

> These attacks and untruthful presentations of so-called history demand refutation, for the South cannot surrender its birthright and we pray the day may never dawn when it will be willing to abandon the truth in a cowardly or sluggish spirit of pacifism. During the Great War [World War I], when the South and all other parts of our country were straining every nerve to defeat a common foe, strange and unbelievable as it may seem at such a time of crisis, there was a most remarkable flood of misrepresentations, false analogy, and distorted historical statements concerning our American history as it particularly relates to the Southern people. Ignorance, as well as deliberate distortion of facts, contributed to this. Innumerable examples are on file and could be quoted but no one who reads at all could have failed to note this mass of unfair and untruthful statements which for years has filled newspapers, magazines and periodicals of the North. Nor has this defamation ceased—it still goes on, unabated, and there is a constant and strong stream of misrepresentation and false historical statement flowing from the North ... false history almost overwhelms us.[10]

In *The Gray Book* we see an example of Southerners two or three generations removed from the War for Southern Independence still complaining against the evil of the North writing Southern history, just as President Davis had warned us. Perhaps some of our opponents would claim that the post-war Confederates were only suffering from "sour grapes" or were "poor losers." But how would they explain away the fact that the Sons of Confederate Veterans felt compelled to issue this defense of the Southern people? If the North were so righteous in its defense of the Union, why has it continued to issue slanderous lies about our history? Why has it continued its slander long after the generations who could remember the sting of battle have passed? Could it be that the North has a political agenda that requires the existence of a myth to justify its continued oppression of the Southern people? The lies and slander must continue; if they ceased, the legitimacy of Northern domination of the Southern people would come under close scrutiny.

I'll Take My Stand was published in 1930. In this book, twelve Southerners defended the South and its agrarian tradition. Frank L. Owsley contributed a section titled "The Irrepressible Conflict."[11] Owsley pointed out that, after the South had been conquered by armed aggression and humiliated and impoverished by peace (Reconstruction), there began a second war in which the North attempted to destroy the spirit of the Southern people. It was a deliberate attempt to reshape the thoughts of the Southern people so that they would conform to Northern standards. Northerners attempted to recast every opinion opposed to the North's myths, to impose Northern ways upon the Southern people, to

> . . . write error across the pages of Southern history which were out of keeping with the Northern legend, and set the rising and unborn generations upon stools of everlasting repentance . . . the rising generations were to receive the proper education in Northern tradition. . . . The rising generations read Northern literature, shot through with the New England tradition. Northern textbooks were used in Southern schools; Northern histories, despite the frantic protests of local patriotic organizations, were almost universally taught in Southern high schools and colleges,—books that were built around the Northern legend and either completely ignored the South or insisted upon the unrighteousness of most of its history. . . . There was for the Southern child very little choice. They had to accept the Northern version of history with all its condemnations and carping criticisms of Southern institutions and life. . . . Lincoln was the real Southern hero because Lincoln had saved the Union. So they were told![12]

Notice how Owsley complained about the insistence of the North that Southerners accept what he called "the Northern legend."[13] Owsley recognized that this Northern legend or myth was the vehicle that the North used to condition each generation of Southerners so that we would dutifully occupy our assigned position upon what he referred to as the "stools of everlasting repentance."[14] Owsley recognized what Jennings, et al., in *The Gray Book* failed to see. Regardless of how loyal the South remained to what Jennings called "our reunited country," no matter how much Southern blood was spilled in foreign wars while fighting under the flag of our "reunited country," the North had no intention of ever allowing Southerners to climb down from their assigned place upon the "stools of everlasting repentance"!

In 1949 the Louisiana State University Press published *Plain Folk of the Old South* by Frank L. Owsley. Here Owsley demonstrated the error in the accepted history of the Southern people. The official history of our people (the history adopted by the Northern publishers who supply our textbooks) claimed that the pre-war South was populated by rich plantation owners, poor whites, and slaves. A Yankee, Frederick Law Olmsted, was the primary proponent of this view of Southern society. Frank Owsley noted that the Yankee Olmsted had the "unusual skill in the art of reporting detail and of completely wiping out the validity of such detail by subjective comments and generalizations."[15] Olmsted's view of the South is important because he went on to identify slavery as the primary source of the miserable condition of the poor whites. He even claimed that Negroes in the North lived better than the average Southerner. Owsley pointed out that other Northern writers had little or no first-hand knowledge of the South and relied instead on the writings of the Yankee Olmsted. An example of the error in Olmsted's assessment of the pre-war South is evidenced when one of the farmers he described as living in poverty actually owned a thousand acres of land and more hogs and cattle than he could count! As a traveler through the area, Olmsted had no idea of property boundaries and did not realize that the farmer's livestock were tending themselves on the open range and were hidden from a casual observer.[16]

The main difference between these two men's views of the South arises from the Yankee Olmsted's analysis of Southern society from the vantage point of Yankee commercialism (i.e., his was an economic view of society). Those who have read pre-war Southern accounts of Northerners are aware that our people often complained of the Yankee mindset as being one of materialistic "money-grubbing." As a Southerner, Owsley was able to evaluate our society using our own standards. He analyzed the pre-war South not from the point of view of economics but from the vantage point of culture. He discovered that the larger part of the "plain folk" (those white Southerners who were not a part of the plantation system) were not class conscious, and they were not in open competition with the larger planters for land or resources. The plain folk enjoyed political, social, and economic independence. But note the difference in his view of "money-grubbing." "Relatively few of the plain folk, however, seem to have had a desire to become wealthy."[17] Their contempt for materialism was a natural part of the cultural heritage of the Celtic people from which the majority of them sprang. This contempt of wealth was a major factor in the true assessment of Southern society, a factor that the Yankee mind refused to understand and therefore would not include in its narrow, self-serving evaluation of Southern society.

Owsley noted further that very few of the plain folk were wealthy, and even fewer were poor enough to suffer want. They were a cordial and hospitable people who enjoyed life. They even had a system of social security whereby they shared work when a member of society became ill or injured. The conditional granting of land was one method used by Southern folk to provide for social security.[18]

The Yankee myth-makers would have us believe that the South was a poor and backward area prior to the war. The facts tell a different story. For example, in 1860, if the South had been an independent nation her economy would have ranked as the third largest on the European and American continents.[19] The purchase of advanced farming implements in the South was twenty-five percent higher than in the North.[20] The South had thirty-three percent of the nation's railroad mileage plus navigable streams that did not freeze, and direct coastal access to the ocean in most of the Southern states.[21] The South was behind the North in per capita railroad mileage but still ahead of every other nation in the world.[22] According to the 1860 census, the South had a per capita income ten percent higher than all states west of New York and Pennsylvania.[23] (Could it be that the New England states were rich as a result of their illicit trade in human flesh—the slave trade?)

The important point for Southerners to remember is that our history has been distorted by our enemies. Whether this was done deliberately (as claimed by Davis, Jennings, et al.) or as a natural result of strangers using their own standards to evaluate a different society, the point is made that Southern history has been perverted to injure us regardless of the motive or causative factors.

An example of how the Yankee myth of history is used consciously or unconsciously to degrade our opinions about the South is in order here. Let us examine a very well-known and popular book on the "Civil War" entitled *Picture History of the Civil War* by the Pulitzer Prize-winning historian Bruce Catton. Naturally any book that treats the subject of the "Civil War" is obliged to give some background to that epic struggle. On page 25 we find the author's background information on the South. The page is captioned "A Static South Lags Behind." On page 20 of Catton's book, we find his glowing caption, "The Growing West Adds New Strength to the North." In his description of the South, Catton quotes from none other than the Yankee Olmsted. Catton tells his readers—true to the Olmsted model—that the plantation South was a "facade" which concealed another South of poor whites, and he goes on to state that "the citizens of the cotton states, as a whole, are poor."[24] The average Southerner will not have the opportunity to read the Apologia or any other pro-Southern books. When a Southerner picks up a book like the one Catton wrote and reads his view of Southern society, what will be the result? The result will be an acceptance of the Yankee myth of history—to the detriment of any hope for the Southern people to regain our lost rights and dignity.

As might be expected, the works of the Southerner Owsley (unlike those of the Yankee Olmsted) have been largely ignored by the Yankee myth-makers. Dr. Grady McWhiney, professor of history at Texas Christian University, noted that Owsley's "defense of southern and agrarian ways combined with his attempt to protect the South's history from distortion brought down upon him the full wrath of many nationalistic historians." He added, "But none of his critics has been able to refute Owsley's basic theme of an Old

South culturally dominated by plain folk whose ways were quite distinctive from those of Northerners."[25]

John Gould Fletcher was also one of the twelve Southerners who contributed to *I'll Take My Stand.* He noted the attempt of the conquerors to imprint their view of history on the minds of Southern youth. He noted that, at a national convention of teachers in Pennsylvania in August 1865, they declared that the late conflict had been "a war of education and patriotism against ignorance and barbarism."[26]

In the mid 1950s the Sons of Confederate Veterans found it necessary to re-issue *The Gray Book*, "in the interest of truth." The preface notes:

> Falsehood is still spewed forth in the United States. . . . It is hoped that this re-published book may serve to inform those who wish to know the facts and to shame those who still wish to spread falsehood and engage in the defamation.[27]

In 1988, The University of Alabama Press published *Cracker Culture: Celtic Ways in the Old South* by Dr. Grady McWhiney. Professor McWhiney again challenged the accepted Northern history of the Southern people. He demonstrated the importance of Celtic culture in Southern society. He noted that Southerners were different from their Yankee counterparts in that our society was leisure-oriented and dominated by a system of open-range grazing with support from low-intensity crop cultivation. This stood in contrast to the money-grubbing Yankee culture that patterned its culture after the English (Anglo-Saxon) culture which insisted upon high-intensity cultivation and valued hard work and economic profit.

Dr. McWhiney wrote that the War for Southern Independence was not so much a war of brother against brother as it was a war of culture against culture. Dramatic as this observation is, it is not a new one. Anthony Trollope, a British citizen who traveled extensively in the North and South during the first part of the war, made a similar observation:

> The South is seceding from the North because the two are not homogeneous. They have different instincts, different appetites, different morals, and a different culture.[28]

Trollope observed that, other than language, there was very little that the two sections held in common:

> They [the South] had become a separate people, dissevered
> from the North by habits, morals, institutions, pursuits, and
> every conceivable differences in their modes of thought and
> action. They still spoke the same language, as do Austria and
> Prussia; but beyond that tie of language they had no bond but
> that of a meagre political union. . . . [29]

The influence of the various cultures that populated Colonial
America has been documented by David Hacket Fisher in his book
Albion's Seed. Fisher, a Northerner, demonstrates the four primary
emigration patterns originating in the British Isles. The various
cultural distinctions of these peoples which he documents influenced such social behavior as dietary preferences, mode of dress,
and religious attitudes.[30] The early emigration patterns to the
South came principally from North Britain (Northern England
and Scotland), Northern Ireland, and the Saxon areas of South
England.[31] The New England colonies received more emigrants
from the traditionally English, East Anglia (Puritans),[32] and the
middle colonies received the bulk of Quakers from the North Midlands of England.[33] Thus the cultural differences between the
North and the South originated in the British Isles. The people
who came to this continent did not forsake their ancient folkways,
attitudes, and grudges, but adapted them to the new environment.

John Adams of Massachusetts, while attending the Continental
Congress, wrote home to his wife describing the stark dissimilarity
between the two peoples of the Northern and Southern colonies.
He confided to his wife his impression that these two peoples were
so different that the political union could not be held together
"without the utmost caution on both sides."[34]

The cultural differences between the colonial peoples were also
described by George Mason of Virginia while warning of the inherent dangers in the proposed Constitution. He noted that this
was an extensive country, "containing inhabitants so very different
in manners, habits, and customs."

Thus we have the evaluation of the cultural differences between
the North and the South made in colonial times by one of the
Founding Fathers, a Virginia Anti-Federalist, an evaluation made
at the time of the war by a foreign observer and two contempora-
neous scholars, one from the North and one from the South. No-

tice that regardless of the time frame or their origins, all four described the North and South as culturally different and as distinct peoples.

McWhiney warns his readers that, in order to understand why Northerners and Southerners are so different, we will have to "put aside some myths."[35] He warns us that what we will be reading will be in contrast to both common knowledge and scholars. He goes on to inform us that "both common wisdom and scholars are wrong."[36] Again we see Southerners willing to place their reputations as academicians on the line in order to correct the inaccuracies in the official and accepted Northern history of our people.

Another book appeared in 1988. Its title left no question in the mind of the reader about its author's feelings. The book is *Southern by the Grace of God* by Michael A. Grissom. In the preface to his book, Grissom laments the fact that the South has been treated so unfairly in the official recordings of history:

> It has been a continuing source of disappointment to see traditional heroes, values, and examples of valor culled every year from southern history texts. Today, virtually every school system in the South is equipped with American history books produced in the North by Northern authors. We definitely have a problem when children in the South are raised on the fables of "Honest Abe" while they're taught that their own forebears were the villains of our country's history.[37]

We have now heard evidence, beginning with the words of President Jefferson Davis and continuing with the voices of generation after generation of Southerners, lamenting the falsehoods, slander, and perversion of our history. We have seen that the myth of Yankee moral superiority has been used to demoralize each new generation of Southerners. We have seen how the myth, once put in place, continues to perform its function of justifying Northern aggression, exploitation, domination, and in a word, tyranny. Most of those who accept the myth do so in complete honesty. We are not alleging a secret conspiracy among politicians and wordsmiths. The myth, once accepted by society, is the perfect propaganda weapon. It needs no defense. Indeed those who dare to challenge the myth will meet with a fate almost as final as those accused of religious heresy during the Middle Ages, or, more accurately, the fate of Galileo during the Scientific Revolution.

This section would not be complete without a few words dedicated to some of the most important aspects of the Yankee myth of history. Therefore we will discuss several of the more common and onerous Yankee myths.

YANKEE MYTH
Lincoln the Emancipator,
Humanitarian, and Protector of Liberty

If you want proof of just how successful the Yankee myth has been, just go into a Southern classroom. On the wall you will very likely find a picture of Abraham Lincoln. Inquire of the history teacher and you will find out that somewhere in their education Southern students are required to study if not to memorize Lincoln's Gettysburg Address. Now ask the teacher, "Where is your picture of President Jefferson Davis?" Now ask when these Southern children will read or study President Davis' farewell address to the U.S. Senate or his inaugural address as president of the Confederate States of America. Let's face it—you don't have to go through this exercise—you already know the answers!

The truth is that most of the teachers who teach our children about the "Great Emancipator" have never read the proclamation! If they did, they would find out that it was a self-styled war measure. Its purpose was to drape the invasion of the Southern nation in the robes of morality. It was an effective propaganda ploy to influence England and France not to recognize the Southern nation and was also an attempt to encourage slave insurrection in the South. The truth is that Lincoln's so-called Emancipation Proclamation was not designed to free slaves. A reading of the proclamation will show that Lincoln declared free those slaves who were held "within any State or designated part of a State the people whereof shall then be in rebellion against the United States."[38] In other words, he declared free those slaves over whom he had no control. But what about those slaves within states or portions thereof in which Lincoln had control and supposedly could have declared free? Not a word is said about these slaves. Indeed the six parishes of Louisiana that were at that time under Yankee control were specifically *excluded* from this great document of freedom, as were the forty-eight counties designated as West Virginia! The proclamation states that these excepted areas are "left precisely as if this proclamation were not issued."[39] For the Lincoln-lovers and other skeptics, we remind you that the Yankee general Ulysses S. Grant's wife held personal slaves at the beginning of the war. *The Gray Book* reveals that Grant's slaves were freed, not by Lincoln's proclamation, but by the Thirteenth Amendment passed after the end of the war.[40] According to *The Gray Book*, Grant's excuse for not freeing his slaves was that, "good help is so hard to come by these days." Be that as it may, a reading of the proclamation will demonstrate that Lincoln declared free those slaves he had no power to free, and he left in bondage those that he could have set free! So much for the myth of Lincoln as the great emancipator.

Yankee myth tells us about Honest Abe, the great humanitarian. Yet, when we look at the record, we find that instead of a humanitarian we find someone guilty of the two unforgivable sins of modern times—a belief in white supremacy and a belief in a system of apartheid!

Lincoln's white supremacist ideas are a well-kept secret. (Let it be known at this point that these views are Lincoln's and not the opinions of the authors.) In an 1858 debate Lincoln made the following statements:

> I will say, then, that I am not, nor ever have been, in favor of bringing about in anyway the social and political equality of the white and black races—that I am not, nor ever have been, in favor of making voters or jurors of negroes, nor of qualifying them to hold office, nor to intermarry with white people; and I will say in addition to this that there is a physical difference between the white and black races. . . . I, as much as any other man, am in favor of having the superior position assigned to the white race.[41]

We all know that the surest way to prevent a Southerner from holding a federal court position is for the candidate to be accused of having held white supremacist convictions. Even though the candidate may protest that these were views commonly held at that time and that he or she has since changed viewpoints, it will make little difference to the mob of liberals circling for a Haynesworth or a Bork feeding frenzy. Yet, when the reality of Lincoln the white supremacist is presented, we can expect the myth-makers to declare that it was not uncommon at the time. So Honest Abe joins the ranks of the Skin-Heads!

Another sin for which the liberal press has no tolerance is support for apartheid. How shocking it is to learn that Lincoln was planning a system of geographical separation similar to that which has been practiced in South Africa. Again, in a debate with Stephen A. Douglas, Lincoln made the following comments:

> Such separation if effected at all, must be effected by colonization: . . . what colonization most needs is a hearty will. . . . Let us be brought to believe that it is morally right, and at the same time favorable to, or at least not against, our interests to transfer the African to his native clime, and we shall find a way to do it, however great the task may be.[42]

Again allow the authors to explain that we have quoted Lincoln's personal view on white supremacy and geographical separation not in an effort to encourage said views but to demonstrate the difference between Yankee myth and reality.

Now let us look at the Yankee myth of Lincoln the protector of liberty. The dictatorial power of Lincoln is evidenced when he suspended the writ of habeas corpus and then moved to silence his critics in the North not in the South. (At that time Southerners were governed by one who was governing with the consent of the governed—what a novel idea! Perhaps we should try it again.) Some writers place the number of Lincoln's political prisoners as high as forty thousand. They were held indefinitely, without knowing what, if any, charges were brought against them and without receiving bail or the services of an attorney. Indeed, many of their families did not even know where they were. More than three hundred newspapers and journals were shut down by executive order. A member of Lincoln's Cabinet had a bell on his desk about which the secretary would brag that he could send any American to prison just by ringing that bell! It was with no small amount of contempt that the *Raleigh* (NC) *News and Observer* wrote some time after the war that, even though the Confederate government was new at the time and faced with invasion, "It is to the honor of the Confederate government that no Confederate secretary ever could touch a bell and send a citizen to prison."[43]

Now let us examine how the dictator Lincoln used his powers to illegally imprison people he hated. A short summary is offered of the fate of Capt. Robert Tansill, U.S. Marine Corps. Captain Tansill served aboard the USS *Congress* when he read Lincoln's inaugural address in 1861. It convinced him that it was time to resign his commission. He presented his letter to Secretary of the Navy Gideon Welles who refused to accept his resignation and dismissed him on the spot (you can't quit—I fire you). That same evening, Captain Tansill was arrested and sent to jail at Fort Lafayette. Captain Tansill wrote letters to Lincoln desiring to know the charges for which he was being held, but to no avail. At last Captain Tansill's wife asked for an interview with the Northern leader. After great effort she finally got an audience with the president. The following is a small portion of her own account:

> He spoke, still looking me full in the face, "I did receive that letter and it has got all the answer it will have." Mr. President, I said, you are aware of the circumstances under which my husband was arrested—of his having just returned from sea after an absence of two years from his family and of his being hurried off like a common felon to prison, without giving him any reason for it. Was it, I asked Sir, for any other reason than his having resigned? His face then turned perfectly livid. He jumped up from the table at which he was sitting, and brought his clenched hand down hard upon it with an oath. . . . He began to walk the room in violent excitement, stamping his feet, and averting his head from me. . . . Mr. Lincoln, you understand, I hope that the only object of my call upon you was to ask if my husband's letter had reached you, and I have received my answer! "You have most positively!" was his reply, with head turned from me. I took my little son by the hand, and closed the door, and thus shut away from my sight, I trust for evermore, the greatest despot and tyrant that ever ruled a nation.[44]

Let us now review an example of how Lincoln used his office to reward men who were conducting a campaign of terrorism against the Southern civilian population. The Southern people were forced to endure innumerable acts of rape, robbery, pillage, and plundering, all at the hands of United States military personnel. These acts were well known in Washington, yet the crimes continued throughout Lincoln's presidency. More detail regarding the terrorist acts of Lincoln's army of invasion are dealt with in Chapter 4, "Yankee Atrocities," and Chapter 13, "The Yankee Campaign of Cultural Genocide."

If Lincoln had been a truly compassionate human being, then he would have tried to prevent this needless human suffering, even the suffering of those who opposed his government's policy of armed aggression. We are speaking of "needless" suffering; we are not speaking of accidental civilian casualties as a result of war. We are speaking of intentional crimes committed by United States forces against civilians held to be enemies of the Federal Union. Such acts were committed by Colonel John B. Turchin.

Colonel Turchin commanded the Eight Brigade, Third Division, of the Army of the Ohio. His command included the Nineteenth Illinois, Twenty-Fourth Illinois, Thirty-Seventh Indiana, and Eighteenth Ohio.[45]

Colonel's Turchin's activities came under question early on in the war. On July 16, 1861, Brig. Gen. Stephen A. Hurlbut, commanding Headquarters Brigade, Illinois Militia, Quincy, Illinois, notified Colonel Turchin of the Nineteenth Illinois that some of his troops "violated private rights of property and of persons. . . ."[46]

The next year, on June 30, 1862, Maj. Gen. Ormsby M. Mitchel informed Gen. Don Carlos Buell, commander of the Army of the Ohio, that "The pillage of the town of Athens [Alabama] by the troops under the command of colonel Turchin is a matter of general notoriety."[47] General Buell issued orders to have Colonel Turchin court-martialed.

On August 6, 1862, General Buell published the findings of the court-martial against Turchin:

> "[He] allowed his command to disperse and in his presence or with his knowledge and that of his officers to plunder and pillage the inhabitants. . . . they attempted an indecent outrage on a servant girl . . . destroyed a stock of . . . fine Bibles and Testaments. . . . Defaced, and kicked about the floor and trampled under foot. . . . A part of the brigade went to the plantation . . . and quartered in the negro huts for weeks, debauching the females. . . . Mrs. Hollingsworth's house was entered and plundered. . . . The alarm and excitement occasioned miscarriage and subsequently her death. . . . Several soldiers . . . committed rape on the person of a colored girl. . . . The court finds the accused [guilty as charged] . . . and does therefore sentence. . . Colonel J.B. Turchin . . . to be dismissed from the service of the United States. . . . It is a fact of sufficient notoriety that similar disorders . . . have marked the course of Colonel Turchin's command wherever it has gone.[48]

The court-martial of a ranking officer was not done overnight or in secret. As we will demonstrate in a later chapter, the officials in Washington were aware of the crimes being committed by their military personnel in the name of the United States. Yet even though Colonel Turchin was under court-martial for horrible crimes against innocent civilians and subsequently found guilty, President Lincoln promoted Colonel Turchin to the rank of Brigadier General of the United States Volunteers on August 5, 1862![49] Turchin accepted his gift from Lincoln on September 1, 1862, and continued his service to the United States in its war of aggression against the Southern nation until October 4, 1864.

Yankee mythology portrays Lincoln as a compassionate fighter for human rights and liberty. It tells us that he was a man full of love and emotions of tender mercies directed toward the downtrodden, the enslaved, the weak and defenseless masses of mankind. Yet Lincoln, the Northern president, has the dubious distinction of being the only American president who personally ordered the mass execution of Americans whose guilt could not be positively determined! Not only did Lincoln order their execution but he personally participated in the selection of the victims![50]

In 1862 several tribes of Native Americans revolted against the cruel policies of the United States government. General John Pope was sent to Minnesota to put down the uprising. After the end of hostilities, Pope sent a message to Lincoln that, after a trial, he had ordered more than three hundred warriors executed by hanging. The whites of Minnesota were clamoring for the execution of the Indians. Lincoln knew that the "trial" had been a sham, but he also knew that he needed the white votes from Minnesota. His "political" comprise was to make a blood offering to the whites in Minnesota. As a token to appease the whites, Lincoln selected thirty-nine Indian prisoners to be executed. Lincoln carried Minnesota in the next election, but the price was paid by Native Americans. Lincoln is America's only president to order a mass execution!

A man of compassion would not release a monster to prey upon innocent women and children; a humanitarian would not allow a convicted criminal to control military forces in an occupied country; a man who believed in charity for all and malice toward none would not release a convicted terrorist and compound the release by re-hiring the terrorist to make war against his enemies; a man of tender mercies would not select victims for mass execution. These facts prove that Lincoln was not a man of compassion.

Remember that this is the same Lincoln whose picture hangs in almost every Southern classroom, the same Lincoln our children are taught to worship, and the same Lincoln who has been deified by Yankee mythology.

The important point to remember is not whether Southern children learn the Gettysburg Address, but that the myth of Yankee history does not allow us to question its gods. If we begin to inquire on one point, who knows what points we may ask about tomorrow! These facts about Lincoln have been presented in an effort to demonstrate just how strong and universally accepted the Yankee myth of history is and how shocking the truth about that myth can be.

YANKEE MYTH

The North Fought the War
to Save the American Constitutional Union

The forces of Northern aggression had to hide their real objectives for conducting the war. Their main concern was that the rest of the world might look with sympathy upon the Southerners as they struggled against their giant Northern adversary and that they might offer official recognition to Jefferson Davis' Confederate government. As we have already seen, the myth of freedom for the slaves was a key war measure used by the Lincoln administration to influence world opinion. The myth that the North was attempting to save the American government was and still is another key myth. Those superficial individuals who accept the Yankee myth of history without question find it very easy to accept the allegation that Lincoln and the North were fighting to maintain the American Union. We must note that the Yankee myth *alleges* that they were fighting to maintain the Union. But as Southerners we must make the distinction that preserving the geographical boundary in which the central government of the United States exercises its authority and maintaining the voluntary union of Sovereign American states within a constitutional framework are quite different concepts. This is the point that Southerners have been forced to ignore for more than 125 years. Yes, the North did maintain the authority of the central government over the South-

ern states. Yet this very act changed that authority from one arising from consent, a bargained exchange between equals, into one
of conquest! Yes, superficially the North did maintain the Union.
But are we discussing real estate or principles of free government?
Are we discussing geographical boundary lines, or are we discussing concepts such as the free and unfettered consent of the governed?

Many Unionists like to quote President Andrew Jackson's words,
"The Federal Union—It must be preserved." Yet few quote from
Jackson's later explanation that the Union could not be preserved
by force. Why? Because the Union he referred to was a voluntary
union, and force, which precludes volition, would in and of itself
destroy the very thing it was supposed to be preserving. C. C.
Burr, editor of Judge Upshur's book, *The Federal Government: Its
True Nature and Character*, noted:

> The name of our federation is not Consolidated States, but
> United States. A number of States held together by coercion,
> or the point of the bayonet, would not be a Union. Union is
> necessarily voluntary—the act of choice, free association. Nor
> can this voluntary system be changed to one of force without
> the destruction of "The Union". The Austrian Empire is com-
> posed of several States, as the Hungarians, the Poles, the Ital-
> ians, etc, but it cannot be called a Union—it is Despotism. Is
> the relation between Russia and bayonet held Poland a Union?
> Is it not an insult and a mockery to call the compulsory rela-
> tion between England and Ireland a Union? In all these cases
> there is only such a union as exist between the talons of the
> hawk and the dove, or between the jaws of the wolf and the
> lamb. A Union of States necessarily implies separate sover-
> eignties, voluntarily acting together. And to bruise these dis-
> tinct sovereignties into one mass of power is, simply, to destroy
> the Union—to overthrow our system of government.[51]

In the first chapter of his book, *Southern History of the War*, Edward
A. Pollard explains the Yankee myth of the perpetual union. The
concept of perpetual union does have an American historical pre-
cedent. The Articles of Confederation, the government that preceded the original Constitutional Republic, did have a clause in its
preamble stating that the Articles of Confederation was establishing a perpetual union! What happened to this perpetual union?
Well, believe it or not, each state seceded from it, dissolved that

union, and established a new union among only those states that subsequently ratified the Constitution. Try as hard as they might, the Unionists have never been able to discover similar language — perpetual union — in the United States Constitution. We might say that the guarantee of a perpetual union is conspicuous by its absence. The Founding Fathers made the mistake of guaranteeing one perpetual union that did not work out, and they were not going to make the same mistake again! So much for the myth of the necessity for a righteous crusade to save the Holy Union. The North fought the war to save its empire. This empire was built upon the ashes of our Southern nation, our freedom, our economic security, and our well-being as a people.

YANKEE MYTH

The South Fought the War to Preserve Slavery

When discussing the motives for fighting the War for Southern Independence (of course, the myth-makers insist upon the incorrect term "Civil War"), the Yankee myth-makers have assigned virtue to the North and vice to the South. One of their favorite myths is to assert that Southerners were fighting to keep people in slavery. This lie has been, and still is, either stated or implied over and over until today most Southerners themselves accept their assigned position of national villains without so much as one word of protest.

The absurdity of this myth can be seen by understanding that it has been estimated that from seventy to eighty percent of the Confederate soldiers and sailors were *not* slave owners![52] Now let's try to put the extent of the Southern sacrifice into some type of modern perspective. During World War II, the United States lost approximately three hundred thousand military personnel. If the United States had lost personnel in World War II at the same rate (per capita) as the South did during the War for Southern Independence, the loss of American lives in World War II would not have been three hundred thousand but instead six million (yes, that is right, six million people)!

Who in his right mind could honestly claim that the Southern soldiers and sailors, the vast majority of whom were not slave owners, went to war against a numerically superior foe and endured four long years of hardships, all in order to allow a few rich men to keep their slaves? Yet, the Yankee myth of history has been so pervasive that this is the message that our children usually receive from the educational system paid for by our taxes.

Jefferson Davis wrote to his wife in February 1861 that, no matter what the result of the conflict was, the slave property of the South "will eventually be lost."[53] President Davis' inaugural address did not mention slavery. (See Addendum III).

A partial list of Southern leaders who were not slave owners includes such notables as:

> General Robert E. Lee, C.S.A.
>
> General Joseph Johnston, C.S.A.
>
> General A. P. Hill, C.S.A.
>
> General Fitzhugh Lee, C.S.A.
>
> General J. E. B. Stuart, C.S.A.

Add to this evidence the testimony of a soldier who served in the Confederate army:

> I was a soldier in Virginia in the campaigns of Lee and Jackson, and I declare I never met a Southern soldier who had drawn his sword to perpetuate slavery. . . . What he had chiefly at heart was the preservation of the supreme and sacred right of self-government. . . . It was a very small minority of the men who fought in the Southern armies who were financially interested in the institution of slavery.[54]

In personal letters, soldiers would express their most private feelings. Occasionally we find these men testifying to the principles for which they were fighting. In a letter home, one young lad made the following comments:

> The hard fighting will come off here and our boys will have a fine opportunity of showing the enemy with what determination we intend to fight for liberty, and independence. . . . History will record this as being the greatest struggle for liberty that was ever made. . . . [55]

In an officer's letter to the family of a dead soldier we find these words:

> He was an excellent soldier and a brave young man. The company deeply mourns his loss but he is gone, another martyr to the cause of Southern Independence.[56]

George Washington Bolton of the Twelfth Louisiana Volunteer Infantry, C.S.A. sent this encouragement home to his people:

> You seem to be in low spirits and fearful we will not gain our Independence. So long as there is an arm to raise in defense of Southern liberties there is still hope. We must prove ourselves worthy of establishing an independent Government.[57]

During the siege of Port Hudson, Louisiana, a soldier wrote home:

> It is a beautiful Sabbath morning indeed. I feel that I ought to be at Alabama Church this morning. The merry birds are sweetly singing their songs of spring. Oh, that I could sing in truth the songs of peace and liberty this morning to our confederate states.[58]

The desire for independence was evident in countless letters early in the war and continued even after years of desperate struggle. For example, in March of 1865, a soldier from Company K, Seventh Louisiana Infantry, C.S.A. wrote home:

> . . . with proud hearts and strong arms we are more determined than ever to apply every energy until our independence is achieved.[59]

From Shreveport, Louisiana, in April of 1865, come these words:

> I firmly believe that we will yet achieve our Independence.[60]

From these few examples it can be seen that these men were fighting for the same principles their forefathers fought for in the War for American Independence—the right of self-government. Another Yankee myth exposed.

YANKEE MYTH

We (Southerners) are Better Off
Because We Lost the War

Perhaps no other Yankee myth brings more anger to the Southern heart than does this one—especially when we know the truth of our colonial existence and when we meet with a "fellow" Southerner who like a Pavlovian dog at the ringing of a bell salivates on cue this Yankee propaganda line, "Yes, but you know we are better off since we lost the war." How do we uncondition an individual who has, for an entire lifetime, accepted the Yankee myth of history?

We will not discuss the loss of political rights and the loss of our Constitutional Republic at this time. That will be covered in later chapters. But we will review a very small portion of the economic consequence of our failure to maintain our independence.

An idea of the human loss as a result of a war that we did not start, we did not want, but we could not avoid is demonstrated by the fact that in the first year after the war the state of Mississippi allotted one-fifth of its revenues for the purchase of artificial arms and legs. The enduring economic impact is demonstrated by the fact that it was not until 1911 that the taxable assets of the state of Georgia surpassed their value of 1860.[61] The state of Louisiana lost $170,000,000 in slave property.[62] Now remember, pious Yankee and Southern Scalawag, the Northern slave owner had been very careful to liquidate his investment in his slave property before allowing for emancipation. Let us not also forget that it was the rich Northern merchants who still held the profits from the sale of these very same slaves! In Louisiana at the beginning of the war there were twelve hundred operating sugar mills. By the end of the war there were only 180 mills left. As a result of the war, at least one-half of the cattle, pigs, sheep, mules, and horses had disappeared from the state of Louisiana alone.[63] The percentage was even higher for other Southern states.

In 1961 *LIFE* magazine published a one-page overview of the economic loss experienced by the South as a result of the war. Shortly after the war ended, Yankee speculators chartered special trains to come down South where they were able to buy over fifty million acres of prime Southern virgin forest for as little as fifty cents an acre. Because the North completely controlled the United States government, they were able to raise high protective tariffs for Northern manufactured goods while Southern cotton was left unprotected. The price of cotton dropped to an all-time low. Three years after the close of the war, the Northern-controlled Congress levied a special tax on cotton. This tax cost the struggling Southern economy approximately seventy million dollars in three years. The effect of the economic exploitation of the postwar South is demonstrated by the fact that ten years after the end of the war more than sixty percent of the town of Greenville, Mississippi, was sold at the sheriff's auction for delinquent taxes! In

Sumter County, Georgia, Dr. David Bagley's 1860 net worth was eighteen thousand dollars. After enduring the devastating effects of Yankee invasion, conquest, and occupation, his 1870 net worth was only nine hundred dollars.[64]

The Yankee myth-makers would have us believe that even if this were true, "It all happened long ago and is no longer relevant to us today." Yet the death, destruction, and poverty that is our legacy from the United States government placed us in a permanent secondary economic class. The South, at worst, was forced from a position of plenty to one of peonage. At best, we were transformed into second-class citizens in the United States economy.

Both black and white Southerners suffered as a result of our second-class economic status. Forrest McDonald and Grady McWhiney, in an article entitled "The South from Self-Sufficiency to Peonage," described this demeaning situation:

> Tenancy and sharecropping reduced most white farmers to a system of virtual peonage. . . . Not one in a hundred makes a crop now without mortgaging for his year's support and supplies. . . . burdened by debts, tenants were essentially fixed to the soil. . . . During the late antebellum period, perhaps 80 percent or more of the farms in the Lower South were operated by owners. During the post-bellum period this figure declined steadily until, in 1930, more than one million white families and nearly seven hundred thousand black families were tenants. In that year only 37 percent of Southern farms were fully owned by their operators, and most of those were heavily mortgaged.[65]

McDonald and McWhiney describe a county in the South that prior to the war was an exporter of food. As a result of the war and the subsequent social upheaval, the county became a net importer of food since the people could no longer raise enough food to feed themselves! A telling account of the war's impact can be seen when we compare per capita corn production and number of hogs per capita in the South during 1860 and 1880. In 1860 the number of bushels of corn produced per capita rural population was 33.1; whereas in 1880 it was down to 23.4 bushels per capita rural population. The number of hogs available for use per capita in 1860 was 1.92; whereas in 1880 it had dropped to 1.14 per capita rural population.[66]

More and more people were working harder and harder to scratch out a living of an ever declining quality. . . . thus the gigantic trap slowly, steadily, inexorably closed upon them, until almost no one in the South remained free.[67]

The 1868 Official Record for the state of Mississippi described how the state attempted to buy its way out of the post-war poverty by allowing the Northern capitalists to purchase all the virgin forest in the state, to cut it down, and to ship it back North. A North flushed with victory and subsequent economic gain was at the same time of our poverty experiencing rapid growth. Today, Mississippi's vast and expansive virgin forest is gone, but Mississippi still has its legacy of Yankee-induced poverty!

The 1960 United States census provides another example of how the effects of the war remain with the South. The per capita income for all of the states in the Union was given. Not a single Southern state appeared in the top fifty percent! At the time when the North was preparing to celebrate the centennial of its glorious victory in the "Civil War," the South was still reeling from the economic impact of Yankee aggression. According to the *Charlotte* (NC) *Observer*, April 25, 1982, the lore of Sunbelt prosperity was not substantiated by the 1980 census. The report stated that the South was still by far the poorest part of the country. The United States Census Bureau found that the poverty rate for the South was twenty percent higher than for the nation as a whole. All of the states with the highest poverty levels were in the South, whereas all of the states with the lowest poverty rates were in the North.[68] (One nation with justice for all? Not if you speak with a Southern accent!)

The bad news continues for the South. In addition to selling our birthright of virgin forest, the South, in more recent times, has attempted to gain economic ground by concentrating on industrial development. Southern governors make annual pilgrimages to the North to beg Northern industries to come down South and take advantage of our cheap labor supply. In addition to taking advantage of this labor supply, Northern industrialists have also been taking advantage of our environment. The *Shreveport* (LA) *Times*, April 12, 1990, page 12A, carried a news report of a recent study of the environment. The report concludes that the South has become America's cesspool!

An economy in ruins, a second-class economic status, the transformation of a people from self-sufficiency to dependency, the lowest personal income in America, the irreplaceable loss of our virgin forest, and the pollution of our environment. These effects and more have been the direct result of (1) Yankee conquest and (2) the inability of Southerners to control our economic destiny. We fail to see how losing our war for independence has made the Southern people "better off"; yet, duped Southerners still dutifully parrot this Yankee myth.

YANKEE MYTH

General Lee was a Reluctant Southern Nationalist

It is rather amusing for Southerners to observe the workings of the Yankee myth-makers as they dutifully ignore those parts of history that show the Yankees in their true light as aggressive, unprincipled invaders. They then invent facts about themselves and thereby create mythical heroes such as "Honest Abe." Even though the Yankee myth-makers have a virtual monopoly in the press, in politics, and in academia, they still have not been able to create a Yankee hero equal to our Gen. Robert E. Lee!

The Yankee myth-makers realized early that even they were no match for General Lee. They could not destroy our faith in him and they knew they could not ignore him. So they have attempted to enlist General Lee to their side by way of inference, implication, and the tacit advancement of falsehoods that Lee reluctantly joined the South and then accepted defeat so graciously because he knew that the South's defeat saved the Union. It is unfortunate, but amusing, that the Yankee myth-makers have had better luck in their efforts to illicitly enlist General Lee to their cause than they have had at creating their own hero!

The myth-makers stress in their argument that General Lee was opposed to secession. While this is true, the myth-makers fail to state that many, if not a majority of Southerners, were opposed to secession—opposed until Yankee aggression left no choice *except* secession. President Davis stated in his inaugural address that secession of the Southern states came "as a necessity, and not a choice" (see Davis' inaugural address in Addendum III). Opposition to secession, when other remedies still remain, does not make one less of a Southern Nationalist.

The myth-makers also suggest that General Lee really was not committed so much to Southern Independence as he was to fighting to protect his native state of Virginia.

General Lee's own words will put to rest this Yankee myth. In a letter to Lord Acton, dated December 15, 1866, General Lee described himself as "a citizen of the South."[69] In the same letter General Lee stated that he believed that the maintenance of the reserved rights (State's Rights) under the Original Constitution was essential "to the continuance of a free government."[70] He then emphasized what would happen if those reserved rights were concentrated into a central government; he believed this action would result in a nation that would be "aggressive abroad and despotic at home."[71] General Lee's letter continues with a strong statement regarding the right of any state to ". . . prescribe for itself the qualifications of suffrage."[72] Hardly the words of a Union apologist!

The Yankee myth-makers have made much of General Lee's silence after the war. They infer by this that General Lee was satisfied with the outcome of the war and therefore was not a true Southern Nationalist. General Lee's letter to Lord Acton, as quoted above, demonstrates Lee's true attitude toward the war and the cause for which he so bravely fought. A little-known incident described in *Life and Letters of Robert Lewis Dabney* helps to clarify General Lee's silence as well as to reveal his true feelings about the South.

The incident occurred in August 1870, when Lee and many distinguished ex-Confederates were meeting together. The Union general William S. Rosecrans was there and asked General Lee to make a statement on behalf of the Southern people proclaiming that they were now glad to be back in the Union and loyal to the old flag. General Lee refused to make any statement but did agree to set up a meeting with the other ex-Confederates and to allow them to speak for themselves.

General Lee met each man as he entered the room and then sat quietly as the conference progressed. At the beginning of the meeting Union general Rosecrans asked each of the ex-Confederates the same question he had posed to General Lee. Governor Fletcher S. Stockdale (former Confederate governor of Texas) stated to Dabney that he thought that many of the replies struck him as entirely too sycophantic and insincere. When the question came to Governor Stockdale, he made the following reply:

> The people of Texas will remain quiet, and not again resort to
> forceful resistance against the Federal Government, whatever
> may be the measures of that government. But, General Rose-
> crans, candor requires me to explain the attitude of my peo-
> ple. The people of Texas have made up their minds to remain
> quiet under all aggressions and to have peace; but they have
> none of the spaniel in their composition. No, sir, they are not
> in the least like the dog that seeks to lick the hand of the man
> that kicked him; but it is because they are a very sensible, prac-
> tical, common-sense people, and understand their position.
> They know that they resisted the Federal Government as long
> as any means of resistance was left, and that any attempt at
> resistance now must be in vain, and they have no means, and
> would only make bad worse. This is the view of the matter
> which is going to keep Texas quiet.[73]

At this point General Lee rose from his chair and General Rosecrans took the hint that the meeting was over. General Lee stood at
the door and bade good-bye to each man as he left the room. Governor Stockdale was the last to move to the door; General Lee,
who had his hand on the door, closed it before Governor Stockdale could exit. With the world shut out and only himself and Governor Stockdale in the room, Lee made the following statement:

> Governor Stockdale, before you leave, I wish to give you my
> thanks for brave, true words. You know, Governor, what my po-
> sition is. Those people [his uniform term for the Yankees]
> choose, for what reason I know not, to hold me as a representa-
> tive Southerner; hence, I know they watch my words, and if I
> should speak unadvisedly, what I say would be caught up by
> their speakers and newspapers, and magnified into a pretext for
> adding to the load of oppression they have placed upon our
> poor people; and God knows, Governor, that load is heavy
> enough now; I want to thank you for your bold, candid words.[74]

At this point General Lee paused for a moment and Governor
Stockdale thought that the general was preparing to bid him good-
bye. But Lee held the door closed, looked up, and continued:

> Governor, if I had foreseen the use those people designed to
> make of their victory, there would have been no surrender at
> Appomattox Courthouse; no, sir, not by me. Had I foreseen

these results of subjugation, I would have preferred to die at Appomattox with my brave men, my sword in this right hand.[75]

Here we see in General Lee's own words, as spoken to a former governor, what his estimation of the results of subjugation and Reconstruction were. We see that Lee viewed the actions of the United States government to be illegal, cruel, and disastrous for the people whom he had served so well. He believed this so strongly that he would have preferred to have died with his face to the Yankee foe than to have submitted to such despotism.

YANKEE MYTH

The Struggle for Southern Independence was a Civil War

Those who do not understand the workings of the Yankee myth of history (its primary function is to create and to maintain a guilt-ridden Southern people and to justify Northern aggression, conquest, and oppression of the Southern people) will think it strange for us to insist upon the use of a specific title to describe the War of 1861-65. The important point is that the name we use conveys an implied message. Repeated over and over again, it soon becomes a "given" (i.e., one of those unquestionable "facts" that the left-of-center wordsmiths rely upon to keep the masses in line). The truth is that the war was not a civil war because there were not two factions attempting to gain control of the government. Yet the vast majority of books, articles, and lectures about the war label it as the "Civil War."

The use of the compromise term "War Between the States" is also incorrect. We have in hand a copy of our great grandfather's parole papers when he surrendered at Vicksburg, Mississippi. The names of two contending nations, the United States and the Confederate States, can be found on this document. Remember, this document was prepared and used by the army of the United States and, as such, is an official document of that government. Nowhere does this document mention the various states.[76] They were not mentioned because the various states were not engaged in a war among themselves. However, *the two nations who were at war are listed!*[77]

O. W. Blacknall in January 1915 published a booklet entitled

Lincoln as the South Should Know Him (reprinted by Manly's Battery Chapter, Children of the Confederacy, Raleigh, North Carolina). In the booklet the author states that it is incredible that the otherwise intelligent and war-like people of the South should so easily abandon the just cause of their forefathers by foreswearing the use of the "high, expressive, and honorable name of the struggle given to their fathers, The War for Southern Independence."[78] The author recognized the term "War Between the States" for what it is, a compromise name. A usual Southern compromise, we surrender something of value, and the Yankee surrenders nothing in exchange. Surely, at one point in time it was necessary for the South to forsake the use of the true title "War for Southern Independence." Blacknall states, "The compromise name, War Between The States, which our perhaps overcautious leaders thought best to use while the South still had her head in the lion's mouth, was, as they must have known, a clear misnomer." Realizing this, Blacknall continues, "Nevertheless, whatever the war was, it was not war between the States. The States, as States, took no part in it, were not even known in it. It was a war between two thoroughly organized governments and for one great principle, that completely overshadowed all others—Southern Independence. . . . To every patriotic Southerner, War for Southern Independence should be a sacred name."[79]

Why is it important that we assign a specific title to the war? The importance is not its historical accuracy, but that the current title, as soon as it is spoken, immediately assigns the aggressor to the position of an equal participant in a struggle to uphold high principles. The title "Civil War" or "War Between the States" relieves the aggressor of the necessity for explaining why he used cruel and barbaric measures in his invasion and conquest of a free people. The acceptance and use of either of these titles has been a major propaganda victory for the Yankee myth-makers who continue winning this victory with the assistance of our fellow Southerners, who should know better.

We are now in a position to take the offensive. By use of a title that is friendlier to our cause, we can put the myth-makers on the defensive. When the myth-makers are confronted with the insistent use of the term "War for Southern Independence," they are forced to explain why self-determination is good in Eastern Europe but not good for the South. Even if they ignore our use of the term, the implied virtue of our cause is transmitted to our fellow Southerners just by the hearing of the term "War for Southern Independence." The term is self-explanatory. It does not require anyone to explain that independence, not slavery, was the cause for which our forefathers fought.

As Southern Nationals, we must insist upon the use of the pro-Southern term, *War for Southern Independence*. This is not to suggest that the occasional use of other terms is wrong or anti-Southern. There are occasions when a short term is desired, but at every opportunity, especially when dealing with the media, we should insist upon the use of the term that best describes the virtue of our cause and the villainy of our oppressors!

YANKEE MYTH

The South Committed
War Crimes at Andersonville

When the self-righteous Yankee is challenged to explain why he thinks he has a right to deny self-determination to the Southern people, he quickly grabs one of his two most valuable scare charges—slavery or Andersonville. With either of these magic wands of Yankee propaganda, the Northerner usually is able to silence rational discussion. We will now examine the travesty which occurred at Andersonville.

Yankee wordsmiths have equated Andersonville with Nazi death camps. They announce the horrible "truth," and we must accept it, as if it were announced from the mouth of God. In the autumn of 1990, the Public Broadcasting System aired "The Civil War." This program was produced by a Northerner with a large anti-Southern bias. In his treatment of Andersonville, he offered only the Yankee side of the story, completely ignoring the Southern viewpoint as if it did not exist!

The story of Andersonville is too long to be treated completely here. A short listing of a few relevant facts will serve to demonstrate how unfair the Confederate commander of Andersonville, Capt. Henry Wirz, was treated while being victimized by Yankee justice. Wirz was placed on trial by the Yankee government for "war crimes."

Wirz's defense made several motions to dismiss the case. One such motion was based upon the fact that the charges against Wirz were unconstitutionally vague and indefinite. For example, he was charged with thirteen allegations of murder but not a single murder victim was named! How could a man murder thirteen people in the presence of several thousand witnesses (who were the fellow comrades of the alleged victims), and yet no one could remember a single victim's name![80]

Wirz was charged with "conspiracy to destroy prisoners' lives in violation of the laws and customs of war."[81] It takes at least two people to "conspire," yet no one other than Wirz was ever brought to trial. Indeed, Jefferson Davis and fourteen others were also charged in this "crime." Why did the prosecution not use the "evidence" it had obtained in the first trial to convict the others? Perhaps the Yankees did not want to subject their evidence to closer scrutiny. One of the unnamed victims that Wirz was convicted of murdering was supposedly killed on February 1, 1864. Captain (later Major) Wirz did not arrive in Andersonville until the following month, March of 1864. In addition, Yankee justice convicted him of the murder of two unnamed prisoners in August of 1864. During the time in question, Wirz was away from the camp on sick leave.[82]

Of the 160 witnesses called by the prosecution, 145 testified that they had no personal knowledge of Wirz ever killing or mistreating anyone. Only one could give the name of a prisoner allegedly killed by Wirz. The problem with this testimony was that the date given by the witness did not agree with any date used in the charges against Wirz. The court "corrected" this situation by simply changing the date in the indictment to match the testimony already given![83]

The Yankee court decided which witnesses it would allow the defense to call. Several key witnesses were not allowed to testify on behalf of the defense. While on the one hand the Yankee court restricted the defense, it would on the other hand compliment prosecution witnesses for their "spirited testimony."[84] One defense witness was arrested and jailed when he arrived to testify on behalf of Wirz.

Perhaps the most outrageous and damning of all the incidents connected with this display of Yankee justice involved the prosecution's key witness. A man claiming to be one De la Baume testified that he personally saw Wirz shoot two prisoners. His testimony was so compelling that the court gave the witness a written commendation for his "zealous testimony" and rewarded him with a government job! Eleven days after Wirz was hanged, De la Baume was recognized by Union veterans as one Felix Oeser, a deserter from the Seventh New York Regiment. The veterans were so outraged they went to the Secretary of the Interior and had the deserter fired. Upon his discovery, the deserter admitted that he had committed perjury in the Wirz trial.[85] (The Union veterans were angry because the deserter was on the government payroll, not because he had perjured himself and thereby had killed an innocent man.)

The unfair treatment accorded the defense caused three of the original five defense attorneys to quit early in the case. The remaining two finally gave up and quit after their motion for time to prepare their closing argument was denied. Not to be outdone, the court allowed the prosecution to present both closing arguments! Oh, the brilliance and versatility of Yankee justice— something all Southerners have come to appreciate while watching our children as they are bused across town!

The myth of Andersonville is yet one more example of how the Yankee wordsmiths create the "truth" to serve their purposes and then use their monopoly of the media and education to enforce their myth. Lincoln's Secretary of War, Edwin Stanton, noted that a higher percentage of Southern POWs died while in Yankee camps than did Northern POWs held by the South. Still the myth-makers have continued to select only the facts that they wish preserved in their official history.

YANKEE MYTH

The North Was Motivated by High Moral Principles to Preserve the Union

The primary task facing the Yankee myth-makers is to maintain the delusion that the North was the champion of virtue and that therefore, the South represented villainy. Their basic technique has been to paint the South with the tar brush of slavery and racism. The North, in contrast, is depicted as engaging in a selfless sacrifice for human freedom and equality. Variations on this theme can be seen in politically correct textbooks throughout the United States. This theme is then routinely re-enforced by "Civil

War documentaries" and twenty-second sound bits on national television networks. All in all, a rather effective propaganda effort—financed by middle-class taxpayers!

The question still remains: Why did the North invade, conquer, and occupy an independent South? Imperialist powers usually attempt to hide their naked aggression with high-sounding moral excuses which allow them to justify their armed aggression. Saddam Hussein's excuse for invading Kuwait was that Kuwait was really a part of Iraq that had illegally broken away; Joseph Stalin claimed that it was necessary to maintain the Soviet Union's military presence in post-war Eastern Europe to protect international socialism; Adolph Hitler claimed that his invasion of Czechoslovakia was only an attempt to protect German nationals and to give Greater Germany living space; and the British claimed that it was necessary to occupy India in order to preserve order and to prevent French domination. Thus, those who send armies off to foreign countries to deny people the right of self-determination can always find a high-sounding moral motive to justify their invasion. The excuses given by an invader should be viewed with great skepticism. We should always look beyond the aggressor's propaganda and attempt to determine if there are any underlying causes that motivated the invasion and occupation of an erstwhile free people.

General Sir James Marshall-Cornwall, in the first chapter of his book *Grant as a Military Commander*, noted that the real issue between the North and the South was political and economic. He described the economic pressure on the North to protect its industrial expansion with high tariffs, whereas Southern agriculture needed free trade. Thus the animosity and tension between the two sections were based upon different cultures with conflicting economic systems.[86]

Senator William Grayson, one of Virginia's first United States Senators, expressed concern that the South would eventually become the "milch cow" of the Union![87] Shortly after the American Revolution, the Northern states decided to transfer all state war debts to the federal government. This meant that the federal government would pay the war debts of the states. This would be a windfall for the North because the federal government would obtain the monies to pay the debt by raising tariffs. The result was that the Southern states were required to pay a disproportionate share of the debt. For example, the export of cotton alone from the South in 1859 was valued at $161,434,923. The total export of all goods from the North in 1859 was a mere $78,217,202.[88] This differential was in place at the beginning of our political union and continued up to the establishment of an independent South. The Virginia legislature reacted to the proposal to transfer state war debts to the newly created federal government by declaring that, if enacted it would cause "the prostration of agriculture at the feet of commerce, or a change of the present form of federal government, fatal to the existence of American liberty."[89] Nevertheless the effort was successful, and thus began the systematic and "legalized" pilfering of Southern resources disguised by any excuse the numerical majority of the North could frame as necessary for the general welfare.[90]

In 1828, Senator Thomas H. Benton declared:

> Before the Revolution [the South] was the seat of wealth, as well as hospitality. . . . Wealth has fled from the South, and settled in regions north of the Potomac: and this in the face of the fact, that the South, in four staples alone, has exported produce, since the Revolution, to the value of eight hundred millions of dollars; and the North has exported comparatively nothing. Such an export would indicate unparalleled wealth, but what is the fact? . . . Under Federal legislation, the exports of the South have been the basis of the Federal revenue. . . . Virginia, the two Carolinas, and Georgia, may be said to defray three-fourths, of the annual expense of supporting the Federal Government; and of this great sum, annually furnished by them, nothing or next to nothing is returned to them, in the shape of Government expenditures. That expenditure flows in an opposite direction—it flows northwardly, in one uniform, uninterrupted, and perennial stream. This is the reason why wealth disappears from the South and rises up in the North. Federal legislation does all this.[91]

The Abolitionists claimed that slavery was the cause of the loss of wealth in the South. Professor Jonathan Elliot, a teacher of science at Harvard University, discounted this theory and stated that it was federal legislation in regard to the Tariff Acts that was the culprit.[92]

A pertinent incident is reported in *The Sectional Controversy*, written by W. C. Fowler and published in 1864. The author recounted an incident when, fifteen or twenty years previously, he met a friend from his college days who was at that time a prominent Northern member of Congress. The Congressman was leaving a heated meeting regarding abolition and other sectional issues. Fowler asked the Congressman what was the real reason that Northerners were encouraging abolitionist petitions. The Congressman replied, "The real reason is that the South will not let us have a tariff, and we touch them where they will feel it."[93]

George Lunt, author of *Origin of the Late War*, noted,

> In 1833 there was a surplus revenue of many millions in the public treasury which by an act of legislation unparalleled in the history of nations was distributed among the Northern States to be used for local public improvements.[94]

President James Buchanan's message to Congress declared,

> The South had not had her share of money from the treasury, and unjust discrimination had been made against her. . . .[95]

When the Northern president Lincoln was asked why the North should not let the South go, his reply was, "Let the South go? Let the South go! Where then shall we get our revenues!"[96]

Patrick Henry warned the South about placing our faith in the good will of the North when he spoke out against the proposed Constitution:

> But I am sure that the dangers of this system [the Federal Constitution] are real, when those who have no similar interest with the people of this country [the South] are to legislate for us—when our dearest rights are to be left, in the hands of those, whose advantage it will be to infringe them.[97]

It is revealing to read Northern newspaper accounts that document the change in the mood of the North during the first months after the South seceded. At first there appears to be a mood to allow the South to exercise its right of self-determination. Then we begin to see predictions of economic loss if the North allows the ten percent tariff established by the Southern Confederacy to remain in place and to compete with its higher tariff. Some writers have noted that there were predictions that grass would grow in the streets of New York, while the port of New Orleans would flourish.[98]

The Northern colonies, from the earliest part of the history of the United States, had a great fear of losing their trade in the Western territories. In 1786, John Jay of New York caused an uproar in Congress among the Southern delegates with his attempt to give up rights to the Mississippi River to Spain in exchange for commercial advantages in Spanish ports.[99] The great fear of the commercial North was that all or a great part of the commerce west of the Appalachian Mountains would pass through New Orleans and leave the Eastern ports with very little commerce. The North made many efforts early in American history to give control of the land and great rivers of the Mississippi Valley to Spain. This, they believed, would keep American commerce in Northern ports. These efforts are recorded in *The New Nation* in part by the following:

> At the same time they [Northerners] wanted to control the trade of the West, and this would be denied them, they felt, if the Mississippi were open to western trade. They believed that only by closing the river could western commerce be forced eastward across the Mountains.
>
> The political and economic implications of agrarian expansion westward were alarming to certain mercantile interests in the East who feared the loss of their political and economic control of an expanding America.[100]

This fear of losing its commercial advantages to the states along the Mississippi was a prime factor in the North's invasion of the South. Just weeks before the firing of the first shots of the war, *The New York Times* ran story after story about how the commerce of the North would be lost to New Orleans and to the rest of the South because of the low Southern tariff. Northerners even admitted that their reasons for fighting the South were not the result of differences in principles of constitutional law but only because their profits might be lost if the South was successful in its move for independence. On March 30, 1861, *The New York Times* made the following statement:

> The predicament in which both the Government and the commerce of the country are placed, through the non-enforcement of our revenue laws, is now thoroughly understood the world over. . . . If the manufacturer at Manchester [England] can send his goods into the Western States through

New Orleans at a less cost than through New York, he is a fool for not availing himself of his advantage. . . . If the importations of the country are made through Southern ports, its exports will go through the same channel. The produce of the West, instead of coming to our own port by millions of tons, to be transported abroad by the same ships through which we received our importations, will seek other routes and other outlets. With the loss of our foreign trade, what is to become of our public works, conducted at the cost of many hundred millions of dollars, to turn into our harbor the products of the interior? They share in the common ruin. So do our manufacturers. . . . Once at New Orleans, goods may be distributed over the whole country duty free. The process is perfectly simple. . . . The commercial bearing of the question has acted upon the North. . . . We now see clearly whither we are tending, and the policy we must adopt. With us it is no longer an abstract question—one of Constitutional construction, or of the reserved or delegated power of the State or Federal Government, but of material existence and moral position both at home and abroad. . . . *We were divided and confused till our pockets were touched.*[101] [emphases added]

In an earlier article, *The New York Times* complained about the loss of revenue because the tariffs were no longer being collected in the Southern states. The article bemoans the fact that new loans were needed but could not be guaranteed because the seceded states could not be forced to collect the "National" tariff.[102]

In an editorial, the Manchester, New Hampshire, *Union Democrat* had this to say about the loss of its commercial advantages if the North were to "let the South go."

The Southern Confederacy will not employ our ships or buy our goods. What is our shipping without it? Literally nothing. The transportation of cotton and its fabrics employs more ships than all other trade. It is very clear that the South gains by this process, and we lose. No—we MUST NOT "let the South go."[103]

The New York *Evening Post* bemoaned the lost of tax dollars if the South was a free and independent nation. In an article titled "What Shall Be Done for a Revenue?" the following statements were made:

That either revenue from duties must be collected in the ports of the rebel states, or the ports must be closed to importations from abroad, . . . If neither of these things be done, our revenue laws are substantially repealed; *the sources which supply our treasury will be dried up* [emphases added]; we shall have no money to carry on the government; the nation will become bankrupt before the next crop of corn is ripe. . . . Allow railroad iron to be entered at Savannah with the low duty of ten per cent, which is all that the Southern Confederacy think of laying on imported goods, and not an ounce more would be imported at New York; the railways would be supplied from the southern ports.[104]

From these statements and the facts already discussed, we can see that the North's true motive for launching an invasion into the South was not one of high moral principles, but one of *greed* and *fear of economic loss.* Thus, Yankee imperialism launched an aggressive campaign to deny the people of the South their right to a government established upon the principle of the consent of the governed:

We hold these truths to be self-evident that . . . Governments are instituted among men, deriving their just powers from the consent of the governed. . . .

YANKEE MYTH

The North Championed the Cause of Equality, Racial Tolerance, and Human Brotherhood

No Yankee myth is more historically ridiculous than the myth of the egalitarian North! Yet, what is the response when you ask the average American what section of the country believed in and fought for human equality? Like the needle on a compass, his finger will automatically point northward, while in the background you will see a slow fade-in of the Lincoln Memorial and hear soft, sweet sounds of "The Battle Hymn of the Republic"—ad nauseum!

Alexis de Tocqueville noted the following:

[T]he prejudice of the race appears to be stronger in the States that have abolished slaves than in the States where slavery still exists. White carpenters, white bricklayers and white

> painters will not work side by side with the blacks in the North
> but do it in almost every Southern State. . . .[105]

Was this an ill-formed conclusion, or did it accurately represent the attitude of the Northern people vis-a-vis blacks? To determine this, we need to return to the early days of the nation, to the colonial times when slavery was still practiced in the North.

We will reserve the discussion of the financial reasons that forced the North to discontinue the system of slavery for the next chapter. We will note, however, that, as soon as the supply of white labor in the North became sufficient to reduce the cost of said labor, then and only then did the abolition of slavery become possible. Again, note that it was financial profits and not moral principles that fueled the Yankee's attitude toward slavery. John Adams of Massachusetts stated that the people would have killed both slave and master had the institution continued.[106] Certainly no sense of human brotherhood can be found in his statement. It is also noteworthy that, when Rhode Island passed a law providing for the gradual emancipation of slaves, the law was very carefully written to preclude any interference with the ongoing slave trade that was enriching the state.[107]

After Northern blacks gained their freedom, they were still viewed as an economic threat to white labor. White laborers of the North resented any competition from blacks. When New Jersey passed a law forbidding the importation of slaves into the state, it noted that it was taking this action ". . . so that white labor may be protected."[108]

The racial bigotry of the Northern population against black workers had the effect of barring blacks from social and economic advancement, thereby contributing to the ever-increasing poverty of free blacks. One commentator of the period stated that free blacks had been better off as slaves.[109] Professor McMaster, University of Pennsylvania, stated that ". . . In spite of their freedom they were a despised, proscrived, and poverty-stricken class."[110]

The attitude of the Northern people toward the free black is best described by the authors of William Lloyd Garrison's biography:

> The free colored people were looked upon as an inferior caste
> to whom their liberty was a curse, and their lot worse than that
> of the slaves. . . .[111]

Not only was entrance into the labor market limited in the North but also the accessibility of education was restricted. Connecticut passed a law declaring that non-resident blacks could not attend public schools because ". . . it would tend to the great increase of the colored people of the state."[112]

The North also passed exclusion laws to forbid free blacks from coming into its states. New Jersey passed one of the first of these laws. It prohibited free blacks from settling in that fair state. Massachusetts passed a law that allowed the flogging of blacks who came into the state and remained for longer than two months.[113] In 1853, Indiana's constitution stated that ". . . no negro or mulatto shall come into or settle in the state. . . ."[114] Illinois in 1853 enacted a law ". . . to prevent the immigration of free negroes into this state. . . ."[115]

Not satisfied with a mere statute, in 1862, and while its boys in blue were pillaging the South, Illinois passed by overwhelming popular vote an amendment to the state's constitution declaring that ". . . No negro or mulatto shall immigrate or settle in this state."[116]

Oregon's 1857 constitution provided that ". . . No free negro or mulatto, not residing in this state at the time of adoption [of the constitution of the state of Oregon] . . . shall come, reside, or be within this state. . . ."[117]

It appears that there was a strain of race paranoia in the North that caused Northerners to fear a black peril, as if Northerners thought their fair states would be engulfed by hordes of free black men, women, and children. The Northern president Lincoln attempted to alleviate this fear in his message to Congress, in December of 1862:

> But why should emancipation South send free people North?
> . . . And in any event cannot the North decide for itself whether to receive them?[118]

This irrational fear of black people was not a phenomenon that appeared during the war. Northerners' fear of black political power can be seen in their laws disenfranchising blacks. Remember, these are Northern states disenfranchising their black population even though the ratio of the black population to the white population was relatively insignificant as compared to that in the

Southern states. The following is a partial listing of Northern states that barred blacks from voting:

STATE	YEAR BLACKS BARRED FROM VOTING
New Jersey	1807
Connecticut	1814
Rhode Island	1822
Pennsylvania	1838 [119]

The precarious condition of free Northern blacks can be demonstrated by reviewing the declining population figures of Northern blacks. The census for the period of 1790 to 1830 indicates a drop of the free black population of New York from 2.13 percent to 0.57 percent of the total population.[120] Similar declines can be seen in other areas of the North. Dr. Edgar McManus declared that many, if not the larger percentage, had been the victims of kidnappers and "forced migration." Free blacks were kidnapped and sold into slavery. In New York City alone, in one year, more than thirty-three cases of such kidnapping were revealed.[121] The Yankee developed the habit early of selling blacks into slavery and found it to be very lucrative practice and a hard habit to break!

The racist attitude of the North was well established and persisted up to and beyond the war. William H. Seward in 1858 declared that "The white man needs this continent to labor in and must have it."[122]

John Sherman, William Tecumseh Sherman's brother, made this declaration on April 2, 1862:

> We do not like the negroes. We do not disguise our dislike. As my friend from Indiana [a Mr. Wright] said yesterday: "The whole people of the Northwestern States are opposed to having many negroes among them and that principle or prejudice has been engraved in the legislation for nearly all the Northwestern States."[123]

During the war, when Gen. John A. Dix proposed to remove a number of escaped slaves from Fortress Monroe to Massachusetts, the governor of Massachusetts objected, stating ". . . the Northern States are of all places the worst possible to select for an asylum for negroes."[124]

Yankee apologists will assure us that these views somehow magically changed during the war. But the facts demonstrate otherwise. Ohio, in 1867, at the very time that Congress was forcing the South to accept unqualified suffrage, rejected by popular vote a law allowing blacks to vote.[125]

The arrogant and racist Yankee attitude was not limited to blacks and crackers but included Native Americans. In 1862 the United States government sent Gen. John Pope to Minnesota to suppress an uprising. In one of his orders he described Native Americans thusly:

> They are to be treated as maniacs or wild beasts, and by no means as people with whom treaties or compromises can be made.[126]

Gideon Wells, United States Secretary of the Navy, admitted that the war waged against the Native Americans in Minnesota was racially motivated. He stated that the Native Americans in Minnesota "have good land which white men want and mean to have."[127]

The Yankee establishment works overtime painting the South with the tar brush of slavery and racism. It does this while wrapping itself in robes of self-righteousness and declaring to the world how glad it is that the Yankee is a pure soul never having indulged in any such form of evil. Historical facts tell a different story!

This "holier-than-thou" attitude is evident throughout the history of the North/South struggle. It continues even today. When the national news media needs an example of racism, you can rest assured that the first place they will look will be down South. Yet, in the late 1960s, it was places like Newark, New Jersey, and Detroit, Michigan, that experienced bloody race riots. Who remembers the violent resistance to forced busing, not down South but in Boston, Massachusetts? Howard Beach and Yonkers, New York, are hardly bastions for redneck Southerners. More recently, social analysis has demonstrated that the North is more segregated than the South.[128] Yet, we are still confronted with the Yankee myth of the egalitarian North versus the hate-filled, racist South. The historical record speaks of a different reality, but reality, these days, is only the vision which those who control the media allow the average American to hear and see. The liberal establishment puts its spin on reported "facts" and then carefully controls access to the

media to prevent the Southern point of view from being expressed. The press is only free for those who control access to it!

SUMMARY

These are only a few of the Yankee myths of history used to justify their crimes against our people. It began with the North's attempt to influence foreign nations not to recognize the Southern
nation. It has been used ever since to convince both Northerners
and Southerners that the war was fought for moral reasons, and
that the North was the champion of that morality. Of course, that
leaves the South in the position of championing immorality. Today
when a television or movie producer needs someone to stereotype
as ignorant, evil, or racist, we can expect to find a convenient redneck, hillbilly, or cracker emerging from the wings. This fictitious
character will usually have a "rebel" flag on his pick-up truck,
hanging behind the bar, or tattooed on his arm.

The myth is taught in every Southern school. Every new generation is conditioned to respond appropriately, and those who dare
challenge the myth will face the wrath of the liberal wordsmith in
education, in the media, and in politics. As long as we accept this
myth, the Northern liberals can justify any of their actions used to
repress the rights of Southerners. If the South is the center of evil
and racism in America, then the South-only Voting Rights Act is
necessary. Forced busing is needed, reverse discrimination only
proper, and never will the liberals allow a pro-Southern conservative to sit on the United States Supreme Court. It is time to reject
Yankee myth and march forward to a reality of Southern freedom!

CHAPTER 2

Slavery:
The Yankee Flesh Merchants

Thus it will be seen that the last capture of a slaver was by a Southern officer and the good people of Massachusetts were engaged in this nefarious business at the beginning of our unhappy war.[1]

J. Julius Guthrie

INTRODUCTORY COMMENTS

The Yankee myth of history teaches Southerners that our ancestors are the villains of American history. It teaches us that we are descendants of cruel slave masters and must remain forever upon "the stools of everlasting repentance" because of the sins of our ancestors.

Perhaps no other point can better demonstrate the hypocrisy of the Yankee myth of history than the issue of who was responsible for slavery in America, who made the profits from slavery, and who treated the slaves more compassionately. In this chapter we will explore these questions and, in so doing, explode a few more Yankee myths.

SLAVERY: WHO IS RESPONSIBLE?

Nothing in American history has stirred, or continues to stir, more passion than the institution of African servitude. With the mention of the word "slavery," rational thought disappears only to resurface after the South has been thoroughly flailed, kicked, and punished for the sin of involuntary servitude.

Conventional wisdom (i.e., Yankee myth) maintains that the entire burden for this institution should be carried by the people of the South. Conventional wisdom states that the "Civil War" was fought by the noble and freedom-loving Yankees to free their

*George Clark, Edgefield District, South Carolina, member
Company G, Seventh South Carolina Volunteer Infantry.
Clark had this picture taken shortly before he died of typhoid
fever. The number of deaths attributed to disease during the
war was as great as that resulting from battle. Was the bou-
quet he holds for his mother, sister, or sweetheart?* (Image
courtesy of South Carolina Confederate Relic Room
and Museum, Columbia, South Carolina)

black brothers from cruel Southern slavery. The Yankee myth of history attempts to justify the North's criminal invasion of the South by claiming that the South was fighting to protect its slave property. Unfortunately, many Southerners have fallen victim to this Yankee propaganda. Only those who accept the Yankee myth of history without question and who refuse to read impartial historical evidence succumb to such shallow thinking.

Because of the manner in which true Southern history is treated by our educational systems, the electronic media, and the print media, the modern-day Southerner does not possess the truth regarding the history of slavery in America. Because of some imagined guilt of their forefathers, Southerners feel that they must hang their heads in shame and accept their punishment. As "living history" enthusiasts, the authors of this book have had the opportunity to talk with school children about the War for Southern Independence. All too often, when asked why the South fought the War, the children reply, "To keep their slaves." If these children were from homes in Massachusetts or New York, this answer would at least be understandable. But when we realize that these Southern children are only four or five generations removed from the generation of Stonewall Jackson, Robert E. Lee, and Jefferson Davis, we begin to understand how effective the Yankee mythmakers have been. This is why we must come to a proper understanding of the slave question in America. Then, and only then, will Southerners no longer feel compelled to "hang their heads in shame." Instead of shame, we will once again become proud of our glorious heritage and demand the respect of our fellow Americans.

A study of the facts will show that the North was co-equally responsible for the system of slavery in America. The facts will demonstrate that Northerners were less humanitarian in their treatment of slaves than were the Southern slave owners.

To understand the subject of African servitude in America better, we shall seek the answers to the following questions:

1. Who first legalized slavery in America?
2. Who first attempted to prohibit the importation of slaves?
3. How was slavery abolished in the North?
4. How were the freed blacks treated in the North?

Once we resolve these questions, we will be able to answer the larger question of:

> Who deserves the burden of guilt for the institution of African slavery in America?

We will demonstrate that the South does not deserve the burden of guilt for African slavery in America. When this fact is established, it is only natural for us to ask:

> Why has the South been forced to carry this unfair burden?

When these questions have been answered, you can then decide for yourself who deserves the burden of guilt.

Who First Legalized Slavery in America?

To the average American, the word "slavery" conjures up visions of antebellum homes, mint juleps, and the taskmaster's whip. All of these visions can only be found in the South. Ask any American where slavery as an institution was practiced, and the answer most often heard is "in the South." Few, if any, will even stop to think of the North as the cradle of slavery. All too often we are bombarded with stories of the righteous Yankee toiling to make a "free" land out of the United States. This righteous crusade for freedom, we are told, was constantly hampered by the South's attempt to keep our country half free and half slave. Even when Northern slavery is mentioned, it is quickly claimed that the virtuous North freed its slaves because it was too humanitarian to suffer the existence of slavery within its boundaries (another Yankee myth).

The existence of African slavery in America can be traced directly to the commercial interests of Europe.[2] The first English colony in America was founded in 1607 at Jamestown, Virginia. Approximately thirteen years after Jamestown was founded, a ship claiming to be Dutch brought twenty Africans to the colony.[3] The slaves were not requested by the colony but were offered for sale and were subsequently purchased.

Most people concentrate on the fact that this was the first time African slaves were brought to America. Another equally important point to realize is that property as well as commerce in slaves was considered legal by the European powers. The Spanish, Dutch, English, and eventually the Yankees would take part in this "legal" commerce. The slave trade and ownership of slaves was protected by international law. Indeed, the slave trade was introduced into the New World in 1503 by the Spanish and in 1562 by the English. Today we find it hard to understand this system of forced labor. However, two hundreds years from now, future generations will probably find it hard to understand social conditions that we take for granted today. Slavery existed in other parts of the New World before it was introduced into the English colonies. So, the purchase of slaves in Jamestown was not an unusual transaction. The African slave trade was so lucrative that the English strove to gain the largest share of the trade, which they achieved with the signing of the Asiento Treaty with Spain in 1713.[4] This near monopoly was to be held until the Crown opened it to all Englishmen in 1749. At that time the New England Yankee quickly joined the ranks of the most infamous traders in the world—the trans-Atlantic slave trader.

The African slave trade has a long and bleak history, and, for the most part, Americans have very shallow knowledge of it. If anything is said about the slave trade, it is said only to implicate the South as the chief villain of that nefarious commerce.

The forced movement of Africans to various parts of the world began in the ninth century and continued legally until the late nineteenth century, or for about a thousand years.[5] Two major waves of the slave trade occurred during that time. The trans-Sahara and trans-Atlantic waves would be responsible for the forced movement of just over twenty million Africans from their native soil. Another five million would die in transit.[6]

The trans-Sahara wave carried Africans from their homeland to be sold at markets by Arabs and Berbers in the Mediterranean Sea area and in the northern countries of Africa.[7] The trans-Sahara wave was responsible for selling over ten million Africans into slavery, and lasted from the ninth until the fifteenth century. These slave traders were non-European Moslems.

The second great wave of African slave trading began in the mid 1400s. Around 1460, Portugal established posts along the coast of western Africa to trade in African slaves.[8] This was the beginning of the European slave trade that would be carried on legally and illegally until the end of slavery in the Western Hemisphere in 1888, the date Brazil banned the practice.[9] Although this ended slavery in the Americas and the trans-Atlantic slave trade, slavery was not halted legally worldwide until 1962 when it was outlawed on the Arabian peninsula.[10]

These two great waves of slave migration are very similar. Each wave, lasting around five hundred years, was responsible for approximately ten million Negroes being taken from Africa. Both were carried on by religious people, one Moslem, one Christian. Both were sanctioned by international law. There are also some differences between the two great waves. The earlier wave followed a land route across the Sahara. The other was an ocean route, across the Atlantic. Nevertheless, Arabs and Berbers were the first to become involved in the slave trade, and they influenced the Europeans who became involved several hundred years later.

Those who place the burden of guilt upon the Europeans for slavery will not find the previous paragraph to their liking. But even more shocking is the fact that, within many African societies, slavery was an accepted way of life. In his book, *Prince Among Slaves*, Terry Alford chronicles the life of a young black warrior who was sold into slavery by his fellow black Africans.[11] Abd Rahman Ibrahima was the son of a great warrior chief and king of the Timbo Nation, now part of Guinea. These people were fierce fighters and made slaves of many of their prisoners of war. These black Africans owned and sold other blacks.[12] They had no more qualms about this practice than any of the Arab or European slave traders had. Unfortunately for Prince Ibrahima, the system of slave trading worked as well for his enemies as it did for the people of Timbo. When captured in a battle, he was sold to a Spanish slaver, and ended up as a slave in Natchez, Mississippi. Ibrahima became overseer of his master's plantation during the next forty years, before gaining his freedom and returning to his homeland. This most unusual story is instructive because an African tells how slavery was a part of his life while in Africa. African slavery was not an invention of the European. As we have just seen, this institution existed and was practiced by both the black African and by the Arab long before the European became involved.

As shocking as the fact that black men owned other blacks in Africa is to some people, the fact that black Americans owned other blacks is even more shocking.

Larry Koger, in his book *Black Slaveowners*,[13] has documented the account of blacks owning other blacks in America. According to the 1830 census record, more than ten thousand slaves were owned by free men of color.[14] In Sumter, South Carolina, in 1860, William Ellison, a free man of color, had seventy slaves working his plantation.[15] In Louisiana, in St. Landry Parish, a free man of color, Auguste Donatto, held seventy slaves to work his five-hundred-acre plantation.[16] Even in New York City, eight free men of color owned seventeen slaves in 1830![17]

When these facts are brought to light, most black and left-of-center "leaders" will tell us that these black slave holders were only doing this for benevolent or kinship reasons. According to Koger's study, "the local documents could not demonstrate the dominance of the benevolent or kinship aspect of black slaveowning."[18] He goes on to show that, according to the census records, eighty-three percent of the black slave masters were of mixed ancestry. Also he noted that ninety percent of these slaves were dark-skinned, pure Negro. Koger goes on to state that "free Negro masters were similar to white slaveowners. Both exploited the labor of slaves with the desire for profits."[19]

As we have shown, African slavery has a long history. We cannot accept the whine of the liberal and the black militant when they try to blame this institution on the people of the South. Nor can we accept the idea that it was a European institution. The system of African slavery goes back to the ninth century with the Arab Moslems being one of the first groups to become involved in the trade. Also when it comes time to point a finger of blame for African slavery, let us not forget those Africans who owned and sold their fellow blacks into slavery, and by all means don't forget all those other slave traders—Arab, Spanish, English, and Yankee.

The pious New Englander had little problem enslaving those whom his religious leaders would describe as savages. Listen to the words of one of New England's great founding fathers, the Reverend Cotton Mather: "We know not when or how these Indians first became inhabitants of these mighty Continent, yet we may guess that probably the Devil decoy'd these miserable Savages hither, in hopes that the Gospel of the Lord Jesus Christ would never come here to destroy or disturb his Absolute Empire over them." (Magnalia, Book III, Part III)[20] These Native Americans were the same people that the New Englanders were enslaving and trading for black slaves in the Caribbean islands. The pious fanatics sold not only Native Americans into slavery, but also children of those who did not agree with their form of religion. On

June 29, 1658, the county court at Salem, Massachusetts, set into motion the sale of two children whose parents were fined for attending a Quaker meeting and for siding with the Quakers. The parents became destitute and died within a year. Before they died, they were caught again with several Quaker ladies, all of whom were given a good public whipping and thrown into prison. (How often have you seen a picture of a man or woman who had been whipped by a Yankee? The Yankee establishment seems to delight in showing off pictures of poor slaves whipped on Southern plantations, but never seem to get around to showing us similar pictures of those whipped by Yankees.) The children of the whipped and imprisoned parents were to be sold into slavery in Barbados.[21] In grief and anguish the Quaker historian Bishop declared, "O ye Rulers of Boston, ye Inhabitants of the Massachusetts! What shall I say unto you? Whereunto shall I liken ye? Indeed, I have no Nation with you to compare, I have no People with you to parallel, I am at a loss with you in this point."[22] And the people at the South say, "*Amen!*"

The *Desire* was the first slave ship to be equipped in America.[23] She was built in 1637, only seventeen years after the Pilgrims had landed at Plymouth Rock, and she sailed from Salem, Massachusetts. The Yankee commercial and industrial system had its roots in the profits made by engaging in the African slave trade. The "Good Ship" *Desire* was only the first of many Yankee ships that would prey upon the hapless people of Africa for the next two hundreds years. The slave trade became the cornerstone of Yankee commerce and furnished the financial capital for future investments in legitimate industries, much as modern-day drug dealers launder their tainted money in legitimate enterprises.[24] The slave trade provided much commerce for many people in New England. Not only the seamen engaged in the act of slaving itself, but all those who worked to provide the goods that were used in the trade profitted. The New England slave trade was based on three commodities: rum, slaves, and molasses. In New England, the slave ships would take on a load of fish and rum to be traded in Africa for slaves, about two hundred gallons of rum per slave. In the West Indies, the slaves were traded for molasses, and the molasses was then taken back to New England to be sold to make more rum.[25] As each transaction was made, the ever-mindful profiteer would make a little margin, so by the time he was back in New England he had earned a handsome dividend for the company that owned his ship.

So important were the New England rum distilleries to the slave trade that, when the English parliament made a serious effort to collect a tax on molasses, the Massachusetts merchants protested that such a tax would ruin the slave trade and cause more than seven hundred ships to rot for lack of work.[26] There were at this time in Massachusetts some sixty-three distilleries producing 12,500 hogsheads (barrels of 63 to 140 gallons) of rum.[27] Also there were thirty-five distilleries in Rhode Island producing rum.[28] In 1763 the colony of Rhode Island protested the imposition of the tax to the English Board of Trade in a resolution of its General Assembly in which it said, "This little colony, only, for more than thirty years past, have annually sent about eighteen sail of vessels to the coast, which have carried about eighteen hundred hogsheads of rum, together with a small quantity of provisions and some other articles, which have been sold for slaves. . . . This distillery is the main hinge upon which the trade of the colony turns, and many hundreds of persons depend immediately upon it for a subsistence."[29]

The New England slave trade, which started in 1640, was maintained legally and illegally for more than two hundred years. Even after Congress had outlawed the importation of slaves into the United States, the Yankee slaver found ready markets in the Caribbean and in South America, where ninety-four percent of the African slaves ended up.[30] Off the coast of Zanzibar in 1836, the Yankee slaver was trading calico from Northern textile mills spun from slave-grown cotton for ivory and slaves. In 1831 an English seaman, Captain Isaacs made the following statement about the Yankee slaver: "Few have visited it [the port of Lamu] except the enterprising Americans whose star-spangled banner may be seen streaming in the wind where other nations would not deign to traffic." There were so many Yankee slavers and traders active in Zanzibar that the local population thought that Great Britain was a subdivision of Massachusetts. For many years, even into modern times, the name for cotton cloth in that part of the world would remain "Americani."[31]

During this time, most civilized nations were trying to put an end to the slave trade. Although the United States had outlawed the trade, the government had not signed an agreement with the great powers of Europe to allow their agents to board and search American vessels. Because of this situation, most European slave ships kept at least one American national and a United States flag handy. If they were stopped by a European naval vessel, the European captain of the slave ship would execute a quick sale of his vessel to the American, hoist up the Stars and Stripes, and be safe from capture. This American was known by the slavers as the "Captain of the Flag,"[32] and the flag was the United States flag, *not* the Confederate battle flag! Daniel Mannix in his book *Black Cargoes* states, ". . . the flag especially if it was American proved to be ample protection for a slaver."[33] It would have been so simple for the United States to have allowed the British or French navies to police the illegal American slave trade. The British and French navies attempted this practice, but the New England states set up such a protest that none other than the acting Secretary of State, John Quincy Adams of Boston, Massachusetts, sent a strong message to those nations that no nation would be allowed to stop and search an American vessel.[34] Some forty years later, a Southerner, Henry A. Wise, consul at Rio de Janeiro in Brazil, reported to President Zachary Taylor about the use of the United States flag by Americans (Yankees) as they were engaged in the African slave trade. On February 18, 1847, this Southerner wrote President Taylor these words: "You have no conception of the bold effrontery and the flagrant outrages of the African slave trade, and the shameless manner in which its worst crimes are licensed here, and every patriot in our land would blush for our country did he know and see, as I do, how our citizens sail and sell our flag to the uses and abuses of that accursed practice."[35] In his message to Congress on December 4, 1849 (just eleven years before South Carolina seceded from the Union), President Taylor made the following statement: "Your Attention is earnestly invited to an amendment of our existing laws relating to the African slave trade with a view to the effectual suppression of that barbarous traffic. It is not to be denied that this trade is still in part carried on by means of vessels built in the United States and owned or navigated by some of our citizens."[36] It is of interest to note that Henry Wise's observation about the slave trade was made in a South American port. In studying the slave trade, we note that only six percent of all the Africans taken from Africa were brought to the United States. A full ninety-four percent of them were sold into slavery in the Caribbean and in South American countries. Those who would try to defend the North for its involvement in the illegal slave trade often attempt to shift the blame upon Southerners by saying, "If you Southerners had not provided the market for our slaves, we would never have been in the slave trade." The truth is that after 1800 the South was never a viable market for the African slave traders.

But the fact that the South was not a major market for the North's black cargo never kept the profit-mindful Yankee peddlers from doing business in African slaves. Some of the more prominent families of New England were engaged in the slave trade and built huge fortunes in the process. The deWolf family, one of the more prominent families in Rhode Island, was very much involved in the slave trade. Members of that esteemed family invested the money earned from the slave trade in distilleries and (of all things) in textile mills.[37] The Brown family, also slavers, invested their slave money in candle factories, the first cotton mills in America, and an iron furnace and foundry. These were used to provide Gen. George Washington with many cannons during the Revolutionary War.[38] Mannix, in *Black Cargoes*, states, "The slave trade in New England, as in Lancashire and the English Midlands, provided much of the capital that helped to create the industrial revolution."[39] Many fortunes were made by various families of New England. From Boston comes the story of Peter Faneuil, a man of great wealth who gave to the city of Boston Faneuil Hall, which became known as the "cradle of liberty." It was in this building, a local and national shrine, that many patriot meetings were held before the Revolutionary War. One such meeting resulted in the famous "Boston Tea Party." What is not told about Faneuil is that he was a major backer of a slaving venture.[40] Now if he had been a Southerner, he would be censured and written off as a racist cur. How often have we heard the cry of the liberal media demanding the removal of a Confederate monument or flag because of some supposed connection with slavery? Yet, even though Faneuil was a Yankee slave trader, he is given official sanction. Faneuil Hall has become an icon of what America is supposed to be about, yet the man for whom it is named was a slave trader! Men such as Josiah Franklin, stepbrother of Benjamin Franklin, and John Hancock of Massachusetts were involved with the slave trade. Even though the Confederate flag never flew over a slave ship, and even though the United States flag did fly over slave ships, it is the Confederate flag that the left-of-center wordsmith refers to as the "flag of slavery." What kind of justice is this?

Never let it be forgotten that the means of Northern industrial growth had its origin in the slave trade. Every nickel of profit that Northerners have made from that time to this day is tainted by the blood money of the slave trade.

We all have seen, heard, or read the Yankee propaganda about the horrors of the taskmaster's whip down in Dixie. But how often will we see on television or read in a magazine about the horrors of the "middle passage"? Most people have never heard about the middle passage, no doubt because it did not occur down South!

The movement of slaves from Africa to America began with the capture of Negroes by stronger black tribes in the interior of the African continent.[41] These Negroes were brought to the coast and sold (traded) for rum and guns. Note that the first step in the slave trade was taken by Africans preying upon their fellow Africans! It was seldom necessary for white men to go into the "jungle" to capture Negroes in this first passage. The middle passage was the movement of the slaves from the African coast to market. During the middle passage the sick slaves, who were near death with a contagious disease, and the dead were sorted out and thrown overboard. The rigors of living for up to one year in the unsanitary "tween deck" of the slave ship took its toll on human life.[42]

It has been estimated that more than thirty-three percent of the Africans taken from their homes died by the end of the middle passage. Cruel as it was, this was still a very effective method of providing merchandise for the Yankee slave merchants. The Northern slave peddlers brought to the slave trade their customary Yankee gift for efficiency in commerce. The combination of the holding areas and the horrors of the middle passage greatly increased the human cost of the slave trade. Yet the efficient Yankee peddler was still able to turn a handsome profit![43]

The Yankee myth of history conveniently chooses to ignore Northern crimes against blacks while concentrating upon the supposed crimes of the evil and vile Southern slave owners. Yet, can anyone imagine a Southern slave owner treating his slaves as cruelly as the Yankee merchants treated their captives? Any good farmer knows that he cannot stay in business if he allows half of his stock to die each year. If not for humanitarian reasons, then for simple economic reasons, the Southern slave owner treated the Negro better than the Yankee did. After all, Southerners had to pay hard cash to the Yankee for their slaves. Southern slave owners could not buy Negroes with cheap rum the way the Yankee slave traders did.

Regardless of how we feel about the subject today, the system of slavery was a legal and accepted system. While we were still colonies, Great Britain passed laws protecting slave property. Some American colonies were so zealous to protect their slave property that they passed additional laws. The first colony to pass such a law was our good ole Yankee neighbor of Massachusetts, which stands out as the first colony in America to legalize slavery, by enacting its own law to protect slavery. This was accomplished in the Code of the Massachusetts Colony in New England,[44] said statute adopted in 1641—a mere twenty-one years after the founding of this Yankee colony.

The people of Massachusetts were so eager to get into the slave business that they began to enslave Native Americans before they entered into the African slave business![45] When the Indian Wars began, the colony of Massachusetts began to capture and enslave the Indian population within its domain. In 1646, the colony passed a law by which Indians could be seized, held as slaves, and exported for sale. Major Richard Waldron (acting on behalf of the general court of the territory, which now is part of the state of Maine) in the winter of 1676 issued an order for the enslavement and export of any Indian "known to be a manslayer, traitor, or conspirator."[46] Now who do you supposed would decide if an accused Native American met these criteria? We can only speculate, but we are sure that these poor, hapless Indians received no better treatment at the hands of their Yankee conquerors than the Southern people received some two hundred years later!

These Yankees enslaved not only Indians who went to war against them, but also those who came voluntarily to them under their offer of amnesty.[47] So many Native Americans were enslaved that the thrifty, righteous men of Yankeedom shipped Indian slaves to Bermuda, Barbados, and other islands of the Caribbean for a neat little profit.[48] The trading of Native Americans was the beginning of the Yankee slave trade. This Yankee slave commerce was to continue legally until 1808 and illegally until the War for Southern Independence.

The contrast between the way the New England Yankee colony of Massachusetts dealt with its native population and the way the Southern colony of Virginia dealt with its native population is worthy of note. Virginia passed a law that made it *illegal* to enslave or deport a Native American under any circumstances.[49] While Massachusetts was still busy kidnapping and enslaving the American Indian, Virginia was busy passing laws to protect its Native American population. Yet, Virginia and the rest of the South are held up for ridicule, scorn, and derision by the self-righteous Yankee. At the same time the liberal media eagerly awaits another opportunity to spread the gospel of South-bashing, it totally ignores the fact that the Yankee colony of Massachusetts was the first to engage in the slave trade. Also hidden from public view is the fact that the industrial and commercial strength of the North is based upon the profits made by kidnapping, enslaving, and selling human beings—both Native Americans and Africans. The Yankee myth of history has made the Southerner the villain, the Yankee the hero, and the truth the victim.

QUESTION NUMBER ONE
Who First Legalized Slavery in America?

ANSWER
The Northern Colony of Massachusetts

If the Yankee state of Massachusetts was the first to use the force of its government to protect slavery, then the second question to ask is:

Who First Attempted to Prohibit
the Importation of Slaves?

The answer to this second question will be as astonishing to most people as is the answer to the first.

When the abolition of slavery is mentioned, most people think of Lincoln, radical Republicans, and the terrorist John Brown. But long before these extremists spoke, the state of Virginia had already gone on record as opposing the African slave trade. By an act of the General Assembly of the state of Virginia, while Patrick Henry was governor, the state outlawed the slave trade in Virginia.[50] This was done on October 5, 1778, ten years before Massachusetts and thirty years before the British parliament acted on the vile trade. The law was entitled "An act for preventing the further importation of slaves." This law not only prevented the importation of slaves, but also stipulated that any slave brought into the state contrary to the law would be then and forevermore *free*.[51]

This action of Virginia was the first taken in the civilized world prohibiting the slave trade. But even this was not the first time Virginia had attempted to stop the slave trade. Notice that the law was passed after Virginia had declared itself independent (i.e., had seceded) from Great Britain. The House of Burgesses had many times before attempted to stop the slave trade only to have its laws overruled by the royal governor.[52] The royal governor, who was appointed by the king, was acting on behalf of the king and parliament. In the months before he wrote the Declaration of Independence, Thomas Jefferson, a Southerner from Virginia, stated that one of the reasons the people of Virginia felt compelled to secede from the established British government was that the British had forced the state to endure the slave trade.[53] Jefferson stated that the king had "refused us permission to exclude by law" the slave trade. James Madison of Virginia spoke of the slave trade: "The British Government constantly checked the attempts of Virginia to put a stop to this infernal traffick."[54]

Virginia led the way for the entire South on the subject of this "infernal traffick." Throughout the South the move was on to end the trade, but the commercial interest of first England and then New England put a stop to this movement. After the American War for Independence was won, it would be the commercial interest of the North, allied with two Southern states, that would take the lead in protecting the slave trade. Years later, blue-clad soldiers from the North would march down South to free the slaves that they had sold into bondage. It has been said that while the invaders from the North sang glory, glory hallelujah, the very money they had made from the sale of slaves was jingling in their pockets. What a warped sense of morality to claim that it is wrong to own a slave but not to kidnap and sell a man into slavery. By now the people of the South should be very accustomed to such Yankee logic.

It should be clear why the United States Constitution protected this infernal traffic for twenty years after the adoption of the Constitution. The commercial interest of the North led the fight to include the provision for the protection of the slave trade in the Constitution. This provision was inserted into the new constitution over the objections of Virginia and other Southern states.[55] With the help of a few Southern representatives, the North won its first constitutional battle with the South. It was only after the South had seceded from the union with the North that a clear and unqualified prohibition was written into the Constitution outlawing the slave trade as Article 1, Section 9, of the Constitution of the Confederate States of America. That's right; it was not the United States Constitution that made the first clear and unqualified prohibition against the slave trade, but the Confederate States Constitution. When was the last time you saw a television program or read a history book which explained that little bit of history?

QUESTION NUMBER TWO
Who First Attempted to Prohibit the Importation of Slaves?

ANSWER
The Southern State of Virginia

Now let us pose the third question:

How Was Slavery Abolished in the North?

Any fifth-grade school child will tell you stories of the wonderful Underground Railroad. We are told that it led the poor, downtrodden slave from the Southern land of slavery to the Northern land of freedom and equality. Such anti-South poison flows from every new television program dealing with the subject of slavery. Again and again—like Pavlovian dogs—Southerners are forced to watch, read, and study about the righteous North struggling to improve the plight of man and save the glorious Union while fighting off vicious attacks of hate-filled Southerners. Yankee myth, Yankee lies, and Yankee propaganda; read on and we will explode these inflated social egos!

Yankees are quick to pat themselves on the back and congratulate themselves on freeing their slaves voluntarily. They are quick to inform us that it did not take an invading army to force them to do the "right thing." Lest Mr. Yankee boast too much, we should remind him that at the signing of the Declaration of Independence there were slaves in every American state. Not one Northern state rushed to free its slaves after signing the Declaration of Independence.

The system of African slavery was never very profitable in the North. If the Yankees have an eye for anything, they have an eye for profits. Soon after the end of the American War for Independence, the Northern states began a gradual removal of their slave population. The modern Yankees would have us believe that their ancestors were acting upon principles of morality in decreasing their slave population. The truth is that the only thing that motivated the Yankee was the principle of profit. This is clearly seen by the way in which the North granted freedom to its slave population. *No law was ever passed in the North that granted freedom to a person already in slavery.* In other words, the property rights of the Northern slave holders were always protected by the Northern states (something they must have forgotten to do when they came down South). After a certain date and after a child reached a given age, he or she would be free. All people who were slaves when the law was passed would remain slaves. For a slave to become free, in New Jersey, for example, he or she would have to be born after 1804 and have reached the age of twenty-one years. A slave woman who was fifteen in 1804 would remain a slave for life. If, at the age of thirty (the year then being 1829), she gave birth to a child, that child had to live in bondage until the age of twenty-one years (in 1850) before it would be free. Now remember that the mother was still a slave in the good ole land of Lincoln. As a matter of fact, just ten years before the War for Southern Independence there were 236 slaves for life in New Jersey.[56]

If the North was indeed the land of equality and freedom that it claims to have been, why did it not just do away with slavery in one quick step? Surely, if slavery was wrong in the South, it was just as wrong in the North. Or did Northerners think that a little evil was acceptable, and not as evil as slavery down South? Why didn't they use the same method to reduce the Southern slave population to a number equal to that in the North? The answer to these questions is both simple and sobering. The North used the method of granting gradual freedom to the unborn for two reasons. One motive was greed, and the other was racism.

By freeing only the people born into slavery after a certain time and age, the Yankee protected and thereby recognized the master's right in his property. No Northerners were deprived of their slave property that they owned at the time the law was passed. Also the law did not prohibit the slave owners from removing their property from the state to be sold in other parts of the country. Even if the children of a slave mother were nineteen or twenty years old, just a few years before the law granted them freedom, their master could remove them from the Northern state and sell them in a Southern state where they would remain slaves. Shocking as it may seem, under the Yankee system there could have been slaves in the North until 1873.

With only one exception, every Northern state of the original thirteen states abolished slavery in this manner. The state of Massachusetts never repealed its law on slavery.[57] One can only speculate as to how many slaves were actually allowed to obtain freedom under this arrangement, but it was a profitable way to emancipate slave property. If the Yankees are nothing else, they are profit-minded.

Other than allowing the Northern slave owners to cash in their slave property, the method of gradual emancipation also allowed the Yankees to rid themselves of a people they did not want to keep in Northern society. It had the effect of preventing a large increase in the numbers of free blacks in the state. The pious and righteous Yankee did not want the Negro in his state.

In 1788, eight years after the state of Massachusetts started its judicial emancipation of its slave population, it passed a law ordering every black, mulatto, or Indian who came into the state and remained two months to be whipped publicly.[58] This punishment was to be repeated if the black, mulatto, or Indian did not leave. This law remained in effect until 1834, by which time it had done its work of purging Massachusetts of "undesirables." While this law was in force the people of Massachusetts were hard at work in the slave trade, from which the state collected large tax revenues. It should now be easy to understand that the people of the North were not driven by humanitarian or egalitarian desires to free their slaves. Their emancipation process was driven by the vile impulse to remove, for profit, a people with whom the Yankees had no desire to associate.

QUESTION NUMBER THREE

How Did the Yankee Abolish Slavery in the North?

ANSWER

By a System of Gradual Emancipation That Allowed the Northern Slave Owners to Remove Their

**Property to the South, Sell the Slaves, and Thereby
Divest Themselves of the Human Responsibility
While Making a Handsome Profit.**

We will now move on to the fourth question in our discussion of slavery:

How was the Freed Black
Treated in the North?

From the prior discussion, you can imagine that the life of the free black in the North was not all that the Yankee would have us believe. In the North, for instance, the free black was not allowed to vote or in many cases to testify in a court of law. Even in Lincoln's home state of Illinois, blacks were banned from moving into the state! In reality the North offered blacks only semi-freedom somewhere between a white man and a slave, but they were always in an inferior social and legal position.

One way to judge the quality of life in those times is to look at the rate of population increase by comparing the number of live births with the number of deaths for a given year. Surely if the evil South was as bad and the North was as wonderful as the Yankee myth-makers would have us believe, then the percentage increase of the black population in the North would be greater than in the South. According to the 1860 census records, the percentage of increase in the black population in the South was twenty-three percent. The increase in the North was a bleak 1.7 percent.[59] A race of people who have proven themselves fruitful under slavery and the present-day welfare system were nearly annihilated by Yankee emancipation!

The returns from the 1850 census show that of white Northerners and Southerners, one person in every thousand was either deaf, dumb, blind, insane, or idiotic. For the free blacks of Yankeedom, one in every 506 was afflicted with one of these conditions.[60] If the North was such a better place for blacks, then it would be natural to assume that the Southern blacks would be in worse condition. Not according to the 1850 census records. It demonstrates that only one in 1,464 had a condition as previously described.[61] To put it bluntly, according the United States census records, the Negro slave in the South was in a better mental and physical condition than his free black brother in the North. Let us look at the numbers once again:

Ratio of persons with disability
(deaf, dumb, blind, insane, or idiotic)

White Northerner and Southerner........1 out of every 1000
Free Northern black ....1 out of every 506
Southern slave...............................1 out of every 1464

ANSWER TO QUESTION NUMBER FOUR

How was the Free Black
Treated in the North?

ANSWER

The Free Northern Black Was Living as a
Second-Class Citizen in Conditions Which
Were in Many Ways Not as Good as Those
for the Southern Slave.

Who Deserved to Bear
the Burden of Guilt for Slavery?

From the facts presented here, it is clear that the Southern people do not deserve the burden of guilt they have been forced to bear. There is guilt enough to go around. The blacks in Africa who kidnapped and sold their own kind into slavery and the Yankee merchants who traded rum and guns for black slaves in North and South America all deserve—yet do not receive—the larger portion of the guilt.

Why is it that the Southern people have been singled out for criticism and guilt? This question has already been answered in Chapter 1, "The Yankee Myth of History." The North needs this myth and other lies to justify its war of conquest, and to continue its oppression of the legitimate rights of the Southern people.

In a world as complex as the one in which we live, it is amazing how often people demand a quick fix or a simple solution to complex problems. For instance, scientists today tell us that the ozone layer of the atmosphere is being destroyed. This ozone layer is responsible for protecting us from cancer-causing radiation and is being eaten away by fossil fuels. There is a simple answer to the crisis; quit using those fuels. But how many of us are willing to stop driving cars and trucks? How many of us are willing to stop using electricity generated by coal? This is just a small example of how complex a "simple" solution can be. The same is true with the issue of slavery. Most Americans, from their simplistic point of view, will say that the South should have freed the slaves. But men such as Thomas Jefferson who stated that "these people are to be free" also said "once free we cannot live in the same government."

A perfect example of how complex the problem of ending the slavery issue was is seen in how John Quincy Adams dealt with the question of British naval vessels in search of slave traders on the high seas. He would not allow the British to stop slave vessels, even though that would result in many slave traders being protected by the United States flag.[62] Remember that the United States had just fought a war with the British over the very question of British naval power as it related to the sovereign rights of America. The United States had made its point that, as a sovereign nation, its commerce was secure on the high seas. Because Adams would not allow the British Navy to stop vessels flying the United States flag, many slavers were allowed to carry on this trade. This does not mean that Adams was in favor of that trade, only that he held the view that, unless both nations had a treaty to police each other's vessels, one nation could not force its right of search upon the other. According to international law, one cannot break one good law in order to pursue a pre-eminent good. Now when the people of the South make the statement that they were against slavery, but that they could not end the system unless it could be done in such a way as to safeguard the rights of all Southerners, Northerners set up a howl. It seemed natural and right for the Yankee (future President) Adams to say the same thing in relation to the slave trade, but never would the North allow Southerners to act in the same manner. The issue of how to end slavery and the slave trade needed time and cool heads more than anything else. Unfortunately the Yankee Abolitionists would allow neither. Those in the North who sought political gain saw in this issue a weak point. They used the South's stand for State's Rights then and continue to use it now as a political weapon against the South.

This discussion of the African slave issue has been offered not to belittle anyone, North or South, black or white. It has been made necessary because the American people have been brainwashed by misinformation about the nature of the issue of slavery.

In particular, Southerners have been told that they and their ancestors are responsible for this most vile of institutions, and that the noble North was fighting the war to end slavery and promote equality. It has been shown that the North did not free its slave property for any other reason than to rid itself of a people who had become unprofitable to keep and with whom it desired to have little or no social contact. In both the North and the South, there were different views on the issue of slavery and how to end it. The only difference is that the North had the opportunity to end slavery without disrupting its economy or social fabric. This was a luxury the Yankee never allowed the South.

Andrew J. Vawter, Company I, Twelfth Tennessee Volunteer Infantry. Vawter was wounded at the Battles of Shiloh and Stones River. After recovering from his wounds, he joined Company B, Twentieth Tennessee Cavalry, for the duration of the war. (Image courtesy of Robert M. Vawter, Milan, Tennessee)

The pride of the slave trade fleet, the Nightingale was built in Maine, bought by a Massachusetts firm, and commanded by a New Yorker. Originally used in the China tea trade, she was bought by a Salem, Massachusetts, firm and fitted out as a slaver. She was captured off the African coast with nine hundred slaves on board, and a death rate of three slaves per day. She was one of many American vessels that, under the protection of the United States flag, brought slaves to the New World, even after the War for Southern Independence had begun. After being brought back to New York, she was bought by the United States and used in its war efforts against the South. The use of the United States flag to protect slave traders caused black historian W. E. B. DuBois to state that between 1860 and 1865 more that twelve hundred slaves were brought into the New World under the protection of the United States flag.[1] (Note the flag flying from the Nightingale! See "Captain of the Flag," Chapter 2. (Image courtesy of Peabody Museum, Salem, Massachusetts)

Sergeant Swimmer, Qualla Lands, North Carolina, Company A, Thomas' Legion, Cherokee troops. Swimmer was one of more than four hundred Cherokee Confederates from the old Cherokee lands of North Carolina-Tennessee. Not only did these people support the Confederacy, but many of the Indians were wealthy planters with many black slaves.[2] (Image courtesy of National Anthropological Archives, Smithsonian Institution, Washington, D.C.)

William A. Norris, Company I, Sixth Arkansas Volunteer Infantry, was from Pocahontas, Arkansas. Norris enlisted at the age of twenty-five and was promoted to the rank of third sergeant. He was wounded at the Battle of Perryville, Kentucky, in 1862. (Image courtesy of Paulyne Lain, Ruston, Louisiana)

John M. Collins, second lieutenant, Company A, Forth-Sixth Alabama Volunteer Infantry, Coosa County, Alabama. "Lieutenant Collins was sometimes detached to command other companies because of his efficiency and was for some months the acting adjutant of the regiment, owing to the disabling wounds of adjutant Brooks." Company A was a large unit consisting of 120 privates, of which there were one preacher, one teacher, two merchants, two blacksmiths, one saddler, three mechanics, and 110 farmers.[4] (Image courtesy of Randy Collins, Ruston, Louisiana)

"I was born in Mississippi, but raised in a Northern State; associations there led me to regard the Southern white man as dire foes to the negroes, but . . . You are our best friends." Thus spoke Rep. L. W. Moore, a black representative from Mississippi, as he presented this silver set to the white Speaker of the House. In his presentation speech, he made note of the "warm, cordial, and unprejudiced relations" they (the black delegates) had experienced at the hands of the white Democrats, especially Speaker James S. Madison.[3] These six black representatives were the same delegates who voted for the erection of the Confederate memorial monument in Jackson, Mississippi, in 1890. (See story in Chapter 3.) (Image courtesy of Mrs. Robert Ragan, Cleveland, Mississippi)

William J. Bunn, Company I, Fourteenth Alabama Volunteer Infantry,
Auburn, Alabama. Captured during
the Battle of Spotsylvania Courthouse,
Virginia, May 1864. As a Confederate
POW he was sent to the infamous
prison at Elmira, New York. Bunn had
two other brothers in Confederate service; one, Marcus, was killed during
the Battle of Richmond, in June of
1862. (Image courtesy of Roy
Bunn, Roanoke, Alabama)

A typical home for the non-plantation white Southerner, known as a dogtrot house. It was from this type of dwelling that seventy to eighty percent
of the rank-and-file Confederate soldiers came. These people were for the
most part non-slaveholding Southerners. Those who did own slaves usually owned only one family and worked with their slaves in the fields (see
Plain Folk of the Old South, Chapter 1). This dogtrot home was built
in 1848 by Absalom Autry after he moved from Alabama to North-Cen-
tral Louisiana. Autry had eight sons, seven of whom were old enough to
volunteer for Confederate service. Three of his sons were sent to Virginia,
three were in the Army of Tennessee, and one fought in the Trans-Mississippi Department. Two of the Autry boys never came home from the war;
another three were POWs. (Absalom Autry house, Dubach, Louisiana; Tim Garlington, Ruston, Louisiana, photographer)

Moses Daniel Tate, Johnson County, Arkansas. In May 1862 Tate enlisted in Carroll's Regiment, Arkansas Cavalry, and was later transferred to the First Arkansas Cavalry, then moved to the Engineer Corps. (Image courtesy of Mary Sanders, Baton Rouge, Louisiana)

George S. Waterman, midshipman, Confederate States Navy. Waterman served on the CSS Gaines during the Battle of Mobile Bay, and was cited for his efforts. No other branch of military service had to do so much with so little as the Confederate States Navy. An agrarian nation had to transform itself into a great naval power even as the enemy was approaching its coasts. At the outbreak of war, the timber for its ships stood in the forest, the iron was still in the ground, and hemp for ropes had yet to be grown and cut; nevertheless, the Confederate Navy produced men, ships, and victories that astounded the world.[5] (Image courtesy of Tulane University Libraries, Howard-Tilton Memorial Library, New Orleans, Louisiana)

No, these are not the children of some Yankee Abolitionist hearing about the "bad old slave days" from a runaway slave. The black man is Frank Loper, a former slave of President Jefferson Davis. Loper is surrounded by the great-grandchildren of President and Mrs. Davis. Loper was born on the Davis plantation of Briarfield, near Natchez, Mississippi. He remained a friend to the family well after the death of President Davis in 1889. The love expressed in the eyes of these people should make any reasonable person question the Yankee myth of a hate-filled, racist South. (Image courtesy of Beauvoir, the Jefferson Davis Shrine, last home of Jefferson Davis, Biloxi, Mississippi)

A Mrs. Shelby of Vicksburg, Mississippi, with her former slaves. This photograph was taken circa 1885. It was not uncommon after the war for black and white families to stay together. Many, as this photograph indicates, did so into old age. (Image courtesy of Old Court House Museum, Vicksburg, Mississippi)

Corporal William F. Kennedy, Company D, Tenth Alabama
Volunteer Infantry, was wounded during Pickett's charge at
Gettysburg. Kennedy's son Fred is a member of the Sons of
Confederate Veterans in Alabama, and is also a "Civil War"
reenactor. Fred has been active in protecting the truth about
our Southern history and heritage for many years. He is a
living example of how close we are to those who fought for
Southern Independence. (Image courtesy of Fred
Kennedy, Reece City, Alabama)

Major George Walker, First Louisiana Heavy Artillery. Born in Ireland, Walker moved to Louisiana in 1858, where he served as a physician on a large plantation. At the outbreak of the war, this Irish medical doctor offered his services to the Confederacy. He was the surgeon of an artillery battery during the war. (Image courtesy of James B. Moore, Longview, Texas)

Bill Yopp, former slave and Confederate veteran, visiting his former master at the Confederate Veterans Home in Atlanta. Bill brought gifts not only to his former master (as shown here) but also to all the elderly Confederate veterans in residence there. Before his death, Bill was admitted to the home; when he died, he was buried in the Confederate Veterans Cemetery in Atlanta. (See Yopp's story in Chapter 3.) (Image courtesy of Charles W. Hampton, Clarkston, Georgia)

James H. Trezevant served as first lieutenant and adjutant of the First Regiment Regulars, Louisiana Infantry, and later as captain of one of the companies of the unit. Trezevant, like so many Southerners, had a strong affinity for his dog. This one was very special to him because the dog came to his rescue one evening in New Orleans during a late-night altercation. (Image courtesy of Tulane University Libraries, Howard-Tilton Memorial Library, New Orleans, Louisiana)

Abd Rahman Ibrahima, son of the king of the African people of Timbo. His people were slave holders and slave traders. While in the process of capturing fellow Africans for the slave trade, he was made a captive himself. He was sold into slavery by his African enemies and remained a slave in Mississippi for approximately forty years before returning to his homeland. (See Ibrahima's story in Chapter 2.) (Image courtesy of the Library of Congress, Washington, D.C.)

Unidentified Confederate cavalryman, Arkansas. May the principles for which this unknown Confederate soldier fought never become unidentifiable or unknown to a future generation of Southerners. (Image courtesy of Dale West, Longview, Texas)

Warning! Cultural bigots at work. The destruction of the Confederate monument at Cedar Grove Cemetery, New Bern, North Carolina, is just one example of anti-South bigotry that has become so commonplace today. (See story in Chapter 13.) (Image courtesy of North Carolina Division, Sons of Confederate Veterans; Dave Davis, photographer)

Andrew M. Gooings, Company I, Thirty-First Louisiana Volunteer Infantry. Gooings was also a veteran of the Mexican War, having served in the First Alabama Volunteer Infantry. Gooings served with his Confederate comrades of the Thirty-First during the siege of Vicksburg, Mississippi, suffering two wounds from which he never fully recovered. Vicksburg is approximately a hundred miles from Gooings' home in Union Parish, Louisiana. During the siege, the people of that area could hear the boom of the big guns. No Southern family was ever far removed from the sounds or effects of Yankee invasion.[6] (Image courtesy of Richard Ballard, Ruston, Louisiana)

James Dinkins, Madison County, Mississippi. After taking part in the Battle of Big Bethel as a member of the North Carolina Military Institute corps of cadets, Dinkins joined Company C, Eighteenth Mississippi Volunteer Infantry, under the command of Colonel, later General, William Barksdale. In 1863 Dinkins was promoted to the rank of lieutenant and transferred to Gen. James R. Chalmers Division of Gen. N. B. Forrest's cavalry. (Image courtesy of Tulane University Libraries, Howard-Tilton Memorial Library, New Orleans, Louisiana)

Hispanic defenders of Dixie, members of the Benavides Texas Cavalry, left to right are Refugio Benavides, Atanacio Vidauri, Cristobal Vidauri, and John Leyendecker. These Hispanic Confederates were part of Brig. Gen. Santos Benavides' Texas Cavalry. The area protected by General Benavides and his men became known as "the Confederacy on the Rio Grande." (Image courtesy of Bruce Marshall, Austin, Texas)

Lt. Col. James T. Adams and wife, Lucy Beckwith Adams. There is no way to calculate the sorrow and tragedy that befell an unknown number of young families like the Adams as they answered the call of their country. The soldiers of the Confederacy were sent off to war by the women of the South like heroes, and in defeat these noble ladies nurtured the broken soldiers back to health and with floral and marble tributes continued their defense of Southern rights. God bless the ladies of Dixie! (Images courtesy of Tulane University Libraries, Howard-Tilton Memorial Library, New Orleans, Louisiana)

"*Johnny Reb was not just a white man, he was black too. Blacks were at home, the only land they knew. Black and white women encouraged their husbands to fight.*"[7]   *Dr. L. L. Haynes, black educator*
Baton Rouge, Louisiana

(Image courtesy of The Institute of Texas Cultures, San Antonio, Texas; Bruce Marshall, artist)

William D. Bryant, Randolph County, Georgia, enlisted in Company H, First Georgia Infantry, on September 26, 1861. Bryant was appointed second corporal in Company G, Fifty-Fifth Georgia Infantry, on May 5, 1862. Corporal Bryant died of typhoid fever while on duty in Knoxville, Tennessee, on December 29, 1862. He was married with five children. (Image courtesy of Robert G. McLendon, Jr., Gainesville, Florida)

What is the message that these Southerners are trying to send to future generations? In word and deed Southerners have proclaimed to the world that they were fighting for the right of self-determination during the War for Southern Independence. (Image courtesy of Confederate Memorial Hall, New Orleans, Louisiana)

Elias Murphy, a native of Kentucky, moved to Louisiana with his family as a child. Murphy enlisted in Company I, Sixteenth Louisiana Volunteer Infantry, in 1861 and went back to Kentucky with his unit. Murphy fought in his native state during the campaign of 1862.[8] It was said of Murphy that he could stand in the line of battle and shoot Yankees with the calmness of a man shooting squirrels. (Image courtesy of George Jacob, Castor, Louisiana)

CHAPTER 3

Race Relations in the Old South

. . . we jes' went on peaceful an' happy til de war come an' rooted ebery blessed thing up by de roots.[1]

Charles Stewart, former slave

INTRODUCTORY COMMENTS

In this chapter we will look at the life and contributions of black men and women of the old South. In so doing, we will call upon expert witnesses of life in the "slave days." We will quote from an official United States document, *The Slave Narratives*, which was obtained by the United States government during the Great Depression. Testimonies from some of the last surviving slaves of the Old South will be used to give us an idea of their life under slavery and after Yankee-induced freedom. To collaborate their testimony we will also quote from the *Official Records: War of the Rebellion*, the official report of the United States relating to the War for Southern Independence. In our research of the slave narratives, we have noted an overwhelming body of evidence (more than seventy percent) in which only positive statements were made about the relationship between slaves and masters. Contrary to what many popular novelists and journalists would have everyone believe, this relationship was very close and mutually respectful. Those who report on life at the mercy of brutal masters and the horrors of slavery are reporting, we believe, on cases that were definitely in the minority (thirty percent or less).

In looking at life under the slave system, we do not pretend that such life was always good, or that masters were always just. Yes, there were cases of mistreatment and abuse by some masters. Just as there are some cases of sexual abuse of children by some parents. But, just because we see abuse by some, that does not indicate that all or a majority are responsible for such activities. As we would not condemn all parents because some are abusive, neither

81

Levy Carnine, Pelican Rifles, Second Louisiana Volunteer Infantry. Carnine was from the Mansfield area of DeSoto Parish. He not only served his master during the war but also became a local hero for his service to the men and families of the Pelican Rifles. After the war Carnine became one of the experts on the activity of his unit. (See his story in Chapter 3.) (Portrait by Jim Whittington, Shreveport, Louisiana)

would we accuse all slave holders of intentional cruelty because a few were abusive. Those who trade in the sensational have cast a vile shadow upon many noble and decent people by blaming all for the sins of the few.

There is one misconception we would like to clarify. In looking at the participants in the slave system of the Old South, we are looking at very few members of Southern society. In 1860, there were 5.3 million whites in the South. Of that number, approximately three hundred thousand (six percent) were slave holders.[2] The number of slave holders who could be classified as aristocratic planters was only 150,000 (three percent). The rest of the slave holders owned five or fewer slaves and worked beside their slaves in order to make a living.

The vast majority of Southerners owned no slaves, and from these people were drawn the vast numbers of soldiers of the Confederacy. Also let us state here that we are not defending the system of slavery, but rather seeking the *truth* about the history of that institution and of life in the Old South.

In the Old South, there were at least three different views of slavery ranging from those who wished the quick abolition of slavery, such as Robert E. Lee, to those like Jefferson Davis who sought to uplift and educate the slaves to make them ready for freedom, to others who believed that black people could never be made ready for freedom. It should be noted that each view of slavery had its followers, but all honorable people regardless of how they felt about the institution of slavery believed that the black people should be accorded the respect due them as taught in the Bible in regard to slaves.

The biblical foundation for the slave-master relationship was deeply rooted in America, being practiced by both Southerners and Northerners. The first defense of slavery in America was made by the Puritan Fathers of Massachusetts, and that defense was based on principles founded in both the Old and the New Testament of the Holy Bible. Such notables as Cotton Mather and Judge John Saffin voiced their approval of the institution of slavery in Massachusetts, basing their arguments on the Bible.[3] The idea that slavery was a moral system based upon biblical standards was held by Americans from Georgia to Maine. Today, of course, we do not see slavery in that light, but it was held so by Americans both North and South during the early part of our history.

Race Relations in the Old South

The contribution to the development of the North and South by black Americans is a subject that for too long has been played down. Some people are motivated by their fear of saying anything pleasant about the system of African servitude, and therefore they refuse to admit that during the "slave days" anything good could have happened. These people, with their negative attitudes, will always take any opportunity to ridicule the South. Because of their misguided idea of what slavery was like during the days of the Old South, these people have a burning hatred for slavery and for the South. To them, nothing good could ever come from either. Their hatred for both slavery and the South is so great that they can never accept the idea that slavery was a real and necessary aspect of life in the early days of the North just as it was in the South. Northern liberals apparently feel that, if they admit that slavery was a necessary part of Northern history, their society will be branded with the same negative characteristics that they have imputed to the South.

When we look at the early development of the Northern colonies, we will find that as long as the need for slaves existed, slavery was an accepted system of labor.[4] It was not until the supply of free labor was large enough to meet the demands of society that the system of African servitude was abandoned. It should be noted here that John Adams stated that slavery in the North was not done away with for moral or ethical reasons, but because Northern workers refused to compete with blacks. Adams stated, "Argument might have some weight in the abolition of slavery in Massachusetts, but the real cause was the multiplication of labouring white people, who would no longer suffer the rich to employ these sable rivals so much to their injury. The common people would not suffer the labor, by which alone they could obtain a subsistence, to be done by slaves. If the gentlemen had been permitted by law to hold slaves, the common white people would have put the slaves to death, and their masters too perhaps."[5]

In this statement of John Adams, we see that the clear intent of those who destroyed slavery in the North was their economic protection, and that alone. Also note that Adams believed that the people of Massachusetts would be willing to put the black people and their masters to death rather than compete with the slave labor system.

Those who refuse to recognize the system of African servitude as a positive contribution to the development of America have done a great disservice to those they pretend to serve, the African-Americans. By not looking at the positive contributions made by African-Americans during slavery in both the North and the South, they have condemned black people to a "no-history" role in early American development. A sub-set of the "no-history" group will advocate a role for the slave in early American society by advancing the theory that slavery was so repulsive that the black people acted in such a way as to sabotage the work they were given. Both parts of this "no-history" theory of black life under slavery are in vogue (i.e., are politically correct today), but both are wrong, as we shall demonstrate.

There is also another group of people who refuse to accept the fact that blacks have played an important role in the development of America. The radical racists seem to find it easier to equate blackness with nothingness than to accept the idea that our society has been positively influenced by the African-American. This group would also like us to believe that the black man has a "no-history" role in the evolution of our society. Both groups, for their own reasons, are equally wrong. The history of the black people of the South and of America cannot and should not be overlooked just because that history does not match a preconceived notion of what the system of slavery was really like. These two groups (liberal politically correct "PC" or radical racist) both display a form of bigotry; the first is a cultural bigot, and the second a racial bigot.

As we look at the life and contributions of the black men and women of the Old South, we will prove their worth and loyalty to the South. In so doing, we will call upon expert witnesses of life in the "slave days." We will quote from an official United States document, *The Slave Narratives*, which was obtained by the United States government during the Great Depression. Testimonies from some of the last surviving slaves of the Old South will be used to give us an idea of their life under slavery and after Yankee-induced freedom. To collaborate their testimony we will also quote from *The Official Records: War of the Rebellion*, the official report of the United States as it relates to the War for Southern Independence. In our research of the slave narratives, we have noted an overwhelming body of evidence (more than seventy percent) in which only positive statements were expressed about the relationship between slaves and masters. Contrary to what many popular novelists and journalists would have us believe, this relationship was very close and mutually respectful. Those who report on life at the mercy of brutal masters and the horrors of slavery are reporting, we believe, on cases that were in the minority (thirty percent or less).

In looking at life under the slave system, we do not pretend that such life was always good, or that masters were always good people. Yes, there were cases of mistreatment and abuse by some masters. Just as there are some cases of sexual abuse documented about some parents toward their children. But just because we see some abuse by some does not indicate that all or a majority are responsible for such activities. Just as we would not condemn all parents because some are abusive, neither would we condemn all slave holders because a few were abusive. Those who trade in the sensational, of course, do so, and in so doing have cast a shadow over many noble and decent people.

In looking at life in the slave system of the Old South, we are looking at a very few white Southerners. One must bear in mind that in the Old South less than six percent of white people owned more than three to five slaves. The vast majority of white people owned no slaves, and these made up the huge numbers of men who fought the War for Southern Independence. Also let us state here that we are not defending the system of slavery, but rather seeking the *truth* about the history of that institution and about life in the Old South.

Schooled in the curriculum of modern "politically correct" history, the average American cannot understand the idea of blacks being anything other than antagonistic to the South. As we have shown in other areas of so-called history (actually Yankee myth), what appears as truth, after close investigation, so often falls under the heading of "myth." Such is the case with the relationship between black Southerners and the Old South.

Most Northerners of the 1860s were schooled in the myth of slavery and the Old South by infamous propaganda tracts and novels such as *Uncle Tom's Cabin*. Filled with such vile misinformation about the South, the average Northerner believed that, with a little effort on his or her part, the vast majority of black people of the

South would join in the North's effort to stamp out all vestiges of the South. Northerners failed to understand that the association between black and white people encompassed a wide range of relationships. The people of the slave-holding South co-existed with their black families in relationships ranging from the few cruel masters to the very paternalistic and loving masters. According to Abolitionist theory, the white/black relations was based on the application of brute force by the slave holders over the slaves. If this had been correct, the slave population would have been much more inclined to revolt against their masters during an invasion.

If the relationship between the slave and master was not predicated solely on brute force, what was the nature of the relationship? The Yankee historian Frederick Law Olmsted noted the closeness of the relationship between slave and master when he visited Virginia in the early part of the 1800s. Olmsted observed a white woman and a black woman seated together on a train. Both ladies had their children with them, and the children were eating candy from a common container. Of this incident one writer states, ". . . the girls munched candy out of the same bag 'with a familiarity and closeness' which would have astonished and displeased most Northerners."[6] This close relationship may have been unheard of in the North, but it was a common sight in the South. Even in Mississippi, a warm relationship existed between the two races. In his work, *The Peculiar Institution: Slavery in the Antebellum South*, Kenneth Stampp stated, "Visitors often registered surprise at the social intimacy that existed between masters and slaves in certain situations. A Northerner saw a group of Mississippi farmers encamped with their slaves near Natchez after hauling their cotton to market. Here they assumed a 'cheek by jowl' familiarity with perfect good will and a mutual contempt for the nicer distinctions of color."[7] This type of relationship could not be enforced with a whip, but it existed and was based on respect and love. Not only Northern historians but also Yankee soldiers spoke with contempt about the closeness of the relationship between slave and master. In his diary Pvt. John Haley of Maine had this to say about the slave/master relationship: "Two-hundred years of slavery have not elevated the nigger or his master. The only advancement has been in the way of unnatural selection; the line of demarcation between white and black is not as positive as true virtue demands, but is dimmed by a kind of neutral tint that cannot but be regarded with suspicion."[8]

Note the flagrant racist appeal this Yankee soldier is making. Haley clearly bemoans the fact that the racial line was not being kept as bold as Northerners desired. He equates both black and white Southerners as debased and backward. This racist attitude was not something new for Northerners. The Northern racist attitude was noted by an English Abolitionist, James S. Buckingham, who in 1842 wrote, "This is only one among the many proofs I had witnessed of the fact, that the prejudice of color is not nearly so strong in the South as in the North. [In the South] it is not at all uncommon to see the black slaves of both sexes, shake hands with white people when they meet, and interchange friendly personal inquiries; but at the North I do not remember to have witnessed this once; and neither in Boston, New York, or Philadelphia would white persons generally like to be seen shaking hands and talking familiarly with blacks in the streets."[9] Is it any wonder that, with such an attitude about Southerners, the Northern army could wreak such havoc on the South?

The North was unwilling to learn from true history about the relationship between slave and master, but instead Northerners chose to perpetuate the Abolitionist lie about the South. If the North had taken the time to look at the way blacks had acted when other invading armies had sought to entice slave revolts in the South, they would have noted a strong history of blacks supporting their "home folks."

During the American War for Independence, when the British army offered "freedom" to the slave population if they would revolt against their masters, very few took up that offer. In truth, slaves just like their masters supported the American effort for independence. During the War of 1812 the British captured Washington, D.C. At that time Washington, D.C., had more than fourteen hundred slaves and nearly a thousand free blacks in the city. The British had hoped that the blacks of Washington would fly to the British flag and help defeat the Americans. Again, the invader was disappointed.[10] At the last battle of the War of 1812, the Battle of New Orleans, free men of color were a part of the American army that defeated the British. When the Northern armies came down South offering "freedom" to the slaves of

Dixie, the words were not new to the slaves. Same song, different verse; but the slaves had heard it before.

BLACK CONTRIBUTIONS
TO THE SOUTHERN WAR EFFORT

The contributions of black Southerners to the war effort between 1861 and 1865 fall into two major categories: (1) civilian support, and (2) military support.

Black support of the civilian effort has often been overlooked or belittled by the detractors of the South. Any modern war, and it has often been said that this war was the first really modern war, cannot be carried on without proper support from the home front. Everything from food to munitions must be provided. To keep a modern army in the field, there must be an adequate and stable labor force at home. The work force must be skilled to provide those materials that an army requires to fight. As an example of such skilled labor, one only has to look at the performance of the blacks on the farms and plantations of the South during the war. With virtually no adult white males (age sixteen to forty-five years) on hand, the black farmers of the South keep food production at a level that allowed the army and civilians to be fed. Shoes, harnesses, ropes, clothes, and other necessities were made and forwarded to the men on the field of battle. The black Southerner supported the civilian war effort in many unacknowledged ways. The Tredegar Iron Works in Richmond, which was the most important iron works for the South, drew nearly one-half of its work force from the ranks of its black population.[11] Without the support of the black population, the war effort of the South would not have lasted nearly as long as it did.

Abolitionists usually insist that the only reason that the blacks performed such acts was because they were intimidated by the whites into acting in this manner. Yet, throughout the South, the mature white males were far away in the army. In many places, the white population consisted of women, children, and elderly men. Does anyone think that a people who had proven themselves fierce in war in Africa could be cowered into doing so much against their will? Of course not. Yes, some blacks ran away from home just as some young people today run away from home, but that does not mean that all blacks of that time were unhappy with their lot or that they were being mistreated. As Prof. Edward C. Smith has said, ". . . blacks could . . . have escaped to nearby Union lines but few chose to do so and instead remained at home and became the most essential element in the Southern infrastructure to resisting Northern invasion."[12]

BLACKS IN GRAY IN THE CONFEDERACY

Given that all this is true, what about the contribution to the Southern military effort by blacks? We will take the testimony of some Northern officers and enlisted men to answer that question.

In 1862 Dr. Lewis Steiner, chief inspector of the United States Army Sanitary Commission, was an eyewitness to the occupation of Frederick, Maryland, by Gen. Thomas J. ("Stonewall") Jackson's army. Steiner makes this statement about the makeup of that army: "Over 3,000 negroes must be included in this number [Confederate troops]. These were clad in all kinds of uniforms, not only in cast-off or captured United States uniforms, but in coats with Southern buttons, State buttons, etc. These were shabby, but not shabbier or seedier than those worn by white men in the rebel ranks. Most of the negroes had arms, rifles, muskets, sabres, bowie-knives, dirks, etc. . . . and were manifestly an integral portion of the Southern Confederacy Army."[13] Can anyone doubt that these blacks, well armed and many mounted, were with this army because some "mean old Southerner" was forcing them to be there? Of course not. They were there because, just like their white counterparts, they were fighting an invader.

Private John W. Haley, Seventeenth Maine Infantry, U.S., gives this account of black resistance to the Yankee invader by a black sharpshooter: "There seemed to be a fatality lurking in certain spots. . . . It wasn't long before Mr. Reb made his whereabouts known, but he was so covered with leaves that no eye could discern him. Our sharpshooter drew a bead on him and something dropped, that something being a six-foot nigger whose weight wasn't less than 300 pounds."[14] Both officers and private Union soldiers report the "impact" that the black Confederates had on the invader.

Black men in service to the South were such common sights that, not only did Northern officers and enlisted men write about the service to the South by blacks, but also a British officer reported on the service rendered the South by its black soldiers. Captain Arthur L. Fremantle was a British observer attached to General Lee's army. In 1863 Captain Fremantle went with Lee's army on the Gettysburg campaign. During this time he witnessed many accounts of black loyalty to the Southern cause, including one case in which a black soldier was in charge of white Yankee prisoners. These acts by the loyal blacks prompted the following remarks by the Englishman: "This little episode of a Southern slave leading a white Yankee soldier through a Northern village, alone and of his own accord, would not have been gratifying to an abolitionist, . . . Nor would the sympathizers both in England and in the North feel encouraged if they could hear the language of detestation and contempt with which the numerous Negroes with Southern armies speak of their liberators."[15]

With such testimony, how can anyone continue to believe the myth that Southern blacks were longing for Yankee-induced freedom? How can anyone continue to accept the Yankee Abolitionist view of a hate-filled and evil South? The truth is that life in the Old South was very different from that which the "politically correct" historians would have us believe. Yes, there were many blacks who fought for the South.

The following list is a small sample of the black men who fought for the Confederacy during the War for Southern Independence. Although many historians try to ignore or play down the significance of the black contribution to the war effort, this small sample will clearly show that they had a direct impact on many of their fellow white comrades. Under the heading of status you will note either a "S" for slave, or "FMC" to indicate *gens de couleur libre*, that is, free man of color. In some cases there is no indication of status because none could be found.

The contribution that these people made to the South, like that of their white counterparts, is worthy of our praise and admiration. The main function played by the slaves who went into service with their masters was that of a body servant. They usually referred to this function as bodyguard. Indeed, investigation of the records of these men show that their action in time of battle and in the face of great emergency was more like that of a bodyguard. Many of those who would like to downplay the importance of the black contribution to the South will tell us that blacks only served as cooks and teamsters. Those roles were very vital to the armies of that age. Many of our own ancestors provided the very same service. As you will note, even a cook can become involved in a battle and be subjected to the same dangers of death, injury, or capture. Also remember that the men in nineteenth-century armies died just as often from camp diseases as from battle wounds. Even a bodyguard was subjected to this great danger. All who served did so at great risk to themselves and to the glory of the cause for Southern independence.

Black Confederate Patriots

STATE	NAME	UNIT	STATUS	SERVICE
GA	Thomas Williamson[16]	Light Artillery	S	Bodyguard
MS	Julia Mason[17]	Nurse		Nurse at Vicksburg, had arm shot off during siege
GA	Neptune King[18]	Inf.	S	Crossed enemy lines & brought back body of master
GA	Richmond Mitchell[19]	Inf.	S	
MS	J. C. Leeper[20]	Cav.	S	Bodyguard
GA	James Clarke[21]	Inf.	FMC	Fifer
TN	Levi Oxendine[22]		FMC	
GA	Alexander Harris[23]	Inf.	S	Bodyguard
MS	Andrew Williams[24]	Inf.	S	Served with master in VA in 1909; applied for C.S. pension; his former master drew up and signed document for him.
GA	George Dwelle[25]	Inf.		
GA	Amos Rucker[26]	Inf.		
MS	Isham Marshall[27]	Cav.	S	Entered C.S. service in 1862 with his master; in 1894 was still living on former master's plantation.
GA	Richmond Elder[28]	Inf.	S	
GA	Tim Billing[29]	Inf.	S	Cook

AR	Hunter Beneux[30]		S	Saved master's life while fighting off Yankees
GA	Bill Yopp[31]	Inf.	S	Stayed with master during war and afterwards in Confederate Home
VA	Dick Poplar[32]		FMC	Cook; POW after battle of Gettysburg for 20 mo. rather than turn his back on the South
MS	Moses Pringle[33]	Inf.	S	Bodyguard
LA	Tom Strother[34]	Inf.	S	Bodyguard
VA	Jim Lewis[35]	Inf.	FMC	Bodyguard and friend of Gen. Jackson; stayed with Jackson's army after Jackson's death
AL	Toney [36]	Cav.	S	Bodyguard; he and his master rode with Forrest
LA	Charles Lutz[37]	Inf.	FMC	Participated in all major VA battles; POW after Fredericksburg; exchanged wounded at Gettysburg; POW exchanged & furloughed
LA	Jean Baptiste Pierre-Auguste[38]	Inf.	FMC	Participated in battle of Vicksburg wounded; paroled
LA	Lufroy Pierre-Auguste[39]	Inf.	FMC	Participated in battles of Shiloh, Farmington, and Murfreesboro
LA	Evariste Guillory, Sr.	Home Guard	FMC	Father and son served their home state throughout war, paroled June 1865
	Evariste Guillory, Jr.[40]	Home Guard	FMC	

LA	Levy Carnine[41]	Inf.	S	Bodyguard for three masters during war; became local hero for efforts in getting mail through Yankee lines

It may prove a little embarrassing to those who claim that the North was fighting for the blacks to note that no less than two African-Americans were taken prisoner from the Southern army at the Battle of Gettysburg, one from Virginia and one from Louisiana.

Dick Poplar was well known in Petersburg before the war as a cook. He took that specialty with him when he entered the Confederate army. However, being a cook did not prevent him from being taken prisoner by the Yanks. At Point Lookout Prison, the Negro guards tried their best to make this black man turn against his people. Dick Poplar maintained during this time that he was a loyal "Jeff Davis man." He stayed in this hellish POW camp for twenty months. A word from him at any time would have set him free, but he never turned his back on the South.

Charles F. Lutz, enlisted in Company F, Eighth Louisiana Volunteer Infantry, on June 23, 1861. Lutz was from St. Landry Parish in Louisiana. He was a free man of color and of mixed ancestry. He could easily pass for either a creole of color or a white man. Early in the war his regiment was sent to Virginia, where it became part of Gen. Richard Taylor's brigade of General Jackson's Valley Army. He participated in all of Jackson's astounding battles during the Valley Campaign. While fighting at Fredericksburg on Marye's Heights during the Battle of Chancellorsville, Lutz was taken prisoner along with two hundred of his fellow Southerners. He remained a POW for two weeks until exchanged. A few weeks later he was wounded and taken prisoner at the Battle of Gettysburg. After he was paroled and furloughed, he went home to recuperate. In 1900 he was awarded a Confederate pension from the state of Louisiana.

One of the more impressive stories about loyal blacks during the War for Southern Independence is the story of Levy Carnine.

Levy Carnine was a young slave of a Mr. Hogan in 1861 when the war broke out. When his young master enlisted in the Pelican

Rifles, the first company to leave DeSoto Parish during the war, young Levy went along with his master as his bodyguard. The Pelican Rifles became one of the companies of the Second Louisiana Volunteer Regiment and as such was sent to Virginia early in the war. Levy was near at hand when his master was killed during one of the early battles of the war. Levy saw to the affairs of burying his master and then reported to Col. Jesse M. Williams of the Second Regiment, Louisiana Volunteer Infantry. The colonel requested that Levy stay with him, which Levy did until the colonel was killed in battle. Again Levy carried out his duties to a dead master by burying and marking the grave of another Southern soldier. Then Levy returned to the Pelican Rifles, the group of men with whom his first master had enlisted. He stated that he "took up with the boys" from his old unit and home town. He served them faithfully, including going into battle with them on several occasions.

After the fall of Vicksburg and Port Hudson, most communications with the western Confederacy were lost. The boys from De-Soto Parish in Northwest Louisiana lost all contact with their families in that part of the Confederacy. The boys collected as much Federal money as they could and asked Levy if he would take the money and letters they had written and "desert" to the Yankees. Their plan was to have Levy cross the Union lines and then make his way back to Louisiana carrying their letters home. A more difficult task could not be asked of a friend, but Levy was up to it and brought home to Northwest Louisiana mail and news to the soldiers' friends and families. Levy became a local hero. People from all over the area came to hear his stories about the "boys" who were fighting in faraway Virginia. As if this were not enough, near the end of the war Levy joined one of the last units to be raised in that area as a bodyguard to Ben R. Hogan, a relative of Levy's first master. After the war, Levy remained in Mansfield, Louisiana, where he had many friends. He was always sought after by those seeking information about the Pelican Rifles. His name was carried on the official roll of the United Confederate Veterans as an honorary member. When Levy Carnine passed away, the expenses for his funeral were paid by the members of the local Confederate veterans unit. The old Confederate soldiers marched en masse to the cemetery where they laid his body to rest. So well respected was Levy that the Confederate veterans insisted that Levy, a black man, be buried with all the other Confederate soldiers. Levy Carnine became one of the very few black men to be buried in the white cemetery at Mansfield, Louisiana, where his grave is marked with the words, "Levy Carnine, C.S.A."

These stories of black and white people struggling against a common foe may seem strange to those who have only read the victor's views of the War for Southern Independence. Volumes could be and are in the process of being written about how well the people of the South got along with each other until the Yankee showed up. Let us once again look at the words of one who lived as a slave during that time: "I suppose dem Yankees wuz all right in dere place, but dey neber belong in de South. . . . An' as for dey a-setting me free! Miss, us [Negroes] . . . wuz free as soon as we wuz bawn. I always been free!"[42]

EX-SLAVES SPEAK OUT FOR THE SOUTH

During the late 1930s the federal government, through its Works Projects Administration (WPA), sent journalists and writers throughout the South, and a few Northern states to collect the firsthand testimony of the remaining ex-slaves of America. Their testimony was collected and is maintained in the National Archives in Washington, D.C. In the following text we reproduce some of the statements of those ex-slaves as a representative sample of the entire "Narratives." We are in debt to the Reverend Steve Wilkins of Monroe, Louisiana, who has completed research on four state narratives, for his help with this information which is quoted from his forthcoming work on the "Slave Narratives." In his research of the "Slave Narratives" Rev. Wilkins has found that a vast majority (more than seventy percent) of ex-slaves had only good experiences to report about life as a slave and about the Old South. We will use the very words of these ex-slaves to give us an idea what their life was like before the war. We will look at how the ex-slaves reported their feelings toward slavery, Yankees, freedom, and the Confederacy.

SLAVERY

Isaam Morgan, Mobile, AL

"Any time a slave worked over time or cut mo' wood dan he s'pose to, Massa pay him money for it, 'cauze when ever one of us slaves

seen somp'n we lak, we did jus lak de white folks does now. Us
bought it. Massa never whupped none of his slaves. . . . No'm none
of our slaves ever tried to run away. Dey all knowed dey was well
off. . . . dey [Yankees] offered me a hoss iffen I would go nawth
wid dem, but I jus' couldn't leave de Massa even dough I did want
dat hoss mighty bad."[43]

Simon Phillips, AL

"People has the wrong idea of slave days. We was treated good. My
Massa never laid a hand on me the whole time I was wid him. . . .
Sometime we loaned the massa money when he was hard
pushed."[44]

Mary Rice, AL

"Massa Cullen and Mistis Ma'y Jane was de bes' Marster and Mistis
in de worl'! Once when I was awful sick, Mistis Ma'y Jane had me
brung in de Big House and put me in a room dat sot on de 'other
side of the kitchen so she could take kere of me herself cause it was
a right fur piece to de quarter and I had to be nussed day and
night. . . . I was happy all de time in slavery days, but dere ain't
much to git happy over now. . . ."[45]

D. Davis, Marvell, AR

". . . de furst of ebery week he [the master] gib each en ebery single
man or family a task fer to do dat week en atter dat task is done
den dey is fru wuk fer dat week en kin den ten de patches whut he
would gib dem for ter raise whut dey want on, en whut de slabes
raise on dese patches dat he gib dem would be deres whut-sum-
eber [whatsoever] hit would be, cotton er taters er whut, hit would
be, dey own, en dey could sell hit en hab de money fer dem selves
ter buy whut dey want."[46]

Elija Henry Hopkins, Little Rock, AR

"I was fed just like I was one of the [master's] children. They even
done put me to bed with them. You see, this discrimination on
color wasn't as bad then as it is now. They handled you as a slave
but they didn't discriminate against you on account of color like
they do now. In slavery times, a poor white man was worse off than
a nigger."[47]

Sarah and Tom Douglas, AL

"Slavery times wuz sho good times. We wuz fed an' clothed an' had
nothin to worry about. . . ."[48]

Jane Georgiana, AL

"Ole Marster dead an' gone an' Ole Mistis too, but I 'members 'em jus' lak dey was, when dey looked atter us whenst we belonged to 'em or dey belong to us, I dunno which it was."

"De times was better fo' de war. . . . I goes to church an' sings an' prays, an' when de good Lord teks me, I'se ready to go, en I specs to see Jesus an' Ole Mistis an' Ole Marster when I gits to de he'benly land'!"[49]

Gus Brown, Richmond, VA

[Brown was a body servant of William Brown, Confederate soldier] "I cannot forget old massa. He was good and kind. He never believed in slavery, but his money was tied up in slaves and he didn't want to lose all he had. I knows I will see him in heaven and even though I have to walk ten miles for a bite of bread, I can still be happy to think about the good times we had then."[50]

YANKEES AND FREEDOM

Hannah Irwin, AL

"I suppose dem Yankees wuz all right in dere place, but dey neber belong in de South. Why Miss, one of 'em axe me what wuz dem white flowers in de fiel'? You'd think dat a gentmen wid all dem decorations on hisself woulda knowed a fiel' of cotton! An' as for dey a-settin' me free! Miss, us niggers on de Bennett place wuz free as soon as we wuz bawn. I always been free!"[51]

"Aunt" Adeline, Fayetteville, AR

"After the war many soldiers [Yankees] came to my mistress, Mrs. Blakely, trying to make her free me. I told them I was free but I did not want to go anywhere, that I wanted to stay in the only home that I ever known. . . . Sometimes I was threatened for not leaving but I stayed on."[52]

Betty Curlett, Hazen, AR (parents were slaves)

"When Mars Daniel come home he went to my papa's house and says 'John, you free.' He says, 'I been free as I wanter be whah I is.' He went on to my grandpa's house and says, 'Toby, you are free!' He raised up and says, 'You brought me here from Africa and North Carolina and I goiner' stay wid you as long as ever I get sompin to eat. You gotter look after me!' Mars Daniel say, 'Well I ain't runnin' nobody off my place as long as they behave.' Purtnigh every nigger set tight till he died of the old sets. Mars Daniel say to grandpa, 'Toby you ain't my nigger.' Grandpa raise up and say, 'I is too.'"[53]

Cora Gillam, Little Rock, AR

"I'll tell you lady, if the rough element from the North had stayed out of the South the trouble of reconstruction would not have happened. . . . they tried to excite the colored against their white friends. The white folks was still kind to them what had been their slaves. They would have helped them get started. I know that. I always say that if the South could of been left to adjust itself both white and colored would have been better off."[54]

THE CONFEDERACY

Tom McAlpin, AL

"Boss, dere ain't never been nobody afightin' lak our 'Federates [Confederates] done, but dey ain't never had a chance. Dere was jes' too many of dem blue coats for us to lick. . . . Our 'Federates was de bes' fightin' men dat ever were. Dere warn't nobody lak our 'Federates. . . . Yassuh, I was sont to Richmond to bring home some of our wounded 'Federates. They sont me caze dey knowed I warn't afeered of nothin'. Dat's de way I've always tried to be, white boss, lak my white people what raised me. God bless 'em."[55]

Gus Brown, Richmond, VA

"The Yankees didn't beat us, we wuz starved out! . . . I am a Confederate veteran. . . ."[56]

Sam Ward, Pine Bluff, AR

"I never did care much for politics, but I've always been for the South. I love the Southland."[57]

James Gill, Marvell, AR

". . . all dem good times ceasted atter a while when de War come and de Yankees started all dere debbilment [devilment]. Us was Confederates all de while. . . . But de Yankees, dey didn't know dat we was Confederates. . . . When de Yankees ud come dey would ax [ask] my mammy, 'Aunt Mary, is you seen any Se-cesh [secessionists] today'? and mammy, sheud say, 'Naw-suh' eben iffen she had seen some of us mens, but when any our sojers ud come and say, 'Aunt Mary, is you seen any Yankees 'round here recent?' she ud allus [always] tell dem de truf."[58]

The statements of these former slaves clearly show that many blacks very actively supported the Southern cause during the war. The modest statements of these people speak volumes about how they felt about their position in life at that time. Elija Hopkins of Little Rock made the statement that "In slavery times, a poor white man was worse off than a nigger." It is clear from this statement that this slave did not feel as if he were at the bottom of Southern society. One song that slave children sang stated "I'd rather be a nigger than a poor white man."[59]

The Abolitionist concept of Southern society placed the master on top and the black on the bottom of society. In reality, the structure of Southern society was not vertical, but rather circular. Each person could feel as if he or she were a little ahead of someone else in society. The white master felt better off than the white middle class, the slave felt better off than the poor white, and the white felt better off than the slave. Each group sensed that there was a group ahead and behind him in society as if they were stand in a circle. This allowed each group to respect another group without the fear of losing its place in society. Thus arose the closeness that has been reported by the Yankee about antebellum Southern society.

NORTHERN TREATMENT
OF SOUTHERN BLACKS

The former Alabama slave, Hanna Irwin, clearly points out her feelings about the Yankee invader: "I suppose dem Yankees wuz all right in dere place, but dey neber belong in de South." Many people believe that the Yankee was a great liberator of the black people. Yet, according to the *Official Records: War of the Rebellion*, nothing could be further from the truth. What the Yankee brought to the blacks was thievery, rape, and murder.

In a letter from J. T. K. Hayward to J. W. Brook, who subsequently forwarded it to United States secretary of war Simon Cameron, Hayward described how Northern troops were ". . . committing rapes on the negroes and such like things. . . . These things are not exaggerated by me, . . . and no punishment, or none of any account, has been meted out to them."[60] In Alabama, Yankee colonel John B. Turchin allowed his men to do as they pleased in the town of Athens. The official records show he allowed his men to ". . . plunder and pillage the inhabitants. . . . They attempted an indecent outrage on . . . her [the mistress of the plantation] servant girl. A part of this brigade went to the plantation . . . and [stayed] in the negro huts for weeks, debauching the females. Several soldiers committed rape on the person of a colored girl. . . ."[61] Colonel Turchin's acts were so appalling that he was court-martialled and convicted for his crimes on July 7, 1862. Clearly his conviction had no ill effect upon his career as a Union officer. One month after his conviction, he was offered a promotion to the rank of Brigadier General of United States Volunteer Troops. Turchin served in that capacity until October 4, 1864.[62] Even after the fall of Richmond, General Grant was notified that "A number of cases of atrocious rape by these men [Yankees] have already occurred. Their influence on the colored population is also reported to be bad."[63]

Throughout the official records one can find reports of such fiendish activity by the "Yankee liberators." Not only did the bluecoats commit heinous acts upon the black women of the South, but their actions against the black males were equally hideous.

It seems to be in vogue today to talk about black Union soldiers. What is not often told is how many of these men were compelled to become soldiers. In a letter from Gen. John A. Logan (U.S.) to General Grant, Logan states, "A major of colored troops is here with his party capturing negroes, with or with out their consent. . . . They are being conscripted."[64] In May of 1862 Secretary of the Treasury Salmon Chase received the following message. "The negroes were sad. . . . Sometimes whole plantations, learning what was going on, ran off to the woods for refuge. . . . This mode of [enlistment by] violent seizure. . . is repugnant."[65] The next day at the same plantation the following was reported:

> On some plantations the wailing and screaming were loud and the [black] women threw themselves in despair on the ground. On some plantations the people took to the woods and were hunted up by the soldiers. . . . I doubt if the recruiting service in this country has ever been attended with such scenes before.[66]

Not since they experienced the degradations of the slave hunter in Africa had this race of people known such treatment. And all of this was being done by those who pretended to be friends of the slaves!

From Nashville, Union general Rousseau wrote to Gen. George Thomas the following: "Officers in command of colored troops are in constant habit of pressing all able-bodied slaves into the military service of the U.S."[67]

Even after the blacks were placed in the Union army, they were still treated worse than they had been on the plantation. A black soldier named Sam Marshall was arrested for trying to visit his family. The following is an account of what happened to him. "About a dozen of the soldiers did escort him. . . . they tied him to a tree, and stripping him to the waist lacerated his back with a cowskin, the marks of which Sam will carry to his grave."[68] Over in Virginia Gen. Innis N. Palmer (U.S.) wrote General Butler in '64 the following:

> The negroes will not go voluntarily, so I am obliged to force them. . . . The matter of collecting the colored men for laborers has been one of some difficulty. . . . They must be forced to go, . . . this may be considered a harsh measure, but . . . we must not stop at trifles.[69]

This letter clearly shows how the Yankees had to resort to force in order to obtain the black soldiers they wanted. This attitude, as displayed in the letter, reveals what little respect these Union men had for the rights of the black men or for legality of any type. Once the Constitution, and the rights it is designed to protect, are disregarded, it becomes very easy to be a tyrant, and this is as true today as it was during the War for Southern Independence.

The preceding statements are but a very few which could be cited as proof of Northern disregard for the rights of the Southern blacks. For a complete review of the brutal and fiendish activity of the United States forces throughout the South, against not only the black but also against white civilians, we suggest reading *The Uncivil War: Union Army and Navy Excesses in the Official Records* edited by Thomas Bland Keys. Its information is derived from the *Official Records: War of the Rebellion*, the official report of the war generated by the federal government.

As we have already said, the relations between master and slave varied widely throughout the South. Unfortunately, most people are taught only about the "Simon Legree" or *Uncle Tom's Cabin* type of relationship. Human nature being what it is, no doubt there were some such men in the Old South and in the North. But what about the other side of the story? What about the masters who did their utmost to care for and to improve the lives of their slaves? Jefferson Davis was just such a slave master.

JEFFERSON DAVIS' VIEW OF SLAVERY

Jefferson Davis was influenced early in his life by his older brother, Joseph, who desired to improve the lot of man. Joseph was inspired by the writings of an English industrialist and social reformer, Robert Owen, the author of the book, *A New View of Society*.[70] Owen's conception of a new society was based upon fair and generous treatment of all people. This in itself was a revolutionary idea, with great potential for improving the lot of downtrodden industrial workers of the world. Joseph Davis met and talked with Owens, and he made a determination to use Owens' approach on his Mississippi plantation. Joseph established as rules for the running of his plantation some of the most liberal regulations known to slavery. "The slave quarters exceeded what was considered ideal by the agricultural journals of the period. A variety of food was made available; in some cases with unlimited quantities. Davis even established a court system where a slave was punished except upon conviction by a jury of his peers."[71] Jefferson Davis patterned the conduct of his plantation after that of his older brother Joseph.

In the South at that time, there were several different views of slavery. From the extreme "Fire Eaters" who desired the continuation and extension of slavery, to those who, like Robert E. Lee, desired a quick end to the system. Like all other philosophies, the "peculiar institution" of slavery had a middle ground. It was here that men such as the Davis brothers stood. In Jefferson Davis' view the system of slavery would have a natural end. For it to arrive at that natural end, the enlightened slave master had to prepare his "people" for freedom. Davis stated, "The slave must be made fit for his freedom by education and discipline and thus be made unfit for slavery."[72] For this reason he attempted to "educate" his slaves in the ways of civilized society. On his plantation, Jefferson Davis instituted a system of slave laws, courts, and juries in an effort to improve the understanding of his slaves for what life under "freedom" would be like. It is worthy of note that, under Davis' slave legal system, he could pardon a convicted person but not increase the punishment administered by the slave jury.

In view of how Davis' slaves were treated on his plantation, is it any wonder that so many blacks had such respect for Davis? When asked by a Yankee how he felt about Jefferson Davis, an elderly slave replied, ". . . I loved him, and I can say that every colored man he ever owned loved him."[73]

The deep respect and love that President and Mrs. Davis had for people is clearly shown in the story of little Jim Limber "Davis."

BLACK CHILD IN THE
CONFEDERATE WHITE HOUSE

Jim Limber was an orphaned black child whom Mrs. Varina Davis rescued from an abusive guardian. Jim Limber was "adopted" by the Davis family and became an integral part of the Davis family while they were in Richmond.

While traveling through Richmond, Mrs. Davis saw a Negro man beating Jim. She at once went to Jim's rescue and brought him to the Confederate White House for care. The following day, she had the appropriate papers registered at city hall in Richmond to insure Jim's status as a free person of color. Mrs. Mary Boykin Chesnut wrote in her diary of seeing little Jim the day following his rescue. She stated that "The child is an orphan Mrs. Davis rescued yesterday from his brutal negro guardian. He was proudly dressed up in little Joe's clothes and happy as a lord. He was very anxious to show me his wounds and bruises [given him by his former guardian]."[74]

From the time little Jim was "adopted" by the Davises, he was treated as one of the family. Even in letters, the family would speak fondly of Jim. In one letter written by ten-year-old Maggie to her brother Jeff, she states, "Jim Limber sends his love to you."[75] Many people reported how happy Jim was with life at the Confederate White House. Unfortunately for all, the war was coming to a sad end, and with it the happy life of little Jim.

After the fall of Richmond, the Davis family tried to make their way across the South beyond the Mississippi River. Near Irwinville, Georgia, President Davis and his family were taken prisoners. Varina Davis told of the sufferings of the next few days by all members of the family, including little Jim. Mrs. Davis was horrified by the statement of Union captain Charles T. Hudson who threatened to take little Jim away and make him his own. Mrs. Davis states, "[Captain Hudson], an extremely rude and offensive man, certainly no military gentleman, threatened to take Jim Limber away from us . . . and keep him as his own."[76] When Jim learned that he was to be taken away, he put up one heck of a fight, clinging to the Davis children, screaming and begging to be left with his "family." But pleas of mercy had done little to stem the tide of infamy that had been poured upon the South over four years of war, and such pleas could do little now, even coming from a little boy. The Davises were told that Jim would be taken to Washington. Northern papers ran stories of "Jim Limber one of Jefferson Davis' slaves" who they said would carry scars on his back from the beatings given him by the Davis family. Mrs. Davis denied that Jim was ever beaten by any of the Davis family, ". . . for the affection was mutual between us, and we had never punished him."[77] None of these statements ever made any headlines. After all, the Northern press had their own agenda to pursue, and telling the truth about Jim would not further that agenda.

Other than a few stories in Northern newspapers, the Davis family could never re-establish contact with Jim Limber. No one to this day has revealed what became of him. As late as 1890, Varina Davis said that they still prayed for Jim and hoped that ". . . lovable little Jim Limber . . . has been successful in the world."[78]

In life, the Davis family displayed a genuine love for the people given to their care. That love was returned and displayed on the occasion of the death of the former president.

On December 8, 1889, in New Orleans, Louisiana, Jefferson Davis died. As the news flashed over the South, telegrams and letters began to pour in offering the sympathies of many people. One such telegram was from the old Davis family plantation signed by thirteen people which read, "We, the old servants and tenants of our beloved master, Honorable Jefferson Davis, have cause to mingle our tears over his death, who was always so kind and thoughtful of our peace and happiness. We extend to you our humble sympathy."[79] Thornton Montgomery, a black man whom Jefferson Davis had helped educate, sent the following message from his home in Christine, North Dakota: "I have watched with deep interest and solicitude the illness of Mr. Davis . . . and I had hoped that with his great will power to sustain him he would recover. . . . I appreciate your great loss, and my heart goes out to you in this hour of your deepest affliction. . . ."[80]

After Davis' death, on the last trip the body of the beloved president was accompanied by his last body servant, Robert Brown. Brown was seen weeping uncontrollably at the outpouring of love that was displayed for his former master.

Yes, the life and death of President Jefferson Davis displays to all who are open-minded enough to look how different the relationship between slave and master actually was as opposed to the way in which it is far too often depicted. But yet, the Abolitionist cult still refuses to admit that they could be wrong about the South, and they continue their vicious attacks against anything Southern. They quickly tell us that these blacks, who displayed love for Davis or for anything Southern, were only lying about their true feelings in order to get ahead or to keep from being brutalized by the "rednecks." For example, liberals will state that the only reason that Robert Brown cried for Jefferson Davis was because as a black man he had to do so to keep from being abused by white Southerners. What they conveniently overlook is the fact that Brown could have just disappeared after Yankee-induced freedom. He did not have to maintain a relationship with the Davis family. Look at the warm letter of condolence from Thornton Montgomery, a black man from North Dakota. Does anyone think that a black man living in North Dakota would fear white Southerners? North Dakota is not exactly a Southern state. If anything, Mongomery would have incurred the wrath of the white community of that Northern state by saying positive things about Jefferson Davis. Yet, the liberals still tell us that these blacks were not sincere in their display of affection for Jefferson Davis or for the South. For those foolish enough to fall for that line, let us consider the life and actions of two black men who were part of the Reconstruction government of the South.

EX-SLAVE PROTECTS HIS WHITE FAMILY

The following account is taken from the Turnley family history, published by the family of Rick Formby of Alabama in 1976. Sam Turnley was a slave of the Turnley family of Jacksonville, Alabama.

As Sherman's army marched toward Atlanta, Georgia, Sam deserted the Turnleys and joined the Yankee army. Here is how the story is reported in the Turnley family history:

> A man named Sam was given to Mrs. Turnley by her father, Benjamin Isbell, at the time of her marriage. For a time he worked as a blacksmith in Rome, and when Sherman's Army came, Sam joined them and marched with a brigade toward Jacksonville where he had lived with the Turnleys. He asked to see the General, and insisted, until finally he was permitted to see and talk with the General. He told him he had to have a squad of soldiers to protect his mistress. When told that he was free, and that he no longer had a mistress, Sam insisted. He had seen what happened when soldiers arrived in new territory. The result was that the Turnley Family, the home, the chickens, cows, and silver, all were protected.
>
> After the War Sam became a Member of the State Legislature. He Visited Grandmothers Isbell and Turnley in Chattanooga, . . . went into the kitchen to eat, thanked his former mistress, and left to make his way to Montgomery to meet with the convening Legislature.[81]

Here we have an account of a slave who ran away to join the Union army, but nevertheless still had a strong desire to protect his "people." Even after the war, as a black member of the Alabama legislature, he continued to visit his old mistress. Can anyone believe otherwise than this man was acting out of love and respect for his people?

BLACK REPRESENTATIVE DEFENDS DIXIE

The sincere respect that many black people had for their "white folks" was clearly displayed by a black Republican in 1890. Representative John F. Harris was a legislator from Washington County, Mississippi. According to the 1870 census Harris was from Virginia and could read and write. While a member of the state House of Representatives, he had an opportunity to vote for a resolution to erect a monument to the Confederate soldiers of Mississippi. Now, if we were to be guided by the Abolitionist view of the South, we would have to believe that this elected black official from Mississippi would take this opportunity to vote against such a resolution. Surely a black man from the South, having been a slave before Yankee-induced freedom, would not want to pay homage to Confederate veterans. But according to the "Journal of House of Representatives State of Mississippi," Representative Harris voted for S.B. NO. 25, "An act for the benefit of the Confederate Monument, now in process of erection on the Capital Square, Jackson, Miss."[82] This bill was passed by a vote of fifty-seven yeas to forty-one nays, with Representative Harris, a black man, voting with the majority.[83] Not only did Representative Harris vote for the funding of a Confederate monument, but also he spoke eloquently for passage of that bill. His speech was reprinted in the *Daily Clarion-Ledger*, Jackson, Mississippi, on February 23, 1890, as follows:

> Mr. Speaker! I have arisen here in my place to offer a few words on the bill. I have come from a sick bed. . . . Perhaps it was not prudent for me to come. But, Sir, I could not rest quietly in my room without . . . contributing . . . a few remarks of my own. I was sorry to hear the speech of the young gentleman from Marshall County. I am sorry that any son of a soldier should go on record as opposed to the erection of a monument in honor of the brave dead. And, Sir, I am convinced that had he seen what I saw at Seven Pines and in the Seven Days' fighting around Richmond, the battlefield covered with the mangled forms of those who fought for their country and for their country's honor, he would not have made that speech.
>
> When the news came that the South had been invaded, those men went forth to fight for what they believed, and they made no requests for monuments. . . . But they died, and their virtues should be remembered. Sir, I went with them. I too, wore the gray, the same color my master wore. We stayed four long years, and if that war had gone on till now I would have been there yet. . . . I want to honor those brave men who died for their convictions. When my mother died I was a boy. Who, Sir, then acted the part of a mother to the orphaned slave boy, but my 'old missus'? Were she living now, or could speak to me from those high realms where are gathered the sainted dead, she would tell me to vote for this bill. And, Sir, I shall vote for it. I want it known to all the world that my vote is given in favor of the bill to erect a monument in honor of the Confederate dead.[84]

What a scene to have witnessed! A former Confederate soldier and an elected black official of Mississippi lecturing a white representative and the son of a Confederate veteran on the duties one generation has for defending the truth about the gallant deeds of another generation. Not only did Representative Harris vote for funding the Confederate monument, but also all six black Republicans voted with Harris on this matter.

On the next day, the House Republicans (six black men) presented the Democratic speaker with a silver set in honor of the warm working relationship they had with the speaker and with other Democrats. In his presentation, Representative Moore stated:

> I was born in Mississippi, but raised in a Northern State; associations there led me to regard the Southern white men as dire foes to the Negroes, but receiving such cordial and unprejudiced association upon this floor [House of Representatives] by the entire Democratic party here these tebidus [sic] suspicions have been eliminated from the bosoms of this feeble six and for them I am authorized to speak. You are our best friends; . . . This has been termed the Jeff Davis Legislature possibly because the Republicans voted for your Confederate Monument Bill. . . . In tendering you this, we tender a grateful hand to every Democratic member, for you have shown to be our friends, not our enemies.[85]

Here we see the spokesman for the six black Republicans of the Mississippi House of Representatives speaking about the warm relationship they enjoyed with the white representatives and about their unanimous vote for the Confederate monument. Indeed, the relationship between the black and white people of the South was much better than many would have us believe.

We have called upon first-hand accounts of black people who lived during the war and after the war to give us an insight into the nature of slavery and of life in the Old South. Yet there are accounts that will seem even more shattering to those who still can see nothing but "bullwhips and lynchings" down South.

GEORGIA SLAVE DEFENDS SLAVERY

In 1861, a slave named Harrison Berry wrote and published a pamphlet entitled "Slavery and Abolitionism, as Viewed by a Georgia Slave."[86] The above statement flies in the face of the currently held opinion about slavery. First, the idea that a slave could read and write in 1860 is something that most Abolitionists conveniently overlook. Second, the very idea that a slave, literate or not, would freely defend the system of African servitude strikes at the heart of a very sacred Yankee myth. Yet, here we have, in black and white, the very words of a slave as he attacks "fanatical abolitionists."

Berry's story is unique and inspirational. Harrison Berry was born a slave in Jones County, Georgia, in November 1816 as the property of David Berry. When his master's daughter married S. W. Price, Harrison Berry was given to her. At the age of ten, Harrison began working in the law offices of John V. Berry, one of David Berry's sons. "These employments were such as to leave a good deal of time at his own disposal, which he was induced to improve in learning to read and write." As he grew up, he was trained as a shoemaker, and spent much time, with the assistance of the Berry family, in improving his reading ability.

> He was induced to write upon the subject of Slavery from a firm conviction that Abolitionist agitators are the worst enemies of the Slave, and from the settled opinion that Slavery is according to the Divine Law. He believes, furthermore, that Southern Slaves are in a much better condition than if they had remained in their native land, and this opinion has been formed after a fair and impartial examination of the subject in the light of history, philosophy, and religion.[87]

Thus wrote H. C. Hornady in the introduction to Berry's pamphlet on slavery.

In his own words, Berry tells the world that ". . . I am a Slave, and have been all my life, and therefore, claim the opportunity, at least, of knowing what Slavery is, and what it is not."[88] Berry goes on to state that he was moved to write upon the subject of the agitation for the abolition of slavery by watching how the "evil dangerous and highly detrimental" attacks by the Abolitionists were hurting the very people they pretended to help. He makes it clear that he was writing his pamphlet for the enlightenment of the Northern Abolitionists who did not understand the nature of Southern slavery. Berry's defense of the South echoed other Southern voices raised during the war. After the war, he became a prominent preacher and continued to write on subjects such as theology.[89]

SLAVE PREACHER DEFENDS HIS MASTER

From Richmond, Virginia, comes the story of one of the South's greatest preachers. Without the benefit of formal training the Reverend John Jasper made his impression on the world not as a political activist, or a civil rights leader, but as a proven warrior of the Christian Church.

Jasper was born a slave in Virginia.[90] For many years as a young man he felt the call to be a Christian. His master, Samuel Hargrove, whom he called "Mars Sam," was a good Christian man and did his utmost to encourage his slaves in Christian ways. During his life as a preacher, Rev. Jasper had only kind and gracious comments about his former master. He gave this account of how his master responded to the news of his giving his life to the Lord:

> Little aft'r I hear Mars Sam tell de overseer he want to see Jasper. Mars Sam was a good man; he was a Baptis,' an' one of de hed men of de old Fust Church down here, an' I was glad when I hear Mars Sam say he want to see me. "John, what was de matter out dar jes' now?" . . . I sez to him: "Mars Sam ever sence de fourth of July I ben cryin' after de Lord, six long weeks, an' jes' now out dar . . . God tuk my sins away, an' set my feet on a rock . . . de fires broke out in my soul, an' I jes' let go one shout to de glory of my Saviour."
>
> "John I b'leve dat way myself. I luv de Saviour dat you have jes' foun', an' I wan' to tell you dat I do'n complain 'cause you made de noise jes' now as you did." He . . . walk over to me and giv' me his han', and he say: "John, I wish you mighty well. Your Saviour is mine an' we are bruthers in de Lord." . . . Mars Sam well know de good he dun me.[91]

During the war, and while John Jasper was still a slave, he could often be found at the Confederate hospitals in Richmond preaching to the sick and wounded Confederate soldiers.[92] Is it any wonder that after the war his church was often filled with both black and white people who came to hear this dynamic preacher?

The warm and cordial relations between John Jasper and his master lasted until Sam's death. Even after the war, Jasper would often tell the story of his Christian master from the pulpit of his church.

Jasper often thought of his old master as he preached. His feelings for his former master were well stated when he said:

Oft'n as I preach I feel that I'm doin' what my old marster tol' me to do. If he was here now I think he would lif' up dem kin' black eyes of his, an' say: "Dat's right, John; still tellin' it; fly like de angel, an' wherever you go carry de Gospel to de people." Farwell, my ol' marster, when I lan' in de heav'nly city, I'll call at your mansion. . . .[93]

The story of the Reverend John Jasper stands out as a clear indictment of the falsehood told about the South and its system of African servitude. The close relationship between black Christians such as John Jasper, and white Christians such as Samuel Hargrove, was not unusual in the Old South. The warm relations between black and white people are manifested in stories all across the South. The history of the Palestine Baptist Church, Simpson County Mississippi, relates such a story. The Palestine Baptist Church was organized in 1786 (one year before the United States Constitution was ratified) by twelve men, eleven white and one black.[94] The church has served the community from that date to the present. In 1858 the church had 175 members, 100 white and 75 black.[95] These black members were a vital part of the ongoing evangelical work of the church. The significance of the black members of the church is obvious: the first Baptist church west of the Mississippi River, for example, was established in Louisiana by Joseph Wills, a black preacher.[96] Some historians have taken note of this close relation between the Christians of the two races and the increasing number of black church members in the Old South.

The Baptists did this less by deliberate missionary efforts than by accepting Negro members on a basis of Christian brotherhood that seems strange in the twentieth-century South. There were many instances in which gifted Negroes were allowed to preach to congregations of both races.[97]

These stories of a warm and close relationship between black and white people in the Old South are not isolated stories. There are many others.

BILL YOPP, FORMER SLAVE AND CONFEDERATE SOLDIER

Bill Yopp was born a slave in Laurens County, Georgia.[98] As a young man he and Thomas Yopp played and grew up together.

When war broke out, Thomas Yopp volunteered in Company H, Fourteenth Georgia Regiment. Bill asked and received permission to go with his master to the war. Bill served his master as cook and assisted him during sickness and when his master was wounded.

As the war progressed, Thomas Yopp was promoted to the rank of captain of his company. Captain Yopp and Bill were sent to what is now West Virginia, where Bill was often between the lines of the Confederates and United States armies. Had Bill wanted to run away from Captain Yopp and the Confederate army he could have done so without any problem, but as Bill said, "I had no inclination to go to the Union side, as I did not know the Union soldiers and the Confederate soldiers I did know, and I believed then as now, tried and true friends are better than friends you do not know."[99] Note how Bill, the slave of a Confederate soldier, describes the Confederate soldiers as "tried and true friends."

Even after Yankee-induced freedom, Bill and many other ex-slaves stayed loyal to their former masters. During this time many former masters were worse off than the freed slaves. Many such white people were protected and fed by their former slaves. In the story of Bill Yopp the author relates how Bill and other ex-slaves cared for their former masters:

> . . . [D]uring the transition period, many of the ex-slaves, Bill among them, supplied the white families with freewill offerings of such supplies as they had. In some plantations for a year or more the writer knows of instances where the negroes brought food each Saturday to the families of their former owners.[100]

Just before the outbreak of World War I, Captain Yopp was admitted to the Confederate Soldiers' Home in Atlanta, Georgia. Bill made many visits to Captain Yopp and all the old soldiers at the home. At Christmas Bill would visit the home and bring gifts of food and money to the residents. At this time Bill would be taken into the chapel, where he would make a speech to the veterans. In honor of his affection and gifts to them, the old Confederate soldiers had a medal struck and given to Bill.[101] By a unanimous vote, the board of trustees offered Bill a permanent residence at the Confederate Soldiers' Home.

Bill Yopp, former slave, Confederate veteran, and friend of the old soldiers of the South, died on June 3, 1936, and was buried in the Confederate Cemetery in Marietta, Georgia.[102]

SUMMARY

No other issue in American history has been abused more than the history of African servitude in the South. People who dare to speak about slavery in a light other than that demanded by the neo- Abolitionist left will find themselves an outcast from modern "P.C." society. Nevertheless, when we look at America, we find that many names that we associate with the development of this country have been associated with slavery. The names of the Puritan Fathers of New England loom foremost in that group of slave holders. Even men such as Josiah Franklin, stepbrother of Benjamin Franklin, was associated with slavery, being active as a slave dealer in Boston.[103] Yet the Franklin name is never held up for scorn because of the action of the Boston Franklin family. John Hancock, the most prominent signator of the Declaration of Independence, was both a participant in a slave trading venture and a slave holder. But have you ever heard the cry to take down any monuments to John Hancock? Hancock was not the only New England signator of the Declaration of Independence who was a slave holder.[104] Samuel Huntington of Connecticut[105] and Stephen Hopkins of Rhode Island[106] were also slave holders, and their names can also be found on the Declaration of Independence.

A list of New England slave holders would read like a "Who's Who" in the early history of that region. Nearly every family name that is cited by any historian can be found among the slave traders or slave holders of New England. Yet, these people, or more properly the descendants of these slave holders and slave traders, are the very ones who take it upon themselves to "teach" the South about lofty ideals of morality and virtue. After New Englanders saw fit to do away with the institution of slavery, at a profit to themselves, they then embarked upon a rabid crusade not only to stamp out slavery, but also to destroy the culture, power, and very lives of the people of the South.

From every part of Northern society there poured forth lies and distortions about the nature of Southern slavery *and* about the South in general. To the average person in the North, the South was a place of wicked, lazy, and ignorant people. A false notion of life down South was advanced as reality. This notion made it easy for the people of the North to rationalize any evil behavior in order to "save" the nation from Southern influence. All this was being done, even though the North was as much involved in the slavery issue and was just as guilty of the actions the South had been accused of perpetrating. This hypocritical action of the rabid Yankee Abolitionist killed any hope for Southern emancipationists in their efforts to bring a peaceful end to slavery.

Even more costly to America than the loss of an easy end to slavery, was the lost of respect by the North for the South. Having embarked on its "moral" crusade, with its false notion of what Southern slavery was like, the North focused on the South and not slavery as the chosen enemy. From that point on, no amount of logic could dissuade the North from its unholy crusade against the South. This Abolitionist view of the South magnified the cultural differences between the North and South until it became possible for the North to view Southerners as less than civilized humans. This then marked the beginning of cultural bigotry. With this attitude in place, the Northern troops had little or no qualms about committing any number of atrocities against Southerners. This attitude remains in vogue today. The cultural bigots of the North will overlook their own culture's faults while they demand the demise of Southern culture.

The cultural bigotry of the North and the enforced "politically correct" dogma of left-of-center politicians, journalists, and academics stem from a distorted view of the South as a people, and Southern slavery. This view is stated and reinforced by all means of information (i.e., propaganda). Repeatedly, Americans in general and Southerners in particular are fed lies about what life in the Old South was really like.

As we have revealed in the preceding pages, what the victor has enforced as truth is not always true. We have used the words of former slaves to prove that life in the South was not the way the neo-Abolitionists love to depict it. On the contrary, we have shown that the system of African servitude was one in which many blacks were happy and free from want and violence. One of the most frequently voiced requests made by blacks in the inner cities of America today is the desire to be free from violence. Inner-city black-on-black crime is epidemic. In the United States of America more blacks die at the hands of fellow blacks in one year than ever died from lynching or beatings in *all* the years of Southern slavery! Never has the family unit been stronger in the black community than it was during slavery days. Crime was never a problem for the black community during the time of slavery as compared to the situation in today's black community where one-fourth of black males have a criminal record by the age of thirty. In the past, venereal disease was never a problem in the black community as it is now. Today more families are broken in one year in the black community than were ever separated by white masters during the slavery era.

Now, if the foregoing sounds as if we are advocating the return of the system of African servitude, let us restate emphatically that this is not what we are suggesting; rather, we desire that people look at Southern slavery with an open mind. If indeed the black people were better off in some respects under the system of slavery, that does not justify or warrant its return. As Jefferson Davis stated, the system of slavery would proceed to a natural end. Just as we would no longer desire to return to the days of oil lamps, we do not desire to restore slavery. Just as in the North, if given time, slavery would have ended in the South. It has done so in every civilization known to man; why should anyone think it would have been any different in the South?

The question of slavery is much like the idea of a glass of water that is half full. If one person sees it as half full, that does not mean that the person who reports it as half empty is preaching a falsehood. As long as each individual will recognize that different people will judge events in a different light, we can hope at least to agree that all have a right to their judgment and perception of the event. For too long the South has been excluded from the arena of public discussion. We have been systematically denied the right to teach our views, by those who only see us as evil and ignorant.

Three different sources make the argument that blacks were well treated as a whole under the system of Southern slavery. The words of Dabney (*A Defense of Virginia and the South*), Nobel Prize-winner R. W. Fogel and Engerman (*Time on the Cross*), and the former slaves themselves (*The Slave Narratives*), all point to the fact that, in many ways, slavery was a positive institution for blacks.

One fact that no historian can dispute is that nowhere in Europe or America were blacks granted the rights that whites enjoyed.

The very nature of civilized society in that day would not allow for equal rights under the law. The principle of the innate worth of each individual was yet to be propounded. Even if every black person had been given freedom, where would they have gone, what rights would have been accorded them, and who would have been their friend when the only family they had known were denied them? These questions the fanatical Abolitionists did not want to ask or answer. The politicians of the North who abused the question of slavery for their own political gain cared little for such considerations. Northern liberals sought only to use the agitation of race as a means to destroy their political enemy, the South.

The time has come for America to put away the divisiveness of the past and to look at the question of slavery with an open mind. If the South is an evil place because it had slaves, then so is the North. If Southerners were wrong for owning slaves, then what about the Northerners who sold them those slaves? If the South is to be castigated because a small minority of its citizens made money from slave-grown cotton, then what about the North whose textile mills made money from that same slave-grown cotton? If all Southerners are evil because of the mistreatment of their slaves by a few slave holders, then what about the Yankee capitalists who mistreated their Irish laborers? Is free enterprise to be condemned as evil because some capitalists abuse their workers? Sober reflection will be enough to convince anyone that there is more to the issue of slavery than the Abolitionists would have us believe.

The issue of slavery, like the issue of race, has been used to keep the people of the South fighting one another while allowing the victors to enjoy the fruits of their victory. But never let us forget that the real issue of the war as the South saw it was liberty and freedom.

We have spoken about how the black Republicans of Mississippi in 1890 spoke and voted for the erection of the Confederate memorial in Jackson. On June 3, 1891, the memorial was dedicated in Jackson, Mississippi, and the ceremony was attended by all officials of the state and city, as well as more than twenty-five thousand people. In his invocation, the Reverend Father H. A. Pitcherit boldly stated why the South fought the War for Southern Independence, when he prayed:

O, Lord Jesus, who whilst upon this earth, didst ever show Thyself the friend and defender of the oppressed, we ardently beseech Thee to look down in love and honor to our lamented brothers-in-arms, who have fallen in the holy cause of right and justice.

Thou, O Lord, who wert falsely charged with being a traitor to Thy country, and didst unjustly suffer a cruel death, Thou at least will sympathize with us in our Lost Cause, and we pray Thee to vindicate and to guard the memory of our comrades, who likewise wrongfully accused and condemned, willingly, aye, cheerfully laid down their lives on the consecrated altar of patriotism and liberty.[107]

Deo Vindice

CHAPTER 4

Yankee Atrocities

The soldiers are hunting for concealed things and these searches are one of the pleasant excitements of our march.[1]

Major George W. Nichols
Aide-de-Camp to General Sherman

INTRODUCTORY COMMENTS

The truism that "to the victor go the spoils" is very true when it comes to writing the history of a conflict. If we never read beyond the "accepted" history of the war, we would likely think that the War for Southern Independence was just a "civil war" in which the noble, freedom-loving North had to force the evil, slave-holding South to free its slaves. Once that deed was accomplished everyone shook hands, and everything since then has been grand.

Yankee myth and Southern reality are not brothers. They are not even related. In the following pages we will look at some of the handiwork of the people who are held up to our school children as noble and righteous defenders of human rights.

Volumes could be written about the hideous actions of the men who came down South to rape, pillage, and burn. No doubt some were sincere (although misdirected) in their desire to assist the slaves in Dixie. But they were to be disappointed by their fellow invaders who saw only loot to be had. Also, the blacks refused to cooperate by not revolting against their masters. Many refused to turn their backs on their white families. The idealistic Yankees became disillusioned. Disillusionment comes easy to those who have been fed a steady diet of lies about how things should be, as opposed to how they actually are. This was the fate of many do-gooders from Yankeedom, and the scenario has been repeated every few decades since then.

The Yankee apologist will attempt to discount this record of Northern atrocities by claiming that both sides committed terrible acts of

The little Confederate
1861

James Dinkins, Madison County, Mississippi, was a member of the corps of cadets, North Carolina Military Institute, Charlotte, North Carolina. At the age of sixteen he took part in the first land battle of the war, the Battle of Big Bethel, which the cadets were instrumental in winning.[9] (Image courtesy of Tulane University Libraries, Howard-Tilton Memorial Library, New Orleans, Louisiana) violence during the war. No doubt this is partly true, human nature and war being what they are, but the United States committed far more such acts and those acts were committed with the knowledge and consent of United States officers and officials. This stands in sharp contrast to the orders of Gen. Robert E. Lee and other Southern officers and officials who instructed their troops to protect the property and civil liberties of the civilian population. Edward Pollard noted that President Jefferson Davis was urged to adopt a cruel war policy similar to the one President Abraham Lincoln had adopted. He was urged to do so in retaliation for the sufferings inflicted upon the Southern people at the hands of United States authorities.[2] Confederate Cabinet member Judah P. Benjamin noted that:

> ... when it was urged upon Jefferson Davis, not only by friends in private letters, but by members of his cabinet in council, that it was his duty to the people and to the army to endeavor to repress ... outrages by retaliation, he was immovable in his resistance to such counsels, insisting that it was repugnant to every sentiment of justice and humanity that the innocent should be made victims for the crimes of such monsters.[3]

Compare this, the official stand of our president, with the Yankee president Lincoln's inquiry to Gen. George McClellan asking if he could get close enough to Richmond to "throw shells into the city."[4]

The facts that will be presented here have been carefully documented. Lest anyone find these stories too hard to believe, we enclose a list of books and documents for the unbeliever to review. There will, of course, be those who will dismiss out of hand any evidence whatsoever because their minds are already made up and they don't care to be bothered with facts. To them, no matter what the evidence of history says, the South was and still is wrong. But it is to those who are open-minded and fair that these pages are submitted.

Yankee Atrocities

THE RAPE AND MURDER OF NEW MANCHESTER, GEORGIA

Most people would not look to the American "Civil War" if they are looking for stories of genocide and of the destruction and death of a town. Most people would look to the invading armies of Nazi Germany or the Soviet Union for such accounts. If they would take the time to look beyond the accepted version of the history of the war, they would find many Nazi-like accounts of brutality in the Yankees' actions during the war. Such is the case of the Union invasion of Georgia. Here we find accounts of wholesale genocide and of kidnapping of women and children.

Early in July of 1864, Gen. William Tecumseh Sherman's army was pressing toward Atlanta. Although greatly outnumbered, the Southern army was making the invader pay dearly for his conquest. As usual, when an invader has difficulty with the standing army of the invaded, he will start to attack those whom he knows he can defeat with little trouble. True to form, General Sherman sent his army into the heartland of the South with the orders to "make Georgia howl." The food supply and factories of the South were the object of Sherman's wrath. Sherman declared that there could be no peace in the country until large parts of the Southern population had been exterminated.[5] He put his words into action. First, all the food that could be found was taken for the Yankee army. Then all means of food production were either taken or destroyed. Then he turned his attention to the destruction of factories that aided in the Southern war effort.

It may be a little difficult for us to understand today what it means to have all the food in one's home taken away and also have the means to replace the food stolen or destroyed. When they needed food, Southerners one hundred and thirty years ago did not run down to the supermarket or corner convenience store. They grew and preserved their food, or they bought from others who grew their own food. Some food could be bought, but in times of war when invading armies made normal commerce impossible, the family unit had to depend on its own resources. Therefore, by depriving people of the means of food production, the Yankee invader was condemning them to death by starvation.

Who were these people upon whom Sherman had pronounced the death sentence? For the most part they were women, children, old men, and the sick and wounded who were unfit for military service. These innocent and defenseless victims were the ones upon whom the full measure of anger was to be poured. It seems strange that while the Yankees wrapped the cloak of self-righteousness around themselves and proclaimed themselves as the beacon of all that was right and good, they would stoop so low as to starve and destroy defenseless women, children, the sick, wounded, and dying!

After the Battle of Kennesaw Mountain, in which the invader was thoroughly punished for being in the wrong place, Sherman sent elements of his army around Atlanta and into the towns of Marietta, Roswell, and New Manchester. Several factories that were important to the war effort of the Confederacy were located in these towns. When the Southern soldiers were forced to evacuate these areas, the Yankees moved in and began their work. Food and the means of food production were taken away, and homes were pulled down or burned. All personal property that could be consigned to the flames was destroyed. The only items that could be taken by the hapless Southerners were the clothes on their backs. Even jewelry, such as wedding bands, was pulled from ladies' hands by the noble defenders of the Union.[6]

If the saga of these poor people were to stop here, it would still rate as one of the low points in American history. But for these Southerners, their odyssey of horror had only begun. Sherman then ordered all those who worked in the factories to be gathered up and shipped out of their country.[7] The invader evidently feared that by some miracle these people might not die of starvation, and by some enormous stroke of luck might rebuild their factories from the ashes. With little or no concern for homes, women and children were torn from their families and shipped north. The vast majority of these people were never to see their loved ones again. In all, more than two thousand women, children, and a few old men were collected. Families were divided. Children were separated from their mothers.[8] Tearful mothers were forced to watch as children, who had worked in the factories, were dragged away from home—almost none of them would ever be heard from again. With no more remorse than that shown by the Yankee slave trader, the invaders went about their dirty work of kidnapping defenseless women and children. Even after the end of the war, the United States government never made any attempt to reunite these families!

In the town of Roswell, over four hundred young women and children were kept in the open town square for nearly a week. Imagine the suffering of those who were cramped in that hot (remember this was July in Georgia), dirty place. As if that were not bad enough, the whiskey stores found their way into the hands of the guards. From that time on, the young girls of Roswell lived a continual nightmare.[9]

All the factory workers of New Manchester were taken off in the same manner as the other towns. So complete was the destruction that the town never recovered from the raid and soon passed from existence. New Manchester became a martyr for the cause of Southern independence.

The following comment appeared in a Louisville, Kentucky, newspaper concerning the women and children whom Sherman had shipped north: "The train which arrived from Nashville last evening brought up from the South 249 women and children, who are sent here by orders of General Sherman to be transferred north of the Ohio river. These people are mostly in a destitute condition, having no means to provide for themselves a support."[10] These people were hired out to perform work at a price that was at no more than a subsistence level, making them virtual white slaves for the Yankees. More than two thousand women and children were sent into the North in this manner. The papers in the area advertised them as if they were any other commodity for sale. And so the Yankees maintained their illicit trade in human flesh even as they were singing glory, glory, hallelujah.

LYNCHING AND OTHER CRIMINAL ACTS

Nothing makes the heart of a Yankee liberal beat with more profound sorrow and grief than the thought of the misuse of a rope down South. Dime-store novels, cheap tabloids, television documentaries, and movies find a ready audience for such trash. Of course, the liberals are interested only if Southerners are portrayed as the villains. Perhaps that is why they refuse to publish anything that shows that no one during the War for Southern Independence committed more such crimes than the Yankee invaders.

In Marion County, Missouri, one of the most hideous of such crimes took place. After Missouri attempted to secede from the Union, the state was quickly overrun by Yankee troops. Anyone who expressed Southern sympathies was quickly persecuted by the "loyal" Missouri (Yankee-backed) government officials. In the little town of Palmyra, Missouri, the war was very personal and ugly. After a certain Union informer in town came up missing, it

was presumed by the Federal authorities that he had been ab-
ducted. The general of the "loyal" Missouri troops at that time demanded the return of his informer; otherwise he would execute
ten Southerners whom he held in jail.[11]

The men Gen. John McNeil held in jail were not criminals; they
had been thrown into jail for expressing a pro-Southern point of
view. We would call that an expression of free speech, but Yankee
invaders obviously didn't believe in constitutional freedoms or
they would not have been invading the South. It should be noted
that the Yankees claimed that the Union informer had been captured by Confederate military forces. The Southern hostages held
by the Yankees had *no* connection with said military forces! Let us
emphasize this fact: They were civilians.

When the Union informer did not return, Yankee general Mc-
Neil ordered ten men to be chosen for execution. The ten were not
selected by a lottery. No, General McNeil had a more sinister design for the deaths of these men. He gave orders that only those of
high social, military, educational, and professional background
were to be chosen. Those selected ranged from nineteen to sixty
years of age. With one exception, all were active in their churches
and most were family men. The two who did not have a wife or
children were Hiram Smith and Thomas A. Sidenor. Hiram Smith
was twenty-two years of age and was chosen to die after the others
had received their death sentence. He had spent much time in
tears trying to assist those who had been given the death sentence,
not knowing that his name was to be added to the list. When the
jailer called him to the cell door and informed him that he too
would die the next day, he ceased his crying and never shed another tear. Those in jail noted that this young hero could weep for
others but remained strong and resolute in the face of his own
fate.[12] Thomas A. Sidenor was a former captain in the Confederate army. His unit had been destroyed in battle and thereafter disbanded. He had taken up the life of a civilian and was engaged to
be married. The new suit of clothes he was wearing had been chosen carefully by himself to serve as his wedding garment. It would
become his burial shroud.

Both pro-Southern and pro-Northern citizens made pleas on
behalf of the innocent men. Those who thought they had some
influence with the Yankee government and who had a sense of de-
cency implored the military authorities not to commit this act. But

the order had the highest backing from all levels of the Yankee government. At 1:00 P.M. on October 18, 1862, the ten men were loaded on wagons, seated on newly made coffins, and taken to the Palmyra fairgrounds where the hideous act was to be carried out. No one doubted the resolve of the Yankee. For after all, this was not the first time such an act had taken place. In Kirksville, some seventy miles from Palmyra, Confederate colonel McCullough and fifteen of his men had been murdered by the invader.[13] No help could be expected from the Yankee high command because Union general Merrill nearby had ordered the execution of ten Southerners himself.[14] No, the time had come for this group of men to pay the supreme price for believing in State's Rights and their Southern homeland.

On reaching the fairgrounds, the men were placed in a row and seated on their coffins. A few feet away stood thirty United States soldiers. Behind the thirty soldiers were an equal number of reserve troops. At the command "ready, aim, *fire*," the order was carried out. The only problem was that only three of the men were killed instantly. One was not even hit. The others were lying in pools of their own blood. Not to be outdone, the reserve troops were called into action. Walking among the wounded men, they took their time, and with their pistols shot each hostage until he stopped moaning. Poor Mr. Baxler was the one who had not been hit by the first volley. Sitting on the ground, he had to watch as the reserve troops moved in and shot his friends at point blank range, with each shot moving him closer to eternity.[15]

This incident did not pass without some protest. Not only in the South, but also in London and even in the North, decent people made loud protests about such a barbaric act. Twice in Lincoln's Cabinet meetings the issue was brought up about how to put the best face on this atrocity. But finally the incident was just ignored, because the South had its hands full and could not pursue the matter. But what about General McNeil? Surely the noble men of Yankeedom would censure this man for such acts. Not really. Shortly after the Palymra massacre, he was given a promotion to the rank of Brigadier General of United States Volunteers. The promotion was made, of course, by none other than the all-loving and tender-hearted Abe Lincoln.[16] Who says that crime does not pay! (The reader is directed to Addendum XI, "I Am Condemned to Be Shot," a previously unpublished letter from a Confederate

POW writing home on the eve of his execution. He had been chosen at random to die in retaliation for Confederate military activity in the area surrounding the POW camp in which he was being held.)

In Tennessee, the Yankee invaders laid their foul hands on a young Confederate soldier by the name of Sam Davis who had entered Confederate service at the age of nineteen. He had fought under some of the most noted Confederate generals. In 1863 he was selected as a member of "Coleman's Scouts," an elite group from Tennessee who entered Yankee-controlled territory to gather information. Sam was captured in his Confederate uniform when he visited his home during one of these raids. Regardless of this fact, he was condemned to be hanged as a spy. The commanding general of the Yankees kept young Sam in jail awaiting his execution, during which time Sam was offered his life, freedom, and many rewards if he would betray his commander and other friends in the Scouts. Over and over he was reminded of his impending death by the Yankees. Over and over he was reminded that he was young and had only begun to live his life. Over and over the Yankees tempted him to sell out his country and friends. Over and over he refused to break. Finally the Yankee commander told young Sam that all he had to do to gain his life and freedom was to give the Yankees the name of the man who was the leader of the Scouts. Young Sam's reply was, "You may hang me a thousand times but I would not betray my friends."[17]

To make matters worse for Sam, his commander (Capt. Henry B. Shaw) was already in the hands of the Yankees. Shaw was being held in the next jail cell but the Yankees did not know whom they had captured. All young Sam had to do to gain all that was promised him was to point a finger toward the next jail cell. He did not. He stood by his country and friends, and, as a result, the invader took a rope and placed it around the young man's neck. Courageous Sam Davis, Confederate hero, was hanged by the neck until dead.

> When the Lord calls up earth's heroes
> To stand before his face,
> O, many a name unknown to fame
> Shall ring from that high place!
> And out of a grave in the Southland,

At the just God's call and beck,
Shall one man rise with fearless eyes,
And a rope about his neck.
(Poem on the statue of Sam Davis in Nashville, Tennessee)

LOUISIANA AND
"THE TERRIBLE SWIFT SWORD"

In June of 1864, Louisiana's governor Henry Watkins Allen appointed commissioners to collect testimonies from eyewitnesses of the Yankee invasion of his state.[18] The conduct of the invader had so appalled the people of Louisiana that Governor Allen felt it necessary to make a written record of such fiendish activities. In his charge to the commissioners, he stated, "I hope the publication of a few hundred copies of this report will preserve for the future historian many facts which might otherwise be forgotten."

A reading of *The Conduct of Federal Troops in Louisiana* will provide a fully documented account of the barbaric conduct of the Yankee invaders in Louisiana. Governor Allen's report has been edited by David C. Edmonds. The following facts have been taken from this report.

A review of the history of the conduct of Yankee troops in Louisiana will bring two facts to light: (1) The invader felt that nothing Southerners owned or cared for was to be held beyond the Yankee's hate. This would include not only homes, furniture, clothes, crops, food, and the tools of food production, but also churches and even tombs of the recent dead. (2) The invader had a strong preconceived notion of what life "down South" was like and would not allow contrary facts to change his mind.

Louisiana has always been divided into two distinct portions: the Southern, or Cajun, area with its rich French and Catholic traditions, and the Northern, Scots-Irish and Protestant section. When war began, both sections joined in the defense of their home state and both suffered for their devotion to constitutional principles.

The Mississippi River offered the invader a natural highway into the lower portion of the state. With the fall of New Orleans, the people got their first taste of Yankee justice. The city of New Orleans had been defended by a small squadron of makeshift naval vessels and by two old forts. With the passage of the Federal fleet beyond the forts, both the forts and the city were forced to surrender to the invader. General Mansfiel Lovell, the Confederate military commander, ordered his forces to evacuate the city. On the morning of April 26, 1862, a force was landed from the USS *Pensacola*. This small force moved into the defenseless city and hoisted the United States flag over the Mint Building and then retired to their ship.[19] Unoccupied and unwilling to see the hated emblem of tyranny flying above the city, a young man of twenty-one years climbed to the roof and removed the United States flag. Being young and patriotic was not considered a virtue by the Yankees. Union general Benjamin Butler demanded that the man responsible for the act be thrown in jail. The young man was arrested and sentenced to death by hanging for the act of lowering the United States flag.[20] News of this decree swept the city and the South. All of the city, including the mayor, leading citizens, and church leaders pleaded with the Yankee invaders for the life of the young man. They might just as well have implored the fires of hell to cool as to beg for mercy from the Yankees. Young William Mumford was hanged. A small portion of the rope which was used to murder this innocent young man is maintained in the Confederate Memorial Hall in New Orleans to this day.

Thus Louisiana came under the rule of its conquerors with the infamous General "Beast" or "Spoons" Butler in full power. General Butler would earn for himself a special place in history. No foreign occupier has ever been held in such contempt as Ben Butler. During his stay in New Orleans, not only did he preside over the usual debauchery of Yankeedom, but he also issued the infamous decree that stated that any officer of the United States could and should treat the ladies of the city as if they were prostitutes "plying their trade." He sent to prison, without a grand jury indictment or trial by jury, both women and leaders of the clergy because they would not accept the invaders with open arms. He closed churches and newspapers at his will if he felt they were not loyal to the Yankee government. Every principle and precept that we as Americans take for granted was trampled upon by this man who some would have us believe was a hero of the Union. Jesus said that a tree could be known by its fruit. The fruit of this Union that Benjamin Butler brought to New Orleans was bitter and deadly.

Like a coiled snake, the invaders struck west from New Orleans, through the quaint Acadiana district toward Texas. As the army moved, they continued their normal and expected activities of plunder and destruction. So normal an activity was this that we will no longer mention it, but only relate some of the more audacious acts of these villains.

As the Yankees entered this region, about twenty thousand strong, they were confronted by Gen. Richard Taylor with about 3,500 men. As the Confederate army moved out, the women, children, and old men were left to contend with the invaders. The people were subjected to all forms of abuse. In St. Mary Parish, ladies stood in fear as Yankee soldiers ransacked their homes and chased the servant girls. To one old and frightened lady an intoxicated soldier stated, "Dry up; we've seen enough of you Southern women's tears." Moving to another part of the home another drunken soldier pushed a goblet to her lips and commanded, "Drink, you damned old rebel, drink to the Union!"[21] In the same parish, a horrified lady seeking help from an officer implored a Union colonel to protect her person and property. The colonel's reply was, "Protect you! Protect you a rebel; never! No protection to rebels!"[22] Thus the army of the Union did battle with the unarmed women and children of the South.

The following is just a sample of some of the degradations perpetrated by the Yankee army in Louisiana during its invasion of the Cajun country:

Lafayette: At the home of an infirm and bed-ridden man, all valuables were taken, including the covering on which the invalid was lying.[23]

Petite-Anse Island: Union soldiers entered the home of a man ninety years old, taking all his clothing and other valuables including the covers from his bed. Then as they left his home they cursed the old man.[24]

St. Mary Parish: Yankee troops ransacked the home of a Mr. Goulas, stripping his family of all their clothes, even the infant's clothes, and all bedding.[25]

Fausse Pointe: While in the process of being robbed, a Mr. Vilmeau heard his wife crying for help. Going to her aid, he found several ruffians fighting with her for her personal jewelry. While one succeeded in getting a ring from her hand by biting her finger, causing it to bleed profusely, another jerked her earrings out of her ears, tearing the flesh and causing them to bleed. Vilmeau was shot twice while trying to assist his bleeding wife.[26]

New Iberia: A Mr. Borel's house was pillaged by Yankees who took with them everything of value, including all the food for the family. On leaving the home, they also took Borel's horse, his only means of support for himself and his children. Borel went to Yankee general Nathaniel Banks and explained how everything he had was taken from him and that his children would starve if he did not get his horse back. Whereupon General Banks explained, "The horse is no more your property than the rest. Louisiana is mine. I intend to take everything."[27]

Morgan City: Even the resting place of the dead was not left alone by the invaders. In this city the late Dr. Brashear's tomb was broken into by the Yankees, and his earthly remains were tossed out. His metal coffin was taken for their own use.[28]

New Iberia: The materials from the graves were used for chimneys and hearthstones for the Yankee army. The cemetery was used as a horse corral. While the families of the deceased watched in horror, the Yankees ransacked the burial vaults of the dead, scattering the remains upon the ground.[29]

Opelousas: A Massachusetts unit turned the Protestant (Methodist) church there into a "den of infamy."[30]

New Iberia: The invaders stole the sacred vessels from the Catholic church and danced in the robes of the priest.[31]

Franklin: Federal soldiers pillaged and ransacked the Methodist church, using the pews and other items to furnish a billiard saloon.[32]

Franklin: The home of a Mr. Theodore Fay was ransacked; even the toys of his grandchildren were taken by the Yankees.[33]

The fates would not suffer the plundering Yankee forever. Finally the Confederates met and defeated the invaders and sent them reeling back toward New Orleans. Union general Nathaniel Banks once again proved to be a better general plunderer than a military leader. General Banks ordered another expedition into Louisiana's heartland. This time he attempted to take his army to Texas via Shreveport. Once again the usual activities of plunder and destruction were visited upon the hapless and defenseless civilians. The invasion of Northwest Louisiana also met with the same disaster for the Yankees. At the Battle of Mansfield, the

Yankees were completely defeated by General Taylor.[34] The following day, the Yankee army was hit again by the Confederates at the Battle of Pleasant Hill, Louisiana. All this pressure was enough to convince the Yankees to beat another retreat down the Red River to Alexandria.[35]

It was in Alexandria that the invaders, with the victorious Confederates hot on their heels, decided to vent their wrath on the defenseless people and town. On the withdrawal of the United States military force from the city, a systematic plan was executed to burn the whole place.[36] Without giving any notice to the inhabitants, the invaders set fires which spread throughout the town. Very little was saved; women and children were forced from their homes by the inferno and driven by the flames down to the river's edge to escape the heat.[37] A Yankee reporter from the *St. Louis Republican* was so moved by this wanton, barbaric act that he wrote an account of the burning. He stated, "Women gathering their helpless babes in their arms, rushing frantically through the streets with screams and cries that would have melted the hardest hearts to tears; little boys and girls running hither and thither crying for their mothers and fathers; old men leaning on a staff for support to their trembling limbs, hurrying away from the suffocating heat of their burning dwellings and homes."[38] He went on to give an account of how the people were driven to the river to save themselves, salvaging only the clothes on their backs. Ninety percent of the city was consumed by the fires of the Yankee terrorists.

Fire, sword, and starvation were employed against the hated "rebels" regardless of their age, race, sex, or status as noncombatants. This is the legacy left by the invader, a legacy of death and destruction. When we understand the enormity of these acts perpetrated on the civilians of the South, we wonder why a few monuments are not raised in memorial to those who had to stand in the path of the Yankees and suffer at home as well as those who stood in the line of battle. There is no way to know how much suffering or how many deaths there were among the loyal civilian population, but no doubt the numbers are high. When counting the Southern dead during the war, we should also take into account those who died because of acts of the Yankee invader which led to starvation, disease, and murder.

Not only did Governor Henry Watkins Allen's report on the conduct of the invader make note of the barbarity of the enemy, but it also shed some light on the preconceived (prejudiced) ideas the Yankee had about life in the South, especially the relations between the black and white people. One thing that bothered the Yankee was that the slave population did not rise up in open rebellion against their white masters.

Having been fed on a daily diet of "hate the South" propaganda from such trash as *Uncle Tom's Cabin* and other lies, the Yankees believed that all the slaves would welcome their "liberators" and rise up to kill their white masters. If this had happened, the war would have lasted no more than a year or so. But the Yankee invaders did not receive the cooperation from the blacks that they had counted on!

The Yankees expected to find blacks being whipped daily, starved, and worked to death by a fat and lazy Southern upper class. What they found was that the blacks were much divided as to what they should do with these Yankees who claimed to be their friends. Some blacks did go over to the Yankees *after* the Yankees were in control, another group remained loyal to their white families, and another group waited to see which way the wind was blowing before doing anything. Usually this group's loyalty depended upon whichever army was in control of the region at that time. This breakdown in loyalty closely parallels the loyalty of the civilian population of the American colonies during the American Revolutionary War.

This situation was not what the Yankees expected to find. They had been told by all the Abolitionist newspapers that the slaves were just waiting to rise up and throw off the chains of slavery. In reality this may have happened *if* the Yankee army had been invading a South American or a Caribbean country. As has been noted by James Walvin in his work *Slavery and the Slave Trade*, the system of slavery in the American South was the most benign of all the systems then in practice. This, he concludes, is why in other countries of the Western Hemisphere there had been so many slave revolts, many of which were successful, but little such activity was seen in the South.[39]

It was a common belief among the Yankees that the Southern blacks were all slaves and could own no property. The fact that many Southern blacks were free men and women of color, with as much freedom as black people in the North (if not more), was shocking to the Yankees. But even more shocking was the fact that many of these free blacks were slave holders themselves. In Louisiana, at the Olivier Plantation, the Yankees were surprised to find that the owner was a widowed, free lady of color who presided over a large plantation run by slave labor. A member of the Twelfth Connecticut in a letter home stated that he had been surprised to find as many free blacks down South as he had seen in the larger cities of the North. He wrote, "Some of the richest planters, men of really great wealth, are of mixed descent."[40] He stated that these Negroes would gather to stare at the Northern soldiers as they passed, and "These are not the former slaves, observe, but the former *masters*."[41] (emphasis added)

As the Yankees were retreating from the disaster in South Louisiana, at the town of Vermilion a "rebel's" home was put to the torch. The man's children and sick wife were in the house. After getting his family to safety, he begged the Yankee soldiers to help him put out the fire, because it was threatening all he had for his children and dying wife. No amount of imploring could move the Yankees to action, but a slave from the next plantation came to the assistance of the white man. After the effort had to be abandoned, the soldiers gathered around the black man and wanted to know why he, a slave, would help this rebel. One Yankee suggested that the black man helped only to steal the man's money. At this point the black man denied that he was a thief or that he had been paid for his actions. He contended that he had helped the white man only because of their friendship. The Yankees would not believe this story and told the slave that if he did not give up his money he would be shot. When he persisted, the troops shot him in the thigh. The slave, Benjamin George, survived the Yankee-inflicted wound but remained a one-legged invalid for the rest of his life.[42]

Another example of Yankee prejudice is found in Governor Henry Watkins Allen's report of Yankee atrocities in Alexandria. In the official report, Affidavit No. 4, a story is related of how the Yankees treated a free woman of color.[43] When they came upon a small but well-furnished dwelling in which they found a Negro lady, they demanded to know where her master was. When she informed them that she had no master and was a free lady of color, they laughed at her and told her that she was just hiding her master. They then set about stealing all of her valuables, destroying what they did not take. She begged them to stop and leave her and her property in peace. They once again told her that they knew that she was a liar, because, *"Niggers could not own property in this state."*[44] (emphasis added) All that this lady had worked for—her home, food, and savings—was taken from her. Before they left, the soldiers even pulled down her house and cut up a pile of lumber that she had accumulated for home improvements.

This arrogant, "know-it-all" attitude has caused more hard feelings between the Yankees and their Southern counterparts than anything else. Once they accept a point of view about the South, Yankees refuse to be bothered with facts to the contrary. We can remember very well in the early 1960s when young college students came down South to correct all the "errors" of Southern life. One such boy could hardly wait to leave campus and go downtown to see for himself how the white people made the "darkies" walk in the street rather than allow them on the sidewalks. No amount of assurance would persuade him that this did not happen. He *knew* what we did to "darkies" in Mississippi. Even after his return from town, he was still convinced that we had pulled a fast one on him, and that after he left, the poor old "darkies" would once again be walking in the dust of the streets (the streets were paved but he still saw dirt roads downtown!).

Lest anyone think that the Yankees in the Trans-Mississippi District were the only ones who treated blacks poorly, consider the actions of the men of the Seventeenth Maine Regiment. Throughout his journal, Pvt. John W. Haley displays his total contempt for both the Irish and the Negroes. On moving into Richmond, after its fall, some Negroes got too close for the bluecoats. Haley stated, "A host of young niggers followed us to camp and soon made themselves too familiar. We bounced them up in blankets and made them butt against each other also against some pork barrels and hard-bread boxes. A couple hours worth of bouncing satisfied them. One young nigger had an arm broke and several others were more or less maltreated."[45] So "offensive" were Haley's words about blacks in his journal, whom he always referred to as "niggers," that the editor felt compelled to apologize to the reader about Haley's views on black people.[46] Notice that she did not feel compelled to apologize to the people of the South for the barbaric actions of the Yankee directed against the Southern people! Obviously using the racial slur "nigger" and being cruel to blacks was wrong (a point we do not disagree with); but the pillage and destruction of homes, and the rape and starvation of noncombatant women, children, the elderly, and the infirm—and other such atrocities too numerous to mention—was acceptable by the editor if perpetrated against Southerners. Only a Yankee or a Southern Scalawag could be so depraved as to believe such a lie.

The Human Shield Policy

During the summer of 1990, the leading news consisted of the events in Iraq and Kuwait. One of the more heinous acts in modern times was committed by Iraq, under the leadership of Saddam Hussein. He had the audacity to take Americans and other foreigners as hostages and use them as human shields to protect his vital military bases. The idea of this inhumane and barbaric policy brought down upon Iraq the condemnation of the entire civilized world. Where do you suppose Hussein got the idea of using prisoners as human shields to protect military installations? Perhaps Hussein had been studying the war measures used by the Yankees in their invasion of the South!

Approximately the same time Hussein was setting up his human shield, the Yankee myth-makers were hard at work making a "documentary" entitled "The Civil War." As we have noted, this propaganda series was produced by a prejudiced man from the North—the place where so many slaves were brought into this country after the Yankee flesh merchants had kidnapped them from their homes in Africa. The Northern myth-makers seem to have trouble remembering such facts that are not in keeping with the official Yankee myth of history.

Now let's see if our Southern history will help us determine where Hussein got his idea about using humans as a shield to protect military installations.

In the summer of 1864 the South was pressed on all fronts. The city of Charleston, South Carolina, was under a Yankee blockade. The combined guns of the Yankee forts and the Union navy were shelling the city. The Confederates were answering the Yankees shot for shot. The Yankee government took six hundred Southern POWs and sent them to Charleston. The Yankee invader had hit upon a great idea—"Why not put Southern POWs in front of our position and make the Confederates fire on their own men?" By this method the Yankees hoped to prevent further shelling of the Yankee position by the Confederates.[47]

Captain Walter MacRae of the Seventh North Carolina was one of the six hundred hostages used by the United States government as a part of its human shield. He gives a vivid account of life under the guns and the resultant horrors visited upon these innocent Southern POWs. The prisoners were placed in a stockade less than two acres square. They were beneath the guns of the Yankee fort and situated so that every shot from the Confederate forts ". . . must either pass over our heads or right through the pen [stockade]. Any which fell short or exploded a tenth of a second too soon, must strike death and destruction through our crowded ranks."[48]

Captain MacRae describes the poor living conditions and food that was issued to the Southern POWs. The men were confined in a very small area (two acres), and no sanitary facilities were provided. They had to eat, sleep, and care for their wounded in the same place where garbage and sewage were dumped. Their only supply of water was from holes they dug in the sand. The water holes quickly filled with a mixture of rain water, salt water, garbage, and sewage. Their food consisted of provisions that had been condemned by the Federal government as unfit for Yankee troops. These "rations" consisted of worm- and insect-infested hardtack, a one-inch square, one-half-inch-thick piece of pork, and eight ounces of sour corn meal.

The POWs were placed under the guard of the Fifty-Fourth Massachusetts (*Glory*) and its cruel commander, Col. E. N. Hollowell. When some of the POWs protested the conditions of the rations to Colonel Hollowell, he replied, in true Yankee fashion, ". . . there was meat enough in the crackers, bugs, and worms."[49]

Within the stockade, the Yankees roped off a perimeter. Any POW who walked too close would be shot. Colonel Hollowell also gave orders to the black troops to shoot into any gathering of POWs larger than ten men or at any POW who broke any other rule of the prison.

This barbaric attempt of the Yankee invader to use Southern POWs as a shield to protect their positions did not work. Captain MacRae noted that the Southern gunners did slow down and take more time to aim (the better to hit the Yankee invader). With each well-placed shot from the Southern guns, a great shout of joy would go up from the Southern hostages. When the Southern guns fired, someone in the stockade would shout and everyone would hit the dirt and watch as the friendly fire would do its work on the invader. After a few months of this bombardment, the Yankees removed the men to another prison where they were treated no better, but at least they were not in danger of being killed by their own men.

The Yankee apologists tell us that the North was justified in using Southern POWs as a human shield because the Confederates were treating Northern prisoners just as badly. This accusation was denied by both the people of Charleston and by the Confederate government. Yankee major general C. V. Foster stated:

> Our officers, prisoners of war in Charleston, have been ascertained to be as follows [rations]: Fresh meat three quarters of a pound or one half pound hard bread or one half pint of meal; beans, one fifth pint.[50]

This amount was about five times the quantity given to the Southern POWs held by the Yankees. Foster, in a letter to his superior, Gen. Henry Halleck, made the following statement:

> Many of the people of Charleston exerted themselves in every way to relieve the necessities of our men, and freely, as far as their means would allow, made contributions of food and clothing.[51]

He also stated that the kind and just treatment the Northern POWs received from the South had induced over half (sixty-five percent) of the men to go over to the Southern cause and sign an oath of allegiance to the Confederacy. It may be noted that only one percent of the six hundred Southern POWs held by General Foster went over to the Yankee side. This, in itself, is evidence that the Northern POWs were treated kindly by the people and government of Charleston.

The next time you hear a liberal news commentator venting his wrath on evil tyrants who use innocent human beings as hostages or human shields, stop and remember the six hundred Southern POWs at Charleston. When you hear or read about terrorists such as Saddam Hussein, stop and ask yourself, "Where do you suppose he got that idea?"

YANKEE ATROCITIES AGAINST
BLACK SOUTHERNERS

The criminal, terrorist activities of the United States military during the War for Southern Independence produced massive suffering that was endured by both the black and the white civilian population. In this section we will focus on examples of the suffering endured by black Southerners. The majority of these accounts come directly from the federal government's own official records. It should be noted that, while the official records contain some of the many accounts of atrocities committed by the Northern troops, it is by no means a complete collection. It was not the intent of the Yankee officers who completed these reports to document their crimes. Also, even if an officer wanted to report such crimes, it is very unlikely that his subordinates were eager to include their confessions in their reports. Therefore the official records could not possibly contain the whole story of our people's sufferings.

Late in the war, the Federal authorities admitted that the influence of the United States army upon the black Southern population had produced an undesirable effect.[52] Sarah Debro, a ninety-year-old former slave, gave this account in 1937: "I waz hungry most of de time an' had to keep fightin' off dem Yankee mens. Dem Yankees was mean folks."[53]

The following is a small sample of the atrocities committed by Northern troops against black Southerners during the War of Northern Aggression.

Northern Missouri: On August 13, 1861, Secretary of War Simon Cameron received a letter containing information about United States military forces "committing rapes on the negroes."[54]

Athens, Alabama: The court-martial record of Lincoln's buddy Turchin dated May 2, 1862, contains information about an attempt to commit "an indecent outrage" on a servant girl. It also notes that a part of the brigade, "quarter[ed] in the negro huts for weeks, debauching the females."[55]

Woodville, Alabama: The activities of the Third Ohio Cavalry in August of 1862 included this entry: "negro women are debauched."[56]

Memphis, Tennessee: The Yankee soldiers had been fed a steady diet of lies about so-called slave breeding plantations and the familiarity of Southern male slave owners with their female slaves. The reality of a black race with high moral standards was incomprehensible to the Yankee invader. Therefore the Yankee ordered much of his conduct to match his preconceived notions of the accepted social relationships down South. This can be seen in this report from Memphis on April 7, 1864: "The [white] cavalry broke en masse in the camps of the colored women and are committing all sorts of outrage."[57] General Rufus A. Saxton sent a report to Secretary of War Edwin Stanton on December 30, 1864, in which he described the attitude of the Yankee soldiers: "I found the prejudice of color and race here in full force, and the general feeling of the army of occupation was unfriendly to the blacks. It was manifested in various forms of personal insult and abuse, in depredations on their plantations, stealing and destroying their crops and domestic animals, and robbing them of their money. . . . The women were held as the legitimate prey of lust. . . ."[58]

Bayou Grande Cailou, Louisiana: The Sixteenth Indiana Mounted Infantry sent invaders into a civilian area which resulted in the following account: "Mr. Pelton . . . reported that a soldier had shot and killed a little girl and had fired at a negro man on his plantation. I . . . proceeded to the place, where I found a mulatto girl, about twelve or thirteen years old, lying dead in a field. I learned from the negro man . . . that the girl had been shot by a drunken soldier, who had first fired at one of the men . . . [who] had witnessed the killing. . . ."[59] On November 20, Gen. Robert A. Cameron reported, "I heard by rumor . . . one of [Capt. Columbus Moore's] men had attempted to rape a mulatto girl and had shot and killed her for resisting."[60]

Augusta, Georgia: "The colored citizens wander around at all hours of the night, and many in consequence have been robbed and abused by scoundrels dressed as United States soldiers. . . . The conduct of the Fourth Iowa Cavalry . . . was such as reflects disgrace on both officers and men. . . . Firing so as to cause a colored woman to lose her arm; likewise committing robberies."[61]

Covington, Tennessee: Late in 1862, a campaign was conducted in the vicinity of Covington that produced the following official report: ". . . some of the men [of the Second Illinois Cavalry] behaved more like brigands than soldiers. They robbed an old negro man. . . ."[62]

Robertsville, South Carolina: The Yankee did not distinguish between white or black Southerner nor between free black or slave when he released the dogs of war upon our Southern homeland. On January 31, 1865, the following report was issued: "The indiscriminate pillage of houses is disgraceful. . . . houses in this vicinity, of free negroes even, have been stripped . . . shocking to humanity."[63]

Hilton Head, South Carolina: Politically correct Yankee propagandists masquerading as historians are quick to boast of the large numbers of Southern blacks who fought for the North during the war. They are also quick to dismiss the contribution to the Confederate war effort made by black Southerners, giving the excuse that Southern blacks were forced to serve the Confederacy. Little attention has been given to the forced conscription of blacks into the service of the United States during the War for Southern Independence. On May 12, 1862, the following report was sent to the United States Secretary of the Treasury concerning the forced induction of black Southerners: "This has been a sad day on these islands. . . . Some 500 men were . . . carried to Hilton Head. . . . The negroes were sad. . . . Sometimes whole plantations, learning what was going on, ran off to the woods for refuge. Others, with no means of escape, submitted passively. . . . This mode of [conscription] is repugnant."[64] The next day's report included this comment: "The colored people became suspicious of the presence of the companies of soldiers. . . . They [the blacks] were taken from the fields without being allowed to go to their houses even to get a jacket. . . . On some plantations the wailing and screaming were loud and the women threw themselves in despair on the ground. On some plantations the people took to the woods and were hunted up by the soldiers. . . ."[65] A letter about this incident written to the Federal agent stated, "This conscription, . . . has created a suspicion that the Government has not the interest in the negroes that it has professed, and many of them sighed yesterday for the 'old fetters' as being better than the new liberty."[66] Old fetters of slavery better than the new liberty of Yankee dominion— what a sad commentary. No wonder Northern propagandists work so hard to keep these facts from becoming public knowledge.

Nashville, Tennessee: "Officers in command of colored troops are in constant habit of pressing all able-bodied slaves into the military service of the United States."[67] Notice the complaint is that officers are in "constant habit," not just given to an occasional infraction.

Huntsville, Alabama: General Ulysses Grant received a communique on February 26, 1864, informing him that, "A major of colored troops is here with his party capturing negroes, with or without their consent. . . . They are being conscripted."[68] Notice that the term used is "capturing negroes," not enlisting or drafting them.

New Bern, North Carolina: On September 1, 1864, Gen. Innis N. Palmer reported to Gen. Benjamin F. Butler about the difficulty he was having convincing Southern blacks to help in the fight for their liberation. He stated: "The negroes will not go voluntarily, so I am obliged to force them. . . . The matter of collecting the colored men for laborers has been one of some difficulty but I hope to send up a respectable force. . . . They will not go willingly. . . . They must be forced to go. . . . this may be considered a harsh measure, but . . . we must not stop at trifles."[69] What is it called when someone forces another human being to labor against his will—sounds like slavery to us but the Yankees called it "trifles."

Beaufort, South Carolina: General Rufus A. Saxton made the following report to Secretary of War Stanton on December 30, 1864: "The recruiting [of former slaves] went on slowly, when the major-general commanding ordered an indiscriminate conscription of every able-bodied colored man in the department. . . . The order spread universal confusion and terror. The negroes fled to the woods and swamps. . . . They were hunted. . . . Men have been seized and forced to enlist who had large families. . . . Three boys, one only fourteen years of age, were seized in a field where they were at work and sent to a regiment . . . without the knowledge of their parents. . . ."[70] What happened to the bleeding-heart Abolitionist, crying about black families being broken up and sold to different masters and about children being forcefully separated from their parents? Evidently, such high moral standards were not allowed to stand in the way of the expanding Yankee empire!

Louisville, Kentucky: Major General Innis N. Palmer on February 27, 1865, issued General Order Number 5 confirming the generally accepted theory of the laws pertaining to the enlistment of civilians for military services in an occupied country: "Officers charged with recruiting colored troops are informed that the use of force or menaces to compel the enlistment of colored men is both unlawful and disgraceful."[71]

Fort Jackson, Louisiana: On December 9, 1863, a United States officer at Fort Jackson became angry with two black drummers and fell upon them, beating them with a mule whip. The black soldiers were forced to stand in formation and watch as the white officer mercilessly flogged the young drummers. When the formation was dismissed, the black men, all Union soldiers, rushed the fort's armory, seized their weapons, and with cries of "kill all the damnyankees" began to fire their weapons into the air. Two companies of black Union soldiers joined in and a general revolt against Yankee racial bigotry was underway. With great effort, the white officers persuaded the black solders to end their revolt and return to their quarters.[72]

Craney Island, Virginia: Both black and white Southerners were needlessly subjected to the terror of starvation by terrorist acts of United States troops. From Virginia we find one of many examples of the sufferings borne by black Southerners: ". . . the colored people . . . have been forced to remain all night on the wharf without shelter and without food; . . . one has died, and . . . others are suffering with disease, and . . . your men have turned them out of their houses, which they have built themselves, and have robbed some of them of their money and personal effects."[73] This communique was sent on November 26, 1862. Some Yankee apologists have claimed that the horror against civilians occurred only after many years of bitter war— though we are curious to know how many years of war are necessary to justify any amount of cruel and inhumane conduct against innocent civilians?

Bisland, Louisiana: During the invasion of Cajun Louisiana, the Yankee targeted slaves as part of the loot to be acquired. "Contraband" was a term used to denote slaves enticed or forced away from their masters' plantations. These poor people very often would end up serving in the Federal army or working on a government plantation. When the Confederate forces recaptured the area around Bisland, Louisiana, they discovered the pathetic condition in which these former slaves were forced to live while enjoying the charity of the United States government. One account states that two thousand of these people perished as a result of following, or being forced to follow, the Federal army in retreat. In view of the shallow graves in which many had been hastily placed, the comment was made, "They have found their freedom." The horror of a local sugar house has been described by at least two separate eyewitnesses who were either Confederate soldiers or masters searching for their former slaves. The small house was filled with dead or dying Negroes. Some were "being eaten by worms before life was extinct." The roads "were lined with Negroes half starved, almost destitute of clothing, sick and unable to help themselves; the only question of the poor wretches, who had been two months experiencing Federal sympathy and charity, was the inquiry if their master was coming after them." The Federal army, in spite of its abundance, did not provide for these people. When their fellow Southerners discovered their plight, the Confederate army, short on every necessity, assigned transportation and such food and medicine as it had at its disposal to the salvation of these poor, suffering people. Let it be remembered that it was the compassion of their fellow Southerners and the assistance of the Confederate army that saved the lives of these black Southerners.[74]

The Yankee myth that the North fought the war because of its belief in human brotherhood and its love for the black race has once again been proven to be a lie.

SUMMARY

If at this point you have a feeling of utter despair, don't feel as if you are alone. While conducting our research it has been difficult to overcome feelings of despair as we reviewed the barbaric acts committed against our Southern people by the United States government. It should be remembered that these acts were committed by those in the service of the United States under the flag of that nation and with the approval of the highest officials of the country. This record should drive an agonizing pain into the heart of all Americans.

To ignore this record will only guarantee that further acts of violence will go unreported. Why should we, the people of the South, be made the butt of many jokes about our poverty, our lack of education, and our love for the Southland? We should remember that this poverty did not just happen to us but was the direct result of the Yankee invasion and wanton pillage of the South. Louisiana and South Carolina were the wealthiest states in the Union in 1861; but since the war they have never climbed back up to the national average. Mississippi, before the war, had more millionaires per capita than New York. Each Southern state has just such a story to tell. What happened to all this wealth? Where did all these poor people come from? Did the sky just open up and rain down poverty and destitution on Mississippi and the rest of the South? Does anyone ever stop to think that one reason education in the South has been held back is because the Yankee invaders lost no time in destroying all schools and colleges within their reach. All books and personal libraries were carried North or put to the torch. Homes, railroads, bridges, courthouses with all their records, and every means of production of food and wealth were destroyed. Look again at Mississippi. We find that the first years after the war, before Carpetbagger rule, one of the largest expenditures of money by the state was for the purchase of artificial arms and legs for Confederate veterans. While the South was being taxed to pay for the support of the Union veterans, her own former defenders were not given a dime of support from the then common treasury of the "reunited" country. After the war the South did not get a Marshall Plan to help rebuild her economy as did Germany and Japan after World War II; instead, she got twelve years of cruel military rule and "Reconstruction" exploitation and oppression.

The first thing a Yankee apologist will tell you when confronted with these facts is that the wealth of the South was based on the evil system of slavery and therefore Southerners "got what they deserved." This has a hollow sound to it because much of the wealth of the industrial North had its beginning in the African slave trade. Also, the pious Yankee did not refuse to buy the slave-grown cotton and use it to make all kinds of products for sale. The invaders indeed came marching down South with the money they made from the slave trade jingling in their pockets, with the factories of the North humming in the background using the raw material grown by slave labor.

Even if the Yankee argument is correct (and it is not), why should the seventy to eighty percent of the South that did not own slaves be punished along with the slave holders? No, slavery was only the smoke screen used by the Yankee invaders to cover up their infamous and odious acts committed against a peaceful and defenseless people. If the Yankees could paint the South as being full of evil men and women, bent on living a life of leisure at the expense of their slaves, then and only then would the world *not* look upon the South as the victim. Up until now, very few people have challenged this Yankee myth. Even the children of the South are taught in Southern schools that their ancestors were the product of this evil (as defined by the Yankee) system. But throughout the South, men and women are coming together and speaking out against this falsehood. The winds of change are beginning to blow. The people throughout the world are beginning to question the propaganda of big government. Surely the truth will not stay buried under a heap of Yankee lies.

CHAPTER 5

A Moral Right to Be Free

The principle for which we contended is bound to reassert
itself, though it may be at another time and in another form.[1]

President Jefferson Davis

INTRODUCTORY COMMENTS

Before we reach that other time and other form spoken of by
President Davis, we must first understand that Southerners
do have a moral right to be free. This is more important than
any legal argument for freedom. In this chapter the authors
present the reasons why it was and still is morally correct for the
Southern people to assert their claim to the right of self-determination.

We will demonstrate to the reader the way in which a government may gain or lay claim to legitimacy, and we will establish what form of government the Southern people have traditionally desired. We will demonstrate that our philosophy of
government has deep roots in antiquity and was not a system dreamed up by the slaveocracy to protect its property or hold-
ings.

We will review the theory of "the consent of the governed," the
concept of limited government with constitutional limits upon the
extent of its powers, and the right of a people to dispose of a government that violates the rights of its citizens.

President Jefferson Davis stated in his farewell address to
the United States Senate that the South was compelled to withdraw from the Union to ensure that the rights his generation
had received would be transmitted to future generations. These
rights represented our original inheritance of liberty. Unfortunately, this wonderful estate of freedom was lost to the invader's sword. It is now time to begin our search to regain our lost
estate.

147

McCool, Bull Hill, Oklahoma, was of mixed ancestry, being of Scottish and Cherokee Indian lineage. He served as a scout for the Confederate army in the Trans-Mississippi Department and was one of many Native Americans who supported the Southern cause. (Image courtesy of Ronald G. Ward, Pocola, Oklahoma)

A Moral Right to be Free

Tragedy is no stranger to the South. As Richard Weaver pointed out in the epilogue to his book, *The Southern Tradition at Bay*, the post-war South committed two great errors. First, it failed to study its position to arrive at a basic philosophy that justified its existence. Second, it surrendered the initiative. The South had no philosophical justification for existence. The South was left with no vision for the future and was forced into a defensive political posture. The most that our leaders have been able to do is to seek meekly the acceptance of the national parties. The price for this acceptance has been for us to remain quiet, to allow both national parties to be dominated by non-Southerners and Scalawags, and to accept the ever-enlarging role of the federal government. Because of her defensive position, the South not only has failed to regain her lost estate, but also has been brought to the brink of John Randolph's prediction of that time when "the little upon which we now barely subsist will be taken from us."

The political pacification of the Southern people has been so successful that today there are no Southern-elected officials who will stand above the murky swamp of political mediocrity that typifies the current Southern political condition to ask the following questions: Is the present political and economic condition best for us and our children? Are we morally obliged to accept the continuing intrusion of the federal government into the political, social, and economic life of the Southern people? Do we, the people of the South, have a right to a government that places our cultural, economic, and political development first and foremost?

The Southern people are today ruled by an overgrown central government that has taken unto itself the power to make decisions for us under the assumption that it knows better than we do what is best for us, our children, and our society. As early in our history as the Battle of King's Mountain in 1780, Southerners demonstrated their desire to be left alone. The average Southerner desires to obey the law, to pay reasonable taxes, and to live his or her life undisturbed by a meddling government. The unfortunate reality is that the central government does not share this view.

Do the people of the South have a moral right to be free, or is this an unreasonable demand? Do we have the right to expect the government to exercise its powers in a restrained manner, or should we recognize that the central government now possesses a divine right to set the limit to the extent of its powers? Should we admit that we no longer have a right to be protected from the arbitrary abuse of governmental power? Are we a free people, free to live our lives in peace and security, free from the meddling directives of an all-powerful government? Or are we a controlled people? Are we a people who have no rights or freedoms except those benevolently and condescendingly extended to us by our watchful masters in Washington? Are we the children of serfs who are at times allowed the appearance of freedom in order to keep us amused and docile, much as a parent would keep a child quiet by giving it a shiny bauble?

The men and women of the South are by right of birth heirs to a great heritage of individual freedom and personal accountability. We have a moral right to these freedoms. Evidence of our moral right to be free is seen in the writings of our political forefathers such as Thomas Jefferson and John C. Calhoun.[2]

When Jefferson penned the Declaration of Independence, he clearly set forth his political philosophy in the second paragraph, part of which reads as follows:

> . . . governments are instituted among Men, deriving their just powers from the consent of the governed.[3]

The key word is "consent." This great Southerner knew that the only legitimate use of governmental power is through the free and unfettered consent of the people governed. Without this consent the government has no moral right to exist. The governed, according to Jefferson, have a right to a government that disciplines itself to the will of the people. Furthermore, it can be seen that the failure of the British Crown and Parliament to so discipline itself was the very justification for the call sent forth through the colonies to secede from the established central government![4]

Jefferson advocated a form of government that sought the will of the people as opposed to a government that sought to impose the government's arbitrary will upon the people. The people, according to Jefferson, have a right to a government they consider good and just.

What type of government have Southerners traditionally held to be good and just? John C. Calhoun both posed the question and provided its answer when he wrote, "How can those who are invested with the power of government be prevented from the abuse of those powers as the means of aggrandizing themselves? . . . Without a strong constitution to counteract the strong tendency of government to disorder and abuse there can be little progress or improvement."[5] A desire for a strong constitution with the resultant respect for State's Rights, state sovereignty, and individual liberty has been the hallmark of Southern political thought.[6]

The history of the American Constitution is a record of the struggle between those who sought to protect the sovereignty of the people within the states and those who desired to extend and to enlarge the power and control of the central government. A review of the current budget deficit is a giveaway (no pun intended) as to who won this struggle.

In addition to a huge deficit, we have received from our political masters in Washington a second-rate Southern economy, a Congress dominated by liberals and Southern Scalawags, a Supreme Court that has not had a traditional Southerner on it since the War for Southern Independence, and a school system controlled by the liberal Supreme Court and the NAACP. Two generations of Southerners have grown up under numerous court orders, guidelines, government edicts, affirmative action programs, minority set-asides, desegregation consent decrees ad nauseum; yet we are still no closer to appeasing the collected wrath of our masters in Washington! One can only wonder if perhaps in their infinite wisdom our Southern leaders should reconsider the effectiveness of appeasement.

Thomas Jefferson taught us that we do indeed have a right to a government ordered in accordance to the will of the people. From John C. Calhoun we know that the people of the South have traditionally desired a government typified by a strong constitution with maximum freedom and civil liberties reserved to the people. Recent history has demonstrated that we do not have that type of government.

Some Southerners have accepted the Northern assertion that Appomattox settled everything and that consequently we have no moral right to discuss the prospect of regaining our lost estate. Yet the political philosopher John Locke rejected this barbaric attitude of "might makes right." If we apply Locke's reasoning to the current federal system, we will see that the federal government could not and has not gained a legitimate and justifiable right to the power and authority it now exercises over us.

Locke reasoned that an aggressor gains no rights by a successful military adventure. Indeed, he even maintained that a victor in a justifiable war could never establish moral validity that would contravene the right of the conquered and occupied people to their liberty and property.[7]

The idea that the Southern people must accept the domination of the North because of their failure in the War for Southern Independence is an unfortunate confusion of force with moral validity. The two are separate and distinct. Force can never give rise to moral validity. A government that is predicated upon force can legalize its existence only by a recognition of the rights of the people making up the sovereign community. A government may indeed possess the power to infringe upon the life, liberty, or property of its subjects, but this very act in and of itself voids any claim of legitimacy by that government. Any government—be it a king, prince, magistrate, or whatever form—that either actively or passively attempts or allows such an infringement upon the rights and liberties of the people forfeits its moral validity and therefore negates its legitimate right to exist!

The current liberal domination of our political and economic life in the South is a direct result of the North's victory in its war of aggression waged against the Southern people. Yet military force cannot bestow moral validity upon the subsequent government. When force is used to impose a government upon a people, the *moral* authority reverts to the sovereign community which must then struggle to institute legitimate government.

John Locke reaffirmed that might does not make right; therefore, the North's successful campaign of military aggression does not bestow moral validity upon the federal system established by it. Further evidence of Southerners' moral right to be free can be seen in the works of John Milton. In his *Tenure of Kings and Magistrates*, he proved from natural law, the Scriptures, and the law of England that a tyrannical king could be legally deposed and that the king stood in legitimate danger of the death penalty. Milton declared that the ultimate right to protect the public good resides with the people, not with the king. This is true because a king (and by implication any other form of government) derives authority from the people for the protection of the common good:

The power of kings and magistrates is nothing else, but what
is only derivative, transferred and committed to them in trust
from the people, to the common good of them all, in whom
the power yet remains fundamentally, and cannot be taken
from them without a violation of their natural birthright.[8]

John Milton announced a fundamental principle of Southern political thought when he proclaimed that the right to protect the
public good resides not with the powers that be, not with some arbitrary central government, but with the people. The people possess an inherent right to dispose of any government that does not
rule with the unfettered consent of those governed.

The moral right of a people to be free has been accepted and
enforced many times in American history. The colonies asserted
this claim even though the Crown owned the colonies! So great is
this moral right of self-determination that it voided the English
Crown's legitimate and legal title to its American colonies! The
United States government recognized this right when it recognized the Republic of Texas which seceded from the legal control
of Mexico and again when the same United States government accepted Texas (formerly Mexican territory) into the Union. The
United States government actually assisted the people of Panama
in their secession from Colombia less than two generations after it
had denied the right of secession to the Southern people.

We, the people of the South, do indeed have a moral right to be
free. This has been demonstrated by the writings of such great
Southerners as Jefferson and Calhoun. This moral right is recognized in the writings of Locke and Milton. We must begin the
struggle to regain our rights. John Naisbitt in *Megatrends* wrote,
"People whose lives are affected by a decision must be part of the
process of arriving at that decision."[9] What part did the Southern
people play in instituting forced busing? What part did we play in
reducing and maintaining an inferior Southern economy? What
part have traditional conservative Southerners played on the
United States Supreme Court? When we Southerners begin to realize the moral veracity of our cause, we will see it not as a "lost
cause" but as the right cause, a cause worthy of the great struggle
yet to come!

James W. Nicholson, Claiborne Parish, Louisiana. With his sophomore class at Homer College, Nicholson joined the Twelfth Louisiana Volunteer Infantry at the age of sixteen. Typical of the early settlers of the Southern frontier, Nicholson's family was of Scottish and Irish ancestry. After the war Nicholson was to distinguish himself as a mathematician and educator, as president of Louisiana State University, and as author of books on higher math and Southern history.[10] (Image courtesy of Claitor's Book Store, Publishing Division, Baton Rouge, Louisiana)

CHAPTER 6

A Legal Right to Be Free

We could have pursued no other course without dishonor. And sad as the results have been, if it had all to be done over again, we should be compelled to act in precisely the same manner.[1]

General Robert E. Lee, C.S.A.

INTRODUCTORY COMMENTS

To understand the logic of our legal right to be free, we will review the formation of the original Constitutional Republic. A distinction is made between the original government and the current fraudulent government. The underlying reasons for the assertion that the current government is fraudulent will be explored and explained.

Again we briefly examine the right to govern. We explore our Founding Fathers' attitude toward government and their primary fear regarding the proposed federal government under the Constitution; how the federal government was formed; and, whether or not the states irrevocably surrendered a part of their rights to the new government.

We then move on to describe how the North worked to destroy the Original Constitution by war and Reconstruction. After the review of Reconstruction, we analyze the political condition of the South under the new centralistic federal government. It will be shown that the North relented in its application of Reconstruction only after it had been successful in radically shifting the power of the government from the states to the central government. All this was done against the expressed will of the Southern people while we were disfranchised and under bayonet rule.

155

A Legal Right to Be Free

THE FORMATION OF
THE CONSTITUTIONAL REPUBLIC

Do the people of the South have a legal right to be free? To answer this question, we must review the history of the present federal government. It should be noted that the federal government is only the agent of our oppression. Government in and of itself is neither good nor bad. Government is the instrument of social order. It is, in fact, the tool used by those holding political power. When a people establish a constitutional republic, the limitations imposed by the constitution of that republic will be an effective instrument for the protection of the people only as long as the political leaders are philosophically loyal to the spirit of that constitution.

Suppose a constitutional republic was established with limited power granted to the federal government, and several years later there was a change in the basic philosophy of a large segment of the ruling political leadership. Suppose the majority desired an increase in the power of the central government. The minority would refuse to yield and thereby would prevent an increase in the power of that government. The smaller element could, by using the guarantees and limitations imposed by the constitution, stop the attempts of the majority to increase the central government's power.

Keep in mind that the reason for including limitations upon the central government is to prevent just this type of power grab. In such cases, the minority segment is faced with the prospect of suffering economic and political loss if the majority is allowed to use the power of the central government to advance the majority's interest. The majority element desires to gain certain financial profits at the expense of the minority. Of course it would mask its intent with grand statements that its plans would be best for the entire country and that the minority should not be allowed to stand in the way of progress. The majority has become afflicted with the same passions that prompt and drive imperialism, passions that are as old as man himself—greed, selfishness, and unbridled ambition. When financial profits are threatened by the adherence to a given philosophy, it unfortunately becomes more reasonable (i.e., more profitable) to abandon the philosophy rather than to renounce the profits. The majority will use its greater numbers and its control of the central government to ensure continued and increased personal gain.

Why would the minority element resist the majority's power grab? The answer is simple enough; the minority element would be forced to accept laws harmful to its own economic and cultural development if it didn't resist. In order to protect its rights, the smaller element would be forced to depend upon the limitations imposed by the constitution to protect it. This, after all, is the reason the safeguards were placed in the constitution.

The cause of this hypothetical conflict is purely economical. It must be remembered that the reason for the existence of the constitution is to protect the political interests of all parties. The constitution is a contract by which parties with divergent interests agree to cooperate in matters of mutual interest and at the same time provide for the protection of those rights reserved by each party. When one party to the agreement attempts to gain an unfair advantage over the remaining parties, then conflict is guaranteed.

We now have an apparent standoff, with one element determined to increase the power of the federal government and the other determined to maintain its own rights. In a political environment, nothing remains static. The element demanding a more powerful federal government would have two options. First, it could, by a loose construction of the constitution, cause certain parts to be interpreted so as to give increasing power to the central government. It could then control the central government by reason of its numerical majority. A persistent campaign to reduce and render non-functional the limitations imposed by the original constitution would be waged by the larger element. Public opinion would have to be aroused by using a highly emotional issue to justify the crusade to change the form of the original government. After all, it would be difficult indeed to inflame the public over the economic profits of a few special interest groups. The second alternative left open to the element demanding more power would be to use its position as the stronger partner to force a settlement in its favor by waging aggressive war upon the smaller element, defeating and destroying that element, and then dictating the terms of the new government.

We now have a thumbnail sketch of what would happen in a constitutional republic if two opposing economic and cultural interests were to come into conflict. As previously noted, the political environment does not remain static. In such a conflict there would be no "breaking even." If the situation remained the same, then the smaller element would win. If the smaller element were forced to seek a compromise, then the larger element would prevail. As long as the two sides held together, each would seek to advance its own interest at the expense of the other.

Historically, the South has been the smaller element. Our forefathers made many gallant efforts to defend and protect our liberty. Yet the reality of present circumstances stands as testimony that those past efforts have failed and that something else must be done! Before our crusade begins, we should establish that the people of the South have a legal right to be free. To establish this freedom, we must answer the question, where does government acquire its right to exercise power over a people?

THE RIGHT TO GOVERN

There is within man a natural tendency to associate with his fellows. This tendency leads to the necessity of forming government. The causes that impel man to form civil governments are primarily protective in nature. Government protects the people from external and internal dangers arising from the tendency of man to be in conflict with his fellows. This conflict is accompanied by the connected passions of suspicion, jealousy, anger, and revenge. While this tendency is not the way things ought to be in a moral sense, it is the way things are in reality. Thus the need arises for some controlling power or government. In *A Disquisition on Government*, John C. Calhoun maintained that the moral necessity for government comes directly from God:

> The Infinite Being, Creator of all, has assigned [to man] the social and political state, as best not only to impel him into the social state, but to make government necessary for man's preservation and well being.[2]

To establish government, man, a free moral agent, transfers a portion of his freedom to government. Man freely consents to delegate a portion of the control he has over his life and allow that control to be exercised by government. Unfortunately for the people, government has within itself a strong tendency to abuse its powers. Those who control the government can use its powerful and dominating nature to establish itself as superior to its creators and to proclaim itself the sole judge of its own powers. Thus tyranny replaces responsible government. In our world, tyranny has been and still is the rule. A democratic republic with constitutional limits on the exercise of power is a rare exception.

The right of any government to exercise its powers over a people can be obtained only with the free and unfettered consent of those people.[3] Any government that does not rule with the consent of the governed fails the test of legitimacy and therefore has no legal right to rule and shall be regarded as a tyranny. When government removes itself from the category of responsible government (i.e., ruling with the consent of those governed) and establishes its own arbitrary will as the sole judge of its own powers—that government has by its own actions renounced any claim to a legal right to govern. The people then may use whatever measure necessary to remove that government and to establish, once again, responsible government.[4] The people are limited only by the exercise of prudence. Extreme measures must not be employed unless lesser measures have proven ineffective.

OUR FOUNDING FATHERS' ATTITUDE TOWARD GOVERNMENT

The Founding Fathers' attitude towards government can best be summed up in the words of Virginia's first citizen, George Washington:

> Government is not reason; it is not eloquence; it is force! Like fire, it is a dangerous servant and a fearful master![5]

The primary desire of the framers of the United States Constitution was to design a government that would possess only those powers necessary to carry out the basic needs of the thirteen states (who were at that time independent nations). Each state would reserve its sovereignty to itself, while delegating a portion of its sovereign authority to the federal government. It was understood that the only way the citizens of a given state could protect their individual liberties, so recently won, was by allowing the people of that state through their local government to be the sole agent of those liberties. The only exceptions were to be those few and specific rights clearly delegated to the federal government under the contract of the Constitution.

The reverence held by the Founding Fathers for individual liberty can be appreciated by understanding the manner in which the British government granted Americans their freedom. The British government recognized each of the thirteen colonies as a free and independent state (i.e., as a separate nation in possession of its own sovereignty). With the recognition of independence, each colony became a free and sovereign state.[6]

It is easy then to understand why the people of the states were so reluctant to surrender their hard-earned independence and individual liberties to yet another central government. It is a matter of historical fact that at no time did the states surrender (i.e., renounce) their claim to sovereignty either directly or indirectly.

The Founding Fathers were determined to hold securely to the claim of state sovereignty. They had the insight to foresee and fear what Southerners are experiencing today. Government has within itself a strong tendency to increase its powers at the expense of personal liberties. There is always the tendency of the controlling group, element, or region to increase its own powers at the expense of the smaller group, element, or region. To protect the people from a power-hungry central government, the states retained their sovereignty and delegated, as opposed to surrendered, a very limited and explicit portion of their sovereign authority to the newly formed federal government.

American independence was not granted to a central government or to the American people en masse, but to the individual states.[7] These states were determined to protect the people from the unbridled power of any central government. The primary desire of the Founding Fathers was to construct a central government that would not become another threat to the liberties of the American people.

THE FORMATION OF THE ORIGINAL
FEDERAL GOVERNMENT

The preamble of the Constitution states that "We the People of the United States" ordained and established the Constitution. The Constitution is the legal document that formed the federal government. But can it be maintained that the American people met and formulated the document or that the people en masse ratified it? No, in fact, only a very small number of people met and formulated it. How then can it be said that the people "ordained and established" the Constitution?

The people acting through their states sent their representatives to draft the legal document. This document was then submitted to the individual states to receive the approval or rejection of the representatives of the people.[8] Each individual state, acting as the agent of the people within it, formed and established the federal government. The federal government therefore was created by the states as their agent to perform only those duties the states individually could not accomplish.

The individual states as agents of the people created the federal government. The states did not intend to create a superior institution to sit in judgment over them, but rather intended to, and in fact did, create a co-ordinate (state/federal) government. This federal government was to have only those powers the states specifically delegated to it.

We have now established that the federal government was created by the states to serve as their collective agent in areas specifically assigned to it. From this situation arises the irrepressible question: Did the states surrender their delegated rights to the central government?

DELEGATED OR SURRENDERED RIGHTS?

If the states surrendered their rights to the newly created federal government, then the South's attempt to recall those rights in 1861 would have had no legal foundation. Therefore, it is imperative that we determine whether or not the South had a legal right to recall its delegated powers.

The term "delegate" implies the action of a superior toward an inferior or an equal toward an equal. It cannot mean the action of an inferior toward a superior in that a superior already has the power to require the inferior to submit. Therefore, the states were acting from a position of superiority or at the very least from a position of equality when they delegated powers to the newly created federal government. From this we can deduce that the strongest position that the federal government was to have in relation to the states was only that of an equal partner.

The reason the states refused to surrender their delegated rights is that there was great concern over how the states would protect their citizens from an all-powerful central government. What recourse would the states and the people thereof have if the central government usurped unto itself enough of the reserved powers to make the central government the sole judge of its own powers? The answer can be found in the Virginia Act of Ratification of the United States Constitution:

> We, the delegates of the people of Virginia, duly elected, . . . in behalf of the people of Virginia, declare and make known, that the powers granted under the Constitution, being derived from the people of the United States, may be resumed by them, whensoever the same shall be perverted to their injury or oppression; and that every power not granted thereby, remains with them and at their will: that, therefore, no right, of any denomination, can be canceled, abridged, restrained, or modified.[9]

John C. Calhoun made the following statement about this resolution:

> It declares that all powers granted by the Constitution, are derived from the people of the United States; and may be *resumed* by them when *perverted* to their injury or oppression; and that every power *not granted* remains with them, and at their will; and that no right of any description can be canceled, abridged, restrained or modified by Congress, the Senate, the House of Representatives, the President, or any department, or officer of the United States. Language cannot be stronger![10]

It should be noted that the only way Virginia could be persuaded to ratify the Constitution was with the inclusion of the strong language of the first ten amendments and the even stronger language of her act of ratification of the United States Constitution. If Virginia had refused to ratify the Constitution, her action would have dealt a death blow to the efforts to secure ratification by the remaining states. In her act of ratification, Virginia drew a protective shield around the sovereign community and declared that sovereignty is derived from the people. The people acting together through their agent the state retained the legal right to recall any portion of their delegated or usurped sovereign authority "whensoever it should be perverted to their injury or oppression."

The federal government was established by the individual states as an equal partner in a co-ordinate system of state and federal governments. The states did not intend to establish a supreme judge to rule over them. Before entering into the proposed constitutional contract, the state of Virginia (along with several other states, both north and south) declared the legal right of the sovereign community (the people of the state) to recall any delegated power if it is used in an act of oppression or injury against the people. The fact that the other states accepted the Virginia Act of Ratification without question is reason enough to maintain the assertion that they were in agreement with Virginia.

We have now seen that any government must receive its legal right to govern from the consent of the governed. If at any time the aforesaid government denies the consent of the governed, that government by its own action repudiates its legal right to exist! We have also seen that the states, as agents of the people who comprise the sovereign community, were not created as inferior appendages of a central federal government; but, quite the contrary, they existed prior to the federal government and by their own voluntary action created the federal government. The states viewed their new creation as an equal partner in a coordinate federal and state governmental arrangement. The origin of our independence, the nature of the constitutional compact, and the language of Virginia's act of ratification all stand as evidence of the South's legal right to be *free!*

We have now shown that the right of a constitutional government to issue edicts, guidelines, affirmative action orders, or to take any other such action must first be based upon the free and unfettered consent of those governed (i.e., the consent of the sovereign community). In light of history and current events, it is possible to demonstrate that the present federal government does not have, nor does it seek to obtain, the consent of the Southern people for any of its many oppressive and illegal actions. By its own actions, the present federal government has negated its legal right to govern the people of the South.

THE DESTRUCTION OF THE
CONSTITUTIONAL REPUBLIC

The contrast between the original federal/state co-ordinate system envisioned and established by the Original Constitution and the current system of centralized and oppressive federalism should cause the observant Southerner (or any American) to realize that a major, fundamental change has occurred in our government. If this change was brought about by legal means, then our claim that the present federal government is illegitimate would be unfounded. But if this change was brought about without the consent of the Southern people and by use of fraud, coercion, military aggression, and other illegal acts, then the Southern people have a legal and moral right to be free of such an oppressive government.

Patrick Henry refused to attend the Constitutional Convention stating, "I smell a rat!" Why did this Southerner, who was one of the great advocates of freedom, refuse to aid in the drafting of the new federal government? His great concern was that the proposed government would become the sole judge of its own power. Patrick Henry demonstrated great political insight when he identified the fatal flaw in the proposed government.

Thomas Jefferson warned that, if the federal government was allowed the right to be the judge of the extent of its own power, it would result in a government "not short of despotism—*since the discretion of those who administer the government and not the Constitution would be the measure of their powers*"[11] [authors' emphasis]. Jefferson feared that the democratic will of the people (the consent of the governed) would be usurped by a non-elected judiciary. The people of the South today are very familiar with the coercive and arrogant power of this non-elected judiciary. The Southern people have and continue to experience what Patrick Henry and Thomas Jefferson warned against.

KENTUCKY AND VIRGINIA
RESOLUTIONS OF 1798

It did not take long for the South to come into conflict with those who wanted to extend the power of the federal government at the expense of personal liberty. An example of this conflict can be seen in the Kentucky and Virginia Resolutions of 1798. The author was none other than Thomas Jefferson and James Madison who used the documents to define the limits of legitimate federal power:

> Resolved, that the several States composing the United States of America are not united on the principle of unlimited submission to their general government; but that by compact under the style and title of a Constitution for the United States, and of amendments thereto, they constituted a general government for special purposes, delegated to that government definite powers, reserving each State to itself, the residuary masses of right to their own self-government; and that whensoever the general government assumes undelegated powers, its acts are unauthoritative, void, and of no force; that to this compact each State acceded as a State, and is an integral party; that this government, created by this compact, was not made the exclusive or final judge to the extent of the powers delegated to itself; since that would have made its discretion, and not the Constitution, the measure of its powers; but that, as in all other cases of compact among parties having no common judge for itself . . . each party has equal right to judge for itself.[12]

A reading of these resolutions will demonstrate that the central premise of the original American government was the right of the state to protect the people of that state from the illegal incursion of a power-hungry federal government. John C. Calhoun made this statement from the Senate floor:

> The Constitution has admitted the jurisdiction of the United States within the limits of the several States only so far as the delegated powers authorize; beyond that they [the federal government] are intruders, and may rightfully be expelled.[13]

He explained that the only way the federal government could circumvent the right of the states to protect the people was by ". . . prostrating the Constitution, and substituting the supremacy of military force in lieu of the supremacy of the law. . . ."[14] (Perhaps Calhoun was prophesying of woes to come.)

Even in the early days of the Original Republic, there were grave doubts about the ability of the federal government to discipline itself in the execution of its powers. As the Northern element strove to gain control of the federal government, the Constitution was constantly being "prostrated" and denounced as a "covenant with Hell!" Thus the Northern element decided that it was time to brush aside the technical limitations imposed by the Constitution and by acts of aggression move directly against the Southern people.

THE NORTH'S ATTITUDE
TOWARD THE CONSTITUTION

Laws comprising any legal system have two distinct aspects. Laws have a strict written denotation known in common usage as the letter of the law. But laws also have a connotation set by the spirit of the age in which the law was written. This is known as the spirit of the law. It may be possible to fulfill the letter of the law while actually destroying the spirit of the law. The spirit of our original Constitution was to limit the power of the central government while protecting the liberties of the people within their states. Prior to the War for Southern Independence, the Northern element used the method of loose construction to attack the spirit of the Constitution. The attempt to destroy the spirit of the Constitution reached its most destructive form when the North chose to use military force against the sovereign community in each of the Southern states to prevent them from recalling their delegated rights.

It should be noted that it is far more reasonable to assume a constitutional right of the Southern states to secede from a union from which they had formally and voluntarily acceded than it is to justify, on constitutional grounds, the act of armed aggression on the part of the dominant Northern element against the Southern people. This is especially true when we realize that the term "perpetual union" was not included in the Constitution even though it had been a part of the Articles of Confederation that preceded it! The act of armed aggression by the North to force a new form of government upon the people of the South was in reality an attack upon the original spirit of the Constitution. The attack was an overwhelming success. By the end of the war the South lay prostrate, her armies were physically exhausted, a large portion of her male population was either dead or maimed, her political leaders were imprisoned, and her economy was totally destroyed. But worst of all, the spirit of the Original Constitution was dead!

The end of the war did not mark the end of hostilities. The death of the spirit of the Original Constitution was not enough to satisfy the dominant Northern element. The letter of the law had to be destroyed as well—lest these Southerners regain their nerve and attempt to use political power to enforce the limitations left in the Constitution. The Northern element knew that in order to complete its conquest the letter of the law had to be destroyed. In a political sense, the second attack was as disastrous for the Southern people as the armed invasion had been.

How was this radical change in the American government accomplished? As we have already noted, the stronger element seeking a change in the form of a constitutional republic has only the following two choices: (1) it can use the slow method of loose construction to gradually erode the limitations imposed by the constitution, or (2) it can use its stronger position to wage aggressive war against the smaller element and, after defeating it, dictate the form of the new government. While both methods have been and still are being used against the Southern people, it is the latter, armed aggression, that has forced the greatest change.

ENTER RECONSTRUCTION

The South's failure in the War for Southern Independence is the primary factor determining the relationship between the Northern and Southern people. The war and Reconstruction marked the end of the American Constitutional Republic. The officially accepted history (myth) conveniently ignores the distinction between the American government after the war, as compared to the government that existed before the war. Just as the Imperialists of ancient Rome attempted to keep the trappings of Republican Rome, the Yankee myth-makers attempt to convince us that the current federal government is a legitimate descendant and a natural continuation of the Original American Republic of 1776. The truth is that the Yankee myth of history is a *lie!*

On March 2, 1867, Congress passed the Reconstruction Act. This act abolished civil government in the Southern states. It divided the South into five military districts with a commander of the rank of brigadier general or higher in each district. The army re-invaded the South, abolished all semblance of civil government, and set up military rule. An example of the dictatorial rule imposed on the South is seen in the manner in which the chief executive of the state of Mississippi was treated. Governor Benjamin G. Humphreys was the duly elected governor of the state, when Maj. Gen. Edward O. C. Ord was put in command of the Fourth Military District, which comprised the states of Mississippi and Arkansas. General Ord was a corp commander under General Grant. Ord was given complete authority over the affairs of these states. The governors of Mississippi and Arkansas were without any power to act for their states. All gubernatorial appointments were subject to military veto, and all offenses against "freedmen" were made subject to military courts, as well as many other offenses as determined by the occupying forces. This scenario was played out throughout the South, with the advent of Reconstruction. The Reconstruction Act disfranchised all voters and directed the army to set up registration of its own. The effect was to disfranchise a large portion of white Southerners and to extend the franchise to illiterates, Scalawags, and Carpetbaggers.

The Reconstruction Act of 1867 declared that the Southern states were not part of the Union. Remember, this was the same Union from which the North had previously said that these states could not withdraw! From 1866 to March 2, 1867, the Southern states were accorded the rights of statehood. They participated in the ratification of the Thirteenth Amendment and in the rejection of the Fourteenth Amendment. The rejection of the Fourteenth Amendment posed a major roadblock to the revolutionary schemes of the radicals in Congress. They knew that, even after their successful military conquest of the Southern people, they could not complete their evil designs as long as the South retained even this slight amount of political power. To further their evil schemes the radicals decided to eject their conquered foe from Congress and then complete their revolution. To further their revolutionary and evil goals, the Northern element treated the Southern states alternately as states and as conquered territories.

When Congress enacted the first so-called Reconstruction Act, it was promptly vetoed by President Andrew Johnson. Congress voted to override the veto that very same day! The fact that Congress so quickly voted to override a presidential veto demonstrates just how committed the Northern element was to its evil scheme.

With the Southern people completely expelled from Congress, the Northern radicals set about completing their work of destroying the original constitutional republic and of legalizing their efforts to rob the Southern people of their liberties and what wealth that remained after the war.

In his veto message to Congress, President Johnson made the following statement:

> The bill also denies the legality of the governments of ten of the States which participated in the ratification of the [Thirteenth] Amendment to the Federal Constitution abolishing slavery forever within the jurisdiction of the United States and practically excludes them from the union. If this assumption of the bill be correct, their concurrence cannot be considered as having been legally given, and the important fact is made to appear that the consent of the three-fourths of the States— the requisite number has not been obtained to the ratification of that amendment, thus leaving the question of slavery where it stood before the amendment.[15]

Thus the Northern Congress recognized the legality of the Southern states as long as their actions did not conflict with the radicals' plans. When the South legally rejected the Fourteenth Amendment and thereby refused to acquiesce to the Northern demand to change the letter of duly established constitutional law, the North denied the legal existence of the Southern states. Even though the spirit of the Constitution was destroyed by the North's aggressive war, the South still refused to voluntarily allow the destruction of the letter of legally enacted constitutional law. The Southern states recognized the Fourteenth Amendment as an attempt by the Northern-controlled Congress to transfer all reserved power to a newly created centralistic federal government and therefore rejected the amendment. The Northern element knew that, if it wished to advance its revolutionary scheme, something else had to be done. Political expediency in the North produced Reconstruction in the South. (See Addendum VII, "Plunder of Eleven States," by U.S. Rep. Dan Vorhees of Indiana, March 23, 1872.)

The treatment afforded the Southern people at the hands of the Northern Congress during Reconstruction stands as historical proof of the extent to which the North is willing to go to destroy those who dare oppose it. The right to vote was denied to a large portion of white citizens, and new elections were ordered with illiterates enfranchised regardless of their lack of education or qualifications. New legislatures composed of illiterates and others who had little or no governmental experience were elected to carry out the demands of the Northern Congress. The United States government (Congress, the president, and the Supreme Court) had no constitutional authority to interfere with the right of the people of the states to form their own governments. Yet, in defiance of the letter and spirit of the Original Constitution, the new puppet legislatures, controlled by the Northern Congress and enforced by Northern bayonets, promptly proceeded to ratify the proposed Fourteenth Amendment. This was done even though the Secretary of State in Washington had in hand from the legitimate Southern legislatures previously enacted resolutions rejecting the proposed amendment.

The Fourteenth Amendment was the legislative procedure used by the Northern-controlled Congress to replace the Original Constitutional Republic with a new government of centralistic federalism. The effect of the amendment was to shift the power from the local level (the sovereign communities) and give it to a central government. The Fourteenth Amendment is one of the longest in the Constitution. A brief review of pertinent sections will demonstrate its radical nature:

Section 1. This section defines for the first time a citizen of the United States. Its prohibitions are solely against the states. There are no provisions against the federal government engaging in oppressive acts or usurping powers not belonging to it.

Section 3. This section provides the legal excuse used to disfranchise white Southerners. It bars from state or federal office any person who, as an official of any kind, had previously taken an oath of office and later participated in the "rebellion." This is what is known as *ex post facto law*. It should be noted that *ex post facto laws* are specifically forbidden in Article 1, Section 9, of the Constitution.

Section 5. This section contains the enabling clause giving Congress a free hand in the internal policies of a state.

The enabling clause is the legal excuse that allows Congress to impose its rules upon the Southern people. The Supreme Court has interpreted the Fourteenth Amendment in such a way as to allow the federal government to control the voting qualifications in the Southern states, and impose forced busing, reverse discrimination, minority set-asides, etc.

This amendment was a radical departure from the original letter and spirit of the Constitution. The actions of the Northern-dominated Congress, in conjunction with the acts of the Northern armies, destroyed the concept of the state as an equal partner in a co-ordinate state/federal governmental arrangement. Gone were the concepts of delegated and reserved powers. Gone were the concepts of a government in which authority arose voluntarily from the people and extended to their agent, the state. And for the Southern people—what happened to the concept of "government by the consent of the governed"? One might say that it too is "gone with the wind!"

THE ENACTMENT OF A FRAUD

A study of the death of the American Constitutional Republic would be incomplete without a review of the arrogant methods used by the Northern Congress and its total disdain for constitutional law in its efforts to secure enactment of the Fourteenth Amendment. The term "enactment" is used as opposed to the legal and constitutional term "ratified." This review will further serve to establish the illegitimacy of the present centralistic federal government.

Congressman Thaddeus Stevens declared, "We shall treat the South as a defeated enemy."[16] The Northern Congress fulfilled this threat with the methods it used to secure the enactment of the Fourteenth Amendment. At the time of the introduction of the amendment, there were thirty-seven states in the Union. By mid-1867, the federal Secretary of State had received official documents from the legislatures of thirty-three of the thirty-seven states giving the states' answer to the proposed Fourteenth Amendment. The result was a rejection of the radical amendment. The results were as follows:

States in the Union 37
Needed to ratify...............................28
States voting yes...............................22
States voting no 12
States not voting................................3

Mississippi's rejection resolution did not reach Washington, and therefore it is numbered with the non-voting states. Even if the three non-voting states are added to the states voting for ratification, the amendment would still be short of the number needed for ratification.

The Northern Congress realized that its attempt to secure passage by legal and constitutional methods had failed. Thus the letter of the constitutional law survived its initial post-war assault. But the Northern Congress was determined to complete the radical change it had initiated. Frivolous technicalities such as constitutional limitations, ethics, and morality had proven no obstacle in the North's war against the Southern people. Certainly these barriers would prove no more difficult to surmount in the political sphere than it had been in the military sphere.

To secure enactment of the amendment, the Northern Congress had to accomplish the following:

1. Declare the Southern States outside of the erstwhile indivisible Union.

2. Deny majority rule in the Southern states by the disfranchisement of large numbers of the white population.

3. Require the Southern States to ratify the amendment as the price of getting back into the Union from which heretofore they had been denied the right to secede.

The third point could be turned into a Yankee brain-teaser. The North, in 1866, removed the Southern states from the Union. This was the same North that in 1861 refused to allow the South to secede from the Union. This same North now declared the Southern States to be non-states. To get back into the Union (that originally the South did not want to be a part of anyway, and from which it had previously been denied the right to secede), it was required to perform the function of a state in that Union, while still officially no longer a part of the Union, by ratifying an amendment that previously as states in the Union it had legally rejected! Words alone fail to meet the challenge of such pure Yankee logic.

During the American Revolution, one of the great battle cries of the colonies was "No taxation without representation." The Yankee myth of history has conveniently chosen to ignore a far greater wrong committed by an arrogant legislative body. The act of disfranchising the white population of the South, which comprised the majority, was nothing less than a deliberate attempt to secure the enactment of a favored piece of legislation without obtaining the consent of the people. The Southern people were denied equal representation in both houses of Congress. For the South this was "legislation without representation."

The flagrant disregard for the spirit and letter of the Original Constitution did produce some criticism in the North. The state of New Jersey passed a joint resolution withdrawing its consent to the adoption of the amendment (see Addendum VIII). The Northern Congress ignored this resolution and counted New Jersey as having voted in favor of ratification. The New Jersey resolution called attention to the fact that one of its United States senators had been excluded from voting and that his seat had been vacated in the federal Senate when the Fourteenth Amendment was proposed. This was done in addition to the exclusion of the senators and representatives from the Southern states. Article V of the Constitution plainly states that "No state, without its permission, may be denied equal suffrage in the Senate." There is no denial that the Northern Congress intentionally and with malice violated Article V of the Constitution.

The New Jersey resolution is a fiery indictment of the Northern Congress. The fifth paragraph of Joint Resolution, Number 1, State of New Jersey, reads as follows:

> That it being necessary, by the Constitution, that every amendment to the same should be proposed by two-thirds of both Houses of Congress, the authors of said proposition, for the purpose of securing the assent of the requisite majority, determined to, and did, exclude from the said two Houses eighty representatives from eleven States of the Union, upon the pretense that there were no such States in the Union; but, finding that two-thirds of the remainder of said houses could not be brought to assent to the said proposition they deliberately formed and carried out the design of mutilating the in-

tegrity of the United States Senate, and without any pretext or justification, other than the possession of the power, without the right, and in palpable violation of the Constitution, ejected a member of their own body, representing this state and thus denied to New Jersey its equal suffrage in the Senate.

In paragraph eleven of the New Jersey resolution the amendment is denounced:

It denounces and inflicts punishment for past offenses [*ex post facto law*, see Article 9, Section 1, United States Constitution] and therefore is guilty of violating a cardinal principle of American liberty that no punishment can be inflicted for any offense, unless it is provided by laws before the commission of the offense.

Paragraph fifteen also criticizes the amendment:

It imposes new prohibitions upon the power of the State to pass laws, and interdicts the execution of such parts of the common law as the national judiciary may esteem inconsistent with the vague provisions of the said amendment, made vague for the purpose of facilitating encroachments upon the lives, liberty, and property of the people.

Paragraph sixteen contains the ominous warning against a future all-powerful Supreme Court:

It enlarges the judicial power of the United States so as to bring every law passed by the State . . . within the jurisdiction of the Federal tribunals.

Paragraph eighteen attacks the amendment for denying the states the right to establish "reasonable qualifications" for voting. These men should have been around when the Northern-controlled Congress passed the punitive Southern-only "Voting Rights Act."

Paragraph nineteen is the strongest attack upon the amendment protesting against its denial of the right of the states of the Union to set up reasonable qualifications for voting and claiming that it

. . . transfers to Congress the whole control of the right of suffrage in the State. . . . a power which they [the states] have never been willing to surrender to the general government, and which was reserved to the states as a fundamental principle on which the Constitution itself was constructed—the principle of self-government.

A Southerner could not have said it better!

New Jersey was not the only Northern state to recognize the fraud and corruption of the Northern Congress. The states of Ohio and Oregon both repealed their ratification of the Fourteenth Amendment. In October 1868, the legislature of Oregon issued a rescinding resolution stating that the amendment had not received ratification by three-fourths of the states and that the forced ratification of the Southern states were "usurpations, unconstitutional, revolutionary and void." We remind the reader that these are the words of a Northern legislative body.

Who can truthfully question those of us who agree with the assessment of this Northern state legislature? These acts were and are unconstitutional, usurpations, revolutionary, and *void!*

There are those who would insist that even if the preceding were true it no longer makes any difference because the Fourteenth Amendment is now a part of the Constitution. These apologists for Yankee imperialism choose to ignore the fact that for laws to have moral and ethical legitimacy, they must be made in pursuance of the Constitution. Even though passed by Congress, blessed by a centralist Supreme court, and enforced by the president, if such laws invade the residuary authority of the sovereign state they are, as Alexander Hamilton declared:

> . . . merely acts of usurpation. . . . There is no position which depends on clearer principles than that every act of a delegated authority, contrary to the tenor of the commission under which it is exercised, is void. No legislative act, therefore, contrary to the Constitution, can be valid.[17]

Here is the judgment of an ardent Federalist (in reality he was a consummate centralist—a monarchist). Yet, even one with such a strong desire to enlarge and create a strong central government admitted that laws enacted against the provisions of the Constitution are void of legitimacy!

The legacy of crime and corruption extended even to the state legislature of Oregon. The two representatives from Grant County were refused their seats. Two imposters, Brentz and Mc-

Kean, filled the vacated seats and (guess what?) voted for ratification. The victory margin for ratification in the Oregon legislature was very close. Even with the two imposters voting for the amendment, it barely passed. Three days later, when the legitimate representatives from Grant County were at last seated, they both signed statements that if they had been allowed to vote they both would have voted against the amendment. Thus it would not have passed the Oregon legislature!

This brief review of what the Yankee myth-makers refer to as Reconstruction demonstrates the gross, unconstitutional, and criminal methods used by the Northern Congress to change the form of the American government. Too many Southerners think that the present federal government is the same one our Founding Fathers established. Nothing could be further from reality. The American government, after the defeat of the South, is to the original American Constitutional Republic what Imperial Rome was to Republican Rome. While the name, geography, and institutions may be similar to those of the past, the exercise of governmental power over the people underwent a radical change in the limits of governmental authority. The current all-powerful behemoth in Washington is void of the letter and spirit of our Original Constitutional Republic. The result of an aggressive war and Reconstruction, in addition to our present political and economic serfdom, proves that *the South was right* in 1861.

THE SOUTH UNDER
THE NEW GOVERNMENT

To understand the radical change that occurred in the American government as a result of the war and Reconstruction, we need only ask the average Southerner to explain the "Bill of Rights." A simple question, yet compare the modern answer to the answer you would have received from Southerners such as Thomas Jefferson or Patrick Henry. The modern idea is that the "Bill of Rights" is a document that protects the rights of American citizens. Yet, before the enactment of the Fourteenth Amendment, there was no such thing as an American citizen. An individual was a citizen of the state, not of the federal government. Why was this important? Recall the origin of the American system of government. The individuals in possession of their liberties made up thirteen separate sovereign communities (i.e., the thirteen states). Authority arose from individuals who came together to form the sovereign community, and as individuals they delegated authority to form the state government. The states, as agents of the people, then formed the federal government. What purpose then did the "Bill of Rights" serve?

With the exception of Article 1, Section 10, all the limitations of the United States Constitution as ratified by the states (which includes the first ten amendments containing the "Bill of Rights") pertained to the powers of the federal government alone! "Congress shall make no law . . ."—these are the first words of the First Amendment. You will find in this amendment what we have come to call "our guarantee of religious freedom." Yet, the early constitutions of several states recognized what was virtually a State Church, requiring each locality to provide for and support the public worship of God. It was not until 1818 that Connecticut, in adopting her new state constitution, placed all religious bodies on a equal level. In Massachusetts a tax for support of the Congregationalist Church was imposed. In Massachusetts, religious equality was first fully recognized by a state constitutional amendment of 1833. The right of a speedy and public trial is provided for in the Sixth Amendment, but this extends only to those who stand accused of crimes against the laws of the United States. In Section 9 of the United States Constitution, we find prohibition against the suspension of the writ of *habeas corpus*, bill of attainder, and *ex post facto law*. Why then are the same prohibitions included in the very next section (Section 10)? Did our Founding Fathers suddenly slip into redundancy? No, of course not; it was necessary to repeat the section because, as we have already noted, Article 1, Section 10, is the only limitation in the Original Constitution that *does not* pertain to the federal government. To extend the prohibitions previously mentioned in Section 9 to the states, the Founding Fathers had to declare specifically, as they did in Section 10, that "no State shall . . ."

The "Bill of Rights" was placed in the Constitution for a very important reason. The Founding Fathers intended to protect the individuals within the sovereign community and their agent, the state, from the natural tendency of a central government to abuse its powers. The fear the "Bill of Rights" sought to alleviate was the fear of oppression from an all-powerful central government. The present federal government is an excellent example of what is to be feared from an all-powerful central government.

There are those who would argue that the religious intolerance in the early New England states is reason enough to include an all-encompassing federal "Bill of Rights" in the Constitution. Yet, it should be remembered that any inequities in the various state constitutions were corrected by the people, which is the proper function of a free society. If corrections are needed in the fundamental law, then it is the people who must make the correction and not a supposedly benevolent, all-powerful, central government. The potential for human oppression is greatly reduced at the local level where the possibility of the political redress of grievances is far greater than it is on a national level. If an error in judgment or a flagrant act of oppression is made on the local level, only a small part of the nation will suffer. But should such an oppressive act issue forth at the national level (which is constantly happening today), then the suffering is immediately transmitted to the entire people, who have little or no hope of effectual redress.

It should always be remembered that legitimate authority arises from the people at the local level in the sovereign community. Whenever government attempts to circumvent the legitimate power of the people, even in the name of good, civil liberty suffers, and the potential for despotism is greatly increased. As the old saying goes, "What has done more harm than the follies of the compassionate?"

The radical change in the form of our original constitutional government is a direct result of the success of the Northern armies in their war of aggression against the Southern people. With military success and the force of bloody bayonets, the Northern philosophy of centralistic federalism became the standard for the new American government. This centralistic philosophy was articulated into its "legal" form by the various Reconstruction acts, the Fourteenth and Fifteenth Amendments, and the subsequent Supreme Court decisions that are based upon these acts and amendments.

The history of the English-speaking people is one of great regard for the democratic tradition. When reviewing the unconstitutional and radical change in our original constitutional government, we find it evident that the actions of the Northern

Congress stand alone as the most brazen acts of legislative tyranny in the history of the English-speaking people! It should be remembered that the effects of these acts have not diminished with the passage of time but continue today as the "legal" excuse for innumerable court orders, guidelines, and federal edicts. Every generation of Southerners since the War for Southern Independence has been forced to live under the penalty imposed upon our people by these illegal and fraudulent acts.

At no time has the Northern majority changed its coercive attitude toward its conquered provinces. The Northern element has been quick to use these acts when it suited their purpose. At other times they have been willing to "put it on the shelf" for the time being. When political necessity again arose in the Northern Congress, these acts have been taken off the shelf, dusted off, and re-applied to the Southern people with great vigor and much self-righteous indignation.

From the end of Reconstruction to the mid-1940s, political confrontation between the North and the South was minimal. The South, to varying degrees, was "left alone." What this meant was that, as long as the South left the control of the national government in the hands of the Northern element, accepted its own second-class status, and kept in "its place," then the Northern element graciously allowed the South to maintain nominal control over its area of the country. In exchange the North relented in the active application of the various Reconstruction acts. An unwritten North/South detente developed in which the South was allowed the delusion of self-government when it was allowed to displace the Reconstruction-era state governments. It should be remembered that in all cases the Southern problem has always been handled with the view of what was best for Northern economic and political interests.

The waging of aggressive war against the Southern people was necessary to destroy the idea of popular sovereignty, which, as we have seen, was the very spirit of the Constitutional Republic. Reconstruction was invoked by the Northern Congress against the Southern people to force a radical change in the form of the American national government, thereby destroying the letter of its constitutional law. The active application of Reconstruction legislation was allowed to subside only after the form of the national government was irrevocably changed and it was apparent that the

Southern people had no choice but to accept their new status or to continue under the unspeakable horror of Reconstruction. The unspoken detente was kept in effect until the late 1940s. At this time it became politically profitable for the dominant, Northern, liberal element to break the detente and to reinstate the active application of political Reconstruction. The Southern people continue to be at the mercy of the controlling Northern element. The liberal element in the North has reserved unto itself the power to adjust the application of the unspoken detente. The South has no choice. Its conquering masters have assigned it to a second-class political and economic position. The will of the Southern people and the destiny of the Southern nation are of no value to its masters, the powers-that-be in Washington.

The sham of self-government had permeated the political life of the Southern people by the 1940s. By this time most Southerners had accepted the new order and honestly thought that they were in control of their political destiny to the same degree that their predecessors had held before the war. The psychology underlying this self-delusion had its origin in the defeat of the Southern people in the War for Southern Independence. Southerners knew that the South had the constitutional right of self-determination. They knew that the North had absolutely no constitutional justification for invading the South and for coercing its people into accepting a new centralistic government with no limit on the federal government's power over the states. They knew also that the Southern soldier had fought with high esteem for honor, heroism, and gallantry, fulfilling the demanding code of military chivalry. Knowing all of this, the South could not accept the idea of defeat. Thus, the heroic efforts to reclaim the state government by unseating the Scalawag and Carpetbag government during Reconstruction was overemphasized to the point of claiming a total victory for the South.

Psychologically, a defeated people needed a victory. The success of the Southern people over the Scalawag and Carpetbag regimes provided that victory. This should not be taken as an attempt to belittle the efforts of those responsible for unseating the Scalawags and establishing sane self-government. We must remember that the evil goals of Reconstruction had already been accomplished by the time the Scalawag governments were unseated. The evil goals were accomplished when the original constitutional government was changed from the initial form of a contract between equals to the new form of a centralistic national government having dominant authority over the states and the people thereof. This was accomplished by giving the new central government a form of legality by enacting the Fourteenth and Fifteenth Amendments and other Reconstruction acts. These actions demonstrated that the dominant Northern element cared very little as to who controlled the Southern state governments. The Northern element had already formed a new centralistic federal government. With its new power, the North could force the Southern people to accept their new position as second-class citizens. Therefore, from the Northern point of view, if the Scalawags could hold on to power in the South, so much the better. But if they could not hold on to power, it mattered not in the least. After all, the North retained the power to enforce its will upon the Southern people; whereas the Southern people, in the words of the Yankee general Philip Sheridan, were left with "nothing but their eyes to cry with!"

We have established that the original form of the American government, a government formed by the free and voluntary association of equal states, was changed by the dominant Northern element into a centralistic federal government, formed by armed aggression, criminal fraud, and political coercion. This, and the continuing train of abuses suffered by the Southern people at the hands of the federal government, is enough to brand the federal government as an illegitimate governmental force. The present federal government does not rule by the consent of the Southern people. The present federal government dictates its governing policy toward the Southern people; it does not govern with the free and unfettered consent of the Southern people. Its claim to the right to govern is based upon the right of conquest—a right that Southern Nationalists reject!

REFLECTING ON THE PAST AND
VISIONS OF THE FUTURE

The historical facts that have been reviewed stand as a continuing indictment of the Northern Congress. And the facts represent much more. The facts stand as a continuing indictment of the Northern-controlled Supreme Court, an arrogant tribunal that refused attempts to grant a review of the legitimacy of the Reconstruction acts and amendments. While on the one hand the court has refused to review these frauds, it has on the other hand been very willing to apply them as the legal excuse for its aggressive and punitive decisions, court orders, and edicts.

The current Northern-controlled federal government was established by fraud, corruption, political coercion, and blatant military aggression. Its continuing existence depends upon maintaining the myth that these crimes against the Southern people never occurred and that the present system is legitimate. The creation of the Northern-controlled government was marked by the death of thousands of Southerners and by the deliberate extinction of a culture and a way of life. Even more importantly, it is marked by the demise of the spirit and letter of our Original Constitution and of the original and legitimate government of our country— the constitutional republic called the United States of America!

Many observers of the American political system freely admit that there is a major difference between the federal system as originally established and the system which operates today. Yet few have ever stopped to analyze why this change has occurred and what it means to the people of the South. A radical change occurred in the philosophical foundation of the American government. The idea that governmental authority resides with the people, making up the sovereign community, was displaced with the new reality of an all-powerful central government having dominant authority over the people of the states. The Constitution was changed from an instrument limiting the power of the federal government to an instrument allowing the federal government to review every action of its now inferior appendages, the states. The destruction of the Original Constitutional Republic brought about the end of constitutional protection of the rights and liberties of the Southern people in particular and of all Americans in general.

The Southern people today know very well the dangerous tendencies of a government to abuse its powers and to oppress its subjects. In addition to the Original Constitutional Republic, something else passed away—a legitimate federal government, a government that ruled by the consent of the governed. The legal right of the federal government to govern the Southern people lost the justification for its very existence.

The people of the South do indeed have a right to be free. It is an innate right, a birthright that existed before the establishment of government itself. The people of the Southern states comprise a sovereign community in each state. This and this alone is the repository of legitimate authority. *A thousand Appomattoxes or a thousand Gulags can never negate the right of a sovereign people to be free!*

The Northern-controlled federal government has never renounced its numerous crimes against the Southern people. It would be foolish indeed for us Southerners to cling to the delusion that we are a free people. To do so would require us to continue to ignore our history, to make a mockery of justice, and to deny the natural right of individual liberty. It would mark this age as a generation of foolish cowards. Our children would grow up to hate us, knowing that for a small effort, infused with courage, we could have saved our Southern nation and made them free!

Yes, the Southern people by right and of necessity ought to be free. The belligerent and aggressive attitude of the federal government, both past and present, demonstrates this truth. Refusal to yield to the will of the sovereign community, coercion, military aggression, innumerable acts of crime, fraud and corruption—all of these and more stand as testimony that the present federal government is an illegal and illegitimate governmental force. Therefore, the federal government has negated its right to govern the Southern people and has by its own action released them from the obligation to maintain allegiance to such an oppressive despotism. This allegiance must now be withdrawn to the respective states. Southerners must look forward to the establishment of a new constitutional government in the United States, or failing that, to the establishment of the second Constitutional Republic within the borders of their common homeland, the South!

William W. Church, Company C, Fifty-Third Alabama Volunteer Infantry. Church's unit served as mounted infantry during part of his service. (Image courtesy of Betty C. Kennedy, Simsboro, Louisiana)

CHAPTER 7

John Milton:
The Father of Secession

> The South possesses an inheritance which it has imper-
> fectly understood and little used. It is in the curious position
> of having been right without realizing the grounds of its right-
> ness.[1]
>
> Richard M. Weaver

INTRODUCTORY COMMENTS

Richard Weaver noted that the post-war/Reconstruction South made two critical mistakes. First, it failed to study its position until it could defend its philosophical logic or reason for being. It needed a Burke or a Hegel, but all it produced were lawyers and journalists. When the average Southerner was forced to defend his region he would become frustrated and explode in anger.

The second mistake was that due to its first failure (i.e., the lack of a philosophical or even revolutionary justification for its exist-ence) the South refused to go on the offensive. The sum total of its efforts was to defend and compromise.

The South was transformed from the fighting South into the hesitant and pacified South. It took the decision of Appomattox too literally. This cast a dark cloud over any efforts or dreams of taking the offensive and regaining its lost estate.

In the next section we will demonstrate the depth and richness of our Southern political philosophy. Our belief in limited govern-ment, reserved and delegated rights, and the right to recall dele-gated powers was not something thought up down South to protect slavery. It has deep historical roots—roots that nourished a beautiful tree of liberty in the South—until the arrival of the drunken Yankee woodsman.

John Milton: The Father of Secession

The political philosophy that would lead to Southern secession was first advocated by John Milton. Although he is best known for his literary works such as *Paradise Lost*, his political works were destined to have an impact on political thought equal to or even greater than his literary achievements.

Early in the seventeenth century, England was beginning to groan under the forces of change. The English Church had renounced the authority of Rome and purists were attempting to rid the English Church of the last vestige of Romanism. The king, James I, had alienated the Puritans by his threats at the Hampton Court Conference of 1604.[2] Turning from religion to politics, he lectured Parliament on the divine right of kings. The Commons replied in their 1604 apology, "The voice of the people, in the things of their knowledge, is said to be as the voice of God."[3] It was an era of tumultuous change.

In 1638, John Milton visited Galileo in Florence. Galileo's work on planetary motion placed him in the forefront of the scientific revolution and on a collision course with the Roman Church. Even though he was forced to recant his theory that the earth orbited the sun, he ended his recantation with these words, "eppur si muove" (and yet it moves). Milton's visit with this man who was willing to challenge accepted authority and present new and bold ideas served as the prelude to his political writings.

John Milton's political philosophy is revolutionary because he presents radically different ideas (under appropriate conditions extreme measures may be necessary) and openly challenges accepted authority. His advocacy of civil liberty establishes him as the first major English libertarian, a classical liberal a hundred years before his time. Milton's work prepared the way for the writings of subsequent men who are more popularly quoted by modern historians.

John Milton's political writings established the foundation upon which Southern political thought was built. The political concepts advocated by him have been reaffirmed by subsequent generations in England and by the American South up to the 1870s.

THE ORIGIN OF GOVERNMENT

Anthropologists inform us that the early form of order in human society was based upon kinship. As the need to control more land and people increased, the kinship system was extended into an enlarged and formal system of government.[4]

Milton was one of the first English political philosophers to address the question of the origin of government. In *The Real and Easy Way* he asserted that the law of nature is man's first principle in his relation to government.[5] In Book XII of *Paradise Lost* the archangel Michael explained to Adam that man would at first be ruled by kinship groups. The change from kinship groups would result from the evil then within man.[6] At first, kings would be appointed or elected by the people. The idea that all men were born free was a bold assertion to make in the age of absolute monarchy. Milton based his belief in the natural freedom of man upon the biblical account of man's creation in the image of God as a free moral agent.[7]

The English philosopher John Locke was born in 1632. Locke became the philosopher of the Glorious Revolution. This revolt removed the Catholic, James II, and placed William and Mary on the English throne. Locke reaffirmed Milton's attack on the divine right of kings by publishing his *First Treatise on Government* followed by the *Second Treatise on Government*.[8] In the *Second Treatise* he again borrowed from Milton by depicting man originally in a state of nature bound by nature's laws.[9]

In 1760 a young Southerner, Thomas Jefferson, entered William and Mary College. This young Southerner was to draw from Milton's political ideas to formulate a Southern political philosophy. In the first line of the Declaration of Independence Jefferson boldly proclaims, "We hold these truths to be self-evident . . ." Compare those words to the first lines of Milton's *Tenure*, ". . . proving that it is lawful and hath been held so through all ages . . . " Here we see Milton's shadow touching the very document announcing the birth of the American Republic! Jefferson goes on to assert that "all men are created equal." Recall Milton's words, "No man who knows aught, can be so stupid to deny that all men naturally were born free."[10] Thomas Jefferson echoed Milton's own words. We can see how the ideas championed by Milton influenced Southerners from the earliest days of the republic.

John C. Calhoun was also influenced by Milton's ideas. Calhoun maintained that due to the evil within man, God had ordained man to live under some form of government.[11] This idea runs parallel to lines eighty-three through ninety-three, Book XII of *Paradise Lost*. Calhoun expanded Milton's natural law[12] into the concept of the sovereign communities.[13] The people of the states represented to Calhoun the natural repository of all natural laws from which government gained legitimacy.

The men who followed Milton took the ideas he had already advocated and adapted them to a new age. While the men and times changed, Milton's principles regarding the origin of government remained useful and influential with each succeeding generation.

THE RIGHT OF REVOLUTION

Milton's purpose in writing *The Tenure of Kings and Magistrates* was to prove that it is and always has been lawful to overthrow and even put to death a wicked king. He replaced the traditional concept of divine right of kings with his own adaptation of natural law. He used Roman history to support the concept that a bad king should be removed, quoting the Roman emperor Trajan, "Take this drawn sword to use for me if I reign well; if not, to use against me."[14] Milton envisioned the act of revolt as an act of popular self-defense; and if an individual's act of self-defense is lawful, so then is the mutual self-defense of an entire people who rise up in revolt.[15]

Milton established for the English-speaking people the right to revolt against tyranny. Years later Locke asserted that when rulers do not abide by the law of reason and attempt to oppress the natural rights of the people then a state of war exists. At this point the people resume their natural rights, that is they withdraw their delegated rights and make an appeal to the God of battle.[16]

When Thomas Jefferson wanted to justify the secession of the American colonies from the established English government, he looked to the philosophy of Locke and Milton. In the Declaration of Independence, Jefferson described a large number of abuses of power by the king against the American people. These abuses were not given as the reason for the secession but stood as evidence that the king had violated the natural rights of Americans. "These truths" were not creatures of Jefferson's mind but were political ideas already established by Locke and earlier by Milton.

In the Declaration of Independence, Jefferson proclaims the right of the people to alter or abolish any government that encroaches upon certain inalienable God-given rights. In Book VII of *Paradise Lost*, Milton shows that man is created a free moral agent in the image of God. Here again we can see another parallel in Jefferson's ideas and Milton's works. Jefferson champions the right to set up new government just as Milton justified the changing of government in *The Tenure of Kings and Magistrates, Eikonoklastes, The Second Defense*, and others.

THE CONSENT OF THE GOVERNED

The most striking example of Milton's influence on Southern political thought can be seen by tracing the political theory of the "consent of the governed." Milton stated that kings were exalted to their high place with the consent of the people.[17] Therefore, the legitimacy of any government is based upon the consent of the people. John Locke followed this same theme by asserting that government is freely created by the people to protect their rights and that it derives its power from the consent of the people.[18] Compare this to the very familiar words of Jefferson:

> . . . governments are instituted among Men, deriving their just powers from the consent of the governed.

But what of the right of the people to withdraw their consent from an existing government (i.e., to secede)? In *Tenure*, Milton explains that one of the conditions for a people to consent to be ruled is to bind the king with oaths to do "impartial justice by law." If the king failed to abide by his oath, "the people would be disengaged."[19] Milton believed that the power exercised by kings "was and is" the people's and that those powers are in the form of a conditional grant. If such powers are used unjustly, the people retain the right to "resume" them. This right to resume delegated powers is a clear and early declaration of the people's right to secede from an oppressive government.[20]

In its resolution ratifying the United States Constitution, Jefferson's native state of Virginia placed this condition upon her consent to the new government:

> The powers granted under the Constitution, being derived from the people of the United States, may be resumed by them, whensoever the same shall be perverted to their injury or oppression.[21]

The same argument was penned by Jefferson in the Virginia and Kentucky Resolutions of 1798. Milton's own words could have been substituted:

> The power of kings and magistrates is nothing else but what is only derivative, transferred, and committed to them in trust, the right remaining in [the people] to reassume it to themselves, if by kings or magistrates it be abused.[22]

John C. Calhoun defended the South's right to withdraw her consent from an oppressive government based upon the works of Jefferson. He attacked the intrusion upon State's Rights on constitutional grounds, declaring:

> The Constitution has admitted the jurisdiction of the United States within the limits of the several states only so far as the delegated powers authorize; beyond that they are intruders, and may rightfully be expelled.[23]

Calhoun believed that:

> All powers granted by the Constitution are derived from the people of the United States; and may be resumed by them when perverted to their injury or oppression; and that every power not granted, remains with them, and at their will; and that no right of any description can be canceled, abridged, restrained, or modified by Congress, the Senate, the House of Representatives, the President, or any department or office of the United States.[24]

Calhoun could have just as easily quoted Milton:

> Thus far hath been considered briefly the power of kings and magistrates, how it was and is originally the people's, and by them conferred in trust only to be employed to the common peace and benefit; with liberty therefore and right remaining in them to reassume it to themselves, if by kings or magistrates it be abused, or to dispose of it by any alteration as they shall judge most conducing to the public good.[25]

Calhoun also believed that:

> Sovereignty, by a fundamental principle of our system, resides in the people and not in the government and the Federal government is the representative of the delegated powers.[26]

Almost two centuries earlier Milton had advocated the same principle when he wrote of his idea of Parliament or Grand Council:

> In this grand council must sovereignty, not transferred but delegated only and as it were deposited, reside.[27]

Again we see not only the same ideas and principles advocated, but quite literally the same words used to express those ideas and principles.

POPULAR DEMOCRACY

Even though these early political philosophers were champions of individual liberty, they were also quick to understand the dangers posed by unbridled popular democracy. Milton based his fear of man's misuse of governmental power upon his belief that man is a fallen creation. This is seen in lines eighty-nine through ninety-three of *Paradise Lost*.[28] Man has within himself "unworthy Powers" according to Milton. Calhoun stated that man is so "constituted that his direct or individual affections are stronger than his sympathetic or social feelings."[29] Therefore even a democracy can become oppressive to personal liberty.

Milton recognized the selfish tendency for men in power to attempt to enlarge their power and to rule for their own good.[30] John Stuart Mill, a contemporary of Calhoun, identified as one of the dangers of representative government the situation in which the representatives' interests are not "identical with the general welfare of the community."[31] Mill agreed with Calhoun's and Milton's assessment of human nature and the inherent danger it holds for personal liberty. Mill thought that "One of the greatest dangers lies in the sinister interest of the holders of power."[32] Calhoun went on to assert that government has a strong tendency to abuse its powers. This tendency arises from the fact that all governments are administered by men who are naturally self-centered.[33] Milton in his *Real and Easy Way* had already asserted that large numbers of men could be corrupted within the walls of a parliament.[34]

APOLOGISTS FROM MILTON TO DABNEY

Webster defines an apologist as one who "speaks or writes in defense of a faith, cause, or an institution." A review of the works of

Milton and Locke will show both to be persistent apologists. *Paradise Lost* was written to justify the acts of God. Prior to that epic, Milton had written several political apologies, the most notable being *Tenure, The Second Defense, Eikonoklastes,* and *An Apology.*

John Locke's *Second Treatise of Government* was written to justify the efforts to remove Charles II from the British throne. In the Declaration of Independence, Jefferson defended the action of the colonies by an appeal to the world to review the evidence of the king's abuses and usurpations. In the Kentucky and Virginia Resolution, Jefferson defended the right of the states against the intrusion of the federal government. Calhoun spent a large portion of his life defending the South. In his last speech before the United States Senate, a speech that was read by a colleague because Calhoun was too weak to speak, he traced the history of the nation and the South's continued retreat before the onslaught of Federalism.[35] Using Calhoun's arguments, the Reverend R. L. Dabney wrote *A Defense of Virginia and Through Her the South.* The efforts to justify the South by the post-war Southern apologists were based upon the ideas of Calhoun and Jefferson. Calhoun and before him Jefferson were the apologists of their day who had drawn their political concepts from even earlier apologists such as Locke and Milton.

The crowning efforts of all Southern political theorists were the writings of the post-war apologists who knowingly or not drew their ideas from Milton. The labors of the Southern apologists have been largely ignored by word merchants subservient to the ruling powers who have taken the coin of the realm to propagate the Yankee myth of history. Yet, the apology was written. After reviewing the work of these last Southern apologists, one can only admit that their work was well done and befitting those descended of so many kings.

CONCLUSION

Southerners such as Jefferson, Calhoun, and Dabney drew upon the works of Locke and Milton to present the principles of Southern political thought. The parallel between Southern philosophy and Milton's political ideas is evidence of the degree of influence these ideas had upon the South. It is a noble heritage unknown by too many Southerners.

The influence of ideas from one generation to the next travels in ever-increasing circles much as the ever-increasing circles produced by ripples on the surface of a pond. Long after the initial splash, the circles continue to spread out over the surface of the water. And so it has been with the political philosophy popularized by Milton, Locke, Jefferson, and Calhoun. With the passage of time, the ripples of influence have continued to widen as these ideas continue to touch generations of Southerners. The question remains as to whether the ripples will yet touch us.

E. F. Reicherd, Fifth Company, Washington Artillery, Louisiana. This young man enlisted on March 6, 1862, and served until his death on September 19, 1863, at the Battle of Chickamauga, Georgia.[11] (Image courtesy of Tulane University Libraries, Howard-Tilton Memorial Library, New Orleans, Louisiana)

CHAPTER 8

Secession: Answering the Critics

A fig for the Constitution! When the scorpion's sting is prob-
ing us to the quick, shall we stop to chop logic? . . . There is no
magic in the word union.[1]

John Randolph of Roanoke

INTRODUCTORY COMMENTS

In the following chapter we will look at some of the arguments
used by those who do not believe that the South, or any other state
or group of states, has or ever has had the right to withdraw
peacefully from the Union. What irony! Americans who oppose
secession for Dixie find themselves in bed with the communist
generals of Yugoslavia and the communist hard-liners of the
former Soviet Union.

We will look at seven of the most popular myths about the nature of secession as it related to the South in 1860. We will demonstrate where and why the critics' arguments are faulty and prove
once again that our Southern ancestors were correct in their claim
to the right of secession.

We will also show how the United States Military Academy at
West Point has in its library a textbook on the Constitution which
teaches that secession was and is a right of each state. This book,
used as a textbook and also kept as a reference, is William Rawle's
Views on the Constitution published in 1825. Rawle's book was used as
a text for one year and is still kept in the library at West Point. Another work which we will refer to is *Commentaries on American Law*
by James Kent. This book, in one of its editions, was used at West
Point from 1827 until just after the War for Southern Independence. Kent did not approach the subject of secession per se, but
left no doubt about his belief in the reserved rights of the states
and the independent nature of the states when they acceded to
the Union. These facts have proven to be more than a little em-

barrassing to the enemies of Southern independence. Be assured that we take great pride in bringing these facts to you!

Secession: Answering the Critics

An overbearing Yankee once asked a Southerner, "When are you people going to stop fighting the war?" The cracker responded, "Oh, I suppose we'll stop fighting when you damn Yankees stop shooting at us."

With far more insight than the average viewer of Yankeefied television, our redneck philosopher cut through innumerable myths and identified the key issue. Indeed, today we Southerners are bombarded by a constant barrage of cultural insults and falsehoods. These attacks come from the liberal media of Yankeedom and their Scalawag running dogs of the "New South" mentality. Yet, when Southerners stand up and defend their heritage and the values of the South, they are met with the condescending question, "Why are you people still fighting the war?"

Secession movements are so common today that no one questions if these movements are correct or not. The secessionists of Quebec, Eastern Europe, the Baltics, and various republics of the former Soviet Union are blessed with official sanction from the liberal media and even the government in Washington. How odd! Odd indeed, when we remember how the liberal establishment falls all over itself in its efforts to prove how evil and wrong secession is for the South.

Why is it that something that was condemned as evil and wrong in 1861 was given official sanction by the same Republican Party in 1991? Why is it that the government in Washington will applaud Vaclav Havel of Czechoslovakia for withdrawing his country from the Soviet Union's orbit, but continue its attack upon Jefferson Davis and his fellow Southerners for doing the same thing for the South? By now you no doubt know why these attacks continue— because our conquering masters must never cease their propaganda about the righteousness of their oppression of the Southern people. In doing so they have promoted several myths about secession. According to Yankee myth, Southern secession was (and therefore still is) wrong for several reasons:

1. Secession would have destroyed the United States and the South.

2. Secession was a way to protect the system of slavery, and the "Civil War" would not have been fought had slavery not existed.

3. Lincoln was justified in using whatever force at whatever cost to save the Union.

4. Secession is an act of a sovereign state, and no state in America was sovereign before or after the Declaration of Independence was signed.

5. The original thirteen states did not secede from the Union when they withdrew from the Articles of Confederation. The perpetual union under the Articles of Confederation is the same union under the United States Constitution.

6. Secession was an action taken by Southerners to save the institution of slavery and/or to destroy America.

7. Nullification and secession had already been proven illegal by the federal government.

The people of the South have a long record of resistance to tyrants that in history extends back to their ancestral homelands. In 1320 in the Declaration of Arbroath, otherwise known as the Scottish Declaration of Independence, the nobles of Scotland stated that they had the right to give their consent to their king and to withdraw it from him. They stated that, if the king who governed them did not rule as they saw fit, they reserved the right to "make some other man who was well able to defend us our King."

In 1570, the French Huguenots were resisting the tyranny of those who believed in the divine right of kings. In that year European Calvinists issued *Vindiciae Contra Tyrannos* (A Defence of Liberty Against Tyrants), in an effort to prove that the people had the right to resist the unlawful act of government (kings). Speaking of the rights of kings, they said, "they [kings] should acknowledge that for them, they as it were borrow their power and authority."[2] *Vindiciae Contra Tyrannos* issued a warning to the believers in centralized power that the people had a right to remove any king who acted beyond the realm of the law. This idea was restated by Thomas Jefferson in the American Declaration of Independence.

In the year 1578 George Buchanan wrote *The Rights of the Crown in Scotland*. This was another defense of the people's right to govern the state, by stating where a king obtained his right to rule,

and in what manner 'and by whom an unjust king could be removed. Buchanan shows that it is from the people that the king
("king" here is used as a synonym for government) derives power,
not an absolute power, but a conditional power. Buchanan states
that "the people, from whom he derived his power, should have
the liberty of prescribing its bounds; and I require that he should
exercise over the people only those rights which he has received
from their hands."[3]

In 1643 the Reverend Samuel Rutherford wrote *Lex Rex* (The
Law and The Prince). Rutherford sounded a theme that would be
repeated by the Founding Fathers of the United States and the
Confederate States by showing how the people had the right to
recall the delegated powers they had "loaned" government, be
that a king, a parliament, or a president. Rutherford stated,
"Those who have power to make, have power to unmake a king.
Whatever the king doth as king, that he doth by a power borrowed
from (or by a fiduciary power which is his by trust) the estates, who
make him king."[4]

Political ideas such as government by the consent of the governed and State's Rights do indeed have a long and rich heritage
for all Americans.

The critics of Southern secession use two broad avenues of attack when wrestling with the idea of secession. First, they use an
appeal to emotion by seeking to take the high moral ground and,
by inference, to leave the South in the position of supporting an
immoral object, be that the destruction of "America," or the support of human slavery (note arguments 1, 2, 3, and 6 above). Second, they make a tortuous and difficult appeal to legality (note
arguments 4, 5, and 7). In other words, "if you can't dazzle them
with brilliance, baffle them with B.S." Let us now take a close look
at these arguments and in so doing expose and explode a few
more Yankee myths.

1. Secession would have destroyed the United States and the
   South.

With this appeal to emotional fantasy, we are urged to disregard
all reasons for which the republic of 1776 was called into being.
Without the opportunity to say good-bye to the principle of government by the consent of the governed, we Southerners are
driven down the dead-end road of regret. At the end of that road

we will be instructed to perch again on our "stools of everlasting repentance."[5] It should be remembered that whenever anyone states this first myth about secession, he or she always fails to take note of the fact that the North's war of aggression did indeed destroy the South. We must question our opponents' vaunted goodwill for "the United States and the South" when they make the statement that secession would destroy "America" (see point 6).

The anti-secessionist argument that the war was necessary in order to save America from self-destruction and from "falling apart" needs closer investigation. Do secession movements cause the destruction of one or both parties involved in the act of secession? In answering this question, we will not make an appeal to raw emotion; rather, we will adhere to historical facts.

Has secession caused the destruction of one or both parties in the past? If we can show that secession has not caused such misery but in actuality has done the opposite, then the anti-secession statement is false.

Let us now look at some successful secession movements:

A. Ireland seceded from the British empire. Neither Ireland nor the British empire were destroyed as a result of the independence of Ireland from Britain. Both nations have taken their places among the free nations of the world and have played important roles in world history.[6]

B. Norway seceded from Sweden. For ninety-one years from 1814 until 1905 Norway was in a union with Sweden.[7] (The North and South had only been in a union for eighty-four years when Dixie seceded.) In 1905, the legislature of Norway declared that country's independence. Sweden, after some thought of war, recognized the independence of Norway. Neither country has "gone to the dogs" because of this secession movement, but rather both countries have learned how to work together for common goals. It is sad that "America" could not have pursued the same course.

C. Texas seceded from Mexico.[8] Does anyone think that Texas would be better off if it had lost its war of secession with Mexico?

D. Portugal seceded from Spanish rule. Portugal had to fight *four* "civil wars" with Spain before it gained independence in

1139. This was well before the great world exploration both countries were to experience as independent nations. Secession kept neither Spain nor Portugal from becoming world powers. In fact, it could be argued that secession is what caused their rise as world powers.

E. Panama seceded from Colombia.[9] Neither country fell into oblivion because of this successful secession movement. A revealing point can be made in this instance. The secession of Panama could never have happened without the backing of the United States. The history of this fact is well documented but seldom spoken of in the Yankees' official record of history. Before the War of Southern Independence, the United States supported the secession movement in Texas, and *after* the War for Southern Independence the United States supported the secession movement in Panama. Strange is the working of the Yankee mind. Over a sixty-five-year period the United States supported secession for Texas from Mexico, opposed secession of the South from the North, and then supported the secession of Panama from Colombia.[10]

The list of inequities could go on, but the point has been made. Secession in and of itself does not cause the destruction of the nation that secedes nor of the nation from which it withdraws. The bloodshed and evil that can result from a secession movement will occur at the discretion of the nation from which the seceding is being done. If cool and rational heads are in control, then war and heartache are avoided as evidenced in the secession of Norway from Sweden. As in the case of Portugal and Spain, however, it may require many wars before the empire will free its subjugated people.

2. Secession was a way to protect the system of slavery, and the "Civil War" would not have been fought had slavery not existed.

The issue of why the South fought the war has already been covered in Chapter 1. But the anti-secessionist's notion that the war would have never been fought had it not been for the issue of slavery should be scrutinized.

To say that a civil war would never have been fought if slavery had not existed is to say that slavery causes civil war. Obviously, more civil wars have been fought in which the issue of slavery played no part than otherwise. Nevertheless, many people will accept the notion that without slavery the so-call "Civil War" would have never been fought. Wars are caused by many reasons. Of all issues that have caused war, none is greater than the economic issue.[11] To protect its economic well-being, the North waged a war of aggression against the South.[12] Economics motivated the war; slavery and maintaining the Union were no more than smoke screens to hide the North's imperialist objectives. Its empire was built on the graves and ashes of the South. On Southern impoverishment, Northern cumulative wealth was built!

In early 1820, before slavery had been seized upon by the North as an issue to use against the South and after the financial panic of 1819 and a House committee report of mismanagement and speculation by the Bank of the United States, a Kentuckian predicted that events would continue ". . . with a steady pace, to civil war and dissolution of the union."[13] At about the same time, Thomas Cooper, president of South Carolina College, said, "We shall ere long be forced to calculate the value of our Union, to ask of what use is an unequal alliance by which the South has always been the loser and the North always the winner."[14]

In 1850 a little-known incident almost caused the secession of Texas from the Union ten years before South Carolina seceded. A dispute arose when a federal army officer called a convention to form the state of New Mexico on land that was claimed by Texas. Governor Peter H. Bell of Texas called for force to be used to maintain the integrity of Texas. War was averted by a compromise giving Texas ten million dollars and 33,333 square miles of land.[15] The point is that this near war, in which the South had stood by Texas against the interests of the federal government, was not about slaves but about land claimed by Texas and the federal government.

These two examples clearly show that issues other than slavery were at play in the United States even as early as 1820. These forces had been set in motion by the North as it advanced its general welfare at the expense of the South. Even at this early date, Southerners were expressing the need to separate from the North. Even if there had been *no* question about slavery, the North and the South would have been on a collision course. Either each region would have had to go its own way, or one region would have had to wage a war of aggression and conquer the other. The North chose war and subjugation.

3. Lincoln was justified in using whatever force at whatever cost to save the Union.

Only if one believes in the barbaric idea that the ends justify the means could it be maintained that Lincoln and the North had a right to do whatever was necessary to win the war and save the Union. If winning at any cost is justifiable, then men such as Saddam Hussein have the right to use poison gas or human shields as long as they are in pursuit of victory. The following quote may not sit well with those who think that might makes right or that the ends justify the means. It is taken from James Kent's *Commentaries on American Law*: "No one nation had a right to force the way of the liberation of Africa, by trampling on the independence of other states; or to procure an eminent good by means that were unlawful; or *to press forward to a great principle, by breaking through other great principles that stood in the way*"[16] [emphasis added]. Kent was making a point about the proper and lawful way to stop the slave trade. As he noted, we cannot, according to international law, break one law or principle even if we are pursuing a greater good. Kent's textbook was used by the United States military cadets at West Point from 1826 through 1865.[17] Such men as Robert E. Lee, Albert Sydney Johnston, Joseph Johnston, and Jefferson Davis were instructed on principles of international law by Kent's textbook.

Although Lincoln and his worshippers believe that no price was too great to save the Union, international law does not uphold that position. In the Le Louis case, British courts established that British vessels of war could not board a French vessel in search of slave traders even if that trade was deemed illegal by British and French law. This case reinforced the principle of free navigation. Only if the countries involved were under treaty obligation to police each other's maritime fleet could one nation's vessel of war stop and search a vessel of another nation during time of peace. The British court stated that the greater good of ending the slave trade did not give a nation the right to trample principles of international law: "The right of visitation and search, on the high seas, did not exist in time of peace. If it belonged to one nation, it equally belonged to all, and would lead to gigantic mischief, and universal war."[18] So, according to internationally recognized principles, the ends do not justify the means. Lincoln could not legally pursue the cause of union at any price. Edmund Burke, in an address to the British Parliament entitled "Conciliation with the Colonies" (1775), stated that the use of force to bring the colonies back under British law was wrong because, ". . . you impair the object by your very endeavors to preserve it. The thing you fought for is not the thing which you recover, but depreciated, sunk, wasted, and consumed in the contest."[19] Burke declared that, to prove that the colonies should not be free, ". . . we are obliged to depreciate the value of freedom itself."[20] Lincoln erred as the British had done; that is, to save the Union, he was willing to "depreciate the value of freedom." Without question, Lincoln and his fellow Northerners were acting outside of internationally accepted principles when they sought to coerce the South back into the Union.

4. Secession is an act of a sovereign state, and no state in America was sovereign before or after the Declaration of Independence was signed.

One fact that bothers the anti-secessionist more than any other is that the colonies acted as independent states before and after the Revolutionary War. Obviously, if the states did function as independent states and did freely enter into a compact with other free states, then only the states could judge for themselves how long they would stay in that compact or union.

The anti-secessionist will throw up many smoke screens and try to dance around the idea that the colonies and then the states did indeed act as independent bodies. First the anti-secessionist will advance the theory that "sovereignty is indivisible," and therefore the several states could not each be sovereign. The anti-secessionist will state that sovereignty resided in the hands of the British while the states were colonies, and it had to remain in the hands of the United States government after the colonies had gained their independence. The idea that all power or sovereignty must be in the hands of one agent and not divided among many is a throwback to the erroneous notion of the divine right of kings. This idea had effectually been refuted by British noteworthies such as Milton and Locke (see Chapter 5). Within the British empire sovereign authority was divided between Parliament and the monarch in the seventeenth century.

The great fear among the American patriots of 1776 focused on the placement of too much power in the hands of government. The colonies and later the states always strove to prevent the accumulation of too much power in the hands of the few. This fear brought forth the idea of shared powers and a government of co-equal partners. Each partner would share in the function of government; each partner was supreme in its own sphere, but the greater bulk of rights and power would always remain in the hands of the agent of the people, the state.

So much for abstract theory. Regardless of what we may think about theory, the facts will speak absolutely on this matter.

One anti-secessionist made this statement about the American colonies: ". . . [they] possess neither independence nor sovereignty nor any other attribute or form of authority commonly associated with states."[21] It is an easy matter to look at the history of the American colonies and see if they did indeed possess any attributes of a state.

The following are some of these attributes. A state:

1. Conducts war or pursues peace
2. Makes laws to regulate society
3. Taxes and spends tax funds
4. Raises military forces
5. Conducts relationships with sovereign nations.[22]

If we can show that the colonies performed any of the above functions, then they cannot be said to have been lacking in those characteristics "commonly associated with states." Proof that the colonies exercised the attributes of sovereignty will be taken from a textbook on Southern history entitled *The History of the South* written by F. B. Simkins.[23]

In 1689, the British Parliament tried to exercise power, which had previously been held by the monarch, over the colonies. The colonies resisted and demanded that their legislative assemblies should be *co-ordinate* with Parliament; each within its own sphere should exercise *sovereign* authority. Parliament gave in to the demands of the colonies.[24] Even at this early date, the clamor for State's Rights could be heard. According to Simkins in *The History of the South*, every Southern colony, by 1700, had an elected legislature and had won two privileges from the British Crown: (1) the right to assent to laws and taxes, and (2) the right to initiate legislation. Here we see the colonies performing two major functions of a state: taxing and spending, and regulating society.[25]

Even so, the anti-secessionist will tell us that these rights were instituted under the watchful eye of the governor of these colonies who was appointed by Britain's monarch; therefore they were functioning as part of the sovereign British nation. But, according to the royal governor of South Carolina, James Glen (1748), "The people have the whole of the administration in their hands."[26] Yes, self-government has a long tradition in the South. Southerners insisted early in the colonial era on the right to govern themselves. Not only had Southerners elected their own legislatures in each colony by 1700, but also by early 1776 *all* royal governors had been removed from office and replaced by governors chosen by the people or their representatives. These actions all occurred before the Declaration of Independence was signed. The following is a list of the royal governors and the dates of their removal by the people of the South:

1. Virginia governor John Murray Dunmore, June 1775
2. North Carolina governor J. Martin, August 1775
3. South Carolina governor W. Campbell, early 1776
4. Georgia governor James Wright, January 1776 [27]

Each of the Southern colonies was demonstrating the attributes of a sovereign state by changing the type of government under which its people would live. These actions were performed by a free people. The theory that the Declaration of Independence formed the Union and that this document called the states into being cannot be justified by historical facts.

Let us look at more evidence to prove that the Southern states existed before the signing of the Declaration of Independence.

In April 1776, the congress of Georgia had *empowered* its delegates to the Continental Congress to vote for American independence.[28] Now, if the states did not exist before the Declaration of Independence, how could the state of Georgia *empower* its delegation to vote for American independence?

The last straw to which the anti-secessionist will cling is the myth that in international matters the colonies always had to depend on either the British government or the Union. Sorry; wrong again! According to James Kent, in *Commentaries on American Law*, Vol. I, the only way the colonial congress could enforce the rule of international law was ". . . to have infractions of it punished in the only way that was then lawful, by the exercise of the authority of the legislatures of the several states."[29] Note that James Kent was from New York, and not a Southerner. Kent states that the only legal way to enforce the rule of international law was through the power of the individual states. We have now demonstrated that the Southern states have been active in the pursuit of the rights of free men since 1700. Before the signing of the Declaration of Independence the Southern states had exercised every attribute of a sovereign power. So much for another Yankee myth.

If the colonies acted as independent states prior to the Declaration of Independence, how did they view themselves while adopting the United States Constitution? A glance at how Massachusetts expressed herself as far as her sovereign rights will demonstrate that even the Northern states considered themselves sovereign. Before it would ratify the United States Constitution, Massachusetts demanded ". . . that it be explicitly declared, that all powers not delegated by the aforesaid Constitution are reserved to the several States, to be by them exercised."[30] Before it would adopt the Constitution, the state of Pennsylvania insisted upon the following amendment to the Constitution: "All the rights of sovereignty which are not, by the said Constitution, expressly and plainly vested in the Congress, shall be deemed to remain with, and shall be exercised by the several States in the Union."[31] Every state insisted that this and similar language be added to the United States Constitution, resulting in the adoption of the Tenth Amendment to the Constitution: "The powers not delegated to the United States, by the Constitution, nor prohibited by it to the States, are reserved to the States, or to the people."

We have now determined that the people of the states acted as sovereign and independent states before the Declaration of Independence and during the ratification process of the Constitution. Let us look at how these states perceived their role once they were in the Union.

The anti-secessionists will tell you that state sovereignty never existed, and, if it did, it surely died with the adoption of the Constitution. Again, they are wrong. The state of New Hampshire adopted her state constitution in 1792, some three years after the United States Constitution went into effect. Yet note the strong assertion of state sovereignty placed into its state constitution, "The people of this Commonwealth have the sole and exclusive right of governing themselves as a free, sovereign, and independent State; and do and forever hereafter shall exercise and enjoy every power, jurisdiction, and right which is not, or may not hereafter be, by them, expressly delegated to the United States."[32] The people of New Hampshire, like the people of the other states, believed that they were members of an independent state (which, of course, they were). No one tried to accuse the people of New Hampshire of being "traitors" because they believed in State's Rights.

One last look at how the people of the states of America viewed their states in relation to the Union will show that the people did believe the states to be co-equal with the federal government and not subservient to the Union.

Even after the adoption of the Bill of Rights, in 1791, the states were very jealous of the acts of the federal government (Union). Just six years after the adoption of the Constitution the states became enraged when the federal Supreme Court stated that Article III of the United States Constitution permitted states to be sued in federal courts by citizens of another state. The state of Georgia was then ordered to appear before the court (*Chisholm v. Georgia*). Georgia refused to appear, stating that the states were co-equal with the federal government, and therefore could not be compelled by the federal government to act against their will. The states of the Union were so incensed by the federal court's action that the Eleventh Amendment was quickly passed. That amendment reaffirmed the sovereignty of the states by declaring that "The judicial power of the United States shall not extend to a suit against a State by citizens of another State."[33] Clearly the people of America at this time believed that the states were indeed independent and sovereign agents.

5. The original thirteen states did not secede from the Union when they withdrew from the Articles of Confederation. The perpetual union under the Articles of Confederation is the same union under the United States Constitution.

How embarrassing it is for those who oppose secession when they consider that nowhere in the Constitution is there a statement about perpetuity. It is doubly embarrassing when they note that there is a statement about perpetuity in the Articles of Confederation, the government that the states seceded from in order to form the government under the Constitution. The anti-secessionist will claim that the Union is the Union regardless of the type of government we have; therefore the Union is perpetual.

A political union is an association of political entities for a predetermined purpose. The Articles of Confederation stated how the union of the states was to act and *how it could be changed*.[34] Each state before it became a partner in this union had to ratify the Articles of Confederation. Note that in the body of the articles the statement that the only way this association could be changed was by the unanimous approval of the members of the union. When the states changed from a union under the Articles of Confederation to the Union under the Constitution, it was done not by unanimous approval of the states but by the approval of nine of thirteen states of the old union.[35] With the approval of nine of the thirteen states of the old union under the Articles of Confederation, a new type of association would then exist between only those states so ratifying the Constitution. This means that from one to four states would be under a different type of national government than the other nine. Can anyone pretend that those two groups were the same? Remember that North Carolina and Rhode Island did not join the new union for over a year after it had been in effect among the other states. They were treated as independent states. The union of states under the Articles of Confederation was disbanded by the secession of nine states from the articles. The states, in doing so, were acting as sovereign entities. They were *not* acting as states of the present Constitutional Union do when they ratify a constitutional amendment because such an act requires a three-fourths majority to pass, and the amendment becomes binding upon *all* states. Note that the act of ratifying the Constitution required the approval of each state, acting on its own, *not* in concert with anyone else, and that this act was binding only on the states ratifying the Constitution. The two unions could be considered the same only if the second union under the Constitution had the same member states and the same form of government as the first under the Articles of Confederation. This was not the case. No one ever suggested that the other states of the union had the right to wage war upon North Carolina and Rhode Island in order to "save the Union." Why not? Because this was a new and different union, and each state had the right to decide for itself if and when it would become a member state.

6. Secession was an action taken by Southerners to save the institution of slavery and/or to destroy America.

The theory that secession was a slaveholders' wicked plot is favored by many liberals and New South Scalawags.

The idea that to withdraw from the Union was an illegal act is based upon the false notion that the Union was to be perpetual—that in America, government was to have some form of everlasting life. Yet when we look at the first union of American colonies, we will find that even though this union was styled as "perpetual," it died a natural death.[36]

In 1643 four New England colonies formed the first union in North America, the United Colonies of New England. This union was declared to be "firm and perpetual."[37] As Kent stated, the colonies that joined this union ". . . acted in fact as independent sovereignties, and free from the control of any superior power."[38] This union existed for more than forty years. Note that, even though the Yankee colonies had stated that their union was perpetual, it was not. Also note that each of these colonies entered into this union, according to Kent, ". . . as Free, and Independent Sovereignties."[39] This puts to rest the Yankee myth that the states were never sovereign before or after July 4, 1776.

Twice in our history, Northern states have left a "perpetual" Union: once in 1686 at the death of the United Colonies of New England and again in 1787 as they withdrew from union formed by the Articles of Confederation. With such a secessionist track record, is it any wonder that in 1814 the New England states met at Hartford, Connecticut, for the purpose of discussing secession from the federal Union? Even still, the Yankee myth-makers persist in claiming that secession was an evil Southern plot.

Northern myth-makers would have a somewhat valid case if secession from the American Union had never been discussed or written about before the 1860 election. Then and only then would the anti-secessionist argument be valid. Is there a record in American history of secession being taught as a right of the states? The answer is a clear-cut *yes*.

Secession as Taught at West Point

Yes, as early as 1825 the right of secession was being taught as a clear-cut right of the states. But, even more shocking is the fact that the federal government itself was paying for that teaching. From 1825 to 1826, the United States Military Academy at West Point, New York, used William Rawle's *Views of the Constitution* as its textbook on constitutional law. Men such as Confederate general Albert Sidney Johnston were taught constitutional law from this book.[40] Rawle, born in 1759, was thirty years old when the United States Constitution was adopted. His book was warmly received when published. The *North American Review*, a journal of Boston political orthodoxy, blessed Rawle's book as, ". . . a safe and intelligent guide."[41] Here is what Rawle had to say about state sovereignty and secession:

> It depends on the state itself to retain or abolish the principle of representation, because it depends on itself whether it will continue a member of the Union. To deny this right would be inconsistent with the principle of which all our political systems are founded, which is, that the people have in all cases, a right to determine how they will be governed.
>
> This right must be considered as an ingredient in the original composition of the general government, which, though not expressed, was mutually understood. . . .[42]

Here you have it from the words of a textbook used at West Point Military Academy. Rawle said that the people held the right to ". . . determine how they will be governed." Rawle goes on to state that this right was an "ingredient in the original composition of the general government." This is merely a reflection of Jefferson's pronouncement from the Declaration of Independence that a just government was one which was based on the consent of the governed. Rawle is restating a historical fact. The United States was founded on the principle that we, the people, acting through our agent, the state, have the right to give or take away the right of any government to rule over us. This is the natural result of our being a free people. To deny this principle is to attack our very freedom.

But what about the act of secession itself? Rawle was even more specific about when and how a state should and could go about seceding from the Union.

> The secession of a state from the Union depends on the will of the people of such state. The people alone as we have already seen, hold the power to alter their constitution.

But in any manner by which a secession is to take place, nothing is more certain than that the act should be deliberate, clear, and unequivocal.

To withdraw from the Union is a solemn, serious act. Whenever it may appear expedient to the people of a state, it must be manifested in a direct and unequivocal manner.[43]

Rawle explains how a state should withdraw from the Union. He clearly notes that if a state did leave the Union, that state would leave many benefits behind. Jefferson Davis also felt the same way. In his farewell address to the United States Senate, Senator Davis said, "A state . . . out of the Union surrenders all the benefits (and they are known to be many), deprives herself of the advantages (and they are known to be great), severs all the ties of affection (and they are close and enduring), which have bound her to the Union."[44] Davis learned well from Rawle. Rawle taught that the secession of a state from the Union had to be carried out carefully. Davis and all Southerners had to weigh the pros and cons of secession and, after doing so, they found the Union wanting. If we look at the manner in which the first eleven states of the South seceded, we would see that they followed Rawle's prescription for secession.

Because of the defeat of the South during the War for Southern Independence, most Americans find it hard to understand how Rawle could be a patriotic American and also believe in secession (the Yankee myth-makers have done their dirty work very well). As an American, Rawle knew that the Union was dear to all and offered many advantages to member states. But, as an American, he also knew that when the people of a state felt that those advantages no longer existed and that the Union had become a threat to their happiness, the very reason for the Union's existence was no longer valid. Listen to the words of the first popular "war" song of the South, "The Bonnie Blue Flag." "As long as the Union was faithful to her trust, like friends and like brethren kind were we and just. But now that Northern treachery attempts our *rights* to mar, we hoist on high the Bonnie Blue Flag that bears the single star."[45] In song and in deed, the South was making the statement that the Union had lost sight of the real reason for its existence, and was embarking on a course of aggression and oppression. Therefore the Southern states acted in the only way they could to protect the liberty of their people—they seceded from the Union.

There are some important points to note about Rawle's textbook on constitutional law. First, Rawle was from Philadelphia, Pennsylvania, and a member of a leading family of that *Northern* city. Even though the book was used by the United States Military Academy as a text to instruct its students in constitutional law and has been used as a reference book since that time, these are not the most important characteristics of Rawle's work. The most important fact for us to remember is that secession was held to be a legal and a constitutional right for all the states of the Union as early as 1825, the publication date of Rawle's textbook. Rawle was a friend of both Benjamin Franklin and President George Washington and a leader in the early abolition movement. His textbook was not only used in the Military Academy at West Point, but also by many other colleges and academies.[46] The right of secession was not first uttered by some "hot-headed" Southern secessionist, but written eloquently by a "cool-headed" Northerner. The fact that this work was used for at least one year as a textbook at West Point and has been used since that time as a reference work is merely lagniappe.

If Rawle really loved the Union, why did he write about how to secede from the Union? Rawle, like the men of the South some thirty-six years later, did love the Union. But he understood the nature of the Original Constitutional Republic of our Founding Fathers. If the states were able to secede from the Union, if and when that Union became oppressive to the people of those states, then they could use this potential to act as a check on the abuse of federal power. Because he loved American liberty more than he loved the Union, Rawle made sure that all those who read his textbook on the Constitution would understand how that liberty could be protected from federal tyranny. Therefore, according to Rawle, only if the liberty of its people were in danger should a state use the extreme measure of secession. Listen to the words of President Jefferson Davis in his inaugural address as Confederate president: "As a necessity, not a choice, we have resorted to the remedy of separation. . . ."[47]

Southerners did not desire secession; it was forced upon them. Like Rawle, Southerners loved American liberty more than governmental institutions. Therefore, when faced with the choice of submission to federal tyranny or secession, they chose secession.

7. Nullification and secession had already been proven wrong by the federal government.

In the confused world of the Yankee myth-maker, an assertion is sometimes made that confuses secession with the act of nullification. It is sometimes expressed that the government in Washington had already proven in the South Carolina tariff nullification crisis that the states did not have the right to nullify laws of the federal government.

Jefferson Davis, in his farewell address to the United States Senate in 1861, explained that the two ideas, secession and nullification, were different. He explained that a state's nullification of acts that it considered unlawful was carried out by a state that was trying to protect its rights within the Union. Further, the act of secession was a final attempt by a state to protect rights that were threatened and that could not be maintained within the Union. As he stated, the act of nullification maintained the Union, whereas the act of secession maintained the rights of the people within the states (see Addendum II).

Most "American" history books will discuss the act of nullification only in the South Carolina context. They will then state that the federal government in Washington was victorious in putting down this Southern act. But little if anything is ever told about the more flagrant acts of nullification by the Northern states.

In the history of the Northern states there is a long record of those states nullifying acts of Congress, parts of the Constitution, and decrees of the federal Supreme Court. Those acts were never the object of an attack by the federal government in Washington. No armies ever marched on or navies blockaded any ports of those Northern states because of their acts of nullification. Article IV, Section 2, of the United States Constitution, known as the Fugitive Slave Law, reads, "No Person held to Service or Labour in one State, under the laws thereof, escaping into another shall, in Consequence of any law or Regulation therein, be discharged from such Service or Labour, but shall be delivered up on claim of the Party to whom such Service or Labour may be due." The Fugitive Slave Law was part of the agreement that the states and people therein committed themselves to maintain and obey when they adopted the Constitution. No one can say that they did not know what they were doing or that they had been tricked by anyone when they agreed to abide by the law of the land. At this point Southerners, acting in accordance with this law, are usually met by cries from self-righteous Yankees protesting that they had a "right" not to enforce an immoral act such as returning slaves to their masters. Yet when we look into the history of the fugitive slave acts, we will clearly see that the first fugitive slave law that was ever passed in America was enacted by the New England states.

George H. Moore was from New York and in 1866 was a librarian of the New York Historical Society and a corresponding member of the Massachusetts Historical Society. In his *History of Slavery in Massachusetts* Moore wrote the following: "The original of the Fugitive Slave Law provision in the Federal (U.S.) Constitution is to be traced to this Confederacy [United Colonies of New England], in which Massachusetts was the ruling colony."[48] It should be noted also that by the authority of the United Colonies of New England, the people of New England used their power to deal with a colony of another nation in order to have a slave returned to his owner. As stated in the "Plymouth Colony Records," a treaty between the Dutch and the English was made in which fugitives, slave or criminal, would be returned to the New England colonies from New Amsterdam (New York).[49] Yet in 1843 the states of Massachusetts and Vermont nullified the national Fugitive Slave Law of 1793. The act of these two Northern states was nothing less than breaking a bargain with the states of the South. Note that this was done well after the slave trade had been almost stopped by the action of Congress, an action supported by most Southerners. As long as there was profit to be made, Massachusetts supported slavery, but when the profits declined, citizens of that state became more aggressive in their attacks on slavery. Nevertheless, when two people strike a deal or bargain, *both* must comply with the agreement; otherwise the agreement is broken. Daniel Webster of Massachusetts expressed this principle clearly: "A bargain broken on one side is broken on all sides."[50] Webster had even stronger words for those in the North who refused to obey the law, yet remained in the Union: "The Union is a Union of States founded upon Compact. If the Northern States willfully and deliberately refuse to carry out their part of the Constitution, the South would be no longer bound to keep the compact."[51] Even the supreme court of the state of Wisconsin participated in the act of nullifying constitutional law when in 1854 it nullified the Fugitive Slave Law of 1850.[52]

Now, every time we start talking about the Fugitive Slave Law, we are met by self-righteous Yankees and "hung-head" Southern Scalawags telling us how virtuous Northerners were for not sending the poor downtrodden slaves back into bondage. In Chapter 2 we proved that Yankees were not driven by their love of liberty in freeing their slaves, but rather wanted only to get rid of people with whom they did not want to associate, and make a little profit in the process. But for those who require a little more proof, please note that, while the people of the Northern states were refusing to follow the law of the land as far as the Fugitive Slave Law was concerned, they were also passing laws to prevent free Negroes from settling in their states. In 1853 the state of Illinois passed a law to prevent free Negroes from ". . . coming into this State and remaining ten days, with the evident intention of residing in the same."[53] This law remained in effect until some time after the War for Southern Independence began. How odd is the workings of Yankee justice. If slaves escaped into Massachusetts or Vermont, they could not be restored to their masters even though the Constitution, acts of Congress, and rulings of the federal Supreme Court declared that they had to be so returned. But if free Negroes moved up North into Illinois, they would be arrested and thrown into jail just for being there! After the state of Kansas was admitted into the Union as a "free" state, a member of that state's legislature stated that Kansas "was and will forever be a white-man's State."[54] Yet time after time Southerners are told that the North would not keep its part of the bargain by obeying the law of the land and returning runaway salves because it was a friend of freedom and the Negro.

As we have proven, the North was not the champion of the black race and freedom, but only used the slave issue as it used many other issues, as a weapon against the people of the South.

SUMMARY

In the preceding pages we have looked at the major arguments used by the promoters of centralized federal power over the rights of the states and people. We have shown that the arguments advanced against secession are so illogical that only a blatant appeal to raw emotion is left to the detractors of the South. This irrational type of argument is the primary reason why such detractors seldom dare discuss the issue of secession by itself. They always try to use the tar brushes of slavery and racism to paint the South as the hotbed of evil ideas and wicked people. Then they will use their last tar brush and paint Southerners as un-American, and unpatriotic, because they fought against the "American" Union. With these two strokes we Southerners are supposed to hang our heads in shame, and humbly sit in the corner on our "stool of everlasting repentance." This was the motivation behind and the desired response of such propaganda as PBS's "The Civil War" series. But something has changed. From across the South and America, people are no longer accepting everything their "benevolent" masters are telling them. People are beginning to question much of the liberal "truth" about such matters as secession and the South.

With the break-up of the old communist empire in Eastern Europe, people are beginning to question the value of "bigger is better" government. Even the new Soviet Commonwealth is having to wrestle with the problem of republics declaring their independence. Americans are having to look again at why the South fought for independence and why the federal government fought against the South. Americans are becoming embarrassed by the thought of their government, in 1861, pursuing the same policy that the communist generals of Yugoslavia and the communist dictators of the Soviet Union followed in repressing movements for independence. If we have learned nothing else from the KGB-led communist coup in Moscow, it should be this: those in power do not take lightly the break-up of their empire (Union) be it Soviet or American. This was the response of those in power in Washington in 1861. The radical party of the North claimed that the South did not have the right to secede and used brute military force to "prove" its point—just as the Chinese communists did in Tiananmen Square and as the communist hard-liners tried to do in Russia.

The North went to war to "prove" that the right of secession did not exist. Then after winning the war with the South, the North required the South to surrender its right of secession in order to rejoin the Union. In order to take their place in the Union, from which the North had fought a war to "prove" that they could not legally leave, Southern states were ordered to give up the right of secession. Each Southern state, before it was allowed back into the Union, had to write into its state constitution a clause surrendering forever the right of secession.[55] How could a state give up that which it never had? The very acts of the Northern government proved that the South did indeed have the right of secession.

It must be pointed out here that, although the North won the war, winning a war is not how one "proves" matters of ethics and principles. If brute force is the measure of virtue and correctness, then why do we have laws and juries? If force is the proper measure of virtue, then trial by combat would be correct and trial by a jury would be only a waste of time and money. No, the North only proved that an industrial society can defeat an agrarian society in a protracted war. Issues of morality and constitutional law cannot be judged by such a barbaric method. Only tyrants such as Adolph Hitler or Saddam Hussein would ever subscribe to that method.

Morgan L. Brand, Company D, Thirty-Fourth Alabama Volunteer Infantry. Brand was the son of a former indentured servant. He was typical of the hardy non-slaveholders who answered their country's call to repel invaders. Brand participated in the Battle of Murfreesboro, Tennessee, and was twice wounded. He was captured and sent to Fort Delaware, the infamous camp where so many Confederate POWs died. Brand was exchanged in late 1864 and served his country until the end of the war.[12] (Image courtesy of Jude W. Brand, Baton Rouge, Louisiana)

CHAPTER 9

State's Rights and Constitutional Liberty

State Sovereignty died at Appomattox.

Supreme Court Justice Salmon P. Chase[1]

The worst fears of those Boys in Gray are now a fact of American life—a Federal government completely out of control.

Professor Jay Hoar of Maine[2]

INTRODUCTORY COMMENTS

The central theme of this book is that the Northern majority used unconstitutional, illegal, and immoral methods to change the Original Constitutional Republic into a centralized national government that it now controls. This radical and revolutionary corruption of the original government changed the very nature of that government from a voluntary compact among sovereign states to an empire established by the Northern majority via the conquest of the numerical minority of the South. Because the states were sovereign, they possessed specific "rights" as a result of their sovereign character, thus the term "State's Rights."

As hard as it may be to believe, there was a time when states were sovereign and the Tenth Amendment was a valid and honored part of the United States Constitution. The demise of state sovereignty leaves the citizen at the mercy of an all-powerful central government. In the following chapter we shall trace the origins of the attack upon state sovereignty and observe the struggle leading to the War for Southern Independence and the death of the Constitutional Federal Republic of the United States of America.

State's Rights and Constitutional Liberty

According to Chief Justice Salmon P. Chase, United States Supreme Court 1864-73, state sovereignty died at Appomattox. As surprising as it may be, we agree with his assessment! Our differences are that while the Republican chief justice was celebrating the conquest of this great Southern principle, we, on the other hand, lament the death of the Constitutional Federal Republic. It is unfortunate that "conservatives" refuse to recognize the fact that the death of the principle of state sovereignty caused a radical transformation in the very nature and character of the resulting government. They insist on living in a fantasy world as if the war and Reconstruction had no effect upon the constitutional nature of the current government. Establishment conservatives have a vested interest in maintaining this fantasy. They must continue to conduct business as usual, all the while pretending that the United States Constitution guarantees a limited central government and that the limitations imposed by the Ninth and Tenth Amendments are just as valid today as they were under the Original Constitution. To do otherwise would force them into an untenable position of admitting that the original compact that created this country (the Constitution) has been illegally altered and is no longer valid for the purpose it was designed. Admitting this, they would be forced to conclude that there is nothing left to conserve. Therefore, they would have to abandon their position and acknowledge defeat.

As Southern Nationalists we must remember that there is no magic in the word "constitution." Even communist Russia had a constitution that guaranteed human rights and religious freedom. Yet, it availed the people very little! The current United States Constitution may resemble the original, it may be titled the same, it may contain certain identical clauses, but it does not effectively limit the power of the federal government, nor does it allow the people of the states an avenue to effectively defend their reserved rights when these rights are trampled upon by an all-powerful central government. Therefore, *beware* of your liberties for indeed there *is* no magic in the word "constitution"! Absent the sovereign state, the individual citizen stands naked and alone, unprotected against the might of a centralized federal government—a government that has assumed unto itself the right to be the exclusive judge of the extent of its own powers. What monarch has ever asked for more?

MONARCHY VERSUS STATE SOVEREIGNTY

We are now centuries removed from the era of royalty and the political doctrine of the divine right of kings. It may seem strange to many Americans that there once was a very influential group of American monarchists who wanted to see some form of monarchy established in the United States. This group attempted to influence the Constitutional Convention to accept a strong central (national) government modeled after the English monarchy.[3] The monarchy faction was defeated, but it still held to its monarchist principles and used every method available to invest the new government with centralized, kingly powers.[4] One of the leading advocates of an all-powerful, monarchist, national government was John Adams of Massachusetts. United States senator John Langdon of New Hampshire wrote:

> Mr. Adams certainly expressed himself that he hoped, or expected to see the day when Mr. Taylor, and his friend, Mr. Giles, would be convinced that the people of America would never be happy without a hereditary Chief Magistrate and Senate; or at least for life.[5]

Later we shall see how President John Adams used his vision of kingly powers to violently and unconstitutionally violate the civil liberties of his "subjects."

Thomas Jefferson also recorded John Adams' monarchist views:

> Mr. Adams had originally been a Republican. The glare of royalty and nobility, during his mission in England, had made him believe their fascination to be a necessary ingredient in government. His book on the American Constitution had made known his political bias. He was taken up by the monarchial Federalist in his absence, and was by them made to believe that the general disposition of our citizens was favorable to monarchy.[6]

The American monarchist looked to England as a model monarchy. How strange that, only a few short years after fighting a war to gain independence from the central government represented by the British Crown, we now find Americans desiring to emulate centralized, kingly power. Thomas Jefferson observed that Alexander Hamilton had declared of the British constitution, "As it stands at present, with all its supposed defects, it is the most perfect government that ever existed." Thomas Jefferson declared that, "Hamilton was not only a monarchist, but a monarchist bottomed on corruption."[7]

In his introduction to the 1868 edition of *The Federal Government: Its True Nature and Character*, by Abel P. Upshur, C. C. Burr describes Hamilton and his monarchist followers thusly:

> General Hamilton, one of the principal writers of the *Federalist*, was undoubtedly at heart a monarchist. On more than one occasion he plainly avowed himself such. In the Convention which framed the constitution he exerted his commanding influence to impart centralized, consolidated, or monarchical powers to the Federal Union. But, signally failing in this, in his subsequent interpretations of the Constitution he did what he could to bend the instrument to suit his views. Judge Story and Chief Justice Kent, and earlier, Chief Justice Jay, belonged to the same political party as General Hamilton. They were Federalist, and so odious did this party become to the American people, that it was driven out of power at the expiration of old John Adams' single presidential term in 1800.[8]

This assessment of Hamilton as a monarchist attempting to form an all-powerful central government is echoed by a contemporary political scientist:

> Hamilton's proposed scheme of government resembled that of eighteenth century Great Britain. . . . Thus, the senate, the executive, and the judiciary would consist of officials not subject to periodic elections. Hamilton's objective was to strengthen the central government at the expense of the states. He claimed that they had become obsolete and that their preponderance over a more efficient and powerful nation could no longer be justified.[9]

The influence that the American monarchist had upon certain groups of citizens can be seen in a portion of a letter sent to President Adams:

> We, the subscribers, inhabitants and citizens of Boston, in the State of Massachusetts . . . beg leave to express to you, the Chief Magistrate and supreme ruler over the United States, our fullest approbation of all the measures, external and internal, you have pleased to adopt, under direction of divine authority.[10]

C. C. Burr stated that "Any one can see that the men who could address the President after this fashion, had a great deal less respect for the restraints and limitations of a written Constitution, than for the will and force of individual power."[11] Even though the monarchists were defeated in the Constitutional Convention, they never ceased their efforts to give the United States a strong, centralized, consolidated, federal government. They ceased their labors as open monarchists and renewed their efforts as consolidationists (i.e., Federalists), years later as Radical Republicans, and today as liberals. The doctrine of state sovereignty stood as a barrier to the dreams of the federal monarchists. The Anti-Federalists knew that the only way a central, national government could ever be established was at the expense of the sovereign states. At this very early stage of United States history Southerners knew that the demise of state sovereignty would mean the death of American liberty.

WERE THE STATES SOVEREIGN?

One of the many arguments used against the Jeffersonian school of limited central government, and later against secession, was that the states were never sovereign. The Yankee president Abraham Lincoln even went so far as to claim that the Union preceded the states. These arguments were answered in Chapter 8 and will not be repeated here. We do feel it necessary to document examples of the states exercising their sovereign authority as evidence of their status as sovereign states. An explanation of what is meant by the term "sovereignty" may be useful at this point. The state government is not sovereign, nor is any citizen individually. By the term "sovereign state" we refer to the citizens of the state collectively. John C. Calhoun described the state as the "sovereign community." The state, as the agent of the people, exercises sovereign authority by the consent of those who created it (i.e., the people of the state). A state, as the agent of the sovereign community, may delegate a portion of its powers to another government, but it can not delegate a portion of sovereignty. Sovereignty, like chastity, is not transferable or divisible.

Prior to the signing of the Declaration of Independence, the colonies had within their control the right of colonial legislation. Many of the colonies had removed their royal appointed governors, and Virginia had gone so far as to declare her independence in May of 1776! All these events were the acts of a sovereign nature, with no reference to a higher governmental authority. When, on July 4, 1776, they declared their independence it was a joint declaration announcing to the world that the thirteen American colonies were now free and independent states (note the plural), not in the aggregate as one nation but individually, yet acting jointly as may best secure for all the blessings of liberty. So from their separate and independent acts prior to and at the time of their declaration of independence, these colonies, now states, acted separately and independently of each other without reference to a superior governmental agency and in their capacity as sovereign entities.

During the Revolutionary War they continued as sovereign states. The monarchist school of thought attempts to advance the theory that the American Declaration of Independence created a nation-state by the action of the sovereign will of the American people in the aggregate. The following examples will demonstrate that the people of the states did not contemplate the establishment of a national government by their joint declaration of independence on July 4, 1776.

While jointly engaged in a common war with the British Crown, and while the Continental Congress was in session, the sovereign states of New York and Vermont almost declared war against each other! Their dispute created tensions so high that in 1784 Massachusetts adopted a formal resolution declaring her neutrality. New York passed a resolution stating that the state was prepared to "recur to force." Vermont's governor John J. Chittenden declared that his state did not desire to "enter into a war with the State of New York." He also advised Congress and the other states to "observe a strict neutrality" in the event of hostilities between the two states.

Another example of a state exercising its sovereign authority during the Revolutionary War was Virginia's declaring herself bound by a treaty with France then under consideration in the Continental Congress. Virginia thought the treaty to be so important that she did not wait for its slow progression through Congress but intervened via her state legislature and unilaterally bound herself to the treaty.[12] These examples demonstrate that the states did not surrender their sovereignty by their joint declaration of independence, but retained and exercised their sovereign authority.

At the close of the Revolutionary War, did His Britannic Majesty recognize the independence of the United States alone according to the *e pluribus unum* model (i.e., as one nation)? No! Each state is named as a free and independent state in the Treaty of Paris signed by the representatives of the British Monarch.

Additional evidence demonstrating the sovereign nature of the individual American states can be found in the language of the Articles of Confederation. In Article II the states make known to all parties that:

> Each State retains its sovereignty, freedom, and independence, and every power, jurisdiction, and right, which is not by this Confederation expressly delegated to the United States in Congress assembled.

Language can not be clearer. There is no room to question the states' intent to maintain their individual "sovereignty." The states acceded to the Articles of Confederation as sovereign entities and reserved all powers unto themselves as separate and independent states. It is also instructive to observe the relationship between these sovereign states in Congress under the Articles of Confederation. Each state voted as a unit, with an equal vote regardless of the size of its population or territory. Why did the states treat each other as equals? The answer is simple if we understand the principle of state sovereignty. How else could sovereign states treat each other absent a treaty, compact, or constitution mutually agreed to that plainly altered international convention? In international relations, when a league between sovereign nations is established, each nation is presumed equal unless the presumption has been specifically altered and agreed to by all parties to the league.

From the preceding discussion we can see that the states exercised their sovereign authority prior to their joint declaration of independence, during the American War for Independence, their sovereignty was recognized by the British Monarch by acknowledging their independence, and the states maintained their sovereign status under the terms of the Articles of Confederation. Now arises the question: Did these sovereign states surrender or renounce state sovereignty by the ratification of the United States Constitution?

The Constitution clearly established a different government from the one which operated under the Articles of Confederation. The preamble to the Constitution boldly states that "We the People of the United States . . . " The monarchists, Federalists, consolidationists, and others favoring a strong central federal government have seized upon these words as evidence that the people of America formed a national government, superior to the states. If this assertion is correct, then it follows that sovereign authority has shifted from the states to the central government. Did the people of America hold a plebiscite and, by virtue of the democratic principle of majority rule, vote to establish the federal government as the national and supreme government of the United States? The answer, as any school child should know, is a simple no. The Constitution was proposed by representatives of the individual states and ratified by the states, becoming binding only on those states which so ratified it. In other words, the people of the United States as a collective body did not participate in the process, the states participated in their independent and sovereign role as the elected agent of the people of their respective states. In their acts of ratification, many states specifically reserved the right to recall their delegated sovereign powers should those powers be used by the federal government to encroach upon the rights and liberties of the people. This reservation of rights is another example of the states exercising their sovereign authority. From these examples we can see that the states did not renounce their sovereign authority by ratifying the Constitution.

We have now observed that the states, acting in their separate and independent capacity, exercised their sovereign authority; prior to their Fourth of July joint declaration of independence, during the Revolutionary War, their separate independence was recognized by the British Crown; they restated their separate and independent nature in the Articles of Confederation and, as separate and independent states, sent representatives to the Constitutional Convention; and subsequently, as sovereign states, they ratified the new Constitution contingent upon certain reservations of rights. Throughout this entire course of events, state sovereignty was in no way reduced, impaired, encumbered, or otherwise compromised. Sovereignty remained where it was originally—with the states and the people thereof. The question now arises: Did the states, by some specific declaration in the newly ratified Constitution, surrender their sovereignty to the central federal government?

International law requires more than an inference or even a series of inferences to determine that a nation has voluntarily surrendered its sovereignty in favor of another government. The same rule holds for the thirteen sovereign states that joined together under the compact of the Constitution to form the federal government. The states, by their own voluntary action, created as their common agent the federal government. By means of a compact the states delegated specific powers to their common agent. Their agent, the federal government, could act only in those specific areas allowed by the Constitution. Notice that nowhere in the Constitution is sovereignty specifically surrendered or transferred to the federal government. Even though this new compact limited the federal government to specific areas, there were numerous demands for an amendment similar to Article II in the Articles of Confederation to ensure that the sovereignty of the states would remain safe from the centralizing (monarchial) tendency of all governments. Thus the Ninth and Tenth Amendments were immediately added to the Constitution. The Tenth Amendment clearly states that all powers not delegated by the Constitution are reserved to the states. At the inception of the United States Constitutional Convention, the sovereign authority of the states, as we have demonstrated, was held to remain with the states. Article V of the Constitution provides that no state shall be denied equal suffrage in the Senate without its consent.[13] This article recognizes the sovereign authority of the state to defend its equal representation in the Senate. Article IV, Section 3.1, provides that no state may be formed within the territory of an existing state without its consent. Who may nullify the will of Congress, the president, the Supreme Court, all other states, and the people of the United States in the aggregate, if they decide to form a new state within an existing state, contrary to the will of that existing state? By its provisions in Article IV, Section 3.1, the Constitution allows the threatened state to nullify the actions of the federal government, combinations of states, and/or the numerical majority of citizens. Article I transfers the war-making power from the sovereign states to the federal government, but the sovereign states retain the right to engage in war if in imminent danger. Such is the nature of a sovereign state—it possesses the right of self-defense!

ATTACKS AGAINST STATE SOVEREIGNTY

As we have seen, the monarchists were defeated in their early attempts to establish a strong central government patterned after the British system. They gradually moved into the Federalist camp and continued to work for a consolidation of power in the federal government. It is difficult today to assess the motives of the Federalists. Some, such as John Adams and Alexander Hamilton, were monarchists. Others, like George Washington perhaps, recalled the difficulty of defending the country when faced with an organized foreign power and feared future foreign invasion if European powers perceived the United States as a weak and disorganized country. Some, like James Madison, honestly believed that the states were a greater threat to the federal government and therefore the central government needed more powers to protect itself from state encroachments upon federal powers.[14] Surely there were many who had honest motives for desiring a stronger (as opposed to an all-powerful) federal government. In the final analysis, the primary motivating factor encouraging the consolidation of power was one of commercial greed—in a word, "money." Patrick Henry made it very clear that the purpose of the Revolutionary War was to secure for Americans not a "great and mighty empire" but the blessings of "liberty"[15] (often described as the right to be left alone). This view was not shared by the writers of the *Federalist Papers* who declared it to be their intention to establish an American commercial empire.[16] The Northeastern states desired to close the Mississippi River by giving control of it to Spain, thereby forcing trade eastward. They were also fearful that an expanding West (a substantial portion of which was then owned by Virginia) would draw off their labor supply and thus increase their cost of labor. In short, the Northeastern mercantile interest feared a loss of their political and economic control of an expanding, agricultural America. Gouverneur Morris of Massachusetts wanted to give control of the Mississippi River to Spain because he thought this would allow the Eastern states to hold the population of the West under their control.[17] Captain James De Wolf, one of Rhode Island's most prosperous slaver traders, realized the potential in developing manufacturing in the United States. He transferred capital from his slaving enterprises and built one of the earliest cotton mills in the New England states:

> He [De Wolf] sensed, too, that the new industry needed political influence. . . . In 1821, he was elected to the United States Senate. Here he was a strong advocate of protection for the new young industries and he opposed the extension of slavery to Missouri and the West. . . . His interest now was no longer in the African slave but in the white mill laborer.[18]

Slowly political philosophy of limited versus centralized government began to take on a commercial character as the Northern states began to turn to the federal government as a source of money for internal improvements and of protection for its emerging commercial empire. The money for internal improvements in the North was derived to a greater extent from the Southern states. In the words of Virginia's senator William Grayson, the South had become the "milch cow of the Union"!

With the ratification of the Constitution, the two opposing political theories stood face to face waiting to see who would draw first blood. It did not take long. One of the very first attempts of the Federalists to enlarge the power of the federal government, to the detriment of the states, was made by none other than the United States Supreme Court in *Chisholm v. Georgia*. A basic principle of sovereignty is that the sovereign power can not be brought under the jurisdiction of a court. In this case, an individual had brought suit in federal court against the sovereign state of Georgia. The states were shocked! They had been assured by no less a personage than Hamilton himself that this immunity from suit was "inherent in the nature of sovereignty."[19] John Marshall, who would later work so hard to enlarge the power of the federal government, had declared thusly:

> I hope that no gentleman will think that a State will be called at the bar of the Federal court. . . . It is not rational to suppose that the sovereign power should be dragged before a court.[20]

The state of Georgia declared that to submit to the jurisdiction of the federal court would be to destroy the "retained sovereignty of the State."[21] The Federalist United States Supreme Court required only fourteen days to hear and decide the case and issue a four to one decision commanding Georgia to submit to the authority of the federal court. The Georgia legislature passed a bill ordering that any federal agent attempting to execute the court's order should ". . . suffer death, without benefit of clergy, by being hanged."[22] (Oh, for such men today.) Eleven of the thirteen states immediately ratified the Eleventh Amendment declaring that the United States Supreme Court has no judicial power to hear a suit against a state brought by an individual. The Supreme Court had acted so unconstitutionally in the Chisholm case that it required an immediate constitutional amendment to protect state sovereignty.

The danger to state sovereignty inherent in the Federalist Supreme Court was recognized by the Virginia's Anti-Federalists, William Grayson and George Mason. While debating the proposed constitution, Grayson declared:

> This court has more power than any court under heaven. . . .
> What has it in view, unless to subvert the State governments?[23]

George Mason's words border upon prophecy:

> When we consider the nature of these courts, we must conclude that their effect and operation will be utterly to destroy the State governments; for they will be the judges how far their laws will operate. . . . The principle itself goes to the destruction of the legislation of the States, whether or not it was intended . . . I think it will destroy the State governments. . . . There are many gentlemen in the United States who think it right that we should have one great, national, consolidated government, and that it was better to bring it about slowly and imperceptibly rather than all at once. . . . To those who think that one national consolidated government is best for America, this extensive judicial authority will be agreeable. . . .[24]

Southerners of today should not find it surprising to discover that the United States Supreme Court was the first federal department to attempt to infringe upon the rights of the sovereign states!

Congress, in 1798, demonstrated its ability to overstep its delegated powers when it passed the Alien and Sedition Acts. Essentially these acts made it a federal crime "to oppose any measure or measures of the government of the United States . . . if any person shall write, print, utter, or publish. . . ." It is evident that this piece of Federalist legislation was a direct assault upon the Bill of Rights.

As we shall see, the federal Supreme Court, who was according to Federalist theory the exclusive guardian of civil liberties, not only refused to overturn these unconstitutional acts but actually engaged in enforcing them! (Who shall guard the guards?) The purpose of these acts, passed while the Federalist John Adams of Massachusetts was president, was to stifle political opposition to Adams and his monarchist, consolidationist party.

The unreliability of the federal Supreme Court as a guardian of constitutional liberty soon became very apparent. Using these acts, federal Supreme Court Justice Chase (Justice S. Chase, Federalist, who served from 1796 to 1810, not to be confused with Justice S. P. Chase, Republican, who served from 1864 to 1873) was instrumental in having James Callender, editor of the *Richmond Examiner*, indicted for sedition. Callender was tried and found guilty. Charles Holt, editor of a New Haven, Connecticut, paper was tried by federal Supreme Court Justice Bushrod Washington. Vermont Congressman Matthew Lyon published an article in the *Vermont Journal* critical of Adams. Lyon was indicted for sedition, tried before federal Supreme Court Justice William Patterson, found guilty, and sentenced to four months in jail. David Brown refused to divulge the names of his friends who shared his Anti-Federalist views. Federal Justice Chase was so enraged that he fined Brown $450 and sentenced him to jail for eighteen months. Barely a decade had passed since the writing of the Bill of Rights and those who desired a strong central federal government (call them monarchists, Federalists, or consolidationists) had already made a mockery of American civil liberties—with the aid and participation of the United States federal Supreme Court, Congress, and the president. After four years of the Federalist John Adams as president, the voters removed King John of Massachusetts and replaced him with a Southern Anti-Federalist named Thomas Jefferson. But even so great a man as Jefferson could not construct a bulwark of sufficient strength to shield the sovereign states of the South from the attacks of the consolidationists. The system was flawed not because it lacked sufficient language in its constitution but because it lacked sufficient integrity on the part of the emerging Northern numerical majority. Commercial profits and greed will never recognize the limitations imposed upon their expansion by constitutions and political philosophy.

After the ratification of the Constitution, the monarchists gradually faded into the background and were replaced by other advocates of a strong, central government. They were known at various times by different names: consolidationists, nationalists, Federalists, Radical Republicans, and currently liberals. The one thing that is common to all is that they are continually searching for and expounding new "constitutional" theories and interpretations that would enlarge the power of the central government while subordinating the states under this newly discovered federal authority.

Federal Supreme Court Justice Joseph Story's *Commentaries on the Constitution* is an example of how the consolidationists perverted the plain meaning of the Constitution and forced it to support their views. Story asserted that the federal government was a national government, supreme in its authority (i.e., sovereign), and could if necessary coerce states into submitting to national laws and policies. To negate the doctrine of state sovereignty, he asserted that (1) the people of the thirteen colonies were one people during the colonial period, (2) the people of America formed a nation by declaring their independence on July 4, 1776, (3) the state governments were organized pursuant to the instructions of the Continental Congress, (4) the preamble of the Constitution proved that "We the People" formed the federal (i.e., a national) government, and therefore, (5) sovereign authority resides in the federal government to the exclusion of the states.[25] Justice Story's perverted logic proved to be the primary source of consolidationists such as Webster and eventually Lincoln. Lincoln's astounding pronouncement that "the Union preceded the States" is rooted in the perverted logic of Federalist Justice Story.

An equally radical and absurd "constitutional" argument was advanced by Sen. William H. Seward, Republican of New York. Seward advanced the notion that the Constitution must be subservient to "higher law," especially those ideas expressed in the Declaration of Independence.

> According to this view, the Declaration of Independence was *the* founding document, established by the sovereign people of America as opposed to being an act of sovereign states. Thus the Declaration supersedes the Articles of Confederation, the state constitutions, and the United States Constitution as fundamental law. The significance of Seward's

inauspicious utilization of the Declaration of Independence is that it struck at the core of . . . the sovereignty of the states. . . . The idea of "higher law" is rooted in a natural law tradition—a tradition full of ambiguity and subject to various interpretations . . . a political movement that articulates a reasonable political ideology from a natural law basis would, indeed, possess the theoretical wherewithal to effectively challenge conflicting positive laws embodied in a written constitution.[26]

Seward's logic served the consolidationist dreams perfectly. Here at last was a method to circumvent the strict reservations of rights so plainly written into the Constitution. The consolidationists transformed the Declaration of Independence from a joint announcement of the independence of thirteen states into a document superior to the Constitution. This transformed the Union from a compact among consenting sovereign states to a national compact of individual American citizens. The South recognized the danger posed by this new school of radical consolidationism. Senator Clement C. Clay of Alabama declared:

When they get control of the Federal Government, which they vauntingly predict, the Southern States must elect between independence out of the Union or subordination within it.[27]

The destruction of the sovereign states and the merging of the American people into one giant nation-state was expressed by Seward as "one country and one Sovereign—the United States of America and the American people."[28] Repeat this Sewardism several times out loud and then repeat this: "God, King, Country." Do you hear the echoes of monarchy in the former phrase? Now repeat this: "Hitler is Germany, Germany is Hitler." Notice the similarity of tone and spirit—whether a monarch or a dictator, tyrants hate anything that would limit the exercise of their power; tyrants love strong, consolidated central governments that they control. Any government that is the exclusive judge to the limits of its own power is in effect a tyranny. John C. Calhoun foresaw this danger:

That the Government claims, and practically maintains, the right to decide in the last resort as to the extent of its powers, will scarcely be denied by anyone conversant with the political history of the country. That it also claims the right to resort to force to maintain whatever power she claims, against all opposition, is equally certain. Indeed, it is apparent, from what we daily hear, that this has become the prevailing fixed opinion of a great majority of the community. Now, I ask, what limitation can possibly be placed upon a Government claiming and exercising such rights? And, if none can be, how can the separate governments of the States maintain and protect the powers reserved to them, and among others, the sovereign powers by which they ordained and established, not only their separate State constitutions and governments, but also the Constitution and Government of the United States? But, if they have no constitutional means of maintaining them against the right claimed by this Government, it necessarily follows that they hold them at its pleasure and discretion, and that all the powers of the system are in reality concentrated in it. It follows that the character of the Government has been changed, in consequence, from a Federal Republic, as it originally came from the hands of the framers, and that it has been changed into a great national consolidated Democracy.[29]

SUMMARY

The struggle between the proponents of state sovereignty and those favoring centralized Federalism would continue until the numerical majority of the North at last seized complete control of the federal government. When the Southern states seceded, the North saw its "milch cow" escaping and waged aggressive war against the South to maintain its commercial empire. The South was at last conquered and turned into a colonial province of the Yankee empire. What most Americans do not understand is that state sovereignty is the primary principle upon which the Constitutional Federal Republic was established. Our liberties and freedoms as Americans can not be guaranteed and protected without state sovereignty. Recall federal Judge Chase's words, "State Sovereignty died at Appomattox." He was right, state sovereignty died with the Confederate States of America—slain by the commercial and political interest of the Northern numerical majority. Therefore it follows that the Constitutional Federal Republic of the United States, a government based upon the principle of the consent of the governed, also died at Appomattox. It then again becomes painfully clear that the current, centralized, federal government is an unconstitutional, unauthorized, illegitimate *de facto* government founded not upon a compact among consenting sovereign states but upon the harsh and cruel fact of conquest and maintained by military force and coercion. It is the task of Southern Nationalists and all true conservatives to use the most efficient political methods possible to return this country to its original form of government—a constitutional federal republic of sovereign states.

William Owen, Georgia. Owen was fifteen years old when he entered Confederate service. From the way he holds his weapon and from the placement of his accouterments, he must have still been a raw recruit when this photograph was taken. (Image courtesy of Rick Formby, Gadsen, Alabama)

CHAPTER 10

New Unreconstructed
Southerners

That the Southern people literally were put to the torture is
vaguely understood, but even historians have shrunk from
the unhappy task of showing us the torture chambers.[1]

Claude G. Bowers

INTRODUCTORY COMMENTS

In the last five chapters we have demonstrated that the Southern people have a moral and legal right to be free. We reviewed
the origins of the political philosophy on which the Original Constitutional Republic was based. We observed that from the very beginning of that government there was a conflict between the
Northern and Southern cultures. We saw that through various
means the Northern element finally accomplished its primary
purpose of destroying the constitutional limits on the power of the
central government. The current federal government is now controlled by Northern liberals and their Southern Scalawag lackeys.

Following the war came the second phase of the Northern attack
against the Southern people—Reconstruction. This action was a
deliberate attempt to remake the Southern people so that they
would conform to the Yankee standard. The attempt continues today as we see the national media proclaiming the wonders of some
"New South" politician every five or ten years. As we might expect,
these New South (Scalawag) idols of the liberal media all parrot
the liberal, Northern party line.

Today, a new type of Unreconstructed Southerner is emerging in
the South. This individual, more than at any time since the war, refuses to apologize for the war and has become aggressive in his demand that "Southerners have rights too!" Though it may at times be
oh so difficult to discern—there is a hint of nationalism in his voice!

237

The New Unreconstructed Southerner

During the military phase of the War for Southern Independence, outspoken Yankee political leaders had already announced their intentions to remake the Southern people into a mass that would be acceptable to the conquering Yankee. Immediately after the close of the military phase of the war, and in the occupied territories prior to the end of the military phase, Northern politicians in conjunction with Southern Scalawags positioned themselves to begin the remaking of Southern society and its people. The Northern radicals and their Southern lackeys were confident that with the aid of Federal bayonets and the blessings of the Northern-controlled Congress, they would soon enjoy complete success. Thus the people of the South were subjected to the cruelest peace ever inflicted upon a nation conquered by the United States. The North prefers to disguise its crimes by referring to this period as Reconstruction. In reality it was a cruel, scandalous, and criminal oppression of an erstwhile free people!

Led by men such as Thaddeus Stevens, the Northern powers declared that they would turn Mississippi (and by inference the entire South) into a "frog pond."[2] The North viewed the war as an opportunity to punish the South and vowed that the Southern states would be treated as "conquered provinces" which would be forced to "eat the fruit of foul rebellion."[3] Thaddeus Stevens had a clear view of how to manage Reconstruction:

> Hang the leaders—crush the South—arm the Negroes— confiscate the land. . . . Our generals have a sword in one hand and shackles in the other. . . . The South must be punished under the rules of war, its land confiscated. . . . These offending States were out of the Union and in the role of a belligerent nation to be dealt with by the laws of war and conquest.[4]

Claude Bowers documented these facts in his book *The Tragic Era*. He described the condition in Louisiana during Reconstruction as ". . . Ruin everywhere—enforced by Federal marshals backed if need be by Federal soldiers."[5] The more things change, the more they remain the same!

Albion W. Tourgee, a former Carpetbagger, admitted the failure of Reconstruction in his book, *A Fool's Errand*. He came South to overthrow the supposedly deplorable social conditions. He imagined it would be done by mass emigration from the North

and by settlement of large numbers of Yankee soldiers in the conquered states. He thought that the only way to prevent a future
generation of Southerners from attempting to re-assert their independence was by rebuilding the Southern states

> . . . from the very ground-sill . . . a thorough change in the
> tone and bent of the people. How much prospect there is of
> such a change being wrought by the spontaneous action of the
> Southern people, I do not know; I fear, not much. . . . what
> the subjugated section most required was Northern capital,
> Northern energy, and Northern men to put it again on the
> high road. . . .[6]

At last, the Fool was forced to admit the differences between the
Northern and the Southern peoples:

> The North and the South are simply convenient names for
> two distinct, hostile, and irreconcilable ideas,—two civiliza-
> tions they are sometimes called, especially at the South. At the
> North there is somewhat more of intellectual arrogance; and
> we are apt to speak of the one as civilization, and of the other
> as a species of barbarism. These two must always be in conflict
> until the one prevails, and the other falls. To uproot the one,
> and plant the other in its stead, . . . We tried to superimpose
> the idea of the North, upon the South. . . . So we tried to build
> up communities there which should be identical in thought,
> sentiment, growth, and development, with those of the North.
> It was A FOOL'S ERRAND.[7]

Perhaps the most telling line in the book is Tourgee's announcement of the then and current Yankee attitude regarding the
Southern people:

> The sick man cannot cure himself. The South will never
> purge itself of the evils which affect it.[8]

Grady McWhiney, in *Cracker Culture: Celtic Ways in the Old South*,
tells of an Englishman who, prior to the war, stated that there was
nothing Northerners "hate with so deep a hatred" as Southerners,
and that Northern journalists spoke of the South as the home of
the "ignorant, illiterate, and barbarian"—a region that "has already sunk three centuries back toward the age of barbarism."
The leisure-oriented, agrarian society of the South was the very
antithesis of the money-grubbing, materialistic Northern lifestyle.

For decades prior to the War for Southern Independence, the Northern mind had been trained to demean the worth of the Southerner as an individual, not just Southern society but the Southerner as a human being—as a person of less value than his Northern counterpart—as a sub-human who desperately needed salvation by conversion to the Yankee gospel of progress. Little wonder then that the modern world should have been introduced to the cruel and inhuman concept of total war not by rampaging Nazis but by the heartless brigades of Abraham Lincoln's army of Northern aggression and occupation.

The Yankee's first experiment with social engineering left an indelible mark upon Southern society. For years after the termination of military activities, the Southern people were forced to tolerate strangers in their midst who were determined to remake the South according to the Yankee image. After suffering military defeat, they were forced to tolerate military occupation and were required to stand aside while others with little or no qualifications were raised to positions of absolute power over their society. Unfortunately, each subsequent generation of Southerners has been forced to watch as missionaries of the Yankee gospel of liberal progress and local Scalawags have attempted to remake the "Old South" into a "New South" more in keeping with the Yankee image of what it should be. The Yankee mind has a fixation on social engineering or, as Admiral Semmes stated, "The Yankee is compelled to toil to make the world go around." This deliberate attempt of the North to remake Southern society after its own image led to the development of a group of people in the South known as "unreconstructed Southerners."

Originally, an unreconstructed Southerner was an individual who refused to accept a pardon. The pardon was offered by the United States to anyone who would renounce prior allegiance and swear new allegiance to the United States government. The response of many Southerners can be heard in the words of a former Confederate soldier. When a friend inquired of him if he had asked the Yankees for a pardon, he curtly replied, "Why should I ask them for a pardon when I haven't pardoned them yet!" These early unreconstructed Southerners represented the soldier class who had experienced the hardships of war, knew first-hand the principles for which they had fought, and retained their loyalty to those principles. To them it was not a "lost cause," but the right cause.

The writings of the Southern Apologia is an example of this tradition at its best. Men such as Jefferson Davis, Edward Pollard, Albert Taylor Bledsoe, R. L. Dabney, and Raphael Semmes turned out great works in an effort to justify the South's efforts to defend itself in the War for Southern Independence. The purpose of their work was to show that the Southern people had a legitimate right to self-determination and independence. Their cause was just, and for their allegiance to it they offered no apology and sought no pardon. They wrote about the past and did not try to project into the future. Being in the position of an occupied people, they could not afford to incur the wrath of the occupying forces.

Some Southerners, such as Gen. P. G. T. Beauregard, would voice their secret desire to renew the struggle:

> Would that I could have said to [my soldiers], resist, and hang out our banners on the outer wall etc! but the day of retribution has not yet come when we shall be able to satiate our spirit of revenge on those fanatics and radicals of the North. Whenever it does, we shall make them drink of the poisoned chalice to the very dregs . . . maybe a counter-revolution would be necessary. . . .[9]

But the reality of military occupation and political domination would soon bring even the strongest Southern Nationalist back to the real world. At most, Southerners could only concentrate on restoring some semblance of order to the local level. Grand strategy had to be left to generations yet to come.

The relationship between the conqueror and the conquered can be very deceptive. On the surface there is an uneasy calm. This "detente" serves both parties. The conqueror is required to expend less resources to maintain control, and the conquered people are allowed to put their lives back together and to go on with living. The new social order is established, though by its very nature it denies the basic right of all people—the right to a government established by the free and unfettered consent of the governed. The casual observer viewing from the victor's perspective will assume that the people are content with the new order and are busy going about the business of reconstructing their lives. After the first few years, the awkward adjustments required to break in a new government will have been completed and the citizens will give every indication of accepting the new order. They will obey the laws, rules, and regulations established by the official government and generally will conduct themselves as loyal subjects. Pacification will be a success!

The prior paragraph is a thumbnail sketch of the results of the invasion, defeat, and occupation of the erstwhile free people of Eastern Europe. The Russian conqueror enforced his will upon the people of the Baltic nations who were forced to accept a new order with a new government which was required to do the bidding of its master in faraway Moscow. The people, seeing the utter futility of further military resistance, accepted the new order and began the long and arduous task of rebuilding their lives. Seemingly, they accepted the government which ruled them. Yet, would anyone today deny that these same people and their descendants are still far removed from being loyal citizens of the Soviet Union? [Since the publication of the first edition of this book, not only have the Baltic nations succeeded in their secession from the Soviet Union, but the perpetual union of the Soviet republics is no more! *Three cheers for secession!*] Even though from 1945 to as late as 1985 it appeared that these people were securely within the Soviet Bloc, it is now evident from the wave of discontent, protest, and secession that they were far from being pacified. Just because they were forced to accept the new order is no reason to presume that the new order was legitimate and should or will remain in power. The necessity of the moment forced them to accept the new order quietly, but they remained unreconstructed in their hearts. When the moment was right, they moved from being merely unreconstructed to being openly nationalistic.

What does this have to do with the modern South? Just as the Baltic peoples, Southerners too were invaded, and their legitimate governments were replaced with a new order that would do the bidding of its masters in a faraway city. Just as the Baltic peoples, Southerners were forced by the necessity of the moment to accept this new order. But unlike the Baltic nations, the South has been occupied beyond living memory. The effects of the conqueror's propaganda are so pervasive that the lies have been accepted unquestioningly by latter-day Southerners. But acceptance can bestow legitimacy upon a government only if it flows from the free and unfettered consent of the governed. Enter the modern unreconstructed Southerner—the Southern Nationalist.

The South still has its share of traditional unreconstructed Southerners. They usually fall into two groups: (1) the closet Confederates:
they are proud of their ancestry, they love to study the "Civil War,"
but they don't do anything that might call public attention to the
cause; and (2) the battlefield junkies: they love to read and study
about the war, but not to the point of appearing politically motivated.
In a word, these Southerners have been pacified. To be sure, there is
nothing wrong with being proud of one's ancestors or loving to study
about the war, or any other such activity. But when the current condition of the South is examined we discover the following facts:

A. The South is the poorest region of the nation.

B. The South has been locked into its poor economic position
   since it lost the War for Southern Independence.

C. The Southern people do not have the same rights as citizens
   of other states regarding the establishment of legitimate
   voter qualifications.

D. The schools of the South suffer to a far greater extent than
   those of other regions from federal court orders and enforced busing.

E. Traditional Southern conservatives are not allowed representation on the United States Supreme Court.

F. Southern natural resources have been used to benefit large
   businesses outside of the South without proper compensation or concern for the Southern environment.

G. Symbols of the Southern nation, such as the playing of
   "Dixie" and the display of the Confederate flag, have been
   banned by the federal courts and local Scalawag politicians.

H. Neither national political party represents the aspirations
   and concerns of the average middle-class Southerner.

When confronted with the reality of the current social, economic, and political domination of the South, contemporary
Southerners must make one of three choices:

1.

Join the New South politicians who have embraced the Northern
liberal political philosophy and proclaim that all the evils of the
South will be cured once it has atoned for its sins and followed the
Yankee's example of material and social progress.

2.

Deny or ignore the economic and political disparity between the South and the other sections of the United States.

3.

Become actively involved in diverse methods and efforts to promote the Southern cause (the Southern national appeal).

Across the South, more and more Southerners are beginning to choose the last option. Their activities are usually limited to the local level, but even in these areas it is possible to detect a resurgence of pride in the South. This resurgence in Southern pride is greatly feared by the Northern liberal and his Southern Scalawag counterpart because national pride strikes at the heart of liberal philosophy—guilt.

Modern liberals are driven by a sense of guilt. When they see starving blacks in Marxist Africa, they feel guilty. They feel that somehow African poverty and suffering is their fault or, to be more exact, that it is the fault of Western Civilization of which they are a part; therefore they feel responsible for that starvation half a world away. Thus every social inequity or accident of nature is somehow translated in their minds as another indictment of Western Civilization and therefore an indictment of themselves. To atone for their sins, liberals are compelled to engage in various attempts to resolve the problems of humanity. Now this in and of itself—while bizarre—is not bad as long as the liberals are using their liberty, time, and money to further their personal need for social atonement. But another tenet of liberal philosophy is that one cannot trust the individual to respond correctly to social needs, but must rely on an overseer in the form of a large government to enforce the needs of society. In other words, liberals have very conveniently removed the necessity of using their liberty, time, and money to atone for their perceived sins and have transferred that responsibility to the middle-class taxpayer. Using the police power of the government, liberals can rob the middle class of its rightful property and transfer it to the so-called oppressed people of the world.

The liberals make use of the sense of guilt to convince weak politicians to transfer the property of the middle class to the underprivileged. This is done in much the same way that the Radical Republicans would rouse public opinion against the South by waving the "bloody shirt" and reminding Northern voters that Southerners (and therefore Democrats) killed their sons during the war. If justification is needed for racial quotas and affirmative action, all the liberals need to do is to invoke this sense of guilt by reminding us Southerners that (according to liberal doctrine) it is our fault that "they" (whatever minority that is in vogue at that time) are so far behind. We must, therefore, accept this new piece of social engineering as part of our atonement for the sins of our past.

Today, the world has a new breed of Southerners to deal with. They are different from those who have gone before. They do not yet make up a majority or even a numerically large segment of our society. However, their potential to do mischief to the ruling Yankee order is tremendous. These new unreconstructed Southerners are better described as Southern Nationalists. This is not to say, however, that they have as yet progressed as far as the Baltic people who are demanding independence for their countries. The Southern Nationalists have rejected the conqueror's myth that the South was wrong and that we are better off as a result of the South's defeat. The new unreconstructed Southerners, or more appropriately Southern Nationalists, are not defined by their membership in a splinter political party. They may be Republicans, Democrats, or Independents. The important distinction is that their loyalty is to their peoples' rights not to a political party. Southern Nationalists cover the entire spectrum of pro-South political thought.

There are those who merely want to improve the standing of the middle-class Southerners in the accepted political parties as well as those who have declared "a plague on both your houses" as far as either of the political parties is concerned. There is a new militancy evident in the South. Southerners are beginning to question their second-class status. They are starting to re-examine with a critical eye the Yankee myth of history and are comparing it to the writings of their own people. The Southern Nationalists are challenging this ever-weakening, ever-decaying Northern liberal-dominated nation to assure us our equality within the nation or to face a new demand for the freedom and independence of the Southern nation!

Silas M. Bunn, Company E, Sixty-Second Alabama Volunteer Infantry, Talladega, Alabama. Bunn entered Confederate service just seven months after his older brother, Marcus, was killed in action. (Image courtesy of Roy Bunn, Roanoke, Alabama)

CHAPTER 11

Equality of Opportunity

They [the people of a Democracy] want equality in freedom, and if they cannot have that, they still want equality in slavery.[1]

Alexis de Tocqueville

INTRODUCTORY COMMENTS

Strange as it may seem, some people would rather live in a slave-like condition of equality rather than live free in a condition of inequality! In the late 1980s, while watching a newscast from the Soviet Union, we heard a Soviet citizen complaining that, even though she liked the new goods that free market workers were providing and she acknowledged that the old system was failing to provide such goods, she still complained that the free market workers were "getting rich." Her solution was that "everyone should be paid equally." Somehow she never realized that it is the inequality in a free society that provides the goods and services we enjoy.

The Northern liberals are now demanding that the central government provide equality of results. No longer satisfied with the concept of equality of opportunity, modern liberals, like the citizen of the former Soviet Union, are now preparing to reduce all to the equality of slavery. This concept, equality of results, is in direct opposition to the traditional individualistic belief of our Southern heritage. This concept has given us racial quotas, affirmative action, minority set-asides, busing, ad nauseam.

In the following chapter we will outline the Southern attitude toward the concept of "equality" as it relates to the individual and to the government. In a phrase, our attitude can be summed up as "equality for all—privilege for none."

Equality of Opportunity

"We hold these truths to be self evident, that all men are created equal."[2] No single phrase in American history contains as much hope and promise and, at the same time, has caused so much anger, frustration, and despair! To promise an entire population that all will be equal (i.e., enjoy equal wealth, influence, services received, etc.) is to guarantee a communal existence. Such a thought has always been and continues to be anathema to the individualistic heritage of the South. What then did Thomas Jefferson mean when he penned this "self-evident" phrase?

In the early days of the American Republic, the term referred to equality before God and the law. It was an open attack against the then-prevalent concept of the divine right of kings. Later in the American setting, it came to mean equality of opportunity (i.e., that no one should be arbitrarily barred from the rights protected by law or from access to public services). In short, it was and still is good public policy to encourage all to compete in the market place because such free enterprise leads to lower prices and to better quality of goods and services.[3]

Jefferson did not mean that all people were endowed with the same qualities, characteristics, and talents. As part of the American aristocracy, he knew that some people possessed skills and talents superior to others. But this fact did not change their standing before God or the law. The concept of equality encourages and protects liberty.

Our modern-day liberals have perverted the original concept of equality of opportunity into their current doctrine of equality of result (i.e., absolute equality similar to that found in a communal setting). Contrast the liberal's view with Milton Friedman's:

> Neither equality before God nor equality of opportunity presented any conflict with liberty. . . . Equality of outcome is in clear conflict with liberty.[4]

Alexis de Tocqueville, in *Democracy in America*, noted the danger posed to liberty by the uncontrolled lust for equality:

> The passion for equality seeps into every corner of the human heart, . . . It is no use telling them that by this blind surrender to an exclusive passion [equality] they are compromising their dearest interest. It is no use pointing out that freedom is slipping from their grasp. . . .[5]

Modern liberals have plagued Southern society with innumerable sociological schemes and experiments to achieve their goal of human equality. The rights and liberties of the Southern people have been the preferred sacrifice to appease the wrath of the gods of liberalism. We have been forced to endure such insults as busing, racial quotas, minority set-asides, affirmative action plans, reverse discrimination, and a discriminatory South-only Voting Rights Act, just to name a few. All this (and so much more that space does not allow its printing) in the name of human equality, and still we are no closer to appeasing the gods of Yankee liberalism than when our political leaders first began their groveling. Do you suppose it is time we try something a little more forceful?

To understand why equality of results is such a strong tenet of the religion of liberalism, we must first understand the chief motivating spiritual force of liberalism—guilt! Liberals are driven by an illogical sense of guilt that will not allow them to leave well enough alone, to mind their own business, or even to realize that, although evil exists and they are right to feel sympathy for its victims, they don't understand everything about it, and that even if they did they do not have the means to correct it. How often have we heard Southerners bitterly and vainly complaining to the Yankee press that all they want is to be "left alone." Yet, to liberal minds this is unacceptable; if they perceive a social problem, then they are guilt-ridden until a solution acceptable to the Yankee mind has been found and enforced. During the War for Southern Independence, Adm. Raphael Semmes of the CSS *Alabama* noted that the Yankee is obsessed with the compulsion to "toil to make the world go around." If liberals see that blacks are per capita poorer than whites, then they feel guilty. If more blacks than whites are on death row, then liberals are overcome by guilt. If people in the underdeveloped parts of the world are starving, liberals assume that surely "we" are to blame. When viewing the reality of the human experience, they realize that life is not fair. They feel guilty and determine that it is "our" fault, and therefore "we owe it to these people" to attempt to relieve the suffering they feel "we" have caused. Some authors have considered this sense of guilt to be a typically Anglo/Saxon (English—and therefore Yankee) attitude as opposed to a Celtic (Welsh, Scottish, and Irish—and therefore Southern) attitude. These authors treat this as a characteristic transmitted via the predominant culture.[6] Guilt is the motivating factor of liberalism. To abate their sense of guilt, liberals can justify any amount of taxes, court orders, affirmative action programs, busing, ad nauseam! American liberals are willing to spend the last dollar belonging to the middle class to abate their sense of guilt. From their world view, the middle class is the universal cause of humanity's woes, so why should liberals concern themselves when the villain (the middle class, especially the Southern middle class) begins to groan under the heavy burden laid upon them by their liberal taskmasters? After all, according to the liberals, those responsible are only repaying the underprivileged for all the crimes they and their ancestors have committed against them.

Ever since the end of the military phase of the War for Southern Independence, the South has been made to feel the stern rod in the hand of its liberal taskmasters. To add insult to injury, the Southern economy, which has never recovered from the war and Reconstruction, has been heavily taxed to maintain these inefficient, pork-barrel, bureaucratic boondoggles.

When the sovereign communities in each of the Southern states regain control of their destiny and begin once again to assert and exercise their legitimate political authority, they must be guided by the principle of equality of opportunity. They shall jealously guard the free entry into the market place and maintain strict scrutiny of equality before the law. But they shall never again allow the force of government to enforce equality of results to the detriment of individual liberty and property rights.

When Mahatma Gandhi, a Hindu, was pressed by certain Moslems to reserve a specific number of jobs for minorities regardless of their qualifications, he objected. Gandhi, who was probably this century's purest (if not only) humanitarian spirit, declared his stand on quotas thusly:

> For administration to be efficient it must be in the hands of the fittest. There should certainly be no favoritism. If we want five engineers we must not take one from each community but we must take the fittest five even if they were all Mussulmans or all Parsis. . . . those who aspire to occupy responsible posts in the government of the country can only do so if they pass the required test.[7]

Gandhi made this decision based not just on pure utility but out of deep insight. He knew what too many liberals refuse to recognize—arbitrary and capricious discrimination (even in the name of good) leads to resentment as better qualified (or for that matter less qualified) members are barred from entry into the market place. When people are denied the opportunity to compete, resentment builds, and hatred encourages strife. Instead of improving relations between two divergent elements of society, government has made matters worse, even to the point of causing open violence! The South will not make this mistake. Equality of opportunity, equality before the law, and especially a realization that all people stand as equals before God are all important aspects of the Southern National political philosophy. (The latter is not meant as a theological statement but only to stress the point that all people are equally valuable and therefore not "expendable" from an ethical perspective). Results in each person's life must depend upon the individual's personal talents, skill, motivation, and intelligence.

The Southern people, who have a long tradition of individual responsibility, also have a tradition of opposition to governmentally enforced equality of results. John C. Calhoun declared:

> But to go further, and make equality of condition essential to liberty, would be to destroy both liberty and progress. . . . It is, indeed, this inequality of condition between the front and rear ranks, in the march of progress, which gives so strong an impulse to the former to maintain their position, and to the latter to press forward into their files. This gives to progress its greatest impulse. To force the front rank back to the rear, or attempt to push forward the rear into line with the front, by the interposition of the government, would put an end to the impulse, and effectually arrest the march of progress.[8]

Legitimate Voting Qualifications

The liberal concept of one man-one vote, or universal franchise, is so deeply entrenched in the liberal dogma of the Yankee government that very few are willing to challenge its legitimacy. This is especially true in the South. Here we are faced with the danger of being labeled as a society attempting to deny the franchise permanently on the basis of race. Where will anyone find a popular politician who is willing to confront charges of racism and bigotry just to promote an improvement in the quality of the electorate?

So here, in our beloved South, the past holds the present hostage to the detriment of the future!

The necessity of ethical government, led by the most able representatives chosen from society, demands an honest and courageous assessment of voting qualifications. We have no doubt that this issue will be the one point most aggressively attacked by the enemies of our country, all hysterically waving the bloody shirt of racism, as if this scare tactic will frighten off yet another generation of Southerners; but this time we are not running!

John Stuart Mill (1806-1873), an English defender of civil liberties, an early (1865) champion of women's suffrage, and author of *On Liberty* (1859) and *Representative Government* (1861), is as far removed from "racism" as the North is from the South. Yet, in Mill we find a vocal proponent of requiring specific qualifications prior to the granting of the franchise. Mill believed that voting was a privilege to be earned and to be held as opposed to being a natural right devolving upon all humanity regardless of condition. Mill drew an implied contrast between representative governments and mob rule that results within an unqualified democracy. Bread and circuses were not Mill's idea of "good government."

The current generation of Southerners has witnessed a continuing reduction of voting qualifications, a concurrent decrease in the percentage of qualified voters who actually cast ballots, and a decline of the quality and ethical standards of government. Should any thinking person find this unusual? The officeholders in a democracy represent the average plus one of the electorate. If the majority of the voters have an eighth-grade education, then the average officeholder will represent the interest, social values, and aspirations of that majority. The purpose of the electoral system is to force officeholders to answer to the public. This has always been essential in a free society, but its importance has dramatically increased in our modern technological society. Since it requires little or no qualifications for voting, the Southern electoral process has been relegated to virtual organized mob rule whereby the election is guaranteed to the politician who can promise the "mostest to the mostest." We must move away from blind faith in the liberal theology of one man-one vote. Voting is the means by which citizens control their elected officials. Those who exercise this privilege must first earn it.

First Qualification for Voting

What then are the reasonable qualifications for voting that we shall adopt for our country? The first requirement is that all who would seek the privilege must be able to read, to write, and to demonstrate certain elementary knowledge of history, geography, and mathematics. Quoting from a non-Southern and non-racist source, we see that Mill would require

> . . . it as wholly inadmissible that any person should participate in the suffrage without being able to read, write, and I will add, perform the common operations of arithmetic. . . . people would no more think of giving the suffrage to a man who could not read, than of giving it to a child who could not speak; and it would not be society that would exclude him, but his own laziness. When society has not performed its duty, by rendering this amount of instruction accessible to all, there is some hardship in the case, but this is a hardship that ought to be borne. . . . No one but those in whom an á priori theory has silenced common sense will maintain that power over others, over the whole community, should be imparted to people who have not acquired the commonest and most essential requisites for taking care of themselves. . . . It would be eminently desirable that other things besides reading, writing and arithmetic could be made necessary to the suffrage; that some knowledge of the conformation of the earth, its natural and political divisions, the elements of general history and of the history and institutions of their own country, could be required from all electors. . . . [A]fter a few years it would exclude none but those who cared so little for the privilege, that their vote, if given, would not in general be an indication of any real political opinion.[9]

Second Qualification for Voting

The second requirement is that being a taxpayer should be a prerequisite to voting. Mill stressed the point that those who are required to pay the taxes will make a more intelligent and thoughtful decision as to whom they put in charge of the tax-collecting authority. Mill also emphasized that he did not consider an indirect or easy tax to be sufficient to fulfill this requirement. In other words, a sales tax or payroll tax that is paid in what amounts to easy installments will not affect the average citizens enough to make them conscious of the fact that their government is depriving them of their property. This point is easy to demonstrate by considering the current federal income tax. The average taxpayer never realizes how much money he has paid in taxes until around April the fifteenth when he finally gets around to filing his income tax statement. Note that when the taxpayer files a form, the money has already been oh-so-gently removed from his pocket by the federal tax collector. Other than uttering a momentary groan, the taxpayer never really displays much resistance to this annual fleecing. But what would happen if all citizens were required to pay their taxes in one lump sum at the end of the year? How long would it take for the recall petitions to be filed? How long would it be before we had a Congress that was willing to cut taxes, reduce spending, and decrease the size of an overgrown federal bureaucracy? Again quoting from Mill,

> It is also important, that the assembly which votes the taxes, either general or local, should be elected exclusively by those who pay something towards the taxes imposed. Those who pay no taxes, disposing by their votes of other people's money, have every motive to be lavish and none to economize. As far as money matters are concerned, any power of voting possessed by them is a violation of the fundamental principle of free government; . . . It amounts to allowing them to put their hands into other people's pockets for any purpose which they think fit to call a public one . . . the indirect taxes. . . . But this mode of defraying a share of the public expenses is hardly felt: the payer, unless a person of education and reflection, does not identify his interest with a low scale of public expenditure as closely as when money for its support is demanded directly from himself; . . . It would be better that a direct tax, in the simple form of a capitation, should be levied on every grown person in the community; or that every such person should be admitted an elector on allowing himself to be rated extra ordiem to the assessed taxes; or that a small annual payment, rising and falling with the gross expenditure of the country, should be required from every registered elector; that so everyone might feel that the money which he assisted in voting was partly his own, and that he was interested in keeping down its amount.[10]

Third Qualification for Voting

The third requirement is that those who support their existence with relief (i.e., welfare, public housing, etc.) should not be allowed to exercise the privilege of voting. Again let us look to Mill:

> I regard it as required by first principles, that the receipt of parish relief should be a peremptory disqualification for the franchise. He who cannot by his labour suffice for his own support has no claim to the privilege of helping himself to the money of others. By becoming dependent on the remaining members of the community for actual subsistence, he abdicates his claim to equal rights with them in other respects. Those to whom he is indebted for the continuance of his very existence may justly claim the exclusive management of those common concerns, to which he now brings nothing, or less than he takes away. As a condition of the franchise, a term should be fixed, say five years previous to the registry, during which the applicant's name has not been on the parish books as a recipient of relief.[11]

Fourth Qualification for Voting

Mill would also deny the privilege of voting to those who take advantage of bankruptcy and thereby shift their personal burden upon society who must, through higher prices, insurance rates, and lending rates, finance another's failure.

> To be certified bankrupt, or to have taken the benefit of the Insolvent Act should disqualify for the franchise until the person has paid his debts or at least proved that he is not now, and has not for some long period been, dependent on eleemosynary support.[12]

The basic principle of the franchise is that citizens should not be disqualified except through their own fault, and no arbitrary barriers should be established by which any person is permanently excluded. The privilege must be open to all who are willing to earn it.

> It is not useful, but hurtful, that the constitution of the country should declare ignorance to be entitled to as much political power as knowledge. . . . Men, as well as women, do not need political rights in order that they may govern, but in order that they may not be misgoverned.[13]

The sovereign community, through its representatives within each state, is the only authoritative source for establishing acceptable qualifications for voting. The only restraint that can legitimately be placed upon the sovereign community is that it must maintain a Republican form of government within its state (U.S. Constitution, Article IV, Section 4).

Some will protest that we are "repealing" the Voting Rights Act; this is not true! You do not repeal a fraud; you correct it. You do not recall a tyrant; you remove him. The same is true with the so-called Voting Rights Act. The Voting Rights Act, as with all other Reconstruction legislation (see Chapter VI), must be annulled to restore the balance between the federal and state governments. These Reconstruction acts violate the principle of the consent of the governed within each of the sovereign communities of the South, and therefore they were invalid in their inception and are discriminatory in their enforcement. Thus, the South must use its political strength to terminate this illegitimate use of governmental force. The federal government does not have the right to deny the sovereign community the right to establish legitimate, non-arbitrary voting qualification!

CHAPTER 12

Life, Liberty, and the Pursuit of Happiness

New England, which had been too conscientious to defend the national honor in the war with Great Britain, poured out almost her whole population to aid the extermination of a people. . . .[1]

Edward A. Pollard

INTRODUCTORY COMMENTS

The Southern people have always taken the lead in the military defense of the United States. The nation knew that "when the chips were down" Southern "rednecks" could always be counted on to take up arms and defend our "reunited" country. Southerners were shocked to see their heritage slandered in the Northern press and by official United States government publications during the "Great War" (World War I). This action led the Sons of Confederate Veterans to issue *The Gray Book* shortly after the end of that conflict and again after World War II.

During the Korean War, seventy-eight Congressional Medals of Honor were awarded. Of these, thirty-two were given to Southerners. There were only three citizens from the city of New York who received this high honor, and one of the three had recently moved to the city from the South. This situation is not unusual. During the War of 1812, the North provided 58,552 soldiers to the war effort, while the South gave 96,812. During the war with Mexico, the North furnished only 23,054 soldiers, while the South provided 43,630.

In return for its willingness to serve the flag of the "reunited" nation, the South asks only to be left alone to enjoy life, liberty, and the pursuit of happiness. Unfortunately, the United States government has answered in the negative.

257

Cadet Thomas G. Jefferson of Amelia County, Virginia, a collateral descendant of President Thomas Jefferson. As a cadet at Virginia Military Institute, Jefferson took part in the Battle of New Market in which the boys of VMI made history by their rout of veteran United States troops. Cadet Jefferson was wounded during the charge of cadets and died three days later in the arms of a comrade; he was seventeen years young. Deo Vindice![13] (Image courtesy of the Virginia Military Institute Archives, Lexington, Virginia)

Life

The Declaration of Independence demonstrates the American belief that government should be based upon the consent of the governed. The Founding Fathers believed that government should be an agent of the people. They also knew that any government would possess the tendency to usurp the freedom and liberty that naturally belongs to the people. Thomas Jefferson thought that the best government was one of limited powers that left the people alone and that allowed them to work out their own destiny without undue meddling. Jefferson stated that it was the duty of government to allow the development of life, liberty, and the pursuit of happiness.[2]

How have the people of the South been treated by their government in respect to their life, liberty, and pursuit of happiness?

In the Declaration of Independence, Jefferson made it clear that a legitimate government must accept the fact that the life of its citizens is an endowment from God. The right to life was given to all men [i.e., people] by their Creator, and therefore must not be arbitrarily taken from them by government. This is an accepted fact of our American political philosophy. We believe that we must not give our support to any form of government which would arbitrarily deny anyone the right to life.

The Constitution, as written by the Founding Fathers, had many features that were designed to protect life. The requirement for a writ of *habeas corpus*, grand jury indictment for capital cases, and the right of speedy and public trials was all designed to protect life.

The Founding Fathers and the people of the South have always held that:

1. Government cannot on its own volition take away a person's life; and
2. Government must act in such a way as not to endanger the lives of its citizens. In the discharge of its function, government must act to protect the lives of the people so as not to have them endangered from external (enemy) powers.

We are not charging the government with wanton killing of Americans. So far we are safe from that form of intimidation. But the hands of the Northern liberal establishment are far from clean. Upon their hands is the blood of over one hundred thousand military youth murdered by the system of government controlled by Northern liberals. Only the commercial interests of the North benefitted from the last two no-win wars this country has fought. Our soldiers were ordered to go halfway around the globe to fight in the defense of freedom, but under no circumstance were they to win. Yes, "our" government is guilty of crimes against the "right to life" as defined by Jefferson. A look at recent history will reveal how our government has done this to our military personnel.

In both the Korean and Vietnamese conflicts, young Americans were sent to wage war—to fight and to die—but not to win. When any government makes that type of demand on its citizens, it is just as guilty of the destruction of their right to life as if it had taken those same citizens away from their home and shot them without benefit of a fair trial.

The Founding Fathers established a government that respected the sanctity of human life. They knew that if a government loses this respect for life, it loses its moral right to govern. It is not immoral for a country to go to war to defend itself, provided it fights to win. Citizens have a duty to defend their country if it is engaged in a morally defensible war. If the government constantly displays a tendency to undermine the well-being of its citizen-soldiers, then that government has no right to rule nor should it expect its people to give it their continued support. Consider the recent history of the liberal Northern government. Americans expect that when we go to war we will fight to win. This is a reasonable assumption because we are a nation of people who stand as equals before the law. The government has the duty to do all within its power to protect the lives of its citizens. If the political leadership of the nation requires its citizens to fight a war for any reason other than to win, then those politicians are toying with the lives of the country's citizens. This is contrary to the purpose of government and as such constitutes an illegal act.

It would be reasonable to presume that a "democratic" government would not involve its citizens in a war in which it allows an unfair advantage to the enemy, such as safe havens from which to draw supplies and mass troops for attack. The reason it should not do so is because such action allows the enemy to increase his ability to kill its citizen-soldiers. This is contrary to the purpose of a "democratic" government, which is to do all within its power to protect the lives of its citizens. Too often in the recent past, our government has failed its duty to do all within its power to protect the lives of its citizen-soldiers.

With the failure of the armies of the South at the close of the War for Southern Independence, the original form of government, with its natural check on the abuse of federal power was, by revolution, removed. What we now have is a centralized federal government that has assumed the right to act as its own judge of the limits of its own power.

The idea of checks and balances within the nation has been reduced to the point that it only exists within the federal government itself. As long as the three branches of the federal government (executive, legislative, and judicial) are in line, one with the other (following the same policy, be it forced busing, or no-win wars), its will is supreme and cannot be checked. This is not as it was intended by the Founding Fathers, nor was this the type of government that our nation enjoyed for the first four decades of its independence. If the federal government could be called into account or could be prevented from usurping the rights of the citizens of the states (State's Rights), there would be no such thing as forced busing, reverse discrimination, no-win wars, or a trillion-dollar national debt.

All of these examples of abuse of power by the central government are examples of just how far we have gone in the wrong direction as a nation. The "Boys in Gray" perceived that this would be the natural outcome if they lost the war. Perhaps that is why they fought so hard and so long for Southern independence.

Liberty

> ... [I]s life so dear, or peace so sweet as to be purchased at the price of chains and slavery? Forbid it Almighty God! I know not what course others may take, but as for me, give me liberty, or give me death.[3]

What is it about liberty that causes some men to prefer to suffer the pains of death than to live without it? What would make rational men such as Patrick Henry become radical and speak of dying as a martyr to freedom rather than living a dull life without liberty? As Thomas Paine has stated, "Only God knows how to put a proper price on such a commodity as liberty." Indeed, all citizens must be willing to pay for their liberty or they will surely lose it.

> The sole end for which mankind are warranted, individually or collectively, in interfering with the liberty of action of any of their number, is self-protection. That the only purpose for which power can be rightfully exercised over any member of a civilized community, against his will, is to prevent harm to others. . . . In the part which merely concerns himself, his independence is, of right, absolute. Over himself, over his own body and mind, the individual is sovereign.[4]

In the world today, true liberty as advocated by John Stuart Mill is almost as rare and unseen as the Loch Ness Monster. Even among the Western "democratic" nations, individual liberty suffers at the hands of a complex, technological, centralized society— shades of *A Brave New World*. As society becomes more complex, it demands that government control more of that society. And what is it that government controls? It controls not its own growth and power but the liberty of the individual citizens within its domain. As government becomes more powerful, the citizens lose more liberty. Once this process has started, it becomes self-perpetuating and increases in a crescendo effect, sweeping under its relentless rush that which it was established to protect and serve, the people and their liberty. As an aside, let us note here that liberty is not meant to represent the absolute right to do anything one pleases, for that would be license, not liberty. Liberty is not license. Liberty, as defined by John Locke, has its own circumscribed limits. Locke teaches us that our liberty ends where it would do harm to others. For example, I have a right to own a car. I do not have the right to drive it in such a manner as to do harm to others. Hence, liberty in a free society is liberty under the law. The law is derived and enforced by the free consent of those governed. The entire force of government vis-a-vis the individual should be directed toward maintaining the sovereignty of that individual. This is the expected action of a "just" government. To do less would stamp that government as "unjust" and therefore as a tyranny.

A "just" government as described by Jefferson is one which rules with the consent of those governed. It does not force or coerce its citizens to accept its will, but reflects the common will of the people. A just government respects the liberty of the individual. As John Stuart Mill said,

> No society in which these liberties are not, on the whole, respected, is free, whatever may be its form of government.[5]

Now let us look at the present government of the United States and see how it respects (or fails to respect) the liberty of the individual. Then we can decide if its rules and edicts deserve the consent of those governed.

One example alone will serve to show the nature of the Northern liberal government's disregard for liberty and the consent of those governed. The example of forced busing is proof enough that the government no longer respects the rights of the people. Like a nightmare on wheels, this institution makes a mockery of the concept of liberty and of the principle of government by the consent of those governed. This evil system, which is forced on Southern children to a greater extent than on Northern children, is by its very nature wrong. The federal courts forced busing upon the South claiming that it would improve education and reduce racism. After a generation of forced busing we now know that these goals have not been met and that in fact the very opposite has occurred! All of this has transpired over the objection of the Southern people and in violation of their rights and liberties. When analyzing the results and the hardships that result from this continuing Yankee social experiment, we are left unable to explain why "our" government continues to persist with these policies.

According to a two-year study done by the Dallas Independent School District, black elementary students in segregated schools showed higher academic achievement and less racial prejudice than did black students in integrated schools. (Study reported from Dallas Texas by UPI 2-25-79.)

Taking children away from the control of their parents is wrong, no matter what the objective of some social bureaucrat might be. Children are a divine trust given to parents by God. They are not property of the federal government or of its judges. Yet "our" government tells us that stealing our children will increase civil rights, and that forcing children into schools according to racial quotas will do away with the evil of segregation. They also tell us that giving special treatment to minorities will eliminate racial discrimination and produce a color-blind society. Does this remind you of Orwellian doublespeak? How could anyone believe that forcing parents to send their children to schools far away from home in a strange environment against their will (exit consent of those governed) really increases freedom and decreases prejudice? In the South, eighty to ninety percent of the white population and forty to sixty percent of the black population is opposed to forced busing. These statistics indicate that a clear-cut majority of Southerners is opposed to this nightmare. Yet "our" federal government, which now is the sole judge of its power and its use of that power, continues to force its will on the people of the South. Are we not a land of "democracy"? Are we not a "free people"? Do we not live in the "land of the free"? The simple and painful answer to each question is "No." Why should we deceive ourselves any longer? We do not control the education of our children, the federal government does. Our consent be damned. Governmental officials do as they please, while we must obey like the humble serfs of our conquering masters.

A just government is one that rules by the consent of the governed. Can we say that this government, which has given us forced busing and demanded equality for homosexuals and communists in our classrooms, is doing the will of the people of the South? If this is the will of the people, then we have a "just" government. Fellow Southerner, consider this: if the federal government is doing all this (and needless to say, it is), against the will and consent of its citizens, it has ceased to be a just government. Liberty cannot survive in such an environment. What would patriots like Patrick Henry or Thomas Jefferson say if their children were used by a government like so many guinea pigs in a grand laboratory experiment? Is this the type of country they fought for? Is this the type of country that Southerners have been so willing to die for in every war since 1865? Of course not! Rightful heirs of liberty should not accept the actions and edicts of such an unjust government. The liberal establishment does not rule by divine right. We must not allow them to be our masters any longer. All Southerners must join with that great Southerner Patrick Henry and say, "Give me liberty, or give me death." The faint of heart and the weak of faith will no doubt cry "treason," but *if we fail to be loyal to the first principles upon which this country was founded, then and only then will we have become traitors.* We must not worship the form and forget the substance from which government derives its very essence. Christians revere their Bible, not because of its form or name, but because of what it is and what it does to and for them. To love a Bible just because it is a book is idolatry, but to love the Bible because it is God's Word and because it speaks God's words, is the essence of a Christian's devotion to his God. Jesus rebuked the Pharisees because, as He said, they were like whited sepulchers, beautiful and clean on the outside, but yet inside were full of dead men's bones. With sadness in our hearts, we must report to our fellow Southerners that this "land of liberty," this "land of the free," this "constitutional republic" is like a whited sepulcher. It has the outward signs of liberty, but this is only surface appearance. Inside, it is full of dead men's bones, the remains of individual liberty murdered at the hands of a central government that admits no limits to its own power.

The Pursuit of Happiness

> Let us question the wives of senior managers in industrial corporation. The advance witnesses of life in the future. Thanks to their improved standard of living, do your husbands have more or less work to do than ten years ago? Do they have more or less time available for family life? Were an industrial organization to be content with such a low return, its output itself would be condemned.[6]

The Founding Fathers knew that people needed, for their sense of psychological equilibrium, the right to pursue a state of mind in which they would be content or happy. Nowhere in the Declaration of Independence do we find a commitment of the state to ensure everyone's "happiness," but what was required was that everyone have the right to "the pursuit of happiness."

Like Jean-Jacques Servan-Schreiber, who is quoted above, the South also questions whether happiness can be found among the sweat shops of industrialism. With its rich tradition of agrarianism, the South has long been warning the world of the dangers inherent in the loss of our relationship with the environment. The traditional South, as defended in *I'll Take My Stand*, knew that the creation of industrial wealth could not produce happiness. The Marxists have attempted to solve the problem of property and happiness by forced collectivization. This has very little appeal to traditional Southerners because of their rich heritage of individual liberty and self-reliance.

The pursuit of happiness is a valid means of expression for a free people. Indeed, today our world seems to have gone to the extreme in its efforts to find "happiness." Why should such an element of life be, apparently, so hard to realize?

One major reason happiness is so elusive in the United States is that Northern industrialism has attempted to sell happiness in little boxes of materialism. Sadly we have found out that an abundance of material things cannot in and of itself produce happiness. People can find true happiness only as they understand themselves in relation to God's world.[7]

In this age of materialism we have increasingly removed ourselves from nature. We are less identified with nature and also less able to define our proper role in nature. The more we remove ourselves from the land and lock ourselves up in the artificial environments of cities and suburbs, the more we lose sight of the divine order in the world. We have created too many artificial barriers between ourselves and our natural environment. We now find it difficult to identify happiness. We have separated ourselves from our natural environment, and, like fish out of water, we flounder helplessly as we attempt to find our proper place in this new and alien world. Our only hope is to return to our natural medium and to be refreshed by its revitalizing influence. Otherwise our work-a-day world will slowly choke us with its dull standardization.

Before the Industrial Revolution, people took much pleasure in the accomplishments of their labor. Today's wage slaves, on the other hand, endure their labor while anxiously awaiting the magical "quitting time" that will allow them to begin their real lives. Medical science has given us longer life spans, but technological industrialism has in effect shortened our lives by eight hours per working day.

Northern industrialism is a dangerous entity because it has a tendency to reduce the whole person to an abstraction.[8] This depersonalization is the result of the loss of the essence of humanity, which is everyone's sovereign individuality. Our society is increasingly becoming a machine economy, with the individual becoming no more than an adjunct of the machine.

Is it any wonder that only two parts of the person are developed in today's society? One is that part trained to aid the machine in its role of production. The other is the consuming portion. We have been conditioned to become the consuming entity of the industrial society. We provide the means of production and consumption. We are colonials (those who exist for the good of others) in our own homes.

In the beginning, industry was created to provide the needs of society. This relationship has since been reversed. Now we exist to consume manufactured goods. There is no need for quality in production because we have been told that happiness exists in having disposable items. Material goods are not made to endure. The Northern industrialist cannot allow us to buy goods that last a lifetime—this would reduce the need for production. Far from controlling production (exit the law of supply and demand), we, especially the people of the South, are at risk of becoming its slaves. Industrialism does not look to our needs; it creates a desire for certain material items and then moves to fill that artificially created "need." If a profit can be had, then the industrialist makes and markets the item. The central theme of Northern industrialism is, "If it makes a profit, produce more, advertise more, create more desire for the 'happiness' this item can bring. If it does not produce a profit, then scrap it, for it is of no value." Happiness cannot and should not be judged by such a materialistic standard.

For generations Southerners have been told to industrialize and thereby bring about a new and better world. Industrialism has been held up as a panacea for all the economic woes and ills of the South. Dutifully obedient to this "New South" gospel, Southern governors have made annual pilgrimages to the North to beg Northern industries to come down South and take advantage of its abundant labor supply, its inexpensive living conditions, its wholesome environment, and its stable society. Has industrialism produced the miracle of happiness for our people? It is true that we all want a better standard of living for our people. We also want to pursue happiness, but remember that not all that glitters is gold. We wish to see industry come to our land, but we must make an effort to humanize industry or else be faced with the prospect of being choked by its dehumanizing and environmentally destructive forces.

The heritage of Southern agrarianism speaks a warning to us about the loss of human values to industrialism and admonishes us not to live our lives as adjuncts of mindless machines. It warns us not to heed the false gospel of "progress." It tells us of the danger of leaving the land where we can commune with nature and with our Creator. It reminds us that through the natural world we can renew our lives and enrich our humanity. We are reminded that we need to maintain the spiritual kinship with our agrarian roots. If we seek after the false gods of industrialism, we will leave more than the land; we will leave the source from which we obtain our essence, our humanity. The loss of our humanity plus worship of the machine will lead to a condition in which we will evermore seek happiness but never find it. When happiness is measured in terms of materialism, it is incumbent upon the producers of material goods to assure that the consuming public never find happiness. For, if happiness is found, then consumption will cease or at least be dramatically reduced. The result will be a net loss to those who produce. If we are allowed to find happiness in things other than the material, then we will become ineffective as consumers and therefore of no use to modern industrialism.

COLONIALISM AND
THE DENIAL OF HAPPINESS

Man is only truly man, in as far as master of his own acts and judge of their worth, he is author of his own advancement.[9]

Most of us are accustomed to hearing representatives of third-world countries complain about colonialism. We seldom stop to consider that the Southern people also suffer under the yoke of colonialism.

To deny people the right to be the author of their own advancement is to deny them the right to be whole. For a free people will, by the irresistible impetus of their freedom, be masters of their lives and destinies. Let us consider the life of a colonial. A colonial must exist for the benefit of someone else, a relationship that Southerners have in regard to the all-powerful central government.

Colonialism is not a new idea but rather an old and dying form of government. Under colonialism, people are usually poor economically and spiritually as compared to the people who constitute the governing power. The current poverty of the Southern people is a result of this colonial relationship in which the powerful North exercises control and dominion over the weaker Southern subjects of the Yankee empire. Even more revealing than this relationship between the stronger and weaker is the fact that colonialism is a relationship in which those who are dominated are not allowed to become the creators of their own history. Colonialism has reduced the Southern people to a position in which they are not allowed to assert their rights or defend their heritage. They can only react, much as a tucked-tail dog does when disciplined by his cruel master. This means that their lives, as colonials, are not planned according to their own needs and best interests, but according to the needs and political desires of the ruling

Northern liberal order. As Southerners, we are a minority in the Yankee empire. We are being exploited for the good of the controlling elements. Our labor and raw material is used, not to build a better South, but to maintain the Northern liberal industrial establishment.

THE PURSUIT OF HAPPINESS
AND SOUTHERN ECONOMIC REALITY

Happiness is indeed more than economics, but the pursuit of happiness cannot be divorced from the economic realm of life. It is in this realm of economics that the South stands like a shoeless urchin in a relentless winter storm.

Economic prosperity has been elusive for the South since Appomattox. Because of our poor economic standing, the youth of the South must start their pursuit of happiness as second-class citizens within the United States.

Much has been said about the booming "Sun Belt," but occasionally some hard and cold facts are revealed that dispel this myth of Southern prosperity. According to the United States Commerce Department, the average income for Southerners is below that of other Americans. As a matter of fact, of the Southern states, all but one is ranked in the bottom fifty percent of states for personal income. The South, after the loss of its war for independence, has always been on the bottom of the economic scale. The people of Canada, who remained loyal to the English Crown during the American Revolutionary War, have a higher personal income than the average Southerner!

If two young people start to work, one in the South and one in the North, the Northerner will have a distinct advantage over the Southerner. This trend will continue throughout their lives. If the young person has the luck of living in Mississippi, he or she will have the dubious honor of living (or trying to exist) on the lowest per capita income in the entire country.

Why should the Southern states always be at the bottom of the economic barrel in America? Year after year, Southern youth who are yoked to a second-class economy must compete against their Northern counterparts. Regardless of whether this situation has come about by accident or by design, the results for young and old alike are the same. As Southerners, we must make our way in an economically depressed region of "our" country. This has been the case since our benevolent masters from the North "saved" the glorious Union! What a terrible price we are paying for their political, military, and economic success! The Yankee myth-makers would have us believe that we should be grateful to them for their willingness to come all the way down South to kill, rob, and burn just to keep us in their land of freedom and prosperity.

We should face the fact that our economic well-being will never be salvaged by anyone other than ourselves. The Southern states at one time had enough natural resources in oil and gas to be as prosperous as any Middle-Eastern Arab nation. What has happened? Our resources have been squandered for the benefit of the Northern industrialist. These resources were not and are not being used to build up our Southern economy. The South has served as a convenient source of natural resources and cheap labor, just like any other victimized colony.

Our only hope of changing our second-class economic status is to quit acting like pacified colonial subjects. We must look to ourselves for our economic salvation. Let us pledge to those yet unborn that they shall not come into this world as second-class citizens; then we must be prepared to take those actions necessary to fulfill that pledge.

The controlling element of the Yankee empire responds, in typical reactionary fashion, to the nationalist views of Southerners by assigning villainy (hate, bigotry, racism, etc.) to our motives. The Southern people do not and have never harbored evil intentions against their Northern neighbors. What we have demanded and continue to insist upon is the right to control our lives, our destiny, and the sovereign right to build for ourselves a better South. We have no desire to enforce our will upon others. We claim the right to use our freedom and liberty to build a better world for ourselves, and we reject the notion that the liberal Yankee imperialists possess the right to nullify our liberty. We desire this expression of liberty for ourselves and for all others who wish to adopt it freely.

CHAPTER 13

The Yankee Campaign of Cultural Genocide

If it costs ten years, and ten to recover the general prosperity, the destruction of the South is worth so much.[1]

Ralph Waldo Emerson

INTRODUCTORY COMMENTS

During the War for Southern Independence, the United States government conducted a successful crusade to deny the Southern people their natural right of self-determination. The armed invasion and conquest of the South brought about the wholesale destruction of its economy, the permanent destruction of its political strength vis-a-vis the Northern numerical majority, and the extermination of large numbers of its population. These occurrences are the natural result of armed aggression. Americans have been conditioned to believe that the "Civil War" re-united "our" country and made "us" one people. The truth is that the two regions were not re-united; the Southern people were bayonetted back into line. The blood on those Yankee bayonets is Southern blood!

As we have demonstrated in prior chapters, the Northern people from the very beginning of this nation were told that Southerners were illiterate, lazy, barbaric slave masters. The antagonism between the two distinct cultures was reinforced by sensational newspaper reports, slanderous novels, and the words and actions of Northern politicians greedy for more Southern tariff money. The present-day continuation of cultural genocide is necessary to justify Yankee aggression and to maintain the unholy alliance between Northern liberals, black militants, and Southern Scalawags.

The Southern political Scalawags and their fellow travelers are

271

Fredrick Swint Hood, Jackson Parish, Louisiana, Twenty-Eighth Louisiana Volunteer Infantry. At the tender age of sixteen Hood began his service to his country, fighting in some of the most important engagements in the Trans-Mississippi Department, such as the Battles of Mansfield and Pleasant Hill,[14] giving the Yankee invaders some of their last bitter defeats. (Image courtesy of Keith Canterbury, Simsboro, Louisiana)

the keys to maintaining Northern liberal political domination of our Southern homeland. These people are Southern by birth but traitors by choice. Many have accepted the liberal philosophy of "guilt" and sincerely believe that they must sacrifice their Southern heritage as part of the atonement for the "sins" committed by prior generations of Southerners. Most, though, are simply greedy, pragmatic politicians much like the French traitors who cooperated with the Nazi invaders of World War II. They look around, identify who is in control, and coddle up to the power brokers in hopes of enriching themselves with power, prestige, and money. Southern Scalawags have led the fight to destroy our precious Southern heritage. The reason? Because they owe their allegiance, not to the people of the South, but to the power brokers of the North. Anything that might cause the Southern people to remember such forbidden fruit as constitutional government, State's Rights, local control of education, the right of self-determination, and a government based on the principle of the consent of the governed; anything that displays the principles fought for by our Confederate ancestors is a direct threat to the Scalawags' power base and therefore must be destroyed!

In this chapter we shall review the vicious campaign of cultural genocide as conducted by the forces of the United States during the war and as it continues today.

The Yankee Campaign of Cultural Genocide

In 1861 the United States Congress passed the Morrill Act which was officially designed to use Federal monies to support local education. The forces of centralized Federalism had, at last, seized complete control of Congress. The old Republic of Sovereign States, in which control of education had been reserved for the people at the local level, was dead. Replacing it was a new Federal Nationalism. Senator Justin Morrill declared that "The role of the national government is to mold the character of the American people."[2]

The real purpose of the act was to use Federal monies to give children in Federally occupied areas of the South an education based on Northern ideas and principles. What this meant was that the United States government would financially support efforts to re-educate Southerners to ensure that they would henceforth have a proper "respect for national authority." The North knew that to maintain its domination of an erstwhile free people something had to be done to break the rebellious spirit of their newly acquired Southern vassals. That "something" would be the imposition of Northern education.

The Yankee obsession with the re-education of the Southern people can be seen early in the war. In 1862 New Orleans was suffering under the yoke of a Yankee tyrant known locally as "Beast" Butler. This Massachusetts politician destroyed the traditional educational system in New Orleans and replaced it with one that followed the Boston model. Local teachers who were accused of being secessionist in sentiment or abusive to the United States were removed. New teachers loyal to the North were brought in. Old Southern textbooks were purged and replaced with (guess what?) new Northern textbooks![3]

This effort to re-educate the Southern populace was one of the methods proposed by the Radicals to rebuild the conquered South "from the very ground-sill." Yankee senator J. P. Wickersmah made this declaration in 1865:

> What can education do for the non-slave-holding whites of the South? The great majority are deplorably ignorant. . . . It is this ignorance that enables the rebel leaders to create a prejudice in the minds of this class of persons against the North and to induce them to enlist in their armies. As long as they are ignorant they will remain tools of political demagogues and therefore be incapable of self-government. . . . With free schools in the South there could have been no rebellion in the future. . . . When our youth learn to read similar books, similar lessons, we shall become one people, possessing one organic nationality.[4]

Northerners viewed Southerners as ignorant because they had fought against their "enlightened" view of centralized federal authority. During a national teachers' convention held in August of 1865 in Pennsylvania it was declared that the late rebellion had been "a war of education and patriotism against ignorance and barbarism."[5] To the victorious Northerners it appeared that they had been granted a mandate to enforce their personal world view upon the ignorant, misguided, and otherwise lesser peoples of the world. They and their Northern culture were supreme and most certainly superior. The victorious Yankees felt the world would greatly benefit from the adoption of their principles, even if those principles had to be forced upon ignorant and inferior peoples. George Hoar from Massachusetts declared that his 1870 bill to support national education ". . . will compel the states to do what they will not do." (Yankees love to use other people's money to force them to do what they otherwise would not do). It was also noted that the bill would have the effect of "extinguishing Catholic or religious education and to form one homogeneous American people after the New England evangelical type."[6]

In 1894 J. L. M. Curry, an Alabama educator, sounded the alarm, warning Southerners of the dangers of allowing their children to be taught from Northern textbooks. He declared that, if Southerners continued the practice, future generations would grow up to be ashamed of their Southern heritage. In 1930 Frank L. Owsley again warned the Southern people that the North was attempting to imprint its views upon the minds of Southern youth. He warned that the North was attempting to teach Southern young people that their history was a history of error. He warned of textbooks designed to give Southerners a proper education in Northern traditions *and* at the same time label the Southern cause as evil or unrighteous. As Owsley pointed out, the North made every attempt to destroy the South with naked military force. After the war came the second attack. The North, by using its control of the newly created national government, labeled the Southern cause as evil, slave-based, and racist; while at the same time, it claimed for itself, the invader, the role of champion of morality, freedom, and equality.

To understand this attack against our Southern culture properly, we must first review the terrorist methods used against the Southern civilian population during the war. We must determine if these heinous crimes, committed against the Southern people by the forces of the United States, were only incidental and not a part of an organized campaign conducted with the knowledge and approval of United States officials.

In Chapter 4 we reviewed examples of the atrocities committed against the Southern people by the forces of the United States. In this chapter we will review the *motives* for those crimes. We will see from the United States government's own official records that the primary motivating factor was a desire of those in power to punish and to exterminate the Southern nation and in many cases to pro-cure the extermination of the Southern people.

The reason for this action is very simple; the campaign of cul-tural genocide was (and still is) necessary to ensure Northern po-litical domination of the national government. We will follow the campaign of cultural genocide from its beginnings during the war up to the present campaign conducted by the left-of-center, intel-lectual fascists who control the media, education, and the United States government.

At the end of the War for Southern Independence, the govern-ment of the United States was in the same position as the English empire was after its conquest of the Scottish people. After a long and bloody conflict, the English finally found themselves masters of Scotland. To maintain their newly acquired empire, they found it necessary to take certain actions that would ensure that future challenges to their rule would be minimized. After destroying Scottish homes and cattle, and killing a large part of the male pop-ulation in war, the English established new laws aimed at the cultural heart of Scotland. The clan system was destroyed, High-landers were disarmed, and traditional dress was outlawed along with many other traditional activities and social customs. It was a campaign of cultural genocide that has been so successful that Scotland has only recently begun to demand political liberty.

The South, like Scotland, fell victim to the forces of invasion, conquest, and oppression. The forces of Yankee imperialism—Lincoln, his party, the war governors, radical politicians, extreme Abolitionists, and Northern industrialists—were determined to use their military might to enforce a final solution to the Southern problem. Those Southerners who managed to survive death by sword or Yankee-induced starvation were to be re-educated by the North to ensure proper respect for national authority. The final solution then was to destroy Southern independence, to extermi-nate as many of the Southern people as possible, and then to re-educate the remaining "crackers" to be ashamed of their Southern heritage. At the close of the war the "nation" declared that North-erners must "colonize and Yankeeize the South . . . in short to turn the slothful, shiftless Southern world upside down."[7] Thus, the stage was set for the ultimate destruction of a culture and a peo-ple. The campaign was initiated during the War for Southern In-dependence and continues even today!

THE WAR AND RECONSTRUCTION

When a nation invades and conquers a formerly free people, the victor is left with the problem of how best to keep its ill-gotten prize. This problem is not a new phenomenon. The solution has been addressed by every tyrant who has successfully extinguished the lamp of liberty. Niccolo Machiavelli in *The Prince and the Discourses* gives rulers the following advice about how to hold on to a people who were formerly accustomed to living under liberty:

> . . . allow them to live under their own laws, taking tribute of them, and creating within the country a government composed of a few who will keep it friendly to you. . . . A city used to liberty can be more easily held by means of its citizens than in any other way. . . .[8]

Machiavelli recommends a technique that has proven very successful for the North. As we discussed in Chapter 10, "New Unreconstructed Southerners," the conquered South was allowed to keep the appearance of liberty while the very document of its liberty, the Original Constitution, was radically changed to prevent the South from mounting any effectual resistance to future exploitation. Today, we pay our tribute (taxes), we are allowed to keep the appearance of statehood and constitutional government, and our own local Scalawag, politically correct politicians assist in maintaining the political status quo.

Machiavelli continues by issuing the following warning to the new rulers:

> . . . [They] must at least retain the semblance of the old forms; so that it may seem to the people that there has been no change in the institutions, even though in fact they are entirely different from the old ones. For the great majority of mankind are satisfied with appearances, as though they were realities, and are often even more influenced by the things that seem than by those that are. . . . [the ruler should] not wish that the people . . . should have occasion to regret the loss of any of their old customs. . . .[9]

Thus the South has been left with the semblance of the old forms but without the power to protect its own social, economic, and political interests. Machiavelli did not discover these techniques; he merely codified them. The Northern conquerors, most likely, did not intentionally follow the edicts of tyranny as outlined by Machiavelli; their actions were the natural responses of any tyrant attempting to hold on to his ill-gotten domain.

There are those who attempt to excuse the excesses of the United States forces during their invasions of the Southern nation by claiming that these excesses were isolated incidents and did not represent the intentions of the United States government. Let us review the official records compiled by the victorious United States government to determine who knew and what they knew.

The story of the holocaust experienced by the Southern people is little known and almost never told by "politically correct" historians. Dr. Allen Nevins notes that the "organized devastation" experienced by the South was similar to the property loss of "the worst chapters of the two world wars." He explains that this tale of horror is untold because the "recounting of the devastation quickly becomes monotonous."[10] Can you imagine what would happen if someone suggested that the story of the World War II Holocaust should not be retold because it has become "too monotonous?"

Although the Southern holocaust is little known today, there were many who knew of its horrors during the war.

THE FIELD COMMANDERS KNEW

On June 4, 1861, Union brigadier general Irvin McDowell communicated to army headquarters his knowledge that

> The presence on this side of some corps indifferently commanded has led to numerous acts of petty depredations, pillage, and etc.[11]

Major General John C. Frémont in St. Louis on August 10, 1861, received a letter from a Unionist containing the following revelation:

> Many [citizens] . . . were fired upon not by single shots but volleys, in the presence but without the command of the officers. . . . Soldiers have repeatedly fired from trains at quiet, peaceful citizens. . . . Mr. McAfee, speaker of the last [Missouri] house of representatives was arrested and required by [Union] General Hurlbut to dig trenches. . . .[12]

Colonel Albert Sigel on September 16, 1862, wrote to Col. John M. Glover detailing his reprimand of Lt. William C. Kerr for

> . . . not having obeyed my orders and yours . . . which were . . . to bring in no prisoners.[13]

Brigadier General Thomas Williams, on May 27, 1862, from Baton Rouge, Louisiana, described some of the Union troops thusly:

> . . . These regiments, officers and men, with rare exceptions, appear to be wholly destitute of the moral sense, . . . they regard pillaging not only right in itself but a soldierly accomplishment.[14]

Colonel George W. Deitzler, on June 26, 1862, wrote to Brig. Gen. Isaac F. Quinby in Columbus, Kentucky, complaining:

> The people complain bitterly of the outrages committed by a portion of General Mitchell's brigade. . . .[15]

When a specific instance of outrage committed against civilian population was reported to Gen. Ormsby M. Mitchell he

> . . . declined to take any notice of the case.[16]

General John A. Dix wired Maj. Gen. John J. Peck, Suffolk, Virginia, on February 19, 1863, that

> . . . Colonel Dodge . . . has allowed his men to plunder the country.[17]

Colonel David B. Morris conducted a campaign in Hyde County, North Carolina, during the month of March 1863. He reported to Gen. J. G. Foster that there was a

> . . . lack of . . . discipline among . . . officers of the 103rd Pennsylvania . . . [and the] 101st Pennsylvania [regiments].[18]

Major General John M. Palmer, while near Chattanooga, Tennessee, published a circular declaring:

> . . . pillaging by soldiers, and in some degree by the officers of this command . . . are chargeable to the negligence or collusion of the officers.[19]

Rear Admiral David D. Porter published General Order Number 158 declaring:

... I have been ... mortified by the conduct of persons in charge of some of the gunboats. These two officers ... have committed offenses against the laws of justice and humanity. ... They have ... converted the vessel ... into an instrument of tyranny. ... .[20]

Brigadier General William H. Emory at Morganza, Louisiana, on June 3, 1864, issued General Order Number 53 in which he admitted that the evil committed by his troops was such that

... [due to] the plunder of innocent women and children. ... Death would not atone for their [United States Army personnel] crimes. ... .[21]

From the evidence presented, it is obvious that the field officers were aware of the conduct of the United States army as it invaded the South. There were many instances where individual field officers made cursory attempts to control their troops, but to little avail. The problem demanded intervention from higher authorities.

SHERMAN AND GRANT KNEW

The two commanders most often associated with the victory of the United States in its war to subjugate the Southern people are William Tecumseh Sherman and Ulysses S. Grant. In this section we will question if perhaps these United States military officers could have possibly known or even encouraged the horrible record of Northern atrocities and genocide.

During World War II one of the techniques used by the Nazis against partisan bands was to punish the local inhabitants when a German military target was attacked. This technique was universally condemned. Many one-hundred-percent Americans find it rather embarrassing to learn that the United States used the technique of punishing innocent civilians in its war of aggression against the South.

Major General W. T. Sherman wrote in October 19, 1862, that the attack and burning of a Yankee gunboat should be punished by bringing about the "utter ruin" of the people in the area, and he ordered:

I hope ... you will proceed to Bledsoe's Landing and then destroy all the houses and cornfields for miles along the river on that side. . . . You should shell the whole river whenever one of these raids occurs.[22]

Often, while reading the official records, you will notice in one place, such as the one quoted above, that the commander is issuing harsh and cruel orders; then in another place he appears to be attempting to control the excesses of the troops under his command. Regardless of the reasons for these inconsistencies, perhaps in an attempt to cover their backsides or out of a genuine sense of guilt, the officers unintentionally documented the fact that they were aware of the excesses of the United States military forces early in the war. On June 18, 1862, Maj. Gen. W. T. Sherman issued his General Order Number 44:

> Too much looseness exists on the subject of foraging. The articles of war make it almost a capital offense for an officer or soldier to pillage, which means taking private property for his own use.[23]

Sherman's General Order Number 2, dated December 6, 1862, stated that

> The indiscriminate and extensive plundering by our men calls for a summary and speedy change.[24]

His General Order Number 3, dated January 12, 1863, states:

> Ignorance of the rules of war as to pillage and plunder can no longer be pleaded.[25]

In his General Order Number 49, Sherman declared that

> Stealing, robbery, and pillage has become so common in this army that it is a disgrace to any civilized people.[26]

General Sherman wrote to General Grant at Vicksburg on August 4, 1863:

> . . . we are drifting to the worst sort of vandalism. . . . You and I and every commander must go through the war justly chargeable with crimes at which we blush.[27]

General Sherman reported to General Grant regarding his destruction of Meridian, Mississippi:

> I . . . began systematic and thorough destruction. . . . For five days 10,000 men worked hard and with a will . . . with axes,

crowbars, sledges, clawbars, and with fire, and I have no hes-
itation in pronouncing the work as well done. Meridian, with
its depots, store-houses, arsenal, hospitals, offices, hotels, and
cantonments no longer exists.[28]

General Sherman issued his General Order Number 127 on November 23, 1864, ordering:

> In case of . . . destruction [of bridges] by the enemy, . . . the
> commanding officer . . . on the spot will deal harshly with the
> inhabitants nearby. . . .[29]

From an entry dated March 6, 1865, we get a little insight as to
why General Sherman might have wished to restrain his troops. In
a communique to Gen. H. W. Slocum, he asked Slocum to try to
control his troops because

> . . . we are now out of South Carolina and . . . a little moder-
> ation may be of political consequence to us in North Caro-
> lina.[30]

From the federal government's own record, we have ample evidence that General Sherman was well aware of the suffering of the
civilian population but never stopped the actions of the troops under his command. In addition, we have seen confessions of the destruction of civilian property, hospitals, and the possible starvation
of thousands of innocent civilian men, women, and children—all
at the hands of American (United States) military officials.

We have also seen that Sherman informed Grant of the extent
of the pillaging occasioned by United States troops and sailors.
Did General Grant have any other indication of the extent of the
pillaging, plundering, and other acts of terrorism committed by
the United States forces against the Southern people?

General Grant issued his General Order Number 3 on January
13, 1862. In it he admitted his knowledge of the conduct of some
of his troops vis-a-vis the civilian population:

> Disrepute having been brought upon our brave soldiers by
> the bad conduct of some of their numbers . . . a total disre-
> gard of rights of citizens, and being guilty of wanton destruc-
> tion of private property. . . .[31]

Again and again we see Yankee officers and officials paying lip

service to the "laws of war and civilized conduct," but again and
again failing to enforce these standards.

General Grant received a report from Gen. S. A. Hurlbut in
March of 1863:

> The amount of plundering and bribery that is going on in
> and about . . . Memphis is beyond all calculation. . . . soldiers
> are bribed, officers are bribed, and the accursed system is de-
> stroying the army.[32]

Lieutenant General U. S. Grant, on August 5, 1864, ordered
Maj. Gen. David Hunter:

> In pushing up the Shenandoah Valley . . . it is desirable that
> nothing should be left to invite the enemy to return . . . such
> as cannot be consumed destroy. . . .[33]

From these revealing examples, we can see that both Grant and
Sherman knew what was happening to the Southern people and
approved of these crimes. Was this a carefully guarded secret
known only to Grant and Sherman, or did higher officials in
Washington know and approve?

UNITED STATES SECRETARY OF WAR
STANTON KNEW

United States Secretary of War Edwin M. Stanton received a report in January of 1862 describing the crimes committed by military personnel in Western Missouri:

> They are no better than a band of robbers: they cross the line,
> rob, steal, plunder, and burn whatever they can lay their
> hands upon.[34]

In February of the same year, the Yankee secretary of war received a personal report, in Washington, D.C., from a Unionist
who told Stanton of the "lawless action of U.S. military forces in
Jefferson County, Missouri."[35]

On May 19, 1862, Maj. Gen. Ormsby M. Mitchell wrote to the
Yankee secretary of war to inform him that

> The most terrible outrages, robberies, rapes, arsons, and
> plundering are being committed by lawless brigands and vaga-
> bonds connected with the army. . . .[36]

Secretary of the Treasury Salmon P. Chase forwarded to Stanton the following report of forced conscription of slaves into the Federal army:

> The negroes were sad. . . . Sometimes whole plantations, learning what was going on, ran off to the woods for refuge. This mode of [enlistment by] violent seizure . . . is repugnant. . . .[37]

The tale of Union captain Harry Truman will leave the reader assured of the guilt of Secretary Stanton. Union general Clinton B. Fisk stated on June 8, 1864, that Captain Truman was "plundering the best men in North Missouri, insults and abuses women. . . ."[38] A Union judge William A. Hall wrote that Truman "killed a number of citizens who were not taken with arms. . . ."[39] In the summer of 1864, Truman was found guilty of murder, arson, and larceny, and sentenced to be hanged. After his trial, the informants against Truman were either burned out or murdered, and Captain Truman was once again in the service of the United States military.

It seems that Captain Truman was indeed tried by a military commission convened by Gen. William S. Rosecrans and was sentenced to be hanged. General Rosecrans disapproved of the findings, stayed the execution, and ordered Truman to be held in Alton Military Prison until further orders were issued. The record of the case was then sent to none other than Secretary of War Stanton. The secretary of war ordered Truman released from confinement and reassigned to Washington, D.C. He was not heard of again until he reappeared in Northern Missouri practicing his old tricks of war crimes![40]

From this record it seems obvious that Secretary of War Stanton knew and approved of the crimes his military forces were committing against the Southern people!

THE NORTHERN
PRESIDENT LINCOLN KNEW

The saga of Brig. Gen. J. B. Turchin has already been discussed in Chapter 1. This evidence alone provides ample support to our claim that Abraham Lincoln knew about the terrorist activities of his officers and men. Add to this evidence the experience of Brig. Gen. John McNeil who received his promotion from Lincoln after he had executed ten Southern POWs. Lincoln was fully aware of these executions prior to promoting (rewarding) McNeil. Let us add to this list the story of Brig. Gen. James H. Lane.

Captain W. E. Prince, on September 9, 1861, sent word to Lane informing him of "atrocities" being committed by troops claiming to be part of Lane's command. On September 24, 1861, Lane reported a skirmish at Osceola, Missouri, that required him to reduce the town to "ashes." On October 9, 1861, Lane, who was a radical Republican United States senator from Kansas, sent a telegram to his friend, Abraham Lincoln, complaining that "Governor Robinson . . . has constantly . . . vilified myself, and abused the men under my command as marauders and thieves."[41]

Major General Henry W. Halleck, commander of the Department of the Missouri, on December 19, 1861, sent a letter to Maj. Gen. George B. McClellan, general in chief of the army in Washington, describing some of Lane's activities:

> The conduct of the forces under Lane . . . has done more for the enemy in this State than could have been accomplished by 20,000 of his own army. . . . I receive almost daily complaints of outrages committed by these men in the name of the United States, and the evidence is so conclusive as to leave no doubt of their correctness. It is rumored that Lane has been made a brigadier-general. I cannot conceive of a more injudicious appointment. . . . its effect . . . is offering a premium for rascality and robbing generally.[42]

General McClellan presented Lincoln with the letter. Lincoln read the letter while in the presence of McClellan. What do you think was the response of this man we are taught to virtually worship, this man who is remembered as a compassionate leader "with charity for all and malice toward none"? He turned the letter over and wrote:

> An excellent letter, though I am sorry General Halleck is so unfavorably impressed with General Lane.[43]

Lincoln's friend, Lane, did receive his promotion—a reward for conducting his campaign of terrorism again the Southern people! We can assert that President Lincoln was aware of the terrorist campaign being conducted by officers and men of the United States military forces as evidenced by the federal government's own official records.

While researching these atrocities, we found several complaints recorded by field commanders about political influence working against those who were attempting to control the United States military forces. In January of 1863, General Rosecrans informed Secretary of War Stanton of the numerous crimes of "murder, arson, rape, and others" which were increasing in his area. Rosecrans then complained:

> The power to check them by inflicting the penalty of death is a nullity, for the delays necessary to get them a regular trial by general court-martial, and then holding them until the matter is reviewed and approved by the President, such a time elapses that the troops are relieved and the culprit escapes.[44]

The use of political influence to deter efforts to control the atrocities can be seen in the case of Gen. Innis N. Palmer. On May 30, 1864, he issued a circular order in which he detailed the many cases of plundering, insults, and arson that occurred at the hands of his troops at Washington, North Carolina. Notice what happened when the news of this order reached Washington:

> My order, No. 5, . . . concerning the outrages committed at Little Washington has been severely commented upon in high places; not by my military superiors, but by Senators of the United States and others. . . .[45]

These cases as cited along with the cases of Lane and Turchin illustrate the fact that official Washington both knew and approved of the terrorist acts of the United States military forces committed against the Southern nation.

WAS GENOCIDE THE NORTH'S GOAL DURING THE WAR?

Thousands of non-combatant Southerners died as a result of the deliberate shelling of civilian targets, the blockade of civilian medical supplies, the burning of civilian homes, the forced displacement of the civilian population, and the starvation that resulted from the deliberate destruction of civilian food supplies and the implements necessary to grow future crops.

The question remains whether this was done as a deliberate policy to destroy the Southern population or simply as a result of senseless, unrestrained hatred and violence against the Southern people by the forces of the United States. One point should be made clear; if you are killed by someone, the motive for the murder makes little difference to you, the victim. The result is the same—you are dead! The effect of the vicious invasion of the Southern nation was the extermination of large numbers of its population. Look again at some examples of the thinking that guided those who were responsible for the conduct of the Yankee War of Invasion.

Early in 1863, the Chicago newspapers were attacking Union general Don Carlos Buell because he attempted to control the conduct of certain officers. Colonel Marcellus Mundy stated:

> ... papers ... condemned ... [Buell] very bitterly for his punishment of Colonel Turchin. The burden of the complaint in the papers was this: that General Buell was protecting the [Southern] people, rather than punishing them. ... they seemed to advocate what they called a "vigorous war policy," by which they seemed to mean general devastation. . . .[46]

Admiral Raphael Semmes, CSS *Alabama*, noted the lack of objectivity of Yankee newspapers:

> The war had been a god-send for newspaperdom. The more extraordinary were the stories that were told by the venal and corrupt newspapers, the more greedily were they devoured by the craving and prurient multitude ... without the least regard for the truth. ... Such is the stuff of which a good deal of the Yankee histories of the late war will be made.[47]

Yankees who for generations had been raised to believe that Southerners were lazy, indolent, and cruel slave masters were now making war upon these Southern barbarians. Is there any wonder that Northerners chose to treat Southern civilians as less than civilized, deserving none of the rights and respect due civilized folk, such as themselves?

General in Chief Henry W. Halleck, in Washington, on March 31, 1863, wrote to General Grant:

> The character of the war has very much changed. . . . There is now no possible hope of reconciliation with the rebels. . . . There can be no peace but that which is forced by the sword. We must conquer the rebels. . . .[48]

General U. S. Grant on April 11, 1863, wrote the following:

> Rebellion has assumed that shape now that it can only termi-
> nate by the complete subjugation of the South. . . . It is our
> duty to weaken the enemy, by destroying their means of sub-
> sistence, withdrawing their means of cultivating their fields,
> and in every other way possible.[49]

Where is the "malice toward none, . . . charity for all" spokes-
person? What is meant by the plain words of Grant when he states
that all means of production must be destroyed? How does he propose to feed the starving multitudes if all means of cultivation are
removed—let them eat cake?

The lot of a civilian population when it is invaded by an unprincipled military force can be seen in this Yankee's report:

> I propose to eat up all the surplus, and perhaps the entire crops
> in the country, take all serviceable stock, mules, horses. . . .
> These people are proud arrogant rebels. . . . The hands of all
> Federal officers should fall justly but heavily upon them, so
> that they should respect us—not from love, for they never will
> do that, but from fear of the power of our Government.[50]

Ever since the War for Southern Independence, the Southern
people have learned to fear the power of the Yankee's government.

Major General W. T. Sherman wrote from Vicksburg on January
31, 1864:

> The Government of the United States has . . . any and all
> rights which they choose to enforce in war—to take their lives,
> their homes, their lands, their everything. . . . war is simply
> power unrestrained by constitution. . . . To the persistent se-
> cessionist, why, death is mercy, and the quicker he or she is
> disposed of the better. . . .[51]

Please note that Sherman is not making these remarks in the
heat of battle but while writing to one of his subordinates. Note
also the fact that he claims the right to execute all secessionists, either male or female!

The super-patriots and other one-hundred-percent Americans
will come to this United States general's defense and claim that he
was not really sincere about his desire to kill innocent men and
women, that he was only exaggerating. Yet, look at his remarks
five months later on June 21, in a letter to Secretary of War Stanton:

There is a class of people [Southerners] men, women, and children, who must be killed or banished before you can hope for peace and order.[52]

Instead of moderating his position, Sherman has expanded his human target to now include children! But that was not the end of the matter. Secretary Stanton, in Washington, replied to Sherman's letter stating:

Your letter of the 21st of June has just reached me and meets my approval.[53]

The Yankee armies made every effort to fulfill the desire of their leaders to leave the Southern people with "nothing but their eyes to cry with." Witness an order from General Halleck, chief of staff in Washington, as he relayed an order from General Grant:

General Grant . . . directs that . . . you . . . make all the valleys south of the Baltimore and Ohio road a desert. . . .[54]

How many men, women and children can survive in a desert? The officials and officers of the United States did not care as long as it was Southerners who were being exiled to the desert. But of course the army notified the people to "move out"—out to where? If a population is displaced and is forced to move, then the population that is forced to take in the refugees is now jeopardized. In other words, by forcefully relocating the civilian population, the Federal forces could put both groups of civilians at risk of starvation—another example of thrifty, efficient Yankee cunning.

More proof of how the Yankee invader attempted to reduce the local Southern population to starvation can be seen in a report from Northern Louisiana by an officer of the United States Army of Aggression who boastfully wrote in his official report:

No squad of men . . . can live anywhere we have been. The people have neither seed, corn, nor bread, or mills to grind the corn in if they had it, as I burned them wherever found. . . . I have taken from these people the mules with which they would raise a crop the coming year, and burned every surplus grain of corn. . . .[55]

Notice that the Yankee's efforts were directed not only at destroying current food supplies but also at destroying all means for recovery. The logical result, of course, was to ensure starvation and

misery for innocent civilians, men, women, and children—glory, glory, hallelujah, the Yankee empire goes marching on!
    Sherman wrote to General Grant on October 9, 1864:

> Until we can repopulate Georgia, it is useless to occupy it, but the utter destruction of its roads, houses, and people will cripple their military resources. . . .[56]

Note the word "repopulate" and the phrase "utter destruction of its . . . people." These words were deliberately chosen to communicate an idea to a friend and colleague. Remember the words of the author of A Fool's Errand, when he admitted that it had been the aim of the post-war Reconstruction leaders to repopulate the South by settling large numbers of Northern soldiers in the South.
    General Philip Sheridan also got in on the action as evidenced by his communique dated October 11, 1864, to General Grant:

> . . . guerrilla parties . . . are becoming very formidable. . . . I know of no way to exterminate them except to burn out the whole country.[57]

Note the use of the word "exterminate" as opposed to the military term "defeat" to refer to the local Southern resistance. Note also the manner in which the invader planned to deal with the local resistance fighters—"burn out the whole country." Who feeds the civilian population when the country from which they have traditionally drawn their sustenance is destroyed? Starvation is the result of a scorched-earth policy. Do you suppose that the United States officials in Washington were ignorant of the result of their vigorous war policy? Or do you think they knew and approved of the results? Which do you think is more likely? Lincoln, on October 27, 1864, sent a letter to General Sheridan declaring, ". . . my own personal admiration and gratitude for the month's operations in the Shenandoah Valley."[58] It is rewarding to be appreciated by one's superior, especially when one is conducting a tough campaign against defenseless men, women, and children!
    General Sheridan received this letter of encouragement from General Sherman:

> I am satisfied . . . that the problem of this war consists in the awful fact that the present class of men who rule the South must be killed outright rather than in the conquest of territory . . . a great deal of it, yet remains to be done. . . . There-

fore, I shall expect you on any and all occasions to make
bloody results.[59]

On January 21, 1865, Sherman sent this communique:

> The people of the South . . . see . . . the sure and inevitable
> destruction of all their property. . . . They see in the repetition
> of such raids the inevitable result of starvation and misery.[60]

These officials and officers of the United States knew that their
intentional war against the Southern civilian population would
produce starvation and misery. They knew it, they planned it, and
they carried it out.

As we have already noted, this was not a war against the white
South but a war against all Southerners, both black and white. The
attitude of the United States government can best be demonstrated by quoting Sherman:

> I have [your] telegram saying the President had read my letter
> and thought it should be published. . . . [I] profess . . . to fight
> for but one single purpose, viz, to sustain a Government ca-
> pable of vindicating its just and rightful authority, indepen-
> dent of niggers, cotton, money, or any earthly interest.[61]

After the war came Reconstruction. We have seen, in Chapter
10, that the radical leaders wanted to "hang" all Southern leaders.
The hatred of the North for the Southern people can be seen in
an incident in Vicksburg, Mississippi, where Joseph Davis was attempting to recover land from the local politically correct Carpetbaggers. Here is what the Carpetbagger thought of Southerners:

> . . . instead of temporizing and arguing with traitors, I would
> urge the most prompt and effective measures of force to quell
> and exterminate them.[62]

Note the use of the word "exterminate." This report pleased the
local Federal official who sent it on to Washington, D.C., where it
was accepted without comment. There was nothing unusual in the
report, just a continuation of the planned destruction of a nation,
a culture, and a people.

This vicious campaign of genocide, conducted by the United
States government, was not limited to black and white Southern-
ers. While it was conducting its campaign of extermination down
South, the United States government was also actively attempting

to solve its "Indian" problem. The solution was strangely familiar. Yankee general John Pope declared, "It is my purpose to utterly exterminate the Sioux."[63] Pope planned to make a "final settlement with all these Indians." His plan was to shoot and hang as many as possible and then remove the rest from their land.[64] The Yankees' "final solution" for the Indian problem was very similar to their "solution" for the Southern problem. They planned to kill as many as possible, deprive those who were left of their land, and then re-educate them so they would become Yankees!

Notice how the Yankee mind will not allow for the existence of a culture differing from his own, especially if that culture stands in the way of the Yankee's economic gain. The Northern reformers were determined to re-make the Native Americans into white (i.e., Yankee) men. The Native Americans were viewed as barbarians because of their nonmaterialistic values. The Yankee sought to re-make them in order to

> change the disposition of the Indian to one more mercenary and ambitious to obtain riches, and teach him to value the position consequent upon the possession of riches.[65]

Throughout this chapter we have documented the cruel and evil attitude of United States leaders during their conduct of the war. This evil attitude or mind set is not pleasant to look upon and serves as a source of national embarrassment for many one-hundred-percent Americans.* This may be one of the reasons why the Northern conduct of the war tends to be ignored. Most authors find it unpleasant and therefore prefer to pretend that the entire episode never occurred. The cruel fact is that these events did happen, and it was the Southern people who suffered at the hands of the United States government!

Lyon G. Tyler of Virginia addressed the question of the United States' willingness to use cruel methods to further its aggressive intent:

---

* Our reference to one-hundred-percent Americans is not intended as an attack upon the legitimate patriotism demonstrated by Southerners in every war prior to and after the War for Southern Independence. It is intended to remind Southerners that it is the principles of constitutional government and liberty that should drive our patriotism and not blind allegiance to a government that has been controlled by the forces of Northern liberalism since the defeat of the South in the War for Southern Independence.

During the war for Southern independence the Northern generals everywhere disregarded the international law. The policy everywhere was cruel imprisonment, waste and destruction. Unlike General Lee, Lincoln revelled in using hard language—"Rebels," "Insurgent Rebels," "Insurgents," etc., occur everywhere in his speeches, letters and messages. Because these terms are recognized as insulting, . . . such words were greatly objected to by our Revolutionary fathers, and a committee of the Continental Congress imputed to this habit of the British the licentious conduct of the British soldiers. They were taught by these words to look down upon the Americans, to despise them as inferior creatures. And the same influences operated upon the Northern soldiers, who plundered the South. Lincoln taught them. The North having no just cause for the invasion and destruction of the South, which only asked to be let alone, has ceaselessly tried to hide its crime by talking "slavery." But logically flowing from this attitude is the idea that slavery deprived the South of every right whatever, which was the doctrine of the assassin, John Brown. General Sheridan's philosophy of war was "to leave to the people nothing but their eyes to weep with over the war." General Sherman's, "to destroy the roads, houses, people, and repopulate the country." General Grant's to leave the Valley "a barren waste" and shoot "guerrillas without trial"; and President Lincoln's the adoption of "emancipation and every other policy calculated to weaken the moral and physical forces of the rebellion." (Nicolay and Hay, *Complete Works of Abraham Lincoln, II*, p. 565.) The damage done by the German troops in France was a trifle compared with the damage done by the Northern troops in the South.[66]

Southerners, who are by custom courteous, have been reluctant to discuss this evil attitude of our Northern adversaries. This reluctance has worked to the general benefit of the Northern mythmakers and to the enormous detriment of the South. When courtesy and politeness allow our adversaries an unfair advantage and assist them in maintaining their social, political, and economic domination of our people, then courtesy and politeness are no longer virtues but damnable vices!

Thus far we have demonstrated that the free Southern nation was invaded, many of our people raped or murdered, private property plundered at will, and their right of self-determination violently denied. We have seen that the leaders and officials of the United States government and military held the Southern people in contempt and that their actions were guided by this disparaging attitude. We have seen how the United States government attempted to destroy the South physically as a people and then made early efforts to re-educate the survivors to ensure that future generations of Southerners would remain loyal to the newly established national authority (or at least be made ashamed of their past and therefore remain docile and pacified). We must now review current events to determine if the Northern-controlled establishment has relented in its early campaign of cultural genocide or if perhaps they are continuing their campaign to destroy our Southern culture and heritage.

The War Continues
Contemporary Cultural Genocide

During the late 1960s, amidst strident cries of "black power" and "burn, baby, burn," there emerged the concept of "black pride." The black community insisted that it had a right to teach its children "black history." The general rationale given was that pride in its heritage would serve as a bulwark against attempts to dominate and exploit the black community.

The liberal media and education establishments actively endorsed and promoted black pride, black studies, and Afro-American cultural programs. This support has resulted in not only the education of black children in various Afro-American studies programs but also the forced indoctrination of all children regardless of their cultural heritage.

Our Southern society has a heritage rich in cultural diversity. The study of the various cultures that comprise this heritage is certainly relevant and laudable. The problem is that the liberal education establishment has assumed unto itself the right to decide which cultures are relevant and which ones must be ignored. It has assumed unto itself the right to teach cultural diversity in a manner that will best support its left-of-center, liberal bias. An example is the manner in which our children are taught about Martin Luther King.

Many Southerners are offended by the way in which the liberal establishment has deified King. For instance, his extreme left-wing views, especially his attempts to undercut the support of our troops during the Vietnam War, were not shared by most Southerners. The various charges that continue to emerge regarding his plagiarism of his doctoral thesis and the assertions by his own friends that the Reverend Dr. King was a voracious "womanizer" all tend to detract from his "heroic" status.

The important point to remember is that, even though certain aspects of King's life are offensive to many Southerners, the liberal establishment still forces us to pay homage to their left-of-center hero. Across the South today, in virtually every city, you will find Martin Luther King avenues, parks, and various other public displays honoring the slain activist. These displays are paid for primarily by taxes paid by middle-class Southerners—many of whom, if not most, did not and do not agree with the left-wing political philosophy promoted by King. Yet even though many Southerners do not agree with his political philosophy, there has been very little, if any, resistance to this liberal-sponsored hero worship. Southerners have generally taken the position that, if this is the type of man the black community desires to hold up as their hero, then let them do so—it is their business.

As we have pointed out, the liberal establishment not only has assumed the right to put a left-wing spin on its teaching regarding King but also more importantly for us, has assumed the right to decide which culture should be ignored. By ignoring and or falsifying our Southern heritage the liberal establishment is engaging in a deliberate campaign of cultural genocide.

Campaigns of cultural genocide are not new. It has been a commonly used tool to maintain the domination of an external power over a subjugated people. The invasion and subjugation of Scotland and Ireland by the English imperialists provide examples of how the destruction of a culture was used to maintain control of a local population. The wearing of kilts, the playing of bagpipes, and the gathering of the clans were at various times outlawed by the English occupation forces. Why? Did kilts and bagpipes pose a threat to the English empire? No, not directly, but as a means to encourage a people to be proud of their heritage—their individualism, their past—it tended to encourage them to think of themselves as a people under bondage and to incite passions for such forbidden fruit as liberty!

After the United States occupied the Southern nation, the Federal authorities issued orders similar to those issued by their English kinsmen who occupied Scotland. The displaying of the Confederate flag and other visible symbols of the Confederacy were forbidden. This included all military insignias, even buttons on uniforms. Often returning Southern soldiers were forced to remove or cover the buttons on the only clothing they possessed. Whitelaw Reid, a Radical Republican and Yankee journalist, was eyewitness to a drunken Union sergeant forcing a former Confederate officer to stand and allow him to remove the buttons from the officer's uniform. One of Stonewall Jackson's former staff officers was thrown in jail and charged with the high crime of treason when he was caught by Federal officials as he returned from having his photo taken while wearing his Confederate uniform. Yankee hatred for Southerners even extended to the dead. Arlington Cemetery has witnessed the spectacle of United States troops standing guard to prevent Southern ladies from placing flowers on the graves of Southern dead! United States authorities at Antietam battlefield were forced to give Southern soldiers a proper burial only after hogs began rooting up the remains of Confederate dead, thereby fouling the area close to where the slain Northerners were buried![67]

The former communist empire of Eastern Europe offers another example of how an invader attempted to destroy local cultural pride to prevent resistance to the empire. The central government in Moscow outlawed the celebration of certain cultural events if these events tended to promote regional pride and awareness. Many tourists during the Cold War era returned from occupied countries with stories of local residents giving them old currency and asking them to take it out of the county to the free world as a reminder that their occupied nation was once free. The communist imperialists made every effort to erase all traces of the occupied nations' history. With their history gone and their culture forgotten, who would remain to challenge the empire's domination of the forgotten nations?

In this respect the black militants were correct: It is easy to dominate a people without cultural pride, but people who are proud of their cultural heritage are not easily dominated and exploited! From this fact arises the irresistible question—if cultural pride is good for some groups, why is it denied to Southerners? The answer is very simple, and it follows the logic of invasion and con-quest. Our Southern cultural heritage is being systematically destroyed by the Northern liberal establishment to enhance its domination and exploitation of the Southern middle class. In our political world, culture is not neutral; it has within it the potential to promote a specific political philosophy. Those who control the media, education, and political agendas will use those cultures that help them and will do all within their power to destroy any culture that has within it the potential of threatening their left-of-center ideology.

It should be noted that this campaign of cultural genocide is not a result of some secret conspiracy. It is in fact the result of con-quest. All empires have been faced with the problem of how best to keep the conquered people quiet, docile, and pacified. People who are taught from infancy to despise their past will not be quick to revolt. Thus arises the need to dominate the cultural history of a conquered people. Cultural genocide, as practiced by the North-ern liberal majority against the Southern people, arises from the necessity to maintain political control of a conquered people.

CULTURAL GENOCIDE IN EDUCATION

An example of how Southern children are taught to despise their heritage is in order. We will look at two different textbooks: one was used to teach Southern students in the early 1900s, and the other is used today in our schools. You will recall that in Chapter 6 we dis-cussed how the South was allowed to maintain the "appearance" of free government after Reconstruction. This situation was acceptable to the Northern majority since the North could reinstitute Recon-struction if it became politically expedient (as a matter of fact, the Northern liberal majority has now done just that very thing). In the early 1900s many local Southern textbooks were teaching the history of the war from the Southern point of view. This, of course, was un-acceptable to the Northern liberal majority.

Let us compare the difference between the way Southern chil-dren were taught when Southerners were in nominal control of their educational system. We will first look at *A History of Louisiana* by Harriet Magruder, copyright 1909, and published by D. C. Heath & Company, in Boston, New York, and Chicago. On page 291 begins a chapter titled "The Causes of the Civil War":

To understand some of the causes which led to this war, we
must go back many years. When the Revolutionary War was
over and America was free from Great Britain, thoughtful
men saw that the States could never prosper or be protected
unless they united and formed a strong government. The colonies, however, had felt the power of England. They feared
that if they united they would not be able to leave the Union at
any time that they wished. They finally decided to join together as the United States of America, but it was understood
that any State could withdraw if it chose. All the States, both
Northern and Southern, made the same claim. In 1811 Josiah
Quincy of Massachusetts said that his State ought to leave the
Union if Louisiana were admitted.[68]

The economic struggle between the two sections is given as a
major cause of the war:

The real difficulty lay in the fact that the country had grown
until both North and South contained a great many people,
and both sections were fighting for power. Their business interests were different, and a tax which would help the Northern manufacturer would perhaps injure the Southern
planter. If the Western territories were settled by Northern
people, the North would have more power in Congress and
could pass laws beneficial to the North and harmful to the
South.[69]

The use of the slavery question as an element of anti-South propaganda is also noted:

Though the slaves, as a rule, had kind masters and were
happy, many people in the North began to write articles telling with what horrible cruelty the negroes were treated. The
South became more angry than before, and determined to
leave the Union. She believed that she had the right to do this,
as the States had entered the Union with the understanding
that each could withdraw at any time that it chose.[70]

Now let us compare this record with a textbook currently used
in Louisiana schools. (This exercise could substitute textbooks
from any Southern state. The authors are using their home state
as an example of politically correct indoctrination that is typical of
most Southern schools.) The textbook is *Our Louisiana Legacy*. The
authors of this politically correct textbook decided to omit any ref-

erence to the threat of Josiah Quincy of Massachusetts that the New England states should secede if the "mixed race Creoles of Louisiana" were admitted to the Union. Strange how the 1909 textbook thought it important to inform the children that it was Northerners who first threatened to secede from the Union while the liberal textbook manages to ignore this embarrassing (to Yankees) fact of history. The liberal textbook then attempts to educate our children about that most vile of institutions—"slavery." The text reluctantly admits that slaves were ". . . for the most part sufficiently fed, clothed, and housed. . . ." It leaves the impression that this was done begrudgingly by the slave owners. The specter of the whip is raised as being the most often used means of punishment, but the fact that on most plantations the whip was very seldom used is conveniently omitted. At last the liberal authors put the question to rest by asking:

> When we discuss the life of the slave, we should ask ourselves if we would like to be slaves. The answer provides us with all the arguments against slavery.[71]

Using the politically correct authors' logic of applying contemporary standards to nineteenth-century issues, let us review the conditions of the nineteenth-century Northern industrial sweat shops:

> When we discuss the life of the nineteenth-century industrial child laborer, we should ask ourselves if we would like to be a child laborer in the New England industrial system. The answer provides us with all the arguments against Yankee capitalism.

Thus, we see the abjectly illogical use of contemporary standards as a measure for nineteenth-century systems. Yet, the politically correct authors find no reason to be embarrassed at their simplistic propaganda techniques used to brainwash and condition Southern children to have low esteem for their Southern heritage.

This modern text devotes twenty-seven lines to explain the opposition to secession and no lines to explain the support for secession! For example, it states that at last Louisiana voted in convention 113 to 17 in favor of secession. The authors then make another attack against the ancestors of the children reading this textbook by declaring:

Louisiana declared itself out of the Union without giving its
people the right to vote on the ordinance of secession from
the United States.[72]

The inference is that the secession convention did not represent
the wishes of the people and that if given an opportunity the people would have overruled the secession convention. The illogic of
this propaganda tactic can be demonstrated by asking, "How
many colonies held a plebiscite (statewide vote) to determine if
they should declare independence from Great Britain"? None,
they seceded from Great Britain at the demand of their legislatures, just as most of the Southern states did when they seceded
from the Union.

We have seen how the liberal, politically correct education establishment is using its monopoly of education to brainwash our children. Example after example can be quoted from texts used
across the South of this virulent anti-Southern bigotry. Year after
year, Southern children are taught to despise their heritage and
their ancestors. Year by year, the insidious campaign of cultural
genocide continues. Slowly, the great heritage of the South is being erased from our memory and a false, politically correct model
is being imposed.

CULTURAL GENOCIDE IN THE MEDIA

Examples of the media (radio, television, movies, and newspapers) engaging in attacks against our Southern heritage are legion. We will select just a few to demonstrate our point. During
Black History Month in 1992, a radio commentator on public radio made the statement that no blacks ever served voluntarily in
the Confederate army. According to this commentator, those who
did serve were forced to go with their masters. Note that public radio is financed by our tax monies. The middle-class Southerner is forced to pay for the politically correct slander of his own
heritage. What recourse is available to us when such an attack is
made? Even though we know the truth, it is of little value to us
because the left-of-center, intellectual fascists control access to the
media!

During the 1992 presidential primary, Republican candidate
Pat Buchanan placed a wreath at a monument honoring his ancestors, who fought for the Confederacy. NBC decided to include

this event in its report and, in the process, attempted to smear this conservative candidate by proclaiming to the world that Buchanan was honoring men who "fought to preserve slavery." The national television media also chose this as an ideal time to report on "flag waving" down South. The story was carried on national news programs during prime time and during a presidential primary election. The story concentrated on the fact that North Carolina, once a year and for a single day, flies the Stars and Bars (the first national CSA flag) over the state capitol to honor her sons who died in the war. The biased report was a rally cry for the left-wing extremist who demanded an end to Confederate Memorial Day. During the night prior to Confederate Memorial Day, the Confederate monument at the state capitol was vandalized. Do you suppose it was merely coincidental, or do you suppose the biased news (propaganda) coverage was a major factor in the attack upon our Southern heritage? Again, what recourse is left to us? How do we reply to the slander against our ancestors? Once again the intellectual fascists control the media to which we, who are not politically correct, are not allowed equal access.

The liberal establishment uses its monopoly of the media to indoctrinate (brainwash) Americans regarding the character of our Southern ancestors and their motive for fighting the War for Southern Independence. The 1991 "made for TV" movie *Ironclads* is an example of such brainwashing disguised as entertainment. Using an interesting story line, the naval battle between the CSS *Virginia* and the USS *Monitor*, the liberal thought-control specialists managed to captivate an unsuspecting audience and skillfully blend in appropriate re-enforcements of Yankee mythology. They made sure one of the leading ladies admitted that even though some Southerners claimed the war had other causes, "slavery is the real reason." Then to re-enforce the stereotype of Southerners as bigots and racists, and to re-enforce the Yankee version of the treatment of Southern blacks, they showed a scene in which a white Southerner abuses a slave, calling him "boy" and taunting him by exclaiming that the slave must think the Yankee Abolitionist has already freed him. This is an excellent example of how the liberal establishment presents its propaganda in the form of entertainment. It is very efficient, and the liberal media makes a profit off of the very people they are brainwashing!

Political Cultural Genocide

Liberalism, which is really latter-day Yankee imperialism, uses its control of the federal government to exclude conservative Southerners from the decision-making circles in Washington, D.C. A conservative from Dixie is automatically viewed with distrust and antagonism by the liberal establishment. Supreme Court Justice Clarence Thomas' greatest fault was his conservative philosophy. Is there any question what the outcome would have been if Judge Thomas had been so unfortunate as to have been born not only a Southerner but white as well?

In 1967 President Richard Nixon appointed Judge Clement Haynesworth of South Carolina to the Supreme Court. The American Bar Association gave him its highest rating. The liberals had other ideas. They denounced him as being too "insensitive" and having the wrong "judicial philosophy." Haynesworth was rejected by a vote of fifty-five to forty-three. Nixon's mistake was that he nominated a white, Southern conservative. Senator Herman Talmadge of Georgia criticized the "geographical discrimination" that defeated Haynesworth. Nearly all Southern senators voted for Haynesworth while most Northern Democrats voted against him.

President Nixon responded by nominating another Southerner, Judge Harrold Carswell. By a vote of fifty-one to forty-five the Senate rejected Carswell. President Nixon concluded that no Southern conservative would be confirmed by the Senate, and nominated Harry Blackmun of Minnesota who was confirmed.

The double standard and hypocrisy of the Northern senators was criticized by Senator Earnest F. Hollings of South Carolina:

> Apparently, if one is from South Carolina, the standards . . . are higher than would be required of a Minnesota Judge.[73]

It is not a question of standards, it is a question of political control! The liberal establishment uses its control of the federal government to assure its continued rule over a conquered and occupied Southern nation!

SUMMARY

The vicious ongoing campaign of cultural genocide perpetuated by the forces of the United States during the war and Reconstruction, and the current campaign conducted by the liberal establishment that controls the United States government were and are natural outgrowths of invasion, conquest, and subsequent oppression of a formerly free people. Andrew Nelson Lytle, in the 1930s, noted that by the close of the war, "The mercy of God did not bring independence. Nor was the war over. One phase was done. . . . The avowed purpose [of Northern policy] was the destruction of Southern civilization."[74] Compare the methods currently being employed to control the Southern political system with Machiavelli's recommendation to a tyrant for maintaining his domination of a people who were formerly free.

The Southern people today have all the trappings of the old government; the symbols, the name, the rituals are all the same. The Constitution is on display as is the Declaration of Independence; the Fourth of July is celebrated with great fanfare; Southerners are allowed to elect their own governors and representatives; generally speaking, all is the same as it was before the War for Southern Independence.

Now recall Machiavelli's recommendation that the new ruler "must at least retain the semblance of the old forms" and that this myth will suffice because most people are more concerned with appearance than with reality. He also recommends that the conquered people are more easily ruled by means of their own citizens than by any other means.

To paraphrase Machiavelli regarding the new order established by the Northern majority after its conquest of the Southern people: Keep all the trappings but none of the safeguards of the original Constitutional Republic. Allow the Southern people to have nominal control of their states, put Scalawag politicians into power who owe their allegiance to the liberal establishment, and have these Scalawag politicians, elected by Southerners, lead the way in extracting an ever-higher level of taxation from the middle class.

All that is left is for the liberal establishment to follow the example of all tyrants and to move against any local display of cultural pride that might cause the local vassals to remember and desire past freedoms and prosperity. Such memories are dangerous to tyrants because they might cause the conquered to think of themselves as a people with a common heritage, a common bondage, and a common desire to be *free*!

Rosanne Osterman tending the wounded in Galveston, Texas. Rosanne, a Jewish lady from Galveston, was one of many people of the Jewish faith who assisted the South during the War for Southern Independence. Southerners of all religious faiths joined in a cooperative effort to help in the common struggle. (Image courtesy of The Institute of Texan Cultures, San Antonio, Texas; Bruce Marshall, artist)

CHAPTER 14

Summary and Call to Action

The form of government having been changed by the revolution there are still other acts of the drama to be performed.[1]

Admiral Raphael Semmes, CSN

We began this book by identifying the propaganda methods used by the Northern majority to brainwash every generation of Southerners since the failure of the War for Southern Independence. We reviewed the Yankee myth of history and saw examples of how Northerners have used lies and half-truths to slander the Southern nation and to assure that each generation of Southerners will go out into the world with the appropriate amount of guilt. We have seen how they have used this sense of guilt to prevent Southerners from asserting their rights and reclaiming their lost estate.

We have seen how the Yankee hated the Southerner from the beginning. We have seen how Northerners treated Southerners during the conduct of their invasion of the free Southern nation. We have seen their deliberate attempts, during war and Reconstruction, to exterminate—if not the Southern people then—the entire Southern culture and political philosophy.

We reviewed the right of the Southern people to a government that rules with the consent of those governed. We demonstrated that the current federal bureaucracy has violated this first principle of free governments. We have shown that, due to its failure to gain the unfettered consent of the Southern people, the current federal government is an illegal governmental force.

We continued our review of the tactics used by the Northern majority to destroy the Original Constitutional Republic and to replace it with a centralist federal government under its control. We saw that this new centralist federal government was forced upon the Southern people against their expressed desire and in violation of their right to equal representation in Congress. This new

305

government is the source of innumerable acts of oppression conducted against the South.

We have seen that the Southern people were removed from a position of equal power in the original Union and were forced into a new position as second-class citizens. We have seen that, as a result, Southerners have been forced to endure an inferior economy, constant poverty, and the absence of political leadership dedicated to the improvement of the Southern condition.

After reviewing these crimes, fraudulent political maneuvers, oppressive acts, unfair legislation, and general attitude of disregard for the condition of the Southern people, you the reader must now make a decision. Either you must decide that everything you have read is substantially untrue, in which case you are now finished, or you must decide that what you have read is substantially true, in which case you now have two choices facing you:

1. You can decide that even though what you read is substantially true, you do not choose to do anything about it, or
2. You can decide that it is time to join the ranks of the New Unreconstructed Southerners.

People who want to do something about the political, social, and economic condition of the Southern nation must begin with an understanding that nothing can be accomplished until the rank and file of the South once again begin to believe in themselves. As New Unreconstructed Southerners, our first task is to instill (or re-instill) in our people a healthy dose of Southern pride.

After we have started the process of restoring Southern pride, we have another task before us. We must begin the Southern political revolution. For more than a century and a quarter, Southerners have placed their faith in party politics and the hope that one day the "powers that be" in Washington D.C. will cease and desist their hostile activities and recognize our legitimate complaints. Business-as-usual, party politics requires the status quo to conduct its affairs. This status quo is the very problem that we, as Southerners, need to change. How then can we expect typical party players (be they Republican or Democratic) to challenge and destroy the very thing that they need to conduct their affairs and maintain their positions of power and prestige? The fact is that (as our recent history demonstrates) they will not. Undoubtedly, at the appropriate time they will make an impassioned appeal for home consumption, but nothing more! For instance—when we had a chance to put a real conservative on the Supreme Court, who do you think led the fight against this conservative? None other than Southern Democrats who all go home at election time and assure their constituents that they are true conservatives and will represent the views of their middle-class, conservative constituency. When a liberal or a black extremist from the NAACP demands that a Confederate flag be removed from a school or public building, how easy is it to find an elected official to stand up for our rights? Take it from two who have been there—such officials are as hard to find as the proverbial hen's teeth! Help will not come from Washington. Help will not come from weak and spineless elected officials. *We must elect Confederate Freedom Fighters!*

First, how do we begin the process of instilling pride in our people? The one advantage we have is that the majority of our people want to feel good about themselves and their native Southland. Even after generations of propaganda in the form of Yankee myth, our people still respond to our flag and the singing of "Dixie." The best way to instill pride is to display the flag at various living-history events, C.S.A. memorial services, and historical re-enactments. Every true Southerner should be an active member of an organization dedicated to the preservation and perpetuation of the truth about the Southern cause. The Sons of Confederate Veterans and the United Daughters of the Confederacy are two examples of such organizations. A word of caution though; remember, you are a New Unreconstructed Southerner, or as we prefer, a Southern Nationalist. You may join a local unit that is dedicated to doing book reviews and hiding their heritage in the closet lest they offend someone. Don't disregard these Southerners—they too can be converted. Remember, this is a new struggle and it will take some time for the rank-and-file Southerner to understand what we are about.

As an activist, you should make yourself available to the local schools to do living-history discussions and demonstrations for their history classes. We have found that the knowledge gained from the S.C.V. and our involvement in War for Southern Independence re-enacting makes for a great opportunity to convey to local Southern school children, black as well as white, the truth about their ancestors and the real reason they fought the War for Southern Independence. If you have enough support from your unit, you will want to march in local parades, making sure to carry several traditional Confederate battle flags. If you have never heard the response of a crowd of Southerners when our nation's emblem is proudly displayed, then you are in for a real treat.

The important thing is to remember that you must start small and work your way up. This year you may have to settle for a letter to the editor on Confederate Memorial Day, but next year you should have enough support to pay for a nice advertisement in addition to your letter to the editor. The opportunities for promoting good pro-Southern public relations are almost endless. The important thing is that a portion of our message is constantly being presented to the public. The message is clear and easy to understand: Be proud of your heritage. The last thing we need is for Skin-Heads and neo-Nazis to be seen as the ones who are represented by our nation's flags. Our aim is to re-establish a constitutional republic in which everyone, including Southerners, is treated equally; or, if we fail to convince our Northern neighbors of the wisdom of such a change, then we will establish our own separate Southern nation.

The second phase will be to move from the educational phase (i.e., the activities designed to restore Southern pride) to active political struggle. This phase must not come too soon; otherwise, we will expend our limited resources before the educational phase has done its work and won for the Southern cause workers and supporters, and generally made the public receptive to the message. Though it sounds as if we are describing two separate activities, in reality the educational phase will continue until the revolution (or counter-revolution as General Beauregard called it—see Chapter 10, "New Unreconstructed Southerners") has completed its task of freeing the Southern people.

Too often in the past our people have placed all their hopes in one person. We have seen them all: Barry Goldwater, George Wallace, Richard Nixon, Ronald Reagan, or some trendy New South Scalawag. This is wrong for two reasons: first, one man will not be able to free an entire nation of people. What is needed most is a belief in a cause. Once a large portion of our people have this belief, then no matter who is elected or not elected, we will know what we want and how to go about getting it. The second reason that it is wrong to place all our hopes in one man is that when we do so our political base becomes like a balloon. It looks very large, but it has no substance and can be ruptured very easily. It is more important to have one elected town alderman than to have a candidate running for the governor's office. The small local offices will be the proving grounds for the next generation of Southern National elected officials. It gives us a chance to explain our cause at the local level. It also allows a small group to exert more clout. If we are running a candidate in a state-wide election, our resources will be spread very thin. But when we run candidates on the local level, we can concentrate our workers and other resources into a small area where our numbers can make a difference.

This summary is not intended to give full details of how to go about conducting a Southern political revolution. It is only to show in the most general of terms how Southerners can, if they believe in themselves, rid themselves of the chains of federal bondage and reclaim for the next generation of Southerners their birthright of liberty. The important thing to remember is that first comes the educational phase in which we instill pride of our cause within our people; then we make our presence felt on the local level. Before we attempt to gain a single governor's office, we must first establish a strong presence in each chamber of that state's legislature. This should come only after we have proven ourselves on even a more local level.

The Southern people have all the power we need to put an end to forced busing, affirmative action, extravagant welfare spending, the punitive Southern-only Voting Rights Act, the refusal of the Northern liberals to allow Southern conservatives to sit on the Supreme Court, and the economic exploitation of the South into a secondary economic status. What is needed is not more power but *the will to use the power at hand!* The choice is now yours—ignore this challenge and remain a second-class citizen, or unite with your fellow Southerners and help start a Southern political revolution.

Deo Vindice

Northern Voices
Advocating the Principles
of Southern Freedom

I do not desire to survive the independence of my country.

General Thomas J. ("Stonewall") Jackson

We had received this free government from our fathers, baptized in their blood; we had received from them the sacred injunction to preserve it. . . . The heritage of freedom which our fathers left us, we have not been able to bequeath to you.

Robert L. Dabney, D.D., LL.D.

June 15, 1882

Freedom of speech and freedom of the press, precious relics of former history, must not be construed too largely.

General William T. Sherman

Sherman's Other War

Addendum I presents selected quotes from notable Northerners all advocating the same principles of self-determination as did the South when it seceded in 1861. Yankee myth-makers find it difficult to explain away these contradictory quotes from such unlikely pro-Southern advocates as Daniel Webster, Abraham Lincoln, and Horace Greeley.

First to Threaten to Secede From the Union

Timothy Pickering, of Massachusetts, was the first to threaten secession.

Josiah Quincy, of Massachusetts, was the first to mention secession in congressional halls. The year was 1811.

John Quincy Adams, of Massachusetts, was the first to petition Congress to dissolve the Union.

Charles Francis Adams testified that there was no doubt but that his grandfather, John Quincy Adams, believed that a state had the right to secede.

The New England states were the first to hold a secession convention. The convention was held in Hartford, Connecticut, for the purpose of discussing the possibility of seceding because of the unpopularity of the War of 1812.

Secession as a Natural Right
Belonging to the States

When the Constitution was outlined and read, the words *Perpetual Union* which had been in the Articles of Confederation were omitted. Alexander Hamilton and others noticing it, and desiring a Union, opposed the adoption of the Constitution. Some one moved to have it made a *National Government*, but this motion was unanimously defeated. Senator Ellsworth of Connecticut and Senator Gorham of Massachusetts have testified to this.

Elliot's Debates, Vol. V, p. 908

The attributes of sovereignty are now enjoyed by every state in the Union.

Alexander Hamilton

The Thirteen States are Thirteen Sovereign bodies.

Oliver Ellsworth

The States are Nations.

Daniel Webster
Commentaries on the Constitution
Vol. III, p. 287

The States acceded to the Constitution.

Benjamin Franklin
Franklin Works
Vol. V, p. 409

If the states were not left to leave the Union when their rights were interfered with, the government would have been National, but the Convention refused to baptize it by the name.

Daniel Webster
U.S. Senate
February 15, 1833

If the Union was formed by the accession of States then the Union may be dissolved by the secession of States.

Daniel Webster
U.S. Senate
February 15, 1833

The Union is a Union of States founded upon Compact. How is it to be supposed that when different parties enter into a compact for certain purposes either can disregard one provision of it and expect others to observe the rest? If the Northern States willfully and deliberately refuse to carry out their part of the Constitution, the South would be no longer bound to keep the compact. A bargain broken on one side is broken on all sides.

Daniel Webster
Capon Springs Speech, 1851

John Quincy Adams, in 1839, and Abraham Lincoln, 1847, make elaborate arguments in favor of the legal right of a State to Secede.

Judge Black of Pennsylvania
Black's Essays

Any people whatever have a right to abolish the existing government and form a new one that suits them better.

Abraham Lincoln
Congressional Records, 1847

Had [President] Buchanan in 1860 sent an armed force to prevent the nullification of the Fugitive Slave Law, as Andrew Jackson threatened to do in 1833, there would have been a secession of fifteen Northern States instead of thirteen Southern States.

Had the Democrats won out in 1860 the Northern States would have been the seceding States not the Southern.

George Lunt of Massachusetts
Origin of the Late War

If the Declaration of Independence justified the secession of 3,000,000 colonists in 1776, I do not see why the Constitution ratified by the same men should not justify the secession of 5,000,000 of the Southerners from the Federal Union in 1861.

We have repeatedly said, and we once more insist that the great principle embodied by Jefferson in the Declaration of Independence that government derives its power from the consent of the governed is sound and just, then if the Cotton States, the Gulf States or any other States choose to form an independent nation they have a clear right to do it.

The right to secede may be a revolutionary one, but it exists nevertheless; and we do not see how one party can have a right to do what another party has a right to prevent. We must ever resist the asserted right of any State to remain in the Union and nullify or defy the laws thereof; to withdraw from the Union is another matter. And when a section of our Union resolves to go out, we shall resist any coercive acts to keep it in. We hope never to live in a Republic where one section is pinned to the other section by bayonets.

Horace Greeley
New York Tribune

We of the North couldn't make it [slavery] pay, so we are convinced that it is the sum of all villainy. Our plan is more profitable; we take care of no children or sick people, except as paupers, while the owners of slaves have to provide for them from birth till death. So how we view the issue depends on what kind of glasses we use.

If we of the North were called upon to endure one half as much as the Southern people and soldiers do, we would abandon the cause and let the Southern Confederacy be established. We pronounce their cause unholy, but they consider it sacred enough to suffer and die for. Our forefathers in the Revolutionary struggle could not have endured more than these Rebels.

A nation preserved with liberty trampled underfoot is much worse than a nation in fragments but with the spirit of liberty still alive. Southerners persistently claim that their rebellion is for the purpose of preserving this form of government.

Private John H. Haley
Seventeenth Maine Regiment, U.S.A.

ADDENDUM II

Jefferson Davis' Farewell Address to the U.S. Senate

Senator Jefferson Davis of Mississippi was considered a moderate Southerner. He remained loyal to the Union until the political extremists in the North left Mississippi no choice but to withdraw her delegated rights. Senator Davis gave the following address to the United States Senate when he learned that Mississippi had voted to secede.

Note that he made a distinction between the doctrine of nullification and the doctrine of secession. The first was a means to preserve the Union, whereas the second was the supreme method by which a sovereign community could preserve the rights and liberties of its citizens.

He was very careful to explain the fact that with secession the laws of the United States are no longer legally enforceable within the limits of the seceded state. The United States might choose to make war against an independent nation, but it had no authority to demand obedience to United States laws.

Senator Davis also reminded the Senate that when Massachusetts chose to nullify the fugitive slave law that had been upheld by the United States Supreme Court and declared that it (Massachusetts) would secede from the Union before complying with the Supreme Court decision, he as a senator had refused to support efforts to use force to compel Massachusetts to obey the United States laws. Indeed, he defended her right to withdraw from a union in which she felt her rights were disadvantaged. This of course stands in sharp contrast to the aggressive and destructive venom soon to issue forth from the state of Massachusetts and her Northern co-conspirators.

Note also the courtly and gentlemanly manner in which Davis ended his address. This alone should have assured this speech a prominent place in the annals of American history.

Jefferson Davis' Farewell
Address to the U.S. Senate
January 21, 1861

I rise, Mr. President, for the purpose of announcing to the Senate that I have satisfactory evidence that the State of Mississippi, by a solemn ordinance of her people, in convention assembled, has declared her separation from the United States. Under these circumstances, of course, my functions are terminated here. It has seemed to me proper, however, that I should appear in the Senate to announce that fact to my associates, and I will say but very little more. The occasion does not invite me to go into argument; and my physical condition would not permit me to do so, if otherwise; and yet it seems to become me to say something on the part of a State I here represent, on an occasion so solemn as this.

It is known to Senators who have served with me here, that I have, for many years, advocated, as an essential attribute of State sovereignty, the right of a State to secede from the Union. Therefore, if I had not believed there was justifiable cause; if I had thought that Mississippi was acting without sufficient provocation, or without an existing necessity, I should still, under my theory of the Government, because of my allegiance to the State of which I am a citizen, have been bound by her action. I, however, may be permitted to say that I do think she has justifiable cause, and I approve of her act. I conferred with her people before that act was taken, counseled them then that if the state of things which they apprehended should exist when the convention met, they should take the action which they have now adopted.

I hope none who hear me will confound this expression of mine with the advocacy of the right of a State to remain in the Union, and to disregard its constitutional obligations by the nullification of the law. Such is not my theory. Nullification and secession, so often confounded, are, indeed, antagonistic principles. Nullification is a remedy which it is sought to apply within the Union, and against the agent of the States. It is only to be justified when the agent has violated his constitutional obligations, and a State, assuming to judge for itself, denies the right of the agent thus to act, and appeals to the other States of the Union for a decision; but when the States themselves, and when the people of the States, have so acted as to convince us that they will not regard our constitutional rights, then, and then for the first time, arises the doctrine of secession in its practical application.

A great man who now reposes with his fathers, and who has often been arraigned for a want of fealty to the Union, advocated the doctrine of nullification because it preserved the Union. It was because of his deep-seated attachment to the Union—his determination to find some remedy for existing ills short of a severance of the ties which bound South Carolina to the other States, that Mr. Calhoun advocated the doctrine of nullification, which he proclaimed to be peaceful—to be within the limits of State power, not to disturb the Union, but only to be a means of bringing the agent before the tribunal of the States for their judgment.

Secession belongs to a different class of remedies. It is to be justified upon the basis that the States are sovereign. There was a time when none denied it. I hope the time may come again, when a better comprehension of the theory of our government, and the inalienable rights of the people of the States, will prevent any one from denying that each State is a sovereign, and thus may reclaim the grants which it has made to any agent whomsoever.

I, therefore, say I concur in the action of the people of Mississippi, believing it to be necessary and proper, and should have been bound by their action if my belief had been otherwise; and this brings me to the important point which I wish, on this last occasion, to present to the Senate. It is by this confounding of nullification and secession, that the name of a great man, whose ashes now mingle with his mother earth, has been evoked to justify coercion against a seceded State. The phrase, "to execute the laws," was an expression which General Jackson applied to the case of a State refusing to obey the laws while yet a member of the Union. That is not the case which is now presented. The laws are to be executed over the United States, and upon the people of the United States. They have no relations to any foreign country. It is a perversion of terms—which cites that expression for application to a State which has withdrawn from the Union. You may make war on a foreign State. If it be the purpose of gentlemen, they make war against a State which has withdrawn from the Union; but there are no laws of the United States to be executed within the limits of a seceded State. A State, finding herself in the condition in which Mississippi has judged she is—in which her safety requires that she should provide for the maintenance of her rights out of the Union—surrenders all the benefits (and they are known to be many), deprives herself of the advantages (and they are known to be great), severs all the ties of affection (and they are close and enduring), which have bound her to the Union; and thus divesting herself of every benefit—taking upon herself every burden—she claims to be exempt from any power to execute the laws of the United States within her limits.

I well remember an occasion when Massachusetts was arraigned before the bar of the Senate, and when the doctrine of coercion was rife, and to be applied against her, because of the rescue of a fugitive slave in Boston. My opinion then was the same that it is now. Not in a spirit of egotism, but to show that I am not influenced, in my opinion, because the case is my own, I refer to that time and that occasion, as containing the opinion which I then entertained, and on which my present conduct is based. I then said that if Massachusetts, following her through a stated line of conduct, choose to take the last step which separates her from the Union, it is her right to go, and I will neither vote one dollar nor one man to coerce her back; but will say to her, God speed, in memory of the kind associations which once existed between her and the other States.

It has been a conviction of pressing necessity—it has been a belief that we are to be deprived, in the Union, of the rights which our fathers bequeathed to us—which has brought Mississippi into her present decision. She has heard proclaimed the theory that all men are created free and equal, and this made the basis of an attack upon her social institutions; and the sacred Declaration of Independence has been invoked to maintain the position of the equality of the races. The Declaration of Independence is to be construed by the circumstances and purposes for which it was made. The communities were declaring their independence; the people of those communities were asserting that no man was born, to use the language of Mr. Jefferson, booted and spurred, to ride over the rest of mankind; that men were created equal—meaning the men of the political community; that there was no divine right to rule; that no man inherited the right to govern; that there were no classes by which power and place descended to families; but that all stations were equally within the grasp of each member of the body politic. These were the great principles they announced; these were the purposes for which they made their declaration; these were the ends to which their enunciation was directed. They have no reference to the slave; else, how happened it, that, among the items of arraignment against George III, was, that he endeavored to do just what the North has been endeavoring of late to do, to stir up insurrection among our slaves. Had the Declaration announced that the negroes were free and equal, how was the prince to be arraigned for raising up insurrection among them? And how was this to be enumerated among the high crimes which caused the colonies to sever their connection with the mother country? When our constitution was formed, the same idea was rendered more palpable; for there we find provision made for that very class of persons as property; they were not put upon the footing of equality with white men—not even upon that of paupers and convicts; but, so far as representation was concerned, were discriminated against as a lower cast, only to be represented in the numerical portion of three-fifths.

Then, Senators, we recur to the compact which binds us together; we recur to the principles upon which our government was founded; and when you deny them, and when you deny to us the right to withdraw from a government, which, thus perverted, threatens to be destructive of our rights, we but tread in the path of our fathers when we proclaim our independence, and take the hazard. This is done, not in hostility to others—not to injure any section of the country—not even for our own pecuniary benefit; but from the high and solemn motive of defending and protecting the rights we inherited, and which it is our duty to transmit unshorn to our children.

I find in myself, perhaps, a type of the general feeling of my constituents toward yours. I am sure I feel no hostility toward you, Senators from the North. I am sure there is not one of you, whatever sharp discussion there may have been between us, to whom I cannot now say, in the presence of my God, I wish you well; and such, I am sure, is the feeling of the people whom I represent toward those whom you represent. I therefore feel that I but express their desire, when I say I hope, and they hope, for peaceable relations with you, though we must part. They may be mutually beneficial to us in the future, as they have been in the past, if you so will it. The reverse may bring disaster on every portion of the country; and if you will have it thus, we will invoke the God of our fathers, who delivered them from the power of the lion, to protect us from the ravages of the bear; and thus, putting our trust in God, and in our firm hearts and strong arms, we will vindicate the right as best we may.

In the course of my services here, associated, at different times, with a great variety of Senators, I see now around me some with whom I have served long; there have been points of collision, but whatever of offense there has been to me, I leave here—I carry with me no hostile remembrance. Whatever offense I have given, which has not been redressed, or for which satisfaction has not been demanded, I have, Senators, in this hour of our parting, to offer you my apology for any pain which, in the heat of discussion, I have inflicted. I go hence unencumbered of the remembrance of any injury received, and having discharged the duty of making the only reparation in my power for any injury offered.

Mr. President and Senators, having made the announcement which the occasion seemed to me to require, it only remains for me to bid you a final adieu.

President Davis' First Inaugural Address

President Davis' inaugural address should be read by every Southerner. In the first paragraph he announced to the world the South's desire for peace and the hope that it would be able to establish its independence in the absence of hostilities.

In the next paragraph he proclaimed the fact that the South was exercising the right of a people to establish a government founded upon the principle of the consent of the governed. He clearly stated that the South was not motivated by an interest or passion to invade the rights of others and that it was anxious to cultivate peace with all nations. He declared that the South was actuated solely by the desire to preserve its own rights, and its actions were not marked by aggression upon others.

Inaugural Address of President Jefferson Davis
February 18, 1861
Montgomery, Alabama

Gentlemen of the Congress of the Confederate States of America, Friends, and Fellow-citizens: Called to the difficult and responsible station of Chief Magistrate of the Provisional Government which you have instituted, I approach the discharge of the duties assigned to me with humble distrust of my abilities, but with a sustaining confidence in the wisdom of those who are to guide and aid me in the administration of public affairs and an abiding faith in the virtue and patriotism of the people. Looking forward to the speedy establishment of a permanent government to take the place of this, which by its greater moral and physical power will be better able to combat with many difficulties that arise from the conflicting interests of separate nations, I enter upon the duties of the office to which I have been chosen with the hope that the beginning of our career, as a Confederacy, may not be obstructed by hostile opposition to our enjoyment of the separate existence and independence we have asserted, and which, with the blessing of Providence, we intend to maintain.

Our present political position has been achieved in a manner unprecedented in the history of nations. It illustrates the American idea that governments rest on the consent of the governed, and that it is the right of the people to alter or abolish them at will whenever they become destructive of the ends for which they were established. The declared purpose of the compact of the Union from which we have withdrawn was to "establish justice, insure domestic tranquillity, provide for the common defense, promote the general welfare, and secure the blessings of liberty to ourselves and our posterity": and when, in the judgement of the sovereign States composing this Confederacy, it has been perverted from the purposes for which it was ordained, and ceased to answer the ends for which it was established, a peaceful appeal to the ballot box declared that, so far as they are concerned, the Government created by that compact should cease to exist. In this they merely asserted the right which the Declaration of Independence of July 4, 1776, defined to be "inalienable." Of the time and occasion of its exercise they as sovereigns were the final judges, each for itself. The impartial and enlightened verdict of mankind will vindicate the rectitude of our conduct; and He who knows the hearts of men will judge of the sincerity with which we have labored to preserve the Government of our fathers in its spirit.

The right solemnly proclaimed at the birth of the United States, and which has been solemnly affirmed and reaffirmed in the Bills of Rights of the States subsequently admitted into the Union of 1789, undeniably recognizes in the people the power to resume the authority delegated for the purposes of government. Thus the sovereign States here represented have proceeded to form this Confederacy; and it is by abuse of language that their act has been denominated a revolution. They formed a new alliance, but within each State its government has remained; so that the rights of person and property have not been disturbed. The agent through which they communicated with foreign nations is changed, but this does not necessarily interrupt their international relations. Sustained by the consciousness that the transition from the former Union to the present Confederacy has not proceeded from a disregard on our part of just obligations, or any failure to perform every constitutional duty, moved by no interest or passion to invade the rights of others, anxious to cultivate peace and commerce with all nations, if we may not hope to avoid war, we may at least expect that posterity will acquit us of having needlessly engaged in it. Doubly justified by the absence of wrong on our part, and by wanton aggression of the part of others, there can be no cause to doubt that the courage and patriotism of the people of the Confederate States will be found equal to any measure of defense which their honor and security may require.

An agricultural people, whose chief interest is the export of commodities required in every manufacturing country, our true policy is peace, and the freest trade which our necessities will permit. It is alike our interest and that of all those to whom we would sell, and from whom we would buy, that there should be the fewest practicable restrictions upon the interchange of these commodities. There can, however, be but little rivalry between ours and any manufacturing or navigating community, such as the Northeastern States of the American Union. It must follow, therefore, that mutual interest will invite to good will and kind offices on both parts. If, however, passion or lust of dominion should cloud the judgement or inflame the ambition of those States, we must prepare to meet the emergency and maintain, by the final arbitrament of the sword, the position which we have assumed among the nations of the earth.

We have entered upon the career of independence, and it must be inflexibly pursued. Through many years of controversy with our late associates of the Northern States, we have vainly endeavored to secure tranquillity and obtain respect for the rights to which we were entitled. As a necessity, not a choice, we have resorted to the remedy of separation, and henceforth our energies must be directed to the conduct of our own affairs, and the perpetuity of the Confederacy which we have formed. If a just perception of mutual interest shall permit us peaceably to pursue our separate political career, my most earnest desire will have been fulfilled. But if this be denied to us, and the integrity of our territory and jurisdiction be assailed, it will but remain for us with firm resolve to appeal to arms and invoke the blessing of Providence on a just cause.

As a consequence of our new condition and relations, and with a view to meet anticipated wants, it will be necessary to provide for the speedy and efficient organization of branches of the Executive department having special charge of foreign intercourse, finance, military affairs, and the postal service. For purposes of defense, the Confederate States may, under ordinary circumstances, rely mainly upon the militia; but it is deemed advisable, in the present condition of affairs, that there should be a well-instructed and disciplined army, more numerous than would usually be required on a peace establishment. I also suggest that, for the protection of our harbors and commerce on the high seas, a navy adapted to those objects will be required. But this, as well as other subjects appropriate to our necessities, have doubtless engaged the attention of Congress.

With a Constitution differing only from that of our fathers in so far as it is explanatory of their well-known intent, freed from sectional conflicts, which have interfered with the pursuit of the general welfare, it is not unreasonable to expect that States from which we have recently parted may seek to unite their fortunes to ours under the Government which we have instituted. For this our Constitution makes adequate provision; but beyond this, if I mistake not the judgment and will of the people, a reunion with the States from which we have separated is neither practicable nor desirable. To increase the power, develop the resources, and promote the happiness of the Confederacy, it is requisite that there should be so much of homogeneity that the welfare of every portion shall be the aim of the whole. When this does not exist, antagonisms are engendered which must and should result in separation.

Actuated solely by the desire to preserve our own rights, and promote our own welfare, the separation by the Confederate States has been marked by no aggression upon others, and followed by no domestic convulsion. Our industrial pursuits have received no check, the cultivation of our fields has progressed as heretofore, and, even should we be involved in war, there would be no considerable diminution in the production of the staples which have constituted our exports, and in which the commercial world has an interest scarcely less than our own. This common interest of the producer and consumer can only be interrupted by exterior force which would obstruct the transmission of our staples to foreign markets—a course of conduct which would be as unjust, as it would be detrimental, to manufacturing and commercial interest abroad.

Should reason guide the action of the Government from which we have separated, a policy so detrimental to the civilized world, the Northern States included, could not be dictated by even the strongest desire to inflict injury upon us; but, if the contrary should prove true, a terrible responsibility will rest upon it, and the suffering of millions will bear testimony to the folly and wickedness of our aggressors. In the meantime there will remain to us, besides the ordinary means before suggested, the well-known resources for retaliation upon the commerce of an enemy.

Experience in public stations, of subordinate grade to this which your kindness has conferred, has taught me that toil and care and disappointment are the price of official elevation. You will see many errors to forgive, many deficiencies to tolerate; but you shall not find in me either want of zeal or fidelity to the cause that is to me the highest in hope, and of most enduring affection. Your generosity has bestowed upon me an undeserved distinction, one which I neither sought nor desired. Upon the continuance of that sentiment, and upon your wisdom and patriotism, I rely to direct and support me in the performance of the duties required at my hands.

We have changed the constituent parts, but not the system of government. The Constitution framed by our fathers is that of these Confederate States. In their exposition of it, and in the judicial construction it has received, we have a light which reveals its true meaning.

Thus instructed as to the true meaning and just interpretation of that instrument, and ever remembering that all offices are but trusts held for the people, and that powers delegated are to be strictly construed, I will hope by due diligence in the performance of my duties, though I may disappoint your expectations, yet to retain, when retiring, something of the good will and confidence which welcome my entrance into office.

It is joyous in the midst of perilous times to look around upon a people united in heart, where one purpose of high resolve animates and actuates the whole; where the sacrifices to be made are not weighed in the balance against honor and right and liberty and equality. Obstacles may retard, but they cannot long prevent, the progress of a movement sanctified by its justice and sustained by a virtuous people. Reverently let us invoke the God of our fathers to guide and protect us in our efforts to perpetuate the principles which by his blessing they were able to vindicate, establish, and transmit to their posterity. With the continuance of his favor ever gratefully acknowledged, we may hopefully look forward to success, to peace, and to prosperity.

President Davis' Second Inaugural Address

President Davis delivered the following address when the permanent government of the Confederate States of America was moved from Montgomery, Alabama, to Richmond, Virginia.

Notice that he speaks of the South fighting for the principles of the revolutionary fathers. He states that the United States government had been taken over by the numerical majority of the North.

Also note that in the third paragraph he announces to the world that even though the Southern nation was at war and suffering from invasion, still the rights and liberties of Southerners were secure. No doubt he was attempting to draw a distinction between his government's policy and the flagrant violation of the civil liberties of Northerners who opposed the Lincoln administration.

President Davis' Inaugural Address
Permanent Government
February 22, 1862
Richmond, Virginia

Fellow-Citizens: On this the birthday of the man most identified with the establishment of American independence, and beneath the monument erected to commemorate his heroic virtues and those of his compatriots, we have assembled to usher into existence the Permanent Government of the Confederate States. Through this instrumentality, under the favor of Divine Providence, we hope to perpetuate the principles of our revolutionary fathers. The day, the memory, and the purpose seem fitly associated.

It is with mingled feelings of humility and pride that I appear to take, in the presence of the people and before high Heaven, the oath prescribed as a qualification for the exalted station to which the unanimous voice of the people has called me. Deeply sensible of all that is implied by this manifestation of the people's confidence, I am yet more profoundly impressed by the vast responsibility of the office, and humbly feel my own unworthiness.

In return for their kindness I can offer assurance of the gratitude with which it is received; and can but pledge a zealous devotion of every faculty to the service of those who have chosen me as their Chief Magistrate. . . . For proof of the sincerity of our purpose to maintain our ancient institutions, we may point to the Constitution of the Confederacy and the laws enacted under it, as well as to the fact that through all the necessities of an unequal struggle there has been no act on our part to impair personal liberty or the freedom of speech, of thought or of the press. The courts have been open, the judicial functions fully executed, and every right of the peaceful citizen maintained as securely as if a war of invasion had not disturbed the land.

The people of the States now confederated became convinced that the Government of the United States had fallen into the hands of a sectional majority, who would pervert that most sacred of all trusts to the destruction of the rights which it was pledged to protect. They believed that to remain longer in the Union would subject them to continuance of a disparaging discrimination, submission to which would be inconsistent with their welfare, and intolerable to a proud people. They therefore determined to sever its bounds and established a new Confederacy for themselves.

The experiment instituted by our revolutionary fathers, of a voluntary Union of sovereign States for purpose specified in a solemn compact, had been perverted by those who, feeling power and forgetting right, were determined to respect no law but their own will. The Government had ceased to answer the ends for which it was ordained and established. To save ourselves from a revolution which, in its silent but rapid progress, was about to place us under the despotism of numbers, and to preserve in spirit, as well as in form, a system of government we believed to be peculiarly fitted to our condition, and full of promise for mankind, we determined to make a new association, composed of States homogeneous in interest, in policy, and in feeling. True to our traditions of peace and our love of justice, we sent commissioners to the United States to propose a fair and amicable settlement of all questions of public debt or property which might be in dispute. But the Government at Washington, denying our right to self-government, refused even to listen to any proposals for peaceful separation. Nothing was then left to do but to prepare for war. . . .

Fellow-citizens, after the struggle of ages had consecrated the right of the Englishman to constitutional representative government, our colonial ancestors were forced to vindicate that birthright by an appeal to arms. Success crowned their efforts, and they provided for their posterity a peaceful remedy against future aggression.

The tyranny of the unbridled majority, the most odious and least responsible form of despotism, has denied us both the right and the remedy. Therefore we are in arms to renew such sacrifices as our fathers made to the holy cause of constitutional liberty. At the darkest hour of our struggle the Provisional gives place to the Permanent Government. After a series of successes and victories, which covered our arms with glory, we have recently met with serious disasters. But in the heart of a people resolved to be free these disasters tend but to stimulate to increased resistance.

With confidence in the wisdom and virtue of those who will share with me the responsibility and aid me in the conduct of public affairs; securely relying on the patriotism and courage of the people, of which the present war has furnished so many examples, I deeply feel the weight of the responsibilities I now, with unaffected diffidence, am about to assume; and, fully realizing the inequality of human power to guide and to sustain, my hope is reverently fixed on Him whose favor is ever vouchsafed to the cause which is just. With humble gratitude and adoration, acknowledging the Providence which has so visibly protected the Confederacy during its brief but eventful career, to thee, O God, I trustingly commit myself, and prayerfully invoke thy blessing on my country and its cause.

(Speech published in "The General John T. Morgan Newsletter," Sons of Confederate Veterans, Camp # 361, Anniston, Alabama, Vol. IV, No. 07, July 1992)

Law Against Slave Trade Upheld

A VETO MESSAGE

Not only did the Constitution of the Confederate States of America outlaw the importation of slaves from Africa into the South, but the very first veto issued by President Jefferson Davis was on a bill that he deemed to be in conflict with that part of the Confederate Constitution that prohibited the importation of African slaves.

In the body of his veto message, President Davis declares the reason he felt justified in refusing to sign the bill. His recommendation that the bill not be passed was upheld by the Confederate Congress.

You will notice that in President Davis' message he notes how the bill in question would be in conflict with Article I, Section VII, of the Constitution. This is in reference to that portion of the Provisional Constitution, which was superseded on February 22, 1862, by the Constitution of the Confederate States of America. The portion of the constitution of the Confederacy that deals with the importation of African slaves is found in Article I, Section IX. The effect of the law was the same whether one is looking at the Provisional Constitution or the Constitution of the Confederate States of America.

This message along with that portion of the constitution of the Confederacy that prohibits the future importation of African slaves makes a clear challenge to those who assert that the Southern Confederacy was trying to promote slavery. Those who believe in the myth of the "Slaveholders Confederacy" will have a hard time understanding why the president of the Southern Confederacy and the very constitution of that Confederacy were both opposed to the importation of African slaves. But cultural bigots have never allowed truth to stand in the way of their prejudice.

Veto Message
Executive Department, February 28, 1861

Gentlemen of Congress: With sincere deference to the judgement of Congress, I have carefully considered the bill in relation to the slave trade, and to punish persons offending therein, but have not been able to approve it, and therefore do return it with a statement of my objections. The Constitution (section 7, article I.) provides that the importation of African negroes from any foreign country other than slave-holding States of the United States is hereby forbidden, and Congress is required to pass such laws as shall effectually prevent the same. The rule herein given is emphatic, and distinctly directs the legislation which shall effectually prevent the importation of African negroes. The bill before me denounces as high misdemeanor the importation of African negroes or other persons of color, either to be sold as slaves or to be held to service or labor, affixing heavy, degrading penalties on the act, if done with such intent. To that extent it accords with the requirements of the Constitution, but in the sixth section of the bill provision is made for the transfer of persons who may have been illegally imported into the Confederate States to the custody of foreign States or societies, upon condition of deportation and future freedom, and if the proposition thus to surrender them shall not be accepted, it is then made the duty of the President to cause said negroes to be sold at public outcry to the highest bidder in any one of the States where such sale shall not be inconsistent with the laws thereof. This provision seems to me to be in opposition to the policy declared in the Constitution— the prohibition of the importation of African negroes—and in derogation of its mandate to legislate for the effectuation of that object. Wherefore the bill is returned to you for your further consideration, and together with objections, most respectfully submitted.

Jeff'n Davis.

ADDENDUM VI

The Constitution of the Confederate States of America

This addendum contains an overview of the Confederate States (C.S.) Constitution, a comparison between it and the original United States (U.S.) Constitution, and is followed by the text of the Confederate States Constitution.

The Constitution of

The

CONFEDERATE STATES OF AMERICA

INTRODUCTION AND OVERVIEW

The history of the Confederate States has been studied in just about every area of its existence; the one exception is the study of the Confederate (C.S.) Constitution. In the following pages we will provide a limited comparative review of the Confederate Constitution and the United States Constitution. The authors are indebted to the Honorable Devereaux D. Cannon, Jr., as much of the information for this overview is from the body of a speech given by Mr. Cannon at the annual convention of the Louisiana Division, Sons of Confederate Veterans, in Monroe, Louisiana, in 1990. Mr. Cannon is the author of *The Flags of the Confederacy* and chairman of the Confederate Heritage Committee of the Sons of Confederate Veterans. The complete text of the constitution of the Confederate States is provided at the end of this article.

The War for Southern Independence was the culmination of the struggle between the forces of a strong centralized federal government and the forces of a limited central government (i.e., State's Rights). With the adoption of the United States Constitution, American republicanism (limited government with delegated central authority and the remainder of rights in the control of the

333

states) was born. With the advent of the Lincolnite revolution, the government was changed from that of American republicanism to that of American imperialism. No longer a federal republic of sovereign states and limited central government, this country became a nation of unlimited federal authority with states existing as no more than mere geographical entities. This was the real beginning of the American empire, which mirrored the growth of European imperialism.

On a national level, there have been three distinct constitutional conventions held in America. The first, in Philadelphia, Pennsylvania, adopted the Articles of Confederation in 1781. The second, also held in Philadelphia, produced the Constitution of the United States in 1787. The third was held in Montgomery, Alabama, in 1861, and formulated the Constitution of the Confederate States of America. There are some similarities between the two latter conventions:

1. Both sought to remodel the nature of the government of which they had been a member. One (U.S.) was trying to increase the power of a weak federal government, and the other (C.S.) was trying to place more limits on a federal government grown too powerful.

2. Both were secession movements. One (U.S.) would build a union from only those states that would ratify the new Constitution. When the 1787 (U.S.) Constitution went into effect, only nine of the thirteen original states adopted it, which meant that the remaining four states were still members of the old union under the Articles of Confederation. They existed as a foreign power in relation to the new union. For example, Rhode Island did not become a member of the new union for a year and a half after all the other states had joined the new union, during which time she remained an independent state.[1] The states of the Confederate constitutional convention would also secede from an old union to form a new union.

There were also some major differences between these two constitutional conventions. The states that seceded from the old (Articles of Confederation) union did so after they had written their constitution and while they were still members of the old union.

This was done even though their commission was to reform the Articles of Confederation, not to write a new constitution.[2] Also, they seceded from a union under the Articles of Confederation despite the fact that the preamble of these Articles stated that the union formed by the Articles was to be perpetual. The Confederate convention was held by states that had already seceded from the union in 1861 when they wrote a new constitution and submitted it to the states for approval.

CLASSES OF CHANGES
IN THE TWO CONSTITUTIONS

In looking at the two constitutions, the United States Constitution of 1787 and the Confederate States Constitution of 1861, we cannot help but note how similar they are. Indeed, it has been said that if the war was a revolution, it was the most conservative revolution that has ever been fought. The changes in the new Confederate States Constitution from the United States Constitution can be classified into two groups: 1) changes in interpretation and 2) reform amendments.

I. Changes in Interpretation

The South had long felt that the North had used certain words and phrases in the United States Constitution in ways that the Founding Fathers did not intend. To correct this error, its framers wrote words and phrases into the Confederate States Constitution that would leave no doubt as to their meaning.

No words had given the South more grief than the phrase in the preamble of the United States Constitution "We the People . . ." Now it should be noted that although both documents have preambles, these preambles carry no legal weight.[3] Still, the preamble to the United States Constitution was seized upon early by those who wished to expand the role of the federal government at the expense of the states and of the people. The term "We the People" was cited by the centralizers as evidence that the government formed by the 1787 constitution was a general government of all the people and not a creation of the states. If this was the case, they claimed, then the central government was more powerful than the states and had authority over them. Note that the Confederate Constitution states, "We the people of the Confederate

States, each State acting in its sovereign and independent character . . ."! This would make it impossible for anyone to doubt that the states were still sovereign and not subject to the whim of an all-powerful central government.

It is of interest to note that the term "We the People" had given men such as Patrick Henry much concern about the nature of the government that was being formed. This was one reason he worked arduously against adoption of the 1787 constitution. "What right do they have to say 'we the people' rather than we the States,"[4] Henry would complain. But his fellow Virginian, James Madison, stated in *The Federalist Papers #39* that Henry was using poor logic because everyone knew that the constitution was to be submitted to the states for ratification and not to the people. Therefore, argued Madison, the new constitution was indeed the creation of the states "acting as sovereign bodies independent of all others."[5] Although Madison's logic won out, history has proven that Henry's fears were to become a cruel reality.

II. Reform Amendments

These changes were amendments to improve the original Constitution. As such, they fall into three categories:

1. Election reform
2. Impeachment power reform
3. Tax and spending power reform

Now if you are like most modern-day Americans, you are probably thinking, "Sounds like something we need today." After reading the Confederate States Constitution, you may indeed wish we had a similar document to guide (or restrict) the boondoggle tax-and-spend nature of our government.

1. Election Reform.

In both the United States and Confederate States Constitutions, Article I is the longest article. It delegates the largest portions of power to the central government and establishes the legislative branch of the central government.

Under the original United States Constitution, the only requirement of a voter to elect a member of the House of Representatives was that he be qualified to vote in the election of the House of

Representatives from the state in which he resided at the time of the election. After ratification, some states allowed non-citizens to vote in state elections. This meant that non-United States citizens could vote for members of the House of Representatives. Even today there is no way to prevent a state from allowing a foreigner to vote in state elections. The Confederate constitution sought to correct this discrepancy. In one of its first acts, the Confederate Constitution placed a limit on the states' right to allow non-citizens to vote. The Confederate States Constitution states, "No person of foreign birth, not a citizen of the Confederate States, shall be allowed to vote for any officer, civil or political, State or Federal." Note that not only was a prohibition imposed on foreign voters for national office, but no state was allowed to let non-citizens vote.[6]

Reform of the Confederate States Senate was a little different. At that time in American history, the United States and Confederate States Senators were elected by the legislature of each state. The major problem was that no time limit was set for when an election could be called to fill a Senate seat. If the Whigs came to power in a state and the United States Senator from that state had just been elected by the last legislature which was Democratic, the Senator's seat could be put up for re-election while the state legislature was in the hands of the Whigs. This meant that the state would have one Democratic senator in Washington and one waiting for the Democrat's seat to expire so he could move into the Senator's seat. The new Senator could be elected five years before the other Senator's term in office was completed. It was just plain political gimmickry. The Confederate States Constitution prevented this situation by specifying when an election for a Senator was to be held.[7]

2. Impeachment Powers

Although Article I, Section 2, of the Confederate States Constitution limited the rights of the states in certain areas of voting qualification, it also increased the rights of the states in the area of the impeachment process. In Article I, Section 2, of the United States Constitution, the sole power to impeach is held by the House of Representatives. In the Confederate States Constitution, impeachment power is given to the House except "that any judicial or other Federal officer resident and acting solely within the limits of any State, may be impeached by a vote of two-thirds of both branches of the Legislature thereof."[8]

The effect of this law meant that any federal (Confederate) judge who had jurisdiction only within a state, or an official of the Confederate government acting only within a state, could be impeached by the state in which he was serving. Remember that the act of impeachment means only to bring charges against; the federal senate is the body which would try the case. So if a Confederate "federal" district judge (one acting only within a state) committed a crime for which he or she could be impeached, the Confederate States House of Representatives *or* the legislature of that state could bring charges against that judge. In the United States system, only the House of Representatives can bring charges and the Senate will try the case. The people of the states have no recourse to initiate the process of recalling a federal judge or official.[9]

3. Tax-and-Spend Power

If it were not for a growing trillion-dollar national (U.S.) debt, the reforms of the Confederate States Constitution may seem a little excessive. Is it not just a little sickening to realize that it only took seventy-five years under the Original Constitution to make the conservative South realize that more limits needed to be placed on the power of Congress to tax and spend? It is obvious that the Confederate South knew what would happen if the federal government was left to itself with the power to tax and spend. The current trillion-dollar national debt is evidence that the South was correct in its appraisal of the dangers of an all-powerful federal government that could not be made accountable by anyone.

The Confederate States Constitution attempted to limit the danger of tax-and-spend politicians by placing necessary restrictions on the power of Congress to tax and spend:

1. The placement of more restrictions on the purposes for which Congress could tax.

2. The placement of more restrictions on the purposes for which Congress could spend money.

3. The placement of a larger role in the budget process for the executive branch.

The Commerce Clause of the United States Constitution had been used by Northerners to give certain advantages to themselves at the expense of Southerners. The North had used this clause to make improvements in roads, canals, railroads, and bridges in the North, while the South was allowed few such improvements. It has been estimated that as much as a million dollars per year were collected from the South and sent North to pay for "internal improvements." In his book, *Memoirs of Service Afloat*, Adm. Raphael Semmes of the CSS *Alabama*, states that fully three-quarters of the expense of maintaining the United States government was paid by the South.[10] Little was ever returned to the South, but as Admiral Semmes pointed out, no excuse was too absurd for Yankees to make self-serving raids on the federal treasury. Even the cod and mackerel fisheries of New England were given a subsidy from the United States Treasury.[11] Therefore, the Confederate States Constitution made sure that the federal government could not use tax monies to make internal improvements.

The General Welfare Clause of the United States Constitution was also used to enlarge the power of the federal government. The Confederate reformers attempted to limit this abuse by changing the term "promote the general welfare" in the United States Constitution to "carry on the government" in the Confederate States Constitution. One way the North promoted the general welfare was to place duties, or taxes, on imports from foreign nations who competed with Northern industrial output. This, you will recall, was the genesis of the first major conflict that South Carolina and the South had with the federal government. The Confederate States Constitution states, "Nor shall any duties or taxes on importations from foreign nations be laid to promote or foster any branch of industry."[12] Duties could be imposed and collected, but not for the purpose of assisting some industry in its competition with foreign manufacturers.

With the following changes, the executive branch was given a larger role in the budget process:

1. The president was given a line item veto;
2. The only way Congress could appropriate money not specifically requested by the president was to pass the funding with a two-thirds vote.

No single item for the reduction of United States budget over-runs has been discussed more in the last few years than the line item veto. The line item veto would allow the president to veto parts of a spending bill without vetoing the complete bill. As it now stands in the United States Constitution, the president can only veto or approve a spending bill. This means that, when a budget leaves the president's office and goes to Congress, the members of Congress can add to it any boondoggle expenditure (i.e., make a raid on the United States Treasury; that's our tax money) to help them get re-elected. The president cannot take any of these items out of his or her budget, only accept it with the "rider" amendments or veto the whole document. Usually the whole inflated budget is just passed on, and we the people pay—and pay dearly. Under the terms of the Confederate States Constitution, the president could use the line item veto to eliminate these unwarranted raids on the taxpayers' money, just as do approximately thirty state governors today. Every United States president with one exception in the last twenty years has asked for the right that Jefferson Davis had under the Confederate States Constitution.[13]

> Congress shall appropriate no money from the Treasury except by a vote of two-thirds of both Houses, . . . unless it be asked and estimated for by some one of the heads of departments, and submitted to Congress by the President.[14]

How long have we been listening to first the (U.S.) president and then the (U.S) Congress as they have tried to place the blame on each other because the budget is out of balance? This one little clause from the Confederate States Constitution would eliminate that escape mechanism for our politicians. If Congress wanted to spend money, it would have to have a two-thirds majority; otherwise, the spending bill would have to come from the president. We the people would know who the culprits were in the tax-and-spend game, and we could get rid of them! As effective as that clause is, there is one other clause in the Confederate States Constitution that will make a fiscal conservative jump for joy. ". . . Congress shall grant no extra compensation to any public contractor, officer, agent, or servant, after such contract shall have been made or such service rendered."[15] *Can you imagine? No cost over-run contracts!* Just think about it. When the United States government makes a contract now, you and I have our pockets picked by those who sign a contract for one price, but at the end of the contract are paid sometimes two or three times as much for that same contract. Our Confederate forefathers had the wisdom to know how to deal with that type of money-grubbing contractor.[16] There go those thousand-dollar toilet seats. Too bad our present-day politicians don't have the Confederate States Constitution to keep them honest.

In Article II of the Confederate States Constitution, the term of the president is determined to be six years. The Confederate States Constitution changed the term of the president because it was believed that four years were too few to define and to implement presidential policy. Also, the need to run for re-election by a United States president meant that he or she would spend the first four years in office trying to please everyone just to get re-elected. Frequently a chief executive must make hard choices. A single six-year term would make those decisions easier because the president would not have to be counting votes but doing what he or she thought was best for the country. Note that after the six-year term the president could not run for re-election.[17]

The judicial branch of the federal government was the most unchanged portion in the Confederate States Constitution when compared to the same portion in the original United States Constitution.

The only major change was in what is known as diversity jurisdiction. A diversity jurisdiction is one in which a federal judge is called into action, not because some federal issue is in debate but because two individuals from different states have a legal matter at issue. Many times this has no bearing on federal law but, since it is between citizens of two different states, the matter must be decided in a federal court.

The Confederate Constitution stripped this jurisdiction from the federal court. There has been and is a move to do the same for the United States federal courts. This change would clear the courts' docket of many cases that should be handled at the state level and would give the federal courts more time to try cases for which they were intended.

The final major difference between the United States and Confederate States Constitutions arises in the amendment process. The United States Constitution gives Congress the leading role in initiating the amendment process. In the Confederate States Constitution, the amendment process would be initiated by the states. When three or more states called for a constitutional convention, Congress was mandated to convene such a meeting. The convention was to be called by the states and not by the elected members of Congress. The convention could only consider such amendments as were requested by the states who called it. There would be no runaway convention called for one reason but resulting in a completely new set of laws or a new constitution. Remember, this process is how we got the original United States Constitution. The call went out to reform the Articles of Confederation, not to write a new constitution. In the amendment process, our Confederate forefathers, taking a lesson from history, placed limits on such a thing happening again.

Once the new amendments were passed by the constitutional convention, they had to be ratified by two-thirds of the states in order to become a part of the Confederate States Constitution.[18]

SUMMARY

The Constitution of the Confederate States of America was only marginally different from the original United States Constitution. The reforms that were added to the Confederate States Constitution were done so with the insight of seventy-five years of struggle with the North. The document has been written off by many as a "State's Rights" reactionary instrument. But, as has been clearly demonstrated, one of the first acts of this constitution was in effect to limit the power of the states in the area of state voter qualifications. The document went on to attempt to correct acts perceived by the South to have been an injustice of the Northern numerical majority over the numerical minority of the South.

The Confederate States Constitution has also been rejected by those who claim that it "legalized" slavery. Only a South-hating Yankee or a masochistic Scalawag would be foolish enough to swallow that little bit of propaganda. Both the United States and the Confederate States Constitutions recognized African servitude. The only difference is that the Confederate States Constitution called a slave a slave, whereas the United States Constitution referred to slaves as "others" or "such persons." The fact remains that, when both constitutions were submitted to the states for ratification, slavery existed in every one of their constituent states.

Yes, even the Northern states contained slaves at the time of the ratification of the original United States Constitution.

There is one major fact about slavery that makes the two constitutions stand apart. They dealt differently with the issue of the slave trade. The United States Constitution had, at the insistence of the commercial community of the North, with the assistance of two Southern states, protected the slave trade for twenty years *after* the adoption of the United States Constitution. It then *did not stop the slave trade*, but gave Congress the right to do so. The Confederate States Constitution declared a clear and unequivocal prohibition on the slave trade. It also gave the Confederate Congress the power to pass such laws as necessary to enforce the prohibition of that trade. The very first veto that President Jefferson Davis issued was of a bill he deemed in violation of the spirit of the prohibition on the slave trade, and the Confederate States Congress upheld his veto.

One other complaint that is voiced by those ignorant of its true nature is that the Confederate States Constitution contains no "Bill of Rights." Now, if you look only at the end of the document, you will conclude that indeed there is no "Bill of Rights." The reason is that those rights are contained within the very document itself and were not added as some afterthought as they were in the United States Constitution. We will not list them, but you can find what we speak of in Article I, Section 9, of the Confederate States Constitution.

The very fact that many of the items in the Confederate States Constitution have been studied and sought by various United States politicians is in itself vindication of the wisdom of our Confederate forefathers. This document is the very epitome of limited central government and individual freedom. The Confederate States Constitution well served our people over one hundred years ago and will do so again when called upon.

Definition of Terms and Phrases Used

1. Constitution: Charter or system of laws, written or unwritten, that forms the foundation of the political and legal life of a government. (All constitutions in the United States and the Confederate States were written, as opposed to the unwritten constitution of Great Britain.)

2. Articles of Confederation: The first union formed by the independent states of America after the American Revolutionary War. This union lasted from March 1, 1781, until all the states that were members of that union had seceded from it to form the union under the Constitution of the United States, approximately seven years. The Articles of Confederation stated that it would form a "perpetual union," but the union it created was not perpetual.

3. The Constitution of the United States: The formal document that embodied the political and legal system of the United States was written at the Philadelphia, Pennsylvania, convention in 1787. It went into effect among the first nine states that ratified it. Other states of the original thirteen came into the union later as they ratified the Constitution.

4. Provisional Constitution of the Confederate States of America: The temporary constitution used by the Confederate Founding Fathers until a permanent constitution could be drafted and submitted to the states. All acts that originated or officers commissioned during this time were styled "Provisional" (e.g., Major of the Provisional Army, Confederate States of America).

5. Constitution of the Confederate States of America: The formal document that embodied the political and legal system of the Confederate States of America. Written on March 11, 1861, it was established as the permanent constitution of the Confederacy on February 22, 1862. Up until that time, the Provisional Constitution of the Confederate States was the law of the land.

6. Republicanism: A system or philosophy in which the people rule themselves by electing delegates or representatives to make laws. This should not be confused with the Republican Party which, like the Democratic Party, may or may not support "republican" ideas. A republic is the outgrowth of republicanism. The original United States Constitution formed a republic, as did the Confederate States Constitution.

7. *Deo Vindice*: Latin for "God Will Vindicate." Motto found on The Great Seal of the Confederacy.

8. Federal Government: A system of government in which power is divided between a central government, with the re-

mainder of power at the local governmental level. This is the system formed by the Founding Fathers of the United States and also by the Founding Fathers of the Confederate States. The term "federal" does not imply United States or Yankee government. The Confederate States government was also federal and is referred to as such in its constitution.

Constitution
of the
Confederate States of America

We, the people of the Confederate States, each State acting in its sovereign and independent character, in order to form a permanent Federal government, establish justice, insure domestic tranquillity, and secure the blessings of liberty to ourselves and our posterity—invoking the favor and guidance of Almighty God—do ordain and establish this Constitution for the Confederate States of America.

Article I

SECTION 1.

All legislative powers herein delegated shall be vested in a Congress of the Confederate States, which shall consist of a Senate and House of Representatives.

SECTION 2.

1. The House of Representatives shall be composed of members chosen every second year by the people of the several States: and the electors in each State shall be citizens of the Confederate States and have the qualifications requisite for electors of the most numerous branch of the State Legislature; but no person of foreign birth, not a citizen of the Confederate States, shall be allowed to vote for any officer, civil or political, State or Federal.

2. No person shall be a Representative who shall not have attained the age of twenty-five years, and be a citizen of the Confederate States, and who shall not, when elected, be an inhabitant of that State in which he shall be chosen.

3. Representatives and direct taxes shall be apportioned among the several States which may be included within this Confederacy, according to their respective numbers, which shall be determined by adding to the whole number of free persons including those bound to service for a term of years, and excluding Indians not taxed, three-fifths of all slaves. The actual enumeration shall be

made within three years after the first meeting of the Congress of the Confederate States, and within three years after the first meeting of the Congress of the Confederate States, and within every subsequent term of ten years, in such manner as they shall by law direct. The number of Representatives shall not exceed one for every fifty thousand; but each State shall have at least one Representative; and until such enumeration shall be made, the State of South Carolina shall be entitled to choose six; the State of Georgia ten; the State of Alabama nine; the State of Florida two; the State of Mississippi seven; the State of Louisiana six; and the State of Texas six.

4. When vacancies happen in the representation from any State, the Executive authority thereof shall issue writs of election to fill such vacancies.

5. The House of Representatives shall choose their Speaker and other officers; and shall have the sole power of impeachment; except that any judicial or other Federal officer resident and acting solely within the limits of any State, may be impeached by a vote of two-thirds of both branches of the Legislature thereof.

SECTION 3.

1. The Senate of the Confederate States shall be composed of two Senators from each State, chosen for six years by the Legislature thereof, at the regular session next immediately preceding the commencement of the term of service; and each Senator shall have one vote.

2. Immediately after they shall be assembled, in consequence of the first election, they shall be divided as equally as may be into three classes. The seats of the Senators of the first class shall be vacated at the expiration of the second year; of the second class, at the expiration of the fourth year, and of the third class, at the expiration of the sixth year; so that one-third may be chosen every second year; and if vacancies happen, by resignation or otherwise, during the recess of the Legislature of any State, the Executive thereof may make temporary appointments until the next meeting of the Legislature, which shall then fill such vacancies.

3. No person shall be a Senator who shall not have attained the age of thirty years, and be a citizen of the Confederate States; and who

shall not, when elected, be an inhabitant of the State for which he shall be chosen.

4. The Vice-president of the Confederate States shall be President of the Senate, but shall have no vote unless they be equally divided.

5. The Senate shall choose their other officers, and also a President pro tempore, in the absence of the Vice-president, or when he shall exercise the office of President of the Confederate States.

6. The Senate shall have the sole power to try all impeachments. When the president of the Confederate States is tried, the Chief-justice shall preside; and no person shall be convicted without the concurrence of two-thirds of the members present.

7. Judgment in cases of impeachment shall not extend further than removal from office, and disqualification to hold and enjoy any office of honor, trust, or profit under the Confederate States; but the party convicted shall, nevertheless, be liable and subject to indictment, trial, judgment, and punishment, according to law.

SECTION 4.

1. The times, places, and manner of holding elections for Senators and Representatives, shall be prescribed in each State by the Legislature thereof, subject to the provisions of this Constitution; but the Congress may, at any time, by law, make or alter such regulations, except as to the times and places of choosing Senators.

2. The Congress shall assemble at least once in every year; and such meeting shall be on the first Monday in December, unless they shall, by law, appoint a different day.

SECTION 5.

1. Each House shall be the judge of the elections, returns, and qualifications of its own members, and a majority of each shall constitute a quorum to do business; but a smaller number may adjourn from day to day, and may be authorized to compel the attendance of absent members, in such manner and under such penalties as each House may provide.

2. Each House may determine the rules of its proceedings, punish

its members for disorderly behavior, and with the concurrence of two-thirds of the whole number, expel a member.

3. Each House shall keep a journal of its proceedings, and from time to time, publish the same, excepting such parts as may in its judgment require secrecy, and the ayes and nays of the members of either House, on any question, shall, at the desire of one fifth those present, be entered on the journal.

4. Neither House, during the session of Congress, shall, without the consent of the other, adjourn for more than three days, nor to any other place than that in which the two Houses shall be sitting.

SECTION 6.

1. The Senators and Representatives shall receive a compensation for their services, to be ascertained by law, and paid out of the Treasury of the Confederate States. They shall, in all cases except treason and breach of the peace, be privileged from arrest during their attendance at the session of their respective Houses, and in going to and returning from the same; and for any speech or debate in either House, they shall not be questioned in any other place.

2. No Senator or Representative shall, during the time for which he was elected, be appointed to any civil office under the authority of the Confederate States, which shall have been created, or the emoluments whereof shall have been increased during such term; and no person holding any office under the Confederate States shall be a member of either House during his continuance in office. But Congress may, by law, grant to the principal officer in each of the Executive Departments a seat upon the floor of either House, with the privilege of discussing any measure appertaining to his department.

SECTION 7.

1. All bills for raising revenue shall originate in the House of Representatives; but the Senate may propose or concur with amendments as on other bills.

2. Every bill which shall have passed both Houses, shall before it becomes a law, be presented to the President of the Confederate States; if he approve, he shall sign it; but if not, he shall return it

with his objections to that House in which it shall have originated, who shall enter the objections at large on their journal, and proceed to reconsider it. If, after such reconsideration, two-thirds of that House shall agree to pass the bill, it shall be sent, together with the objections, to the other House, by which it shall likewise be reconsidered, and if approved by two-thirds of that House, it shall become a law. But in all such cases, the votes of both Houses shall be for and against the bill shall be entered on the journal of each House respectively. If any bill shall not be returned by the President within ten days (Sundays excepted) after it shall have been presented to him, the same shall be a law in like manner as if he had signed it, unless the Congress, by their adjournment, prevent its return; in which case it shall not be a law. The President may approve any appropriation and disapprove any other appropriation in the same bill. In such case he shall, in signing the bill, designate the appropriations disapproved; and shall return a copy of such appropriations, with his objections, to the House in which the bill shall have originated; and the same proceedings shall then be had as in case of other bills disapproved by the President.

SECTION 8.

The Congress shall have power:

1. To lay and collect taxes, duties, imposts, and excises, for revenue necessary to pay the debts, provide for the common defense, and carry on the Government of the Confederate States; but no bounties shall be granted from the Treasury; not shall any duties or taxes on importations from foreign nations be laid to promote or foster any branch of industry; and all duties, imposts, and excises shall be uniform throughout the Confederate States.

2. To borrow money on the credit of the Confederate States.

3. To regulate commerce with foreign nations, and among the several States, and with the Indian tribes; but neither this, nor any other clause contained in the Constitution, shall be construed to delegate the power to Congress to appropriate money for any internal improvements intended to facilitate commerce; except for the purpose of furnishing lights, beacons, and buoys, and other aids to navigation upon the coasts, and the improvement of harbors, and the removing of obstructions in river navigation, in all

which cases such duties shall be laid on the navigation facilitated thereby as may be necessary to pay the cost and expenses thereof.

4. To establish uniform laws of naturalization, and uniform laws on the subject of bankruptcies throughout the Confederate States, but no law of Congress shall discharge any debt contracted before the passage of the same.

5. To coin money, regulate the value thereof, and of foreign coin, and fix the standard of weights and measures.

6. To provide for the punishment of counterfeiting the securities and current coin of the Confederate States.

7. To establish post-offices and post-routes; but the expenses of the Post-office Department, after the first day of March, in the year of our Lord eighteen hundred and sixty-three, shall be paid out of its own revenues.

8. To promote the progress of science and useful arts, by securing, for limited times, to authors and inventors, the exclusive right to their respective writings and discoveries.

9. To constitute tribunals inferior to the Supreme Court.

10. To define and punish piracies and felonies committed on the high seas, and offences against the law of nations.

11. To declare war, grant letters of marque and reprisal, and make rules concerning captures on land and water.

12. To raise and support armies; but no appropriation of money to that use shall be for a longer term than two years.

13. To provide and maintain a navy.

14 To make rules for the government and regulation of the land and naval forces.

15. To provide for calling forth the militia to execute the laws of the Confederate States, suppress insurrections, and repel invasions.

16. To provide for organizing, arming, and disciplining the militia, and for governing such part of them as may be employed in the service of the Confederate States, reserving to the States respectively the appointment of the officers, and the authority of training the militia according to the discipline prescribed by Congress.

17. To exercise exclusive legislation, in all cases whatsoever over

such district (not exceeding ten miles square) as may, by cession of one or more States, and the acceptance of Congress, become the seat of the Government of the Confederate States; and to exercise like authority over all places purchased by the consent of the legislature of the State in which the same shall be, for the erection of forts, magazines, arsenals, dock-yards, and other needful buildings, and

18. To make all laws which shall be necessary and proper for carrying into execution the foregoing powers, and all other powers vested, by this Constitution, in the Government of the Confederate States, or in any department or officer thereof.

SECTION 9.

1. The importation of negros of the African race, from any foreign country, other than the slaveholding States or Territories of the United States of America, is hereby forbidden, and Congress is required to pass such laws as shall effectually prevent the same.

2. Congress shall also have power to prohibit the introduction of slaves from any State not a member of, or Territory not belonging to, this Confederacy.

3. The privilege of the writ of habeas corpus shall not be suspended, unless when, in cases of rebellion or invasion, the public safety may require it.

4. No bill of attainder, or ex post facto law, or law denying or impairing the right of property in negro slaves, shall be passed.

5. No capitation or other direct tax shall be laid, unless in proportion to the census or enumeration herein before directed to be taken.

6. No tax or duty shall be laid on articles exported from any State, except by a vote of two-thirds of both Houses.

7. No preference shall be given, by any regulation of commerce or revenue, to the ports of one State over those of another.

8. No money shall be drawn from the Treasury but in consequence of appropriations made by law; and a regular statement and account of the receipts and expenditures of all public money shall be published from time to time.

9. Congress shall appropriate no money from the treasury except by a vote of two-thirds of both Houses, taken by yeas and nays, unless it be asked and estimated for by some one of the heads of departments, and submitted to Congress by the President; or for the purpose of paying its own expenses and contingencies; or for which shall have been judicially declared by a tribunal for the investigation of claims against the government, which it is hereby made the duty of Congress to establish.

10. All bills appropriating money shall specify in Federal currency the exact amount of each appropriation, and the purposes for which it is made; and Congress shall grant no extra compensation to any public contractor, officer, agent, or servant, after such contract shall have been made or such service rendered.

11. No title of nobility shall be granted by the Confederate States; and no person holding any office of profit or trust under them shall, without the consent of the Congress, accept of any present, emolument, office, or title of any kind whatever, from any king, prince, or foreign state.

12. Congress shall make no law respecting an establishment of religion, or prohibiting the free exercise thereof; or abridging the freedom of speech or of the press; or the right of the people peaceably to assemble and petition the Government for a redress of grievances.

13. A well-regulated militia being necessary to the security of a free State, the right of the people to keep and bear arms shall not be infringed.

14. No soldier shall, in time of peace, be quartered in any house without the consent of the owner; nor in time of war, but in a manner prescribed by law.

15. The right of the people to be secure in their persons, houses, papers, and effects against unreasonable searches and seizures, shall not be violated; and no warrant shall issue but upon probable cause, supported by oath or affirmation, and particularly describing the place to be searched, and the person or things to be seized.

16. No person shall be held to answer for a capital or otherwise infamous crime, unless on a presentment or indictment of a grand jury, except in cases arising in the land or naval forces, or in the

militia, when in actual service, in time of war, or public danger; nor shall any person be subject for the same offence to be twice put in jeopardy of life or limb; nor be compelled in any criminal case to be a witness against himself; nor be deprived of life, liberty, or property, without due process of law; nor shall private property be taken for public use without just compensation.

17. In all criminal prosecutions the accused shall enjoy the right to a speedy and public trial, by an impartial jury of the State and district wherein the crime shall have been committed, which district shall have been previously ascertained by law, and to be informed of the nature and cause of the accusation; to be confronted with the witnesses against him; to have compulsory process for obtaining witnesses in his favor; and to have the assistance of counsel for his defense.

18. In suits at common law, where the value in controversy shall exceed twenty dollars, the right of trial by jury shall be preserved; and no fact so tried by a jury shall be otherwise re-examined in any court of the Confederacy than according to the rules of the common law.

19. Excessive bail shall not be required, nor excessive fines imposed, nor cruel or unusual punishments inflicted.

20. Every law, or resolution having the force of law, shall relate to but one subject, and that shall be expressed in the title.

SECTION 10.

1. No State shall enter into any treaty, alliance, or confederation; grant letters of marque and reprisal; coin money; make any thing but gold and silver coin a tender in payment of debts; pass any bill of attainder, or ex post facto law, or law impairing the obligation of contracts; or grant any title of nobility.

2. No State shall, without the consent of Congress, lay any imposts or duties on imports or exports, except what may be absolutely necessary for executing its inspection laws; and the net produce of all duties and imposts laid by any State on imposts or exports shall be for the use of the Treasury of the Confederate States; and all such laws shall be subject to the revision and control of Congress.

3. No State shall, without the consent of Congress, lay any duty of

tonnage, except on sea-going vessels, for the improvement of its rivers and harbors navigated by the said vessels; but such duties shall not conflict with any treaties of the Confederate States with foreign nations; and any surplus of revenue thus derived, shall, after making such improvement, be paid into the common treasury; nor shall any State keep troops or ships of war in time of peace, enter into any agreement or compact with another State, or with a foreign power, or engage in war, unless actually invaded, or in such imminent danger as will not admit of delay. But when any river divides or flows though two or more States, they may enter into compacts with each other to improve the navigation thereof.

Article II.

SECTION 1.

1. The Executive power shall be vested in a President of the Confederate States of America. He and the Vice-president shall hold their offices for the term of six years; but the President shall not be re-eligible. The President and Vice-president shall be elected as follows:

2. Each State shall appoint, in such manner as the Legislature thereof may direct, a number of electors equal to the whole number of Senators and Representatives to which the State may be entitled in Congress; but no Senator or Representative, or person holding an office of trust or profit under the Confederate States, shall be appointed an elector.

3. The electors shall meet in their respective States and vote by ballot for President and Vice-president, one of whom, at least, shall not be an inhabitant of the same State with themselves; they shall name in their ballots the person voted for as President, and in distinct ballots the persons voted for as Vice-president, and of the number of votes for each; which list they shall sign, and certify, and transmit, sealed, to the Government of the Confederate States, directed to the President of the Senate who shall, in the presence of the Senate and House of Representatives, open all the certificates, and the votes shall then be counted; the person having the greatest number of votes for President shall be the President, if such number be a majority of the whole number of electors appointed; and if no person have such majority, then, from the per-

son having the highest numbers, not exceeding three, on the list of those voted for as President, the House of Representatives shall choose immediately, by ballot, the President. But, in choosing the President, the votes shall be taken by States, the representation from each State having one vote; a quorum for this purpose shall consist of a member or members from two-thirds of the States, and a majority of all the States shall be necessary to a choice. And if the House of Representatives shall not choose a President, whenever the right of choice shall devolve upon them, before the fourth day of March next following, then the Vice-president shall act as President, as in case of the death or other constitutional disability of the President.

4. The person having the greatest number of votes as Vice-president shall be the Vice-president, if such number be a majority of the whole number of electors appointed; and if no person have a majority, then, from the two highest numbers on the list, the Senate shall choose the Vice-president; a quorum for the purpose shall consist of two-thirds of the whole number of Senators, and a Majority of the whole number shall be necessary for a choice.

5. But no person constitutionally ineligible to the office of President shall be eligible to that of Vice-president of the Confederate States.

6. The Congress may determine the time of choosing the electors, and the day on which they shall give their votes; which day shall be the same throughout the Confederate States.

7. No person except a natural born citizen of the Confederate States or a citizen thereof at the time of the adoption of this Constitution, or a citizen thereof born in the United States prior to the 20th December, 1860, shall be eligible to the office of President. Neither shall any person be eligible to that office who shall not have attained the age of thirty-five years, and been fourteen years a resident within the limits of the Confederate States, as they may exist at the time of his election.

8. In case of the removal of the President from office, or of his death, resignation, or inability to discharge the power and duties of the said office, the same shall devolve on the Vice-president; and the Congress may, by law, provide for the case of the removal, death, resignation, or inability, both of the President and Vice-

president, declaring what officer shall then act as President, and such officer shall act accordingly until the disability be removed, or a President shall be elected.

9. The President shall, at stated times, receive for his services a compensation, which shall neither be increased nor diminished during the period for which he shall have been elected; and he shall not receive within that period any other emolument from the Confederate States, or any of them.

10. Before he enters on the execution of the duties of his office, he shall take the following oath or affirmation: "I do solemnly swear (or affirm) that I will faithfully execute the office of President of the Confederate States, and will, to the best of my ability, preserve, protect, and defend the Constitution thereof."

SECTION 2.

1. The President shall be commander-in-chief of the army and navy of the Confederate States, and of the Militia of the several States, when called into the actual service of the Confederate States; he may require the opinion, in writing, of the principal officer in each of the Executive Departments, upon any subject relating to the duties of their respecting offices; and he shall have power to grant reprieves and pardons for offences against the Confederate States, except in cases of impeachment.

2. He shall have power, by and with the advice and consent of the Senate, to make treaties, provided two-thirds of the Senators present concur; and he shall nominate, and, by and with the advice and consent of the Senate, shall appoint ambassadors, other public ministers, and consuls, judges of the Supreme Court, and all other officers of the Confederate States, whose appointments are not herein otherwise provided for, and which shall be established by law; but the Congress may by law vest the appointments of such inferior officers, as they think proper, in the President alone, in the courts of law, or in the heads of departments.

3. The principal officer in each of the Executive Departments, and all persons connected with the diplomatic service, may be removed from office at the pleasure of the President. All other civil officers of the Executive Department may be removed at any

time by the President, or other appointing power, when their services are unnecessary, or for dishonesty, incapacity, inefficiency, misconduct, or neglect of duty; and when so removed, the removal shall be reported to the Senate, together with the reasons therefor.

4. The President shall have power to fill all vacancies that may happen during the recess of the Senate, by granting commissions which shall expire at the end of their next session; but no person rejected by the Senate shall be reappointed to the same office during their ensuing recess.

SECTION 3.

The President shall, from time to time, give to the Congress information of the state of the Confederacy, and recommend to their consideration such measures as he shall judge necessary and expedient; he may, on extraordinary occasions, convene both Houses, or either of them; and, in case of disagreement between them, with respect to the time of adjournment, he may adjourn them to such time as he shall think proper; he shall receive ambassadors and other public ministers; he shall take care that the laws be faithfully executed, and shall commission all the officers of the Confederate States.

SECTION 4.

The President, Vice-president, and all civil officers of the Confederate States, shall be removed from office on impeachment for, and conviction of, treason, bribery, or other high crimes and misdemeanors.

Article III.

SECTION 1.

The judicial power of the Confederate States shall be vested in one Superior Court, and in such inferior courts as the Congress may from time to time ordain and establish. The Judges, both of the Supreme and inferior courts, shall hold their offices during good behavior, and shall, at stated times, receive for their services a compensation, which shall not be diminished during their continuance in office.

SECTION 2.

1. The judicial power shall extend to all cases arising under this Constitution, the laws of the Confederate States, and treaties made or which shall be made under their authority; to all cases affecting ambassadors, other public ministers, and consuls; to all cases of admiralty and maritime jurisdiction; to controversies to which the Confederate States shall be a party; to controversies between two or more States; between a State and citizens of another State where the State is plaintiff; between citizens claiming lands under grants of different States, and between a State or the citizens thereof, and foreign States, citizens, or subjects; but no State shall be sued by a citizen or subject of any foreign State.

2. In all cases affecting ambassadors, other public ministers, and consuls, and those in which a State shall be a party, the Supreme Court shall have original jurisdiction. In all the other cases before mentioned, the Supreme Court shall have appellate jurisdiction, both as to law and facts, with such exceptions and under such regulations as to law and fact, with such exceptions and under such regulations as the Congress shall make.

3. The trial of all crimes, except in cases of impeachment, shall be by jury, and such trial shall be held in the State where the said crimes shall have been committed; but when not committed within any State, the trial shall be at such place or places as the Congress may by law have directed.

SECTION 3.

1. Treason against the Confederate States shall consist only in levying war against them, or in adhering to their enemies, giving them aid and comfort. No person shall be convicted of treason unless on the testimony of two witnesses to the same overt act, or on confession in open court.

2. The Congress shall have power to declare the punishment of treason, but no attainder of treason shall work corruption of blood, or forfeiture, except during the life of the person attainted.

Article IV.

SECTION 1.

Full faith and credit shall be given in each State to the public acts, records, and judicial proceedings of every other State. And the Congress may, by general laws, prescribe the manner in which such acts, records, and proceedings shall be proved, and the effect thereof.

SECTION 2.

l. The citizen of each State shall be entitled to all the privileges and immunities of citizens of the several States, and shall have the right of transit and sojourn in any State of this confederacy, with their slaves and other property; and the right of property in said slaves shall not be thereby impaired.

2. A person charged in any State with treason, felony, or other crime against the laws of such State, who shall flee from justice, and be found in another State, shall, on demand of the Executive authority of the State from which he fled, be delivered up to be removed to the State having jurisdiction of the crime.

3. No slave or other person held to service or labor in any State or Territory of the Confederate States, under the laws thereof escaping or unlawfully carried into another, shall, in consequence of any law or regulation therein, be discharged from such service or labor; but shall be delivered up on claim of the party to whom such slave belongs, or to whom such service or labor may be due.

SECTION 3.

l. Other States may be admitted into this Confederacy by a vote of two-thirds of the whole House of Representatives, and two-thirds of the Senate, the Senate voting by States; but no new State shall be formed or erected within the jurisdiction of any other State; nor any State be formed by the junction of two or more States, or parts of States, without the consent of the Legislatures of the States concerned as well as of the Congress.

2. The Congress shall have power to dispose of and make all need-

ful rules and regulations concerning the property of the Confederate States, including the lands thereof.

3. The Confederate States may acquire new territory; and Congress shall have power to legislate and provide governments for the inhabitants of all territory belonging to the Confederate States, lying without the limits of the several States, and may permit them, at such times, and in such manner as it may by law provide, to form States to be admitted into the Confederacy. In all such territory, the institution of negro slavery, as it now exists in the Confederate States, shall be recognized and protected by Congress and by the territorial government; and the inhabitants of the several Confederate States and Territories shall have the right to take to such territory any slaves lawfully held by them in any of the States or Territories of the Confederate States.

4. The Confederate States shall guarantee to every State that now is or hereafter may become a member of this Confederacy, a republican form of government, and shall protect each of them against invasion; and on application of the Legislature (or of the Executive when the Legislature is not in session,) against domestic violence.

Article V.

SECTION 1.

Upon the demand of any three States, legally assembled in their several Conventions, the Congress shall summon a Convention of all the States, to take into consideration such amendments to the Constitution as the said States shall concur in suggesting at the time when the said demand is made; and should any of the proposed amendments to the Constitution be agreed on by the said Convention—voting by States—and the same be ratified by the Legislatures of two-thirds of the several States, or by Conventions in Two-thirds thereof—as the one or the other mode of ratification may be proposed by the general Convention—they shall thenceforward form a part of this Constitution. But no State shall, without its consent be deprived of its equal representation in the Senate.

Article VI.

SECTION 1.

1. The Government established by this Constitution is the successor of the Provisional Government of the Confederate States of America, and all the laws passed by the latter shall continue in force until the same shall be repealed or modified; and all the officers appointed by the same shall remain in office until their successors are appointed and qualified, or the offices abolished.

2. All debts contracted and engagements entered into before the adoption of this Constitution, shall be as valid against the Confederate States under this Constitution as under the Provisional Government.

3. This Constitution, and the laws of the Confederate States made in pursuance thereof, and all treaties made, or which shall be made under the authority of the Confederate States, shall be the supreme law of the land, and the judges in every State shall be bound thereby, anything in the Constitution or laws of any State to the contrary notwithstanding.

4. The Senators and Representatives before mentioned, and the members of the several State Legislatures, and all executive and judicial officers, both of the Confederate States and of the several States, shall be bound, by oath or affirmation, to support this Constitution; but no religious test shall ever be required as a qualification to any office of public trust under the Confederate States.

5. The enumeration, in the Constitution, of certain rights, shall not be construed to deny or disparage others retained by the people of the several States.

6. The powers not delegated to the Confederate States by the Constitution, nor prohibited by it to the States, are reserved to the States respectively, or to the people thereof.

Article VII.

SECTION 1.

1. The ratification of the Conventions of five States shall be suffi-

cient for the establishment of this Constitution between the States so ratifying the same. When five States shall have ratified this Constitution in the Manner before specified, the Congress, under the provisional Constitution, shall prescribe the time for holding the election of President and Vice-president, and for the meeting of the electoral college, and for counting the votes and inaugurating the President. They shall also prescribe the time for holding the first election of members of Congress under this Constitution, and the time for assembling the same. Until the assembling of such Congress, the Congress under the provisional Constitution shall continue to exercise the legislative power granted them; not extending beyond the time limited by the Constitution of the Provisional Government.

Adopted unanimously, March 11, 1861

At Montgomery, Alabama

ADDENDUM VII

Plunder of Eleven States

The Yankee myth-makers would have us to believe that the complaints about Reconstruction come from Southern racists, and that, therefore, such complaints should be dismissed out of hand. By using this stratagem they can avoid the necessity of manning their indefensible position. We have included a portion of a speech delivered by a Northern Congressman who was brave enough to challenge the radicals of his day.

Those who think that Reconstruction was a time of re-building and progressive political movements will find no comfort in these brave words.

Plunder of Eleven States
by
Rep. Dan Vorhees, Indiana
U.S. House of Representatives
March 23, 1872

From turret to foundation you tore down the government of eleven States. You left not one stone upon another. You not only destroyed their local laws, but you trampled upon their ruins. You called conventions to frame new Constitutions for these old States. You not only said who should be elected to rule over these States, but you said who should elect them. You fixed the quality and the color of the voters. You purged the ballot box of intelligence and virtue, and in their stead you placed the most ignorant and unqualified race in the world to rule over these people.

Let the great State of Georgia speak first. You permitted her to stand up and start in her new career, but seeing some flaw in your handiwork, you again destroyed and again reconstructed her State government. You clung to her throat; you battered her fea-

365

tures out of shape and recognition, determined that your party should have undisputed possession and enjoyment of her offices, her honors, and her substance. Then bound hand and foot you handed her over to the rapacity of robbers. Her prolific and unbounded resources inflamed their desires.

In 1861 Georgia was free from debt. Taxes were light as air. The burdens of government were easy upon her citizens. Her credit stood high, and when the war closed she was still free from indebtedness. After six years of Republican rule you present her, to the horror of the world, loaded with a debt of $50,000,000, and the crime against Georgia is the crime this same party has committed against the other Southern States. Your work of destruction was more fatal that a scourge of pestilence, war or famine.

Rufus B. Bullock, Governor of Georgia, dictated the legislation of Congress, and the great commonwealth of Georgia was cursed by his presence. With such a Governor, and such a legislature in perfect harmony, morally and politically, their career will go down to posterity without a rival for infamous administrations of the world. That Governor served three years and then absconded with all of the gains. The Legislature of two years spent $100,000 more than had been spent during any eight previous years. They even put the children's money, laid aside for education of white and black, into their own pockets.

There is no form of ruin to which she has not fallen a prey, no curse with which she has not been baptized, no cup of humiliation and suffering her people have not drained to the dregs. There she stands the result of your handiwork, bankrupt in money, ruined in credit, her bonds hawked about the streets at ten cents on the dollar, her prosperity blighted at home and abroad, without peace, happiness, or hope. There she stands with her skeleton frame admonishing all the world of the loathsome consequences of a government fashioned in hate and fanaticism, and founded upon the ignorant and vicious classes of manhood. Her sins may have been many and deep, and the color of scarlet, yet they will become as white as snow in comparison with those you have committed against her in the hour of her helplessness and distress.

I challenge the darkest annals of the human race for a parallel to the robberies which have been perpetrated on these eleven American States. Had you sown seeds of kindness and good will they would long ere this have blossomed into prosperity and peace. Had you sown seeds of honor, you would have reaped a golden harvest of contentment and obedience. Had you extended your charities and your justice to a distressed people you would have awakened a grateful affection in return. But as you planted in hate and nurtured in corruption so have been the fruits which you have gathered.

ADDENDUM VIII

Joint Resolutions, No. 1
State of New Jersey

The following resolution from a Yankee state is instructive as to the degree of disregard that the Radicals had for the Original Constitution. The work of destruction carried on by the Northern Congress was so bad that even some of their own kinsmen were revolted by it.

Even though New Jersey rescinded its ratification, the Radicals nonetheless continued to count New Jersey as having ratified the Fourteenth Amendment. This resolution also supports the Southern claim that the actions of the federal Congress regarding the Southern states and the Constitution were (and still are) unconstitutional, illegal, revolutionary, and void!

Senate
Joint Resolutions, No. 1.
State of New Jersey

Joint Resolutions withdrawing the consent of this State to the proposed Amendment to the Constitution of the United States, entitled article fourteen and rescinding the Joint Resolution, approved September eleventh, Anno Domini eighteen hundred and sixty-six, whereby it was resolved that said proposed Amendment was ratified by the Legislature of this State.

The Legislature of the State of New Jersey having seriously and deliberately considered the present situation of the United States, do declare and make known:

That the basis of all government is the consent of the governed; and all constitutions are contracts between the parties bound thereby; that until any proposition to alter the fundamental law, to which all the States have consented, has been ratified by such number of the States as, by the Federal Constitution, makes it

370 THE SOUTH WAS RIGHT!

binding upon all, any one that has assented is at liberty to withdraw that assent, and it becomes its duty to do so, when, upon mature consideration, such withdrawal seems to be necessary to the safety and happiness of all; prudence dictates that a consent once given should not be recalled for light and transient causes; but the right is a natural right, the exercise of which is accompanied with no injustice to any of the parties; it has therefore, been universally recognized as inhering in every party, and has ever been left unimpaired by any positive regulation.

The said proposed amendment not having yet received the assent of the three-fourths of the States, which is necessary to make it valid, the natural and constitutional right of this State to withdraw its assent is undeniable.

With these impressions, and with a solemn appeal to the Searcher of all Hearts for the rectitude of our intentions, and under the conviction that the origin and objects of said proposed amendments were unseemly and unjust, and that the necessary result of its adoption must be the disturbance of the harmony, if not the destruction, of our system of self-government, and that it is our duty to ourselves and our sister States to expose the same, do further declare:

That it being necessary, by the Constitution, that every amendment to the same should be proposed by two-thirds of both Houses of Congress, the authors of the said proposition, for the purpose of securing the assent of the requisite majority, determined to, and did, exclude from the said two Houses eighty representatives from eleven States of the Union, upon the pretence that there were no such States in the Union; but, finding that two-thirds of the remainder of said Houses could not be brought to assent to the said proposition, they deliberately formed and carried out the design of mutilating the integrity of the United States Senate, and without any pretext or justification, other than the possession of the power, without the right, and in palpable violation of the Constitution, ejected a member of their own body, representing this State, and thus practically denied to New Jersey its equal suffrage in the Senate, and thereby nominally secured the vote of two-thirds of the said Houses.

The objective of dismembering the highest representative assembly in the nation, and humiliating a State of the Union, faithful at all times to all its obligations, and the object of said amendment were one—to place new and unheard of powers in the hands of a faction, that it might absorb to itself all executive, judicial and legislative power, necessary to secure to itself immunity for the unconstitutional acts it had already committed, and those it has since inflicted on a too patient people.

The subsequent usurpations of these once national assemblies in passing pretended laws for the establishment, in ten States, of martial law, which is nothing but the will of the military commander, and therefore inconsistent with the very nature of all law, for the purpose of reducing to slavery men of their own race in those States, or compelling them, contrary to their own convictions, to exercise the elective franchise in obedience to the dictation of a faction in those assemblies; the attempt to commit to one man arbitrary and uncontrollable power, which they have found necessary to exercise to force the people of those States into compliance with their will; the authority given to the Secretary of War to use the name of the President to countermand the President's orders and to certify military orders to be the direction of the President, when they are notoriously known to be contrary to the President's direction, thus keeping up the form of the Constitution to which the people are accustomed, but practically deposing the President from his office of Commander-in-Chief, and suppressing one of the great departments of the government that of the executive; the attempt to withdraw from the supreme judicial tribunal of the nation the jurisdiction to examine and decide upon the conformity of their pretended laws to the Constitution, which was the chief function of that august tribunal as organized by the fathers of the republic; all are but ample explanations of the power they hoped to acquire by the adoption of the said amendment.

To conceal from the people the immense alterations of the fundamental law they intended to accomplish by the said amendment, they gilded the same with prepositions of justice, drawn from the State Constitutions; but like all the essays of unlawful power to commend its designs to poplar favor it is marked by the most absurd and incoherent provisions.

It proposes to make it a part of the Constitution of the United States, that naturalized citizens of the United States shall be citizens of the United States; as if they were not so with out such absurd declaration.

It lodges with the legislative branch of the government the power of pardon, which properly belongs, by our system, to the executive.

It denounces, and inflicts punishment for past offenses, by constitutional provision, and thus would make the whole people of this great nation, in their most solemn and sovereign act, guilty of violating a cardinal principle of American liberty: that no punishment can be inflicted for any offence, unless it is provided by law before the commission of the offence.

It usurps the power of punishment, which, in any coherent system of government, belongs to the judiciary, and commits it to the people in their sovereign capacity.

It degrades the nation, by proclaiming to the world that no confidence can be placed in its honesty or morality.

It appeals to the fears of the public creditors by publishing a libel on the American people, and fixing it forever in the national Constitution, as a stigma upon the present generation, that there must be constitutional guards against a repudiation of the public debt; as if it were possible that a people who were so corrupt as to disregard such an obligation would be bound by any contract, constitutional or otherwise.

It imposes new prohibitions upon the power of the State to pass laws, and interdicts the execution of such parts of the common law as the national judiciary may esteem inconsistent with the vague provisions of the said amendment, made vague for the purpose of facilitating encroachments upon the lives, liberties and property of the people.

It enlarges the judicial power of the United States so as to bring every law passed by the State, and every principle of the common law relating to life, liberty, or property, within the jurisdiction of the Federal tribunals, and charges those tribunals with duties, to the due performance of which they, from their nature and organization, and their distances from the people, are unequal.

It makes a new apportionment of representation in the national councils, for no other reason than thereby to secure to a faction a sufficient number of the votes of a servile and ignorant race to out weigh the intelligent voices of their own.

It sets up a standard of suffrage dependent entirely upon citizenship, majority, inhabitancy and manhood, and any interference whatever by the State, imposing any other reasonable qualifications as to time of inhabitancy, causes a reduction of the State's representation.

But the demand of the supporters of this amendment in this State, that Congress should compel the people of New Jersey to adopt what is called "impartial suffrage," makes it apparent that this section was intended to transfer to Congress the whole control of the right of suffrage in the State, and to deprive the State of a free representation by destroying the power of regulating suffrage within its own limits, a power which they have never been willing to surrender to the general government, and which was reserved to the States as the fundamental principle on which the Constitution itself was constructed—principles of self-government.

This section, as well as all others of the amendment, is couched in ambiguous, vague and obscure language, the uniform resort of those who seek to encroach upon public liberty; strictly construed, it dispenses entirely with a House of Representatives, unless the States shall abrogate every qualification, and especially that of time of inhabitance, with out which the right of suffrage is worthless.

This Legislature, feeling conscious of the support of the largest majority of the people that has ever given expression to the public will, declare that the said proposed amendment being designed to confer, or to compel the States to confer the sovereign right of the elective franchise upon a race which has never given the slightest evidence, at any time, or in any quarter of the globe, of its capacity for self-government, and erect an impracticable standard of suffrage, which will render the right valueless to any portion of the people, was intended to overthrow the system of self-government under which the people of United States have for eighty years enjoyed their liberties, and is unfit, from its origin, its object and its matter, to be incorporated with the fundamental law of a free people; therefore,

1. BE IT RESOLVED, by the Senate and General Assembly of the State of New Jersey, That the joint resolution approved September eleventh, Anno Domini eighteen hundred and sixty-six, relative to amending the Constitution of the United States, which is in the following words, to wit:

(there follows a recitation of the original ratification resolution of the Fourteenth Amendment which is here omitted)

Be and the same is hereby rescinded, and the consent, on behalf of the State of New Jersey, to ratify the proposed fourteenth amendment to the Constitution of the United States, is hereby withdrawn.

2. AND BE IT RESOLVED, That copies of the foregoing preamble and resolution certified to by the president of the Senate and Speaker of the General Assembly, be forwarded to the President of the United States, the Secretary of State of the United States, to each of our Senators and Representatives in Congress, and to the Governors of the respective States.

3. AND BE IT RESOLVED, That these resolutions shall take effect immediately.

(Followed by the appropriate attestation documentation)

ADDENDUM IX

U.S. News and World Report Editorial September 27, 1957, and January 26, 1970

The following is an abstract from an editorial written by David Lawrence, former editor of *U.S. News and World Report*. Here we see that a major American journal took an editorial stand in support of the claim that the federal government used fraudulent methods to enact the Fourteenth Amendment. Of course, the Yankee myth-makers have done a great job in making sure that these facts are kept out of public sight.

ABSTRACT

U.S. News and World Report
The Worst Scandal in Our History

The fraudulent methods used to enact the Fourteenth Amendment were the subject of a two-page editorial in the September 27, 1957 (re-published January 26, 1970), issue of *U.S. News and World Report*. David Lawrence, editor, openly admitted that "No such amendment was ever legally ratified."

The editorial noted that the Fourteenth Amendment was the legal excuse used by the Supreme Court in its various "desegregation decisions." As we have already noted: It is these Reconstruction acts that have been repeatedly used by the Northern-controlled liberal government to impose and re-impose various forms of Reconstruction upon the Southern people.

David Lawrence noted that to achieve its purpose the Northern Congress:

1. Expelled the South from Congress (an open and flagrant violation of Section V of the U.S. Constitution).

2. Illegally used military forces to occupy peaceful states (remember, the war was over and new civil state governments had been established and their representatives and senators sent to Congress).

3. Disfranchised a large portion of the population (i.e., those who had supported the Confederate government—a violation of the constitutional prohibition against the enactment of *ex post facto* law).

4. Declared that no Southern state could have its seats back unless such state ratified the Fourteenth Amendment (i.e., yielded to forced ratification).

5. Counted as ratifying the Fourteenth Amendment the states of Ohio and New Jersey, both of which had rescinded their ratifications. In addition, the Oregon legislature rescinded its ratification three months later due to the "illegal and revolutionary" methods used by the proponents of enactment.

According to David Lawrence, the history of the Fourteenth Amendment ". . . is a disgrace to free government," but he reminds us, "It is never too late to correct injustice."

---

abstracted from
U.S. News and World Report
January 26, 1970
pages 95-96

ADDENDUM X

ABSTRACT

The Georgia Journal of Southern Legal History

SPRING/SUMMER 1991
VOLUME 1 NUMBER 1

Was the Fourteenth Amendment
Constitutionally Adopted?

BY FORREST MCDONALD

Dr. Forrest McDonald is a professor of history at the University of Alabama. The above captioned article is one of the latest to demonstrate the illegal methods used by the radical Congress to force a major change in the balance of power between the federal and state governments.

Dr. McDonald reminds his readers that the Southern states were not the exclusive advocates of the concept of State's Rights and interposition. In the early days of the Constitution it was the New England and Northern states who were the first to advocate these principles. They were also more successful in their efforts to use said principles to protect their vested interests. In 1808 Connecticut and Massachusetts endorsed interposition; the famous New England Secession Convention was held at Hartford, Connecticut, in 1814; the House of Representatives of Massachusetts in 1846 declared the war with Mexico to be unconstitutional; and many Northern states successfully nullified the fugitive slave acts, thereby overruling both the federal Congress and the federal Supreme Court.

Dr. McDonald notes that in their "zeal to punish, plunder, and reconstruct the South," the radical Congress "greatly increased the powers of Congress at the expense of the states" and that the process of adopting the Fourteenth Amendment was "marred by repeated irregularities." It is here that he gives fresh insight to the old, yet still valid, arguments regarding the legitimacy of this and all Reconstruction era congressional acts. Dr. McDonald notes that

in *Ex parte Milligan* the United States Supreme Court ruled that
martial law could not be constitutionally imposed in the absence of
war or rebellion and in areas where the civilian courts were functioning. The Reconstruction Act of March 1867 was a brazen and
flagrant violation of this decision. He also noted that by declaring
that the Southern states were without legal governments, Congress had trapped itself in a contradiction—earlier Congress had
accepted the ratifications by the Southern states to the Thirteenth
Amendment, but now Congress had declared these same states to
be illegal. Dr. McDonald also notes that the act denied civil rights
to upwards of nine million Southerners. As such, it violated the
Fifth Amendment guarantee of due process and was in direct violation of constitutional prohibitions against bills of attainder.*

To make the point of just how absurd it is to contend that the
Fourteenth Amendment was legally ratified, Dr. McDonald asks
us to make some very interesting assumptions:

First, assume that the amendment had been constitutionally
proposed, then;

Assume that the ratifications of Tennessee, Oregon, and West
Virginia were proper, then;

Assume that the rescission by New Jersey and Ohio were
illegal—then, you are left with the problem that still Congress is
six votes short of the number necessary for ratification!

Now comes the interesting part: to obtain the remaining states,
Congress required the Southern states to ratify in order to get
back into the Union. But remember, states can vote on ratification
of a constitutional amendment "only if they were duly recognized
as governments at the time they acted on the amendment." But
Congress had already declared these "states" to be illegal governments and not a part of the Union—therefore their ratifications,
according to constitutional principle, cannot be counted toward final ratification. Thus we are left with an amendment that was
never ratified!

After learning that the South had rejected the Fourteenth
Amendment, Senator James R. Doolittle of Wisconsin declared

---

*Bill of Attainder: A legislative act, no matter what its form, that applies either to
named individuals or to easily ascertainable members of a group in such a way as
to inflict punishment on them without a judicial trial.

that the North would "march upon them and force them to adopt it at the point of the bayonet."

In his concluding remarks, Dr. McDonald states, "Clearly, then, the Fourteenth Amendment was never constitutionally ratified, even if it had been constitutionally proposed."

ADDENDUM XI

I Am Condemned to Be Shot

Asey V. Ladd, Private, C.S.A.
OCTOBER 29, 1864

The following previously unpublished letters have been transcribed from photocopies of the originals. Asey V. Ladd was a POW held by the Yankee government. He had served three years in the Confederate army. He enlisted on March 10, 1861, and was serving with Company A, Fourth Missouri Calvary when taken prisoner. His official record states that he "died while prisoner of war." The truth is that he was murdered by officials of the United States government in retaliation for local Confederate military activities. The family stressed that Asey was a POW at the time and had nothing to do with the raid that resulted in the death of several Yankee soldiers.

It should be noted that these letters were dated well after Gen. John McNeil had received his promotion from Abraham Lincoln, a promotion given as a reward for an earlier and similar execution of innocent Southern POWs (see Chapter 4, "Yankee Atrocities"). Perhaps the commander of this Yankee POW camp was trying for a promotion from President Lincoln!

St. Louis, Mo.
Oct. 29, 1864

Dear Wife and Children:

I take my pen with trembling hand to inform you that I have to be shot between 2 & 4 o'clock this evening. I have but few hours to remain in this unfriendly world. There is 6 of us sentenced to die in [retaliation] of 6 union soldiers that was shot by Reeves men. My dear wife don't grieve after me. I want you to meet me in Heaven. I want you to teach the children piety, so that they may meet me at the right hand of God. I can't tell you my feelings but you can form some idea of my feeling when you hear of my fate.

I don't want you to let this bear on your mind anymore than you can help, for you are now left to take care of my dear children. Tell them to remember their dear father. I want you to go back to the old place and try to make a support for you and the children.

I want you to tell all my friends that I have gone home to rest. I want you to go to Mr. Conner and tell him to assist you in winding up your business. If he is not there get Mr. Cleveland. If you don't get this letter before St. Francis River gets up you had better stay there until you can make a crop, and you can go in the dry season.

It is now half past 4 AM. I must bring my letter to a close, leaving you in the hands of God. I send you my best love and respect in the hour of death. Kiss all the children for me. You need have no uneasiness about my future state, for my faith is well founded and I fear no evil. God is my refuge and hiding place.

> Good-by Amy.
>
> Asey Ladd

Gratiot Street Prison
St. Louis, Mo.
Oct. 29th, 1864

My Dear Father,

I am condemned to be shot today between the hours of two and four o'clock P.M. in retaliation for some men shot by Reeves (Major Wilson and six men). I am an innocent man and it is hard to die for anothers sins. You can imagine my feelings when I think of you, my wife and children. I want my family to come back to my old place. If you live till peace is made I want you to settle up and pay off all my debts. You need have no uneasiness as to my future state for my faith is well founded and I fear no evil, God is my refuge and hiding place. Meet me in Haven.

> Good bye
>
> Asey Ladd

ADDENDUM XII

A Former Slave's Letter Home

According to Yankee mythology, pre-war Southerners were cruel slave masters, and black Southerners were awaiting any opportunity to rise up and destroy both the system of slavery and their cruel masters.

In the booklet *Bill Yopp: Narrative of a Slave* the author tells about the wife of a Connecticut minister who arrived in the South prior to the war. This poor misguided lady imagined herself to be a missionary to a foreign land where an enslaved people were oppressed and suffering daily the cruelties of barbaric masters. She was astonished to find that, generally speaking, white Southerners were generous and kind and regarded black Southerners not as slaves but as servants. Added to this was her surprise to find that black Southerners were generally contented and happy.

The following letter has been transcribed from the original.* It was written on November 17, 1929, by Jim Holliman, a former slave. He was writing back to his "white folks" to find out what had happened since his moving from Tennessee to Texas. He was eighty-nine years old at the time of this writing. This letter shines through the darkness of lies espoused by the Yankee myth-makers and illuminates a time when people, even though different in skin color and station of life, possessed a sense of mutual respect and admiration that is the very essence of human love. No wonder the Yankee myth-makers are so determined to suffocate such truth!

Henderson, Texas
November 17, 1929

Mr. Henry Holleman, Dear sir,

I received a letter from you some few months ago which I was

---

*The original is held by James K. Turner of Nashville, Tennessee, the great-grandson of Henry Samuel Holleman, to whom the letter is addressed.

very proud of. But being very much crowded in business I have failed to answer at once as I should have done. But I hope you will not think hard of me etc. I am in a condition now to reply to your letters at any returning mail. I still wants to hear from my old home state and white and colored friends and if you will be so kind as to correspond with [me] I will make it [a] history for you and for me also. My father was born in the Holleman family and was never owned by any other until old man Mark Holliman died. Mark's father raised him and he was treated as one of the white children and at the old man's death he fell to Mark who also treated [him] as a white man. He was allowed to carry his gun which was strictly against the Slave rule. Grandma was the cook for white and black. The table was set 3 times a day for black as well as for the white.

I must not tell you too much now if I do I want leave enough for history. But I will say that the Hollemans were good white people.

I am a native of Tenn. the best state in the union. But I been in Texas the best part of my life. I want to hear from you and all the rest of the Holliman[s], is any of Joel Hollimans folks living? Bill, whom they call scrap when he was a boy, he use to run business. Please write me a few lines and I may have something good to answer.

Jim Holliman

(P.S.) I want you to give me the date of Mark Holliman's Sale [the sale of Mark Holleman's estate] for I was, at the time of the Sale, a boy of 10 or 12 years old, all of the property was sold and my papa, Abe, and Sue were Sold to new masters. Dr. Shelby bought papa, next I want you to get on your horse or on some way and go to the Smith cemetery and give me the dates of old master and mistress deaths and I will pay you and if you think it will be too big a job write me first and let me know what it will cost me and we will make a trade. Let me hear from you at once.

Jim Holliman

ADDENDUM XIII

Recommended Reading
for the Southern Nationalist

1. *A View of the Constitution of the United States of America*, William Rawle, H. C. Carey and Lea, Philadelphia, Pennsylvania, 1825. One of the first texts on the United States Constitution. Judge Rawle, a Northern Abolitionist, unequivocally stated in this work that the states have a right to secede from the Union.

2. *Abandoned, The Betrayal of the American Middle Class Since World War II*, William Quirk and Randall Bridwell, Madison Books, New York, New York, 1992. The authors demonstrate how liberalism's experiment with non-democratic government created a fatal schism between the government and the majority of Americans. "Now, a failed government has led this rich country into bankruptcy."

3. *A Defense of Virginia and the South*, Professor Robert L. Dabney, D.D., Sprinkle Publications, Harrisonburg, Virginia, 1977. The author explains how slavery was forced upon the South first by England and later by New England.

4. *A Fool's Errand*, Albion W. Tourgee, The Belknap Press of Harvard University Press, Cambridge, Massachusetts, 1961. A Carpetbagger's story of the failure of Reconstruction. *The Fool* is not friendly toward the South, but it is instructive as to the thinking of the Northern people at the time.

5. *Cracker Culture: Celtic Ways in the Old South*, Grady McWhiney, The University of Alabama Press, Tuscaloosa, Alabama, 1988. An excellent attempt to explain North/South differences in terms of antagonistic cultures.

6. *The Conduct of Federal Troops in Louisiana*, edited by David Edmonds, The Acadiana Press, Lafayette, Louisiana, 1988. Sworn

testimony from eyewitnesses to the outrages committed by the Yankee invaders of Louisiana.

7. *Free to Choose*, Milton Friedman, Harcourt Brace Jovanovich, New York, New York, 1980. Friedman explains why it is necessary to protect individual freedom and its importance to economic prosperity. Though he is not a Southerner, his views on economics and civil liberties are worthy of study.

8. *I'll Take My Stand*, Louisiana State University Press, Baton Rouge, Louisiana, 1983. Twelve Southerners in 1930 warn us about the dangers of abandoning our Southern folkways while seeking after the Yankee god of progress.

9. *Memoirs of Service Afloat*, Admiral Raphael Semmes, The Blue and Gray Press, Secaucus, New Jersey, 1987. The author uses the first six chapters to explain why the South found it necessary to establish an independent nation.

10. *Plain Folk of the Old South*, Frank L. Owsley, Louisiana State University Press, Baton Rouse, Louisiana, 1949. A study of the non-plantation white South.

11. *Southern by the Grace of God*, Michael A. Grissom, Pelican Publishing Company, Gretna, Louisiana, 1988. The author celebrates being a Southerner. This book cannot be read while hiding in a closet!

12. *Southern History of the War*, Edward A. Pollard, The Fairfax Press, New York, New York, 1978. The title reveals the author's viewpoint—an excellent work, originally published in 1866.

13. *The Confederate States Constitution of 1861*, Marshall L. DeRosa, University of Missouri Press, Columbia and London, 1991. The author explains that the Confederate States Constitution was a natural extension of the original United States Constitution.

14. *The Federal Government: Its True Nature and Character*, Abel P. Upshur, St. Thomas Press, Houston, Texas, 1977. Judge Upshur refutes those of the Story and Webster school who believe that the Constitution made the federal government the supreme ruler of the people of the United States.

15. *The Gray Book*, Arthur H. Jennings, Chairman, The Gray Book Committee, Sons of Confederate Veterans, Hattiesburg, Mississippi. Originally published immediately after World War I and re-

published during the 1950s, it attempted to correct the anti-Southern slander issuing from the Yankee myth-makers.

16. *The Last Rebel Yell*, Michael A. Grissom, Rebel Press, Nashville, Tennessee, 1991. The author picks up where he left off in *Southern by the Grace of God*.

17. *The Southern Tradition at Bay*, Richard Weaver, Regnery Gateway, Inc., Washington, D.C., A history of postbellum thought. A must for all serious students.

18. *The Tragic Era*, Claude Bowers, Halcyon House, New York, New York, 1929. A documented account of Reconstruction.

19. *The Real Lincoln*, Charles L. C. Minor, Sprinkle Publications, Harrisonburg, Virginia, 1992. Lincoln's use of brute force against his enemies both North and South is documented in this study.

20. *The Uncivil War: Union Army and Navy Excesses in the Official Records*, Thomas B. Keys, The Beauvoir Press, Biloxi, Mississippi, 1991. The United States' own records are used to demonstrate how cruelly and viciously the Yankee invaders treated the Southern people.

21. *Time on the Cross*, Fogel & Engerman, Little Brown and Company, Boston, Massachusetts, 1974. A contemporary study of African-American slavery that has caused the Yankee liberals to howl!

22. *Yankee Autumn in Acadiana*, David Edmonds, The Acadiana Press, Lafayette, Louisiana, 1979. An in-depth study of the outrages committed by the Yankee invaders of Louisiana using the federal government's own records.

23. *War for What?*, Francis W. Springer, Bill Coats Ltd., Nashville, Tennessee, 1990. An honest appraisal of why the North invaded and conquered the South.

The Southern Nationalist should also study the works of John Stuart Mill (*On Liberty* and *Representative Government*) and the works of John C. Calhoun (*A Disquisition on Government* and *Discourses on the Constitution*) to form a better idea of the Southern National political ideal.

Notes

CHAPTER ONE

1. Grady McWhiney, *Journal of Mississippi History*, "Jefferson Davis the Unforgiven," vol. XLII, May 1980, p. 124

2. Michael A. Grissom, *Southern by the Grace of God* (Pelican Publishing Company, Gretna, LA: 1988), p. iv

3. Niccolo Machiavelli, *The Prince and the Discourses* (Modern Library, New York, NY: 1950), pp. 18-19, 153, 197

4. Richard M. Weaver, *The Southern Tradition at Bay* (Arlington House, New Rochelle, NY: 1968), p. 116

5. Varina Davis, *The Davis Family Newsletter*, Vol. I, # 11, Rosemont Plantation

6. General Stephen D. Lee in an address to the Sons of Confederate Veterans, 1896

7. Raphael Semmes, *Memoirs of Service Afloat* (The Blue and Gray Press, Secaucus, NJ: 1987), preface

8. J. L. M. Curry, *The Southern States of the American Union* (B. F. Johnson Publishing Company, Richmond, VA: 1890).

9. Sons of Confederate Veterans, *The Gray Book*, p. 3

10. Ibid

11. Davidson, Fletcher, et al., *I'll Take My Stand* (Louisiana State University Press, Baton Rouge, LA: 1983), p. 61

12. Ibid, pp. 66-67

13. Ibid, p. 63

14. Ibid

15. Frank L. Owsley, *Plain Folk of the Old South* (Louisiana State University Press, Baton Rouge, LA: 1982), p. 2 [Also see Andrew Nelson Lytle, et al., *I'll Take My Stand* (Louisiana State University Press, Baton Rouge, LA: 1983), p. 211]

16. Ibid, pp. 36-39, 44-48

17. Ibid, p. 134

18. Ibid, p. 19

19. Fogle, R. W. and Engerman, S. L., *Time on the Cross* (Little, Brown and Company, Boston, MA: 1974), p. 250

20. Ibid, p. 255

21. Ibid, p. 254

22. Ibid, p. 256

23. Ibid, pp. 248-49

24. Bruce Catton, *Picture History of the Civil War* (Bonanza Books, New York, NY: 1982), p. 25

25. Grady McWhiney, *Cracker Culture: Celtic Ways in the Old South* (Tuscaloosa, AL: The University of Alabama Press, Tuscaloosa, AL: 1988), p. xvii

26. Davidson, Fletcher, et al., *I'll Take My Stand* (Louisiana State University Press, Baton Rouge, LA: 1983), p. 112

27. Sons of Confederate Veterans, *The Gray Book*, preface by Dr. William D. McCain

28. Anthony Trollope, as cited in *Grant as a Military Commander*, General Sir James Marshall-Cornwall (Van Nostrand Reinhold Company, New York, NY: 1970), p. 5.

29. Anthony Trollope, *North America* (Alfred A. Knopf, New York, NY: 1951), p. 351

30. David H. Fisher, *Albion's Seed* (Oxford University Press, Oxford and New York: 1989), p. 6

31. Ibid

32. Ibid

33. Ibid

34. John Adams, as cited in *Lagniappe, A Journal of the Old South*, Spring 1974, Oxford, MS, p. 32.

35. Grady McWhiney, *Cracker Culture: Celtic Ways in the Old South* (The University of Alabama Press, Tuscaloosa, AL: 1988), p. 2

36. Ibid

37. Michael A. Grissom, *Southern by the Grace of God* (Pelican Publishing Company, Gretna, LA: 1988), p. v

38. Abraham Lincoln, "Emancipation Proclamation" as cited in *The Gray Book*, Sons of Confederate Veterans, p. 9

39. Ibid

40. Ibid. p. 36

41. Abraham Lincoln, as cited in *The Lincoln-Douglas Debates of 1858*, edited by R. W. Johannsen (Oxford University Press, New York, NY: 1965), pp. 162-63

42. Abraham Lincoln, *Abraham Lincoln Speeches, Letters, and State Papers*, vol. I, p. 458

43. *Raleigh* (NC) *News and Observer*, as cited in *The Memorial Volume of Jefferson Davis*, William J. Jones (W. M. Cornett and Company, Dallas, TX: 1890), p. 352

44. *Confederate Veteran*, March-April 1990, p. 19

45. *Official Records: War of the Rebellion* (hereinafter cited as O.R., Series I unless otherwise noted), vol. XVI, pt. II, p. 6

46. O.R., Ser. II, vol. I, p. 186

47. O.R. vol. XVI, pt. II, p. 80

48. Ibid, pp. 273, 274, 275, 277

49. Ibid, p. 277

50. David A. Nichols, *Lincoln and the Indians* (University of Missouri Press, Columbia & London: 1978), p. 117

51. C. C. Burr, ed., Abel P. Upshur, *The Federal Government: Its True Nature and Character* (1840, St. Thomas Press, Houston, TX: 1977), pp. 104-105

52. John S. Tilley, *Facts Historians Leave Out* (Bill Coats, Ltd., Nashville, TN: 1990), p. 9

53. Sons of Confederate Veterans, *The Gray Book*, p. 36

54. Ibid

55. Thomas McGuire, *McGuire Papers* (Mrs. Herman McGuire, Louisiana Society, N.S.D.A.R., 1966), pp. 19-20

56. George Washington Bolton, as cited in *In Defense of My Country*, Eakin and Peoples (Corney Creek Festival, Bernice, LA: 1983), p. 27

57. Ibid, p. 28

58. Daniel Smith, as cited in *E. M. Graham North Louisianian*, W. Y. Thompson (Southwestern University Press, Lafayette, LA: 1984), p. 60

59. *History of Livingston Parish Louisiana* (Curtis Media Corp., Dallas, TX: 1986), p. 23

60. John D. Winters, *Civil War in Louisiana* (Louisiana State University Press, Baton Rouge, LA: 1963), p. 418

61. Georgia Comptroller General's report, 1911

62. John D. Winters, *Civil War in Louisiana* (Louisiana State University Press, Baton Rouge, LA: 1963), p. 428

63. Ibid

64. David King Gleason, *Antebellum Homes of Georgia* (Louisiana State University Press, Baton Rouge, LA: 1987), p. 117

65. Forrest McDonald and Grady McWhiney, "The South From Self-Sufficiency to Peonage," p. 1113

66. Gavin Wright, *Old South, New South* (Basic Books, Inc., New York, NY: 1986), p. 35

67. Forrest McDonald and Grady McWhiney, "The South From Self-Sufficiency to Peonage," p. 1113

68. *Charlotte* (NC) *Observer*, April 25, 1982

69. Lord Acton's letter, original on file, Washington-Lee University, Lexington, VA

70. Ibid

71. Ibid

72. Ibid

73. Governor Fletcher S. Stockdale of Texas, as cited in *The Life and Letters of Robert Lewis Dabney*, Thomas C. Johnson (Banner of Truth Trust, Edinburgh, Scotland: 1977), pp. 497-500

74. Ibid

75. Ibid

76. Records of the National Archives, Washington, D.C., John W. Kennedy

77. Ibid

78. *Lincoln as the South Should Know Him*, Third Edition (Manly's Battery Chapter, Children of the Confederacy, Raleigh, NC), p. 15

79. Ibid

80. *Confederate Veteran*, January-February 1989, "The Trial of Major Henry Wirz," p. 27

81. Ibid

82. Ibid, p. 29

83. Ibid

84. Ibid

85. Ibid

86. General Sir James Marshall-Cornwall, *Grant as a Military Commander* (Van Nostrand Reinhold Company, New York, NY: 1970), p. 4

87. Lyon G. Tyler, *A Confederate Catechism* (Holdcroft, VA, 1935), p. 6

88. Ibid, p. 37

89. Jesse T. Carpenter, as cited in *A History of the South*, Francis Butler Simkins (Alfred A. Knopf, New York, NY: 1959), p. 93

90. Raphael Semmes, *Memoirs of Service Afloat* (The Blue and Gray Press, Secaucus, NJ: 1987), p. 60

91. Sen. Thomas H. Benton, as cited in *Memoirs of Service Afloat*, Raphael Semmes (The Blue and Gray Press, Secaucus, NJ: 1987), pp. 57-58

92. Mildred L. Rutherford, *Truths of History* (M. L. Rutherford, Athens, GA: 1907), pp. 44-45

93. Ibid, p. 98

94. George Lunt as cited in Mildred L. Rutherford, *Truths of History* (M. L. Rutherford, Athens, GA: 1907), p. 12

95. Ibid

96. Abraham Lincoln, as cited in *Memoirs of Service Afloat*, Raphael Semmes (The Blue and Gray Press, Secaucus, NJ: 1987), p. 59

97. Patrick Henry, as cited in *Memoirs of Service Afloat*, Raphael Semmes (The Blue and Gray Press, Secaucus, NJ: 1987), p. 61

98. Lyon G. Tyler, *A Confederate Catechism* (Holdcroft, VA: 1935), p. 37

99. Merrill Jensen, *The New Nation* (Northeastern University Press, Boston, MA: 1981), p. 418

100. Ibid, p. 10

101. *The New York Times*, "The Great Question," March 30, 1861, p. 4

102. *The New York Times*, "An Extra Session of Congress," March 23, 1861, p. 4

103. *Union Democrat*, "Let Them Go!" Manchester, NH, February 19, 1861, recorded in *Northern Editorials on Secession*, Howard C. Perkins, ed., 1965, pp. 591-92

104. *Evening Post*, "What Shall Be Done for a Revenue?" New York, NY, March 12, 1861, recorded in *Northern Editorials on Secession*, Howard C. Perkins, ed., 1965, pp. 598-99

105. Alexis de Tocqueville, as cited in *Truths of History*, Mildred L. Rutherford (M. L. Rutherford, Athens, GA: 1907), p. 92

106. Edgar J. McManus, *Black Bondage in the North* (Syracuse University Press, Syracuse, NY: 1973), p. 166

107. Ibid, p. 168

108. Ibid, p. 180

109. Ibid, p. 185

110. Professor McMaster, as cited in *Virginia's Attitude Toward Slavery and Secession*, Beverly B. Munford (L. H. Jenkins, Inc., Richmond, VA: 1915), p. 162

111. *William Lloyd Garrison*, vol. I, pp. 253-54, as cited in *Virginia's Attitude Toward Slavery and Secession*, Beverly B. Munford (L. H. Jenkins, Inc., Richmond, VA: 1915), p. 163

112. Ibid, p. 169

113. George H. Moore, *A History of Slavery in Massachusetts* (D. Appleton and Company, New York, NY: 1866), pp. 228-29

114. Beverly B. Munford, *Virginia's Attitude Toward Slavery and Secession* (L. H. Jenkins, Inc., Richmond, VA: 1915), p. 171

115. Ibid

116. Ibid, p. 172

117. Ibid

118. Ibid, p. 173

119. Edgar J. McManus, *Black Bondage in the North* (Syracuse University Press, Syracuse, NY: 1973), p. 184

120. Ibid, p. 182

121. Ibid

122. William H. Seward, as cited in *Truths of History*, Mildred L. Rutherford (M. L. Rutherford, Athens, GA: 1907), p. 92

123. Ibid, p. 99

124. Ibid, p. 98

125. Ibid, p. 93

126. David A. Nichols, *Lincoln and the Indians* (University of Missouri Press, Columbia & London: 1978), p. 87

127. Ibid, p. 96

128. "Legal Lynching," Bryant Burroughs, *Southern Partisan*, Third Quarter, 1991, p. 44

CHAPTER TWO

1. J. Julius Guthrie, as cited in *The Gray Book*, published by the Sons of Confederate Veterans, pp. 16-17. This was the son of Capt. J. Julis Guthrie C.S.N. [Authors' note: *The Gray Book* has been revised several times, without benefit of notation.]

2. George F. Dow, *Slave Ships and Slaving* (Kennikat Press, Inc., Port Washington, NY: 1969), pp. 1-4

3. R. L. Dabney, *A Defense of Virginia and the South* (Sprinkle Publications, Harrisonburg, VA: 1977), p. 27

4. W. E. B. DuBois, *The Suppression of the African Slave Trade to the United States of America* (Russell and Russell Inc., New York, NY: 1965), p. 3

5. James Walvin, *Slavery and the Slave Trade* (University Press of Mississippi, Jackson, MS: 1983), p. 40

6. Ibid

7. Ibid, p. 41

8. R. W. Fogel and S. L. Engerman, *Time on the Cross* (Little, Brown and Company, Boston, MA: 1974), p. 17

9. James Walvin, *Slavery and the Slave Trade* (University Press of Mississippi, Jackson, MS: 1983), p. 152

10. R. W. Fogel and S. L. Engerman, *Time on the Cross* (Little, Brown and Company, Boston, MA: 1974), p. 131

11. Terry Alford, *Prince Among Slaves* (Oxford University Press, New York, NY: 1986), p. 23

12. Ibid. p. 5

13. Larry Koger, *Black Slaveowners* (McFarland and Company Inc., Jefferson, NC: 1985), p. 1

14. Ibid, p. 3

15. Ibid, pp. 1, 144-45

16. Ibid, p. 1

17. Ibid

18. Ibid, p. xiii

19. Ibid

20. George H. Moore, *Notes on the History of Slavery in Massachusetts* (D. Appleton and Company, New York, NY: 1866), p. 31

21. Ibid, pp. 32-34

22. Ibid, p. 34

23. Ibid, p. 5

24. Daniel P. Mannix, *Black Cargoes* (The Viking Press, New York, NY: 1962), p. 166

25. Ibid, p. 160

26. Ibid

27. Ibid

28. Ibid, p. 161

29. Ibid

30. R. W. Fogel and S. L. Engerman, *Time on the Cross* (Little, Brown and Company, Boston, MA: 1974), p. 14

31. Daniel P. Mannix, *Black Cargoes* (The Viking Press, New York, NY: 1962), p. 245

32. Ibid, p. 202

33. Ibid, p. 201

34. Ibid, p. 205

35. Henry A. Wise, as cited in *Virginia's Attitude Toward Slavery and Secession* (L. H. Jenkins, Inc., Richmond, VA, 1915), p. 39 [Also see W. E. B. DuBois, *Suppression of the African Slave Trade to the United States of America*, pp. 147-48 and John R. Spears, *Scribner's Magazine*, vol. XXVIII, No. 1, July 1900, p. 456]

36. President Zachary Taylor, as cited in *Virginia's Attitude Toward Slavery and Secession* (L. H. Jenkins, Inc., Richmond, VA: 1915), p. 39

37. Daniel P. Mannix, *Black Cargoes* (The Viking Press, New York, NY: 1962), pp. 162-66

38. Ibid

39. Ibid. p. 166

40. Ibid, p. 162

41. Ibid, p. 30 [Also see John R. Spears, *Scribner's Magazine*, vol. XX-VIII, No. 1, July 1900, pp. 10-11 and James Walvin, *Slavery and the Slave Trade* (University Press of Mississippi, Jackson MS: 1983), pp. 40-46]

42. Daniel P. Mannix, *Black Cargoes* (The Viking Press, New York, NY: 1962), pp. 104-30

43. W. E. B. DuBois, *The Suppression of the African Slave Trade to the United States of America* (Russell and Russell Inc., New York, NY: 1965), p. 2

44. George H. Moore, *Notes on the History of Slavery in Massachusetts* (D. Appleton and Company, New York, NY: 1866), p. 11

45. Ibid, pp. 1-5

46. Ibid, p. 47

47. Ibid

48. Ibid, pp. 3-6

49. R. L. Dabney, *A Defense of Virginia and the South* (Sprinkle Publications, Harrisonburg, VA: 1977), p. 36

50. W. E. B. DuBois, *The Suppression of the African Slave Trade to the United States of America* (Russell and Russell Inc., New York, NY: 1965), p. 14

51. Ibid

52. Ibid

53. R. L. Dabney, *A Defense of Virginia and the South* (Sprinkle Publications, Harrisonburg, VA: 1977), p. 44

54. Ibid

55. Ibid, pp. 57-58

56. Ibid, p. 85

57. Ibid, p. 81

58. George H. Moore, *Notes on the History of Slavery in Massachusetts* (D. Appleton and Company, New York, NY: 1866), pp. 228-29

59. R. L. Dabney, *A Defense of Virginia and the South* (Sprinkle Publications, Harrisonburg, VA: 1977), p. 342

60. Ibid, p. 343

61. Ibid

62. Daniel P. Mannix, *Black Cargoes* (The Viking Press, New York, NY: 1962), p. 205 [Also see Isidor Paiewonsky, *Eyewitness Accounts of Slavery in the Danish West Indies* (Fordham University Press, New York, NY: 1989) p. 62]

CHAPTER THREE

l. Charles Stewart, as cited in *Harper's Magazine,* "My Life as a Slave," Vol. LXIX, No. CCCCXIII, October l884

2. J. Steven Wilkens, *America: The First 350 Years* (Covenant Publications, Monroe, LA: 1988), p. 153

3. George H. Moore, *Notes on the History of Slavery in Massachusetts* (D. Appleton and Company, New York, NY: l866), pp. 30, 88

4. Edgar J. McManus, *Black Bondage in the North* (Syracuse University Press, Syracuse, NY: 1973), pp. 1-3

5. John Adams, as cited in *The Negro in Colonial New England 1620-1776,* Lorenzo Johnston Green (Kennikat Press, Inc., Port Washington, NY: 1966), pp. 113, 322

6. Frederick Law Olmsted, as cited in *Civil War, the Magazine of the Civil War Society,* "Calico, Black and Gray: Women and Blacks in the Confederacy," by Edward C. Smith, vol. VIII, No. 3, Issue XXIII, pp. 11, 12

7. Kenneth Stampp, *The Peculiar Institution: Slavery in the Antebellum South* (Alfred A. Knopf, New York, NY: 1956), p. 323

8. John W. Haley, *The Rebel Yell and Yankee Hurrah,* edited by Ruth L. Silliker (Down East Books, Camden, ME: l985), p. 163

9. J. S. Buckingham, *The Slave States of America* (Negro University Press, New York, NY: l968), vol. II, p. 112

10. Edward C. Smith, "Calico, Black and Gray: Women and Blacks in the Confederacy," *Civil War Magazine,* vol. VIII, No. 3, Issue XXIII, p. 12

11. Ibid, p. 11

12. Ibid, p. l3

13. Ibid, p. l4

14. John W. Haley, *The Rebel Yell and Yankee Hurrah,* edited by Ruth L. Silliker (Down East Books, Camden, ME: l985), p. 167

15. Arthur L. Freemantle, as cited in *Civil War Quarterly,* vol. VIII, pp. 47, 50

16. Francis W. Springer, *War for What?* (Bill Coats Ltd., Nashville, TN: 1990), p. 172

17. Gordon Cotton, *Vicksburg Sunday Post,* Vicksburg, MS, September 23, l984

18. Francis W. Springer, *War for What?* (Bill Coats Ltd., Nashville, TN: 1990), p. 172

19. Ibid

20. Gordon Cotton, *Vicksburg Sunday Post,* Vicksburg, MS, September 23, l985

21. Francis W. Springer, *War for What?* (Bill Coats Ltd., Nashville, TN: 1990), p. 172

22. Ibid

23. Ibid, p. 173

24. Gordon Cotton, *Vicksburg Sunday Post*, Vicksburg, MS, September 23, 1985

25. Francis W. Springer, *War for What?* (Bill Coats Ltd., Nashville, TN: 1990), p. 173

26. Ibid

27. Gordon Cotton, *Vicksburg Sunday Post*, Vicksburg, MS, September 23, 1985

28. Francis W. Springer, *War for What?* (Bill Coats Ltd., Nashville, TN: 1990), p. 173

29. Ibid

30. Ibid

31. Ibid

32. Ibid

33. Ibid

34. Ibid

35. Ibid

36. Ibid

37. Arthur W. Bergeron, Jr., "Free Men of Color in Grey," *Civil War History*, vol. XXXII, No. 3, 1986, The Kent State University Press, p. 248

38. Ibid, p. 249

39. Ibid, p. 250

40. Ibid

41. *Confederate Veteran*, vol. XXXII, No. 10, October 1924, p. 393

42. *SLAVE NARRATIVES: A FOLK HISTORY OF SLAVERY IN THE UNITED STATES FROM INTERVIEWS WITH FORMER SLAVES*, the Alabama Narratives, pp. 218-19

43. Ibid, pp. 282-85

44. Ibid, pp. 312-15

45. Ibid, pp. 329-30

46. *SLAVE NARRATIVES: A FOLK HISTORY OF SLAVERY IN THE UNITED STATES FROM INTERVIEWS WITH FORMER SLAVES*, The Arkansas Narratives, Vol. II, pp. 100-108

47. Ibid, Vol. III, pp. 308-16

48. *SLAVE NARRATIVES: A FOLK HISTORY OF SLAVERY IN THE*

UNITED STATES FROM INTERVIEWS WITH FORMER SLAVES, The Alabama Narratives, Vol. II, pp. 196-200

49. Ibid, Vol. I, pp. 224-26

50. Ibid

51. Ibid, pp. 218-19

52. *SLAVE NARRATIVES: A FOLK HISTORY OF SLAVERY IN THE UNITED STATES FROM INTERVIEWS WITH FORMER SLAVES*, The Arkansas Narratives, Vol. I, pp. 11-16

53. Ibid, Vol. II, pp. 72-78

54. Ibid, Vol. III, pp. 27-33

55. Ibid, pp. 268-271

56. Ibid, Vol. I, pp. 49-50

57. Ibid, Vol. VII, pp. 235-41

58. Ibid, Vol. III, pp. 19-26

59. Ibid, Vol. III, p. 308

60. *Official Records: War of the Rebellion* (hereinafter cited as O.R., Series I unless noted), Series I, Vol. III, p. 459

61. O.R., vol. XVI, pt. II, pp. 273-75

62. Ibid, p. 277

63. O.R., vol. XLVI, pt. III, p. 1005

64. O.R., vol. XXXII, pt. II, p. 477

65. O.R., Series III, vol. 11, p. 53

66. O.R., p. 57

67. O.R., vol. XXXII, pt. II, p. 269

68. O.R., vol. XXXIV, pt. II, pp. 587-58

69. O.R., vol. XLII, pt. II, pp. 653-54

70. Janet Sharp Hermann, *Joseph E. Davis Pioneer Patriarch* (University Press of Mississippi, Jackson and London: 1990), pp. ix, 57

71. *Vicksburg Evening Post*, Vicksburg, MS, June 28, 1985

72. Ibid

73. William Sampson, quoted in *Confederate Veteran*, November-December 1990, p. 18

74. Mary Boykin Chesnut, *Mary Chesnut's Civil War* (Yale University Press, New Haven and London: 1981), p. 568

75. Maggie Davis in a letter to Jeff Davis Jr., cited in *Southern Partisan*, Second Quarter, 1989, p. 28

76. Varina Davis, as cited in *Southern Partisan*, Second Quarter, 1989, p. 30

77. Ibid

78. Ibid

79. *Confederate Veteran*, November-December 1989, p. 18

80. Thornton Montgomery, as cited in *Confederate Veteran*, November-December 1989, p. 18

81. *Stewart Family History* (Stewart University Press, Centre, AL: 1976), p. 242

82. *Journal of the House of Representatives, of the State of Mississippi, Regular Session Thereof*, convened January 7, 1890, p. 377

83. Ibid, p. 378

84. *Daily Clarion-Ledger*, Jackson, MS, February 23, 1890

85. Ibid, February 25, 1890

86. *Afro-American History Series*, "Slavery and Abolitionism, as Viewed by a Georgia Slave" (Scholarly Resources, Inc., Wilmington, DE), vol. 7

87. Ibid, Introduction

88. Harrison Berry, "Slavery and Abolitionism, as Viewed by a Georgia Slave," as cited in *Afro-American History Series* (Scholarly Resources, Inc., Wilmington, DE), vol. 7, Preface

89. Maxwell Whiteman, as cited in *A Georgia Slave Defends Slavery*, a bibliographical note (Scholarly Resources, Inc., Wilmington, DE: 1861)

90. William E. Hatcher, *John Jasper* (Sprinkle Publications, Harrisonburg, VA: 1985), p. 16

91. Ibid, pp. 26-27

92. Ibid, p. 97

93. Ibid, pp. 28-29

94. *Palestine Baptist Church Pictorial Directory 1988* Harrisville, Simpson County, MS, p. 2

95. Ibid

96. Francis B. Simkins, *A History of the South* (Alfred A. Knopf, New York, NY: 1959), p. 159

97. Ibid

98. Charles W. Hampton, *Bill Yopp: Narrative of a Slave* (DeKalb Litho and Advertising, Avondale Estates, GA: 1969), p. 2

99. Bill Yopp, as cited in *Bill Yopp: Narrative of a Slave*, Charles W. Hampton (DeKalb Litho and Advertising, Avondale Estates, GA: 1969), p. 7

100. Charles W. Hampton, *Bill Yopp: Narrative of a Slave* (DeKalb Litho and Advertising, Avondale Estates, GA: 1969), p. 10

101. Ibid, p. 15

102. Ibid, p. 2

103. Lorenzo J. Greene, *The Negro in Colonial New England 1620-1776*, (Kennikat Press, Inc., Port Washington, NY: 1966), pp. 15, 42

104. Ibid, pp. 58-59, 221, 354

105. Ibid, p. 352

106. Ibid, p. 357

107. *Times Democrat*, Memphis, TN, June 4, 1891

CHAPTER FOUR

1. Major George W. Nichols, as cited in *Truths of History*, Mildred L. Rutherford (Mildred L. Rutherford, Athens, GA: 1907), p. 37

2. Edward Pollard, *A Southern History of the War* (The Fairfax Press, New York, NY: 1977), pp. 203, 393

3. Grady McWhiney, "Jefferson Davis—The Unforgiven," *The Journal of Mississippi History*, vol. XLII, May 1980, p. 118

4. *McClellan's Own Story*, as cited in *A Confederate Catechism*, Lyon G. Tyler (Lyon G. Tyler, Holdcroft, VA: 1935), p. 35

5. Ibid, pp. 34-35

6. Edward A. Pollard, *A Southern History of the War* (The Fairfax Press, New York, NY: 1977), pp. 351-53

7. Ibid

8. Ibid

9. Ibid

10. Ibid, p. 352

11. C. M. Baker, D.D., *Confederate Veteran*, vol. XXXVI, No. 1, January-February, 1988, p. 27

12. Ibid, p. 31

13. Ibid, p. 28

14. Ibid

15. Ibid, p. 33

16. Ibid, p. 34

17. Sam Davis, as cited in *Southern by the Grace of God*, Michael A. Grissom (Pelican Publishing Company, Gretna, LA: 1988), p. 361

18. David C. Edmonds, ed., *The Conduct of Federal Troops in Louisiana* (The Acadiana Press, Lafayette, LA: 1988), p. x

19. Edward A. Pollard, *A Southern History of the War* (The Fairfax Press, New York, NY: 1977), p. 323

20. John D. Winters, *The Civil War in Louisiana* (Louisiana State University Press, Baton Rouge, LA: 1963), p. 134

21. David C. Edmonds, ed., *The Conduct of Federal Troops in Louisiana* (The Acadiana Press, Lafayette, LA: 1988), p. 30

22. Ibid, p. 32

23. Ibid, p. 38

24. Ibid

25. Ibid, p. 39

26. Ibid, p. 40

27. Ibid

28. Ibid, p. 44

29. Ibid, pp. 51-52

30. Ibid, p. 51

31. Ibid

32. Ibid

33. David C. Edmonds, *Yankee Autumn in Acadiana* (The Acadiana Press, Lafayette, LA: 1987), p. 52

34. John D. Winters, *The Civil War in Louisiana* (Louisiana State University Press, Baton Rouge, LA: 1963), p. 347

35. Ibid

36. David C. Edmonds, ed., *The Conduct of Federal Troops in Louisiana* (The Acadiana Press, Lafayette, LA: 1988), pp. 153, 155-65

37. Ibid, p. 180

38. Ibid, pp. 178-80

39. James Walvin, *Slavery and the Slave Trade* (University Press of Mississippi, Jackson, MS: 1985), p. 49

40. David C. Edmonds, *Yankee Autumn in Acadiana* (The Acadiana Press, Lafayette, LA: 1987), pp. 61-62

41. Ibid, p. 62

42. Ibid, p. 318

43. David C. Edmonds, ed., *The Conduct of Federal Troops in Louisiana* (The Acadiana Press, Lafayette, LA: 1988), p. 168

44. Ibid, p. 169

45. John W. Haley, *The Rebel Yell and Yankee Hurrah*, edited by Ruth L. Silliker (Down East Books, Camden, ME: 1985), p. 273

46. Ibid, p. 2

47. T. H. Pearce, *Confederate Veteran*, vol. XXXIV, No. 1, January-February 1986, p. 7

48. Ibid, p. 9

49. Ibid, p. 10

50. Ibid, p. 11

51. Ibid

52. *Official Records: War of the Rebellion* (hereinafter cited as O.R., Series I unless otherwise indicated), vol. XLVI, pt. III, p. 1005

53. "Former Slave Speaks," *Southern Partisan*, Vol. X, Third Quarter 1990, p. 39

54. O.R., vol. III, p. 459

55. O.R., vol. XVI, pt. II, pp. 274, 275

56. O.R., vol. XVI, pt. II, p. 319

57. O.R., vol. XXXII, pt. III, p. 286

58. O.R., Ser. III, vol. IV, p. 1029

59. O.R., vol. XLI, pt. I, p. 933

60. Ibid, p. 928

61. O.R., vol. XLVII, pt. III, p. 667

62. O.R., vol. XVII, pt. I, p. 147

63. O.R., vol. XLVII, pt. II, pp. 184-85

64. O.R., Ser. III, vol. II, pp. 52-53

65. Ibid, p. 57

66. Ibid, p. 59

67. O.R., vol. XXXII, pt. II, p. 269

68. Ibid, p. 477

69. O.R., vol. XLII, pt. II, pp. 653, 654

70. O.R. Ser. III, vol. IV, p. 1028

71. O.R., vol. XLIX, pt. I, p. 782

72. John D. Winters, *The Civil War in Louisiana* (Louisiana State University Press, Baton Rouge, LA: 1963), p. 313

73. O.R., vol. XVIII, p. 464

74. David C. Edmonds, ed., *The Conduct of Federal Troops in Louisiana* (The Acadiana Press, Lafayette, LA: 1988), pp. 116-19 [Also see, Arthur W. Bergeron, Jr., *A History of the Eighteeth Louisiana Infantry Regiment* (Arthur W. Bergeron, Jr., Baton Rouge, LA), p. 131]

CHAPTER FIVE

1. Jefferson Davis, as cited in *A Southern History of the War*, Edward A. Pollard (The Fairfax Press, New York, NY: 1978), p. 582

2. Thomas Jefferson, as cited in the Declaration of Independence

3. Ibid

4. Ibid

5. John C. Calhoun, *The Works of John C. Calhoun* (D. Appleton and Company, New York, NY: 1844), vol. I, pp. 10-11

6. Francis Butler Simkins, *A History of the South* (Alfred A. Knopf, New York, NY: 1959), p. 58

7. G. H. Sabine, *A History of Political Theory* (Rinehart and Winston, New York, NY: 1961), pp. 250-51

8. Merritt Hughes, ed. *John Milton Complete Poems and Major Prose* (The Odyssey Press, Indianapolis and New York: 1957), pp. 755-56

9. John Naisbitt, *Megatrends* (Warner Communications Company, New York, NY: 1984), p. 175

CHAPTER SIX

1. Robert E. Lee, as cited in *The Memorial Volume of Jefferson Davis*, J. William Jones, 1889 (Sprinkle Publications, Harrisonburg, VA: 1993), p. 309

2. John C. Calhoun, *The Works of John C. Calhoun*, vol. I, "A Disquisition on Government" (D. Appleton and Company, New York, NY: 1854), pp. 6-7

3. Thomas Jefferson, as cited in the Declaration of Independence

4. Ibid

5. George Washington, as cited in *The Fearful Master*, Edward G. Griffin (Western Islands Publishers, Boston, MA: 1964), p. ii

6. James J. Kilpatrick, *The Sovereign States* (Henry Regnery Company, Chicago, IL: 1957), pp. 7-8

7. Ibid

8. Raphael Semmes, *Memoirs of Service Afloat* (The Blue and Gray Press, Secaucus, NJ: 1987), p. 31

9. Thomas Jefferson, as cited in John C. Calhoun, *The Works of John C. Calhoun*, vol. I, "A Discourse on the Constitution and Government of the United States" (D. Appleton and Company, New York, NY: 1854), p. 248

10. Ibid, pp. 249-50

11. Ibid, p. 355

12. Ibid, pp. 354-58

13. John C. Calhoun, as cited in *Political History of Secession*, W. D. Howe (Putman's Sons, New York, NY: 1927), p. 29

14. Ibid

15. Andrew Johnson, as cited in *The Unconstitutional Fourteenth Amendment*, Kenneth S. Coe (unpublished manuscript copy in possession of the authors)

16. Thaddeus Stevens, as cited in *The Tragic Era* (Halcyon House, New York, NY: 1929), p. 63

17. Alexander Hamilton, as cited in James J. Kilpatrick, *The Sovereign States* (Henry Regnery Company, Chicago, IL: 1957), p. 27. [Also see, *The Hundred Years Hoax*, Patrick Henry Omlor (Aladextra Press, Menlo Park, CA: 1966), p. 25]

CHAPTER SEVEN

1. Richard M. Weaver, *The Southern Tradition at Bay* (Harper and Row, New York, NY: 1960), p. 388

2. "English History," *Encyclopaedia Britannica*, 1972 ed., vol. 8, p. 499

3. Ibid

4. Roger Pearson, *Introduction to Anthropology* (Holt, Rinehart, and Winston, New York, NY: 1974), p. 188

5. Merritt Hughes, ed. *John Milton Complete Poems and Major Prose* (The Odyssey Press, Indianapolis and New York: 1957), p. 881

6. Ibid, p. 454

7. Ibid, p. 359

8. Maurice Cranston, "John Locke and Government by Consent," in *Political Ideas*, David Thompson, ed. (Basic Books, New York, NY: 1966), p. 71

9. J. Bronouski and Bruce Mazlish, *The Western Intellectual Tradition* (Harper and Row, New York, NY: 1960), p. 210

10. Merritt Hughes, ed. *John Milton Complete Poems and Major Prose* (The Odyssey Press, Indianapolis and New York: 1957), p. 754

11. John C. Calhoun, *The Works of John C. Calhoun* (D. Appleton and Company, New York, NY: 1844), vol. I, p. 130

12. Merritt Hughes, ed. *John Milton Complete Poems and Major Prose* (The Odyssey Press, Indianapolis and New York: 1957), p. 754

13. John C. Calhoun, *The Works of John C. Calhoun* (D. Appleton and Company, New York, NY: 1844), vol. I, p. 130

14. Merritt Hughes, ed. *John Milton Complete Poems and Major Prose* (The Odyssey Press, Indianapolis and New York: 1957), p. 757

15. Ibid, p. 778

16. J. Bronouski and Bruce Mazlish, *The Western Intellectual Tradition* (Harper and Row, New York, NY: 1960), p. 212

17. Merritt Hughes, ed. *John Milton Complete Poems and Major Prose* (The Odyssey Press, Indianapolis and New York: 1957), p. 811

18. J. Bronouski and Bruce Mazlish, *The Western Intellectual Tradition* (Harper and Row, New York, NY: 1960), p. 212

19. Merritt Hughes, ed. *John Milton Complete Poems and Major Prose* (The Odyssey Press, Indianapolis and New York: 1957), p. 755

20. Ibid, p. 759

21. John C. Calhoun, *The Works of John C. Calhoun* (D. Appleton and Company, New York, NY: 1844), vol. I, p. 248

22. Merritt Hughes, ed. *John Milton Complete Poems and Major Prose* (The Odyssey Press, Indianapolis and New York: 1957), p. 759

23. W. D. Howe, *Political History of Secession* (Putnam's Sons, New York, NY: 1927), p. 31

24. John C. Calhoun, *The Works of John C. Calhoun* (D. Appleton and Company, New York, NY: 1844), vol. I, p. 249

25. Merritt Hughes, ed. *John Milton Complete Poems and Major Prose* (The Odyssey Press, Indianapolis and New York: 1957), p. 759

26. Ibid, p. 302

27. Ibid, p. 303

28. Ibid, p. 888

29. John C. Calhoun, *The Works of John C. Calhoun* (D. Appleton and Company, New York, NY: 1844), vol. I, p. 3

30. Merritt Hughes, ed. *John Milton Complete Poems and Major Prose* (The Odyssey Press, Indianapolis and New York: 1957), p. 890

31. John S. Mill, *Representative Government*, in *Great Books of the Western World*, Maynard Hutchins, ed. (Encyclopaedia Britannica, Chicago, IL: 1952), vol. 43, p. 363

32. Ibid, p. 369

33. John C. Calhoun, *The Works of John C. Calhoun* (D. Appleton and Company, New York, NY: 1844), vol. I, p. 7

34. Merritt Hughes, ed. *John Milton Complete Poems and Major Prose* (The Odyssey Press, Indianapolis and New York: 1957), p. 882

35. John C. Calhoun, "The Causes by Which the Union Is Endangered," in *The Causes of the American Civil War*, E. C. Rozwenc, ed. (D.C. Heath and Company, New York, NY: 1961), pp. 1-4

CHAPTER EIGHT

1. John Randolph, as cited in *John Randolph of Roanoke*, Russell Kirk (Liberty Press, Indianapolis, IN: 1978), p. 61.

2. Junius Brutus, *Vindiciae Contra Tyrannos*, reprint of 1689 translation (Still Waters Revival Books, Edmonton, Canada: 1989), p. 60

3. George Buchanan, *De Jure Regni Apud Scotos*, reprint of 1799 edition (Sprinkle Publications, Harrisonburg, VA: 1982), p. 252

4. Samuel Rutherford, *Lex Rex*, reprint of 1644 edition (Sprinkle Publications, Harrisonburg, VA: 1982), pp. 126-27

5. Frank L. Owsley, et al., *I'll Take My Stand* (Louisiana State University Press, Baton Rouge, LA: 1983), p. 63

6. Carson, Taylor, and Wallband, *Civilization Past and Present*, Sixth Edition (Scott, Foresman and Company: 1969), vol. 2, pp. 104-106

7. *Collier's Encyclopedia*, "Norway"

8. Ibid, "Texas"

9. Ibid, "Panama"

10. Carson, Taylor, and Wallband, *Civilization Past and Present*, Sixth Edition (Scott, Foresman and Company: 1969), vol. 2, p. 294

11. Francis W. Springer, *War for What?* (Bill Coats Ltd., Nashville, TN: 1990), pp. 52-54

12. Ibid

13. Francis B. Simkins, *A History of the South* (Alfred A. Knopf, New York, NY: 1959), p. 97

14. Ibid, p. 100

15. Thelma Jennings, *The Nashville Convention* (Memphis State University Press, Memphis, TN: 1980), pp. 169-72

16. James Kent, *Commentaries on American Law* (Da Capo Press, New York, NY: 1971), vol. I, p. 186

17. Edgar S. Dudley, "Was 'Secession' Taught at West Point?" as cited in *The Century Magazine*, 1900, p. 633

18. James Kent, *Commentaries on American Law* (Da Capo Press, New York, NY: 1971), vol. I, p. 185

19. Edmund Burke, "Speech on Conciliation with the Colonies" in *The Norton Anthology of English Literature*, Third Edition (W. W. Norton and Company, New York, NY: 1974), vol. 1, pp. 2352-366

20. Ibid

21. James Morgan, "Lithuania and the Confederacy: Thoughts on the Meaning of Secession," *Camp Chase Review*, vol. XVII, #10, September 1990, pp. 19-20

22. James Kent, *Commentaries on American Law* (Da Capo Press, New York, NY: 1971), vol. I, pt. I, Lecture II, "Of the Law of Nations"

23. Francis B. Simkins, *A History of the South* (Alfred A. Knopf, New York, NY: 1959), pp. 43-58

24. Ibid, p. 47

25. Ibid

26. Ibid

27. Ibid

28. Ibid

29. James Kent, *Commentaries on American Law* (Da Capo Press, New York, NY: 1971), vol. I, p. 171

30. Raphael Semmes, *Memoirs of Service Afloat* (The Blue and Gray Press, Secaucus, NJ: 1987), p. 26

31. Ibid, p. 27

32. Ibid, pp. 25-26

33. Ferguson and McHenry, *The American Federal Government*, Tenth Edition (McGraw-Hill, New York, NY: 1969), p. 73

34. Ibid, Appendix 2, Articles of Confederation, Article XIII

35. Ibid, Appendix 3, The Constitution of the United States, Article V

36. George H. Moore, *Notes on the History of Slavery in Massachusetts* (D. Appleton and Company, New York, NY: 1866), pp. 27-28

37. James Kent, *Commentaries on American Law* (Da Capo Press, New York, NY: 1971), vol. 1, p. 190

38. Ibid, p. 191

39. Ibid

40. Edgar S. Dudley, "Was 'Secession' Taught at West Point?" as cited in *The Century Magazine*, 1900, p. 635

41. *The North American Review*, vol. XXII, April 1826

42. William Rawle, *A View of the Constitution* (H. C. Carey and Lea, Philadelphia, PA: 1825), p. 296

43. Ibid, p. 302

44. Jefferson Davis, "Farewell Address to the United States Senate." See Addendum II.

45. Harry MaCarthy, "The Bonnie Blue Flag." See *Songs of the Confederacy*, edited by Henry S. Humphreys (The Willis Music Company, Cincinnati, OH: 1961), p. 20

46. *The National Cyclopedia*, vol. VII, p. 442

47. Jefferson Davis, "Inaugural Address." See Addendum III.

48. George H. Moore, *Notes on the History of Slavery in Massachusetts* (D. Appleton and Company, New York, NY: 1866), p. 27

49. Ibid

50. Daniel Webster, as cited in *Memoirs of Service Afloat*, Raphael Semmes (The Blue and Gray Press, Secaucus, NJ: 1987), pp. 65-66

51. Ibid, p. 66

52. H. Newcomb Morse, "The Foundations and Meaning of Secession," *Stetson Law Review*, vol. XV, No. 2, 1986, p. 423

53. Ibid
54. Mildred L. Rutherford, *Truths of History* (M. L. Rutherford, Athens, GA: 1907), p. 92
55. H. Newcomb Morse, "The Foundations and Meaning of Secession," *Stetson Law Review*, vol. XV, No. 2, 1986, p. 432

CHAPTER NINE

1. Chase, as cited in James Jackson Kilpatrick, *The Sovereign State* (Henry Regnery Company, Chicago, IL: 1957), p. x
2. Personal conversation between Walter Donald Kennedy and Professor Jay Hoar. [Similar views of Professor Hoar can be found in *Confederate Veteran*, September-October 1990, p. 30]
3. Abel P. Upshur, *The Federal Government*, C. C. Burr, editor of 1868 edition (Van Evrie, Horton and Company, New York, NY: 1868), p. ii
4. Ibid, p. iii
5. Ibid
6. Ibid, p. iv
7. Ibid, p. v
8. Ibid, p. 21, footnote
9. Marshall L. DeRosa, *The Confederate Constitution of 1861* (University of Missouri Press, Columbia and London: 1991), p. 35
10. Abel P. Upshur, *The Federal Government*, C. C. Burr, editor of 1868 edition (Van Evrie, Horton and Company, New York, NY: 1868) p. vi
11. Ibid
12. James Brown Scott, *Sovereign States and Suits Before Arbitral Tribunals and Court of Justice* (The New York University Press, New York, NY: 1925), p. 37, footnote
13. Abel P. Upshur, *The Federal Government*, C. C. Burr, editor of 1868 edition (Van Evrie, Horton and Company, New York, 1868), p. 157
14. Madison, as cited by Marshall L. DeRosa, *The Confederate Constitution of 1861* (University of Missouri Press, Columbia and London: 1991), p. 62
15. Abel P. Upshur, *The Federal Government*, C. C. Burr, editor of 1868 edition (Van Evrie, Horton and Company, New York, NY: 1868), p. viii
16. Marshall L. DeRosa, *The Confederate Constitution of 1861* (University of Missouri Press, Columbia and London: 1991), p. 157, footnote 23
17. Merrill Jensen, *The New Nation* (Northeastern University Press, Boston, MA: 1981), p. 10
18. Isidor Paiewonsky, *Eyewitness Accounts of Slavery in the Danish West Indies* (Fordham University Press, New York, NY: 1989), p. 75

19. Hamilton, as cited in James Jackson Kilpatrick, *The Sovereign State* (Henry Regnery Company, Chicago, IL: 1957), p. 54

20. John Marshall, as cited in James Jackson Kilpatrick, *The Sovereign State* (Henry Regnery Company, Chicago, IL: 1957), p. 42

21. Herman V. Ames, *State Documents on Federal Relations* (Northeastern University Press, Philadelphia, PA: 1911), p. 7

22. Ibid, p. 9

23. William Grayson, as cited in Jackson Kilpatrick, *The Sovereign State* (Henry Regnery Company, Chicago, IL: 1957), p. 40.

24. George Mason, as cited in James Jackson Kilpatrick, *The Sovereign State* (Henry Regnery Company, Chicago, IL: 1957), p. 41, footnote 55

25. Abel P. Upshur, *The Federal Government*, C. C. Burr, editor of 1869 edition (Van Evrie, Horton and Company, New York, NY: 1868), pp. 100-102

26. Marshall L. DeRosa, *The Confederate Constitution of 1861* (University of Missouri Press, Columbia and London: 1991), p. 13

27. Clay, as cited by Marshall L. DeRosa, *The Confederate Constitution of 1861* (University of Missouri Press, Columbia and London: 1991), p. 15

28. Seward, as cited by Marshall L. DeRosa, *The Confederate Constitution of 1861* (University of Missouri Press, Columbia and London: 1991), p. 15

29. Calhoun, as cited by Marshall L. DeRosa, *The Confederate Constitution of 1861* (University of Missouri Press, Columbia and London: 1991), p. 10

CHAPTER TEN

1. Claude G. Bowers, *The Tragic Era* (The Literary Guild of America, Inc., New York, NY: 1929), p. vi

2. Ibid, p. 63

3. Ibid, p. 93

4. Ibid, p. 72

5. Ibid

6. Albion W. Tourgee, *A Fool's Errand* (The Belknap Press of Harvard University Press, Cambridge, MA: 1961), pp. 27, 39

7. Ibid, p. 381

8. Ibid, p. 386

9. P. G. T. Beauregard, as cited in T. Harry Williams, *Napoleon in Gray* (Louisiana State University Press, Baton Rouge, LA: 1954), p. 267

CHAPTER ELEVEN

1. Alexis de Tocqueville, *Democracy in America* (Harper and Row, New York, NY: 1966), vol. II, p. 476

2. Thomas Jefferson, Declaration of Independence

3. Milton Friedman, *Free to Choose* (Harcourt Brace Jovanovich, New York, NY: 1980), pp. 128-49

4. Ibid

5. Alexis de Tocqueville, *Democracy in America* (Harper and Row, New York, NY: 1966), vol. II, p. 475

6. Forrest McDonald and Grady McWhiney, *History Today*, July 1980, p. 13

7. Gandhi, as cited in Louis Fischer, *The Life of Mahatma Gandhi* (Harper and Row, New York, NY: 1983), p. 220

8. John C. Calhoun, *The Works of John C. Calhoun* (D. Appleton and Company, New York, NY: 1844), vol. I, pp. 56-57

9. John S. Mill, *Representative Government*, in *Great Books of the Western World*, Maynard Hutchins, ed. (Encyclopaedia Britannica, Inc., Chicago, IL: 1952), vol. 43, pp. 382-83

10. Ibid, p. 383

11. Ibid

12. Ibid, p. 384

13. Ibid, pp. 387, 388

CHAPTER TWELVE

1. Edward A. Pollard, *A Southern History of the War* (The Fairfax Press, New York, NY: 1978), p. 64

2. Thomas Jefferson, Declaration of Independence

3. Patrick Henry, Virginia Convention, Richmond, Virginia, March 1775

4. John S. Mill, *On Liberty*, as cited in *Great Books of the Western World*, R. M. Hutchens, ed. (William Benton, Publisher, Chicago, IL: 1952), vol. 43, p. 271

5. John S. Mill, *On Liberty*, as cited in *Great Books of the Western World*, R. M. Hutchens, ed. (William Benton, Publisher, Chicago, IL: 1952), vol. 43, p. 271

6. Jean-Jacques Servan-Schreiber, *The Radical Alternative* (W. W. Norton and Company, Inc., New York, NY: 1971), p. 27

7. Lyle H. Lanier, et al., *I'll Take My Stand* (Louisiana State University Press, Baton Rouge, LA: 1977), pp. 146-54

8. Ibid, p. 148

9. Pope Paul VI, as cited in *Populorum Progressio*

CHAPTER THIRTEEN

1. Ralph Waldo Emerson, as cited in *The Secret Six*, Otto Scott (Times Books, New York, NY: 1979), pp. 319-20 [Why is it that men like Emer-

son could have so much hatred for the South but say nothing about Northerners such as his great-grandfather, Cornelius Waldo, who was a slave merchant in Boston, Massachusetts (see *The Transatlantic Slave Trade* by James A. Rawley, p. 336)?]

2. John Chodes, "Education for a Conquered Nation," *Chronicles*, March 1989, p. 21

3. John D. Winters, *The Civil War in Louisiana* (Louisiana State University Press, Baton Rouge, LA: 1963), pp. 131-32

4. John Chodes, "Education for a Conquered Nation," *Chronicles*, March 1989, pp. 20-21

5. Davidson, Fletcher, et al., *I'll Take My Stand* (Louisiana State University Press, Baton Rouge, LA: 1983), p. 112

6. John Chodes, "Education for a Conquered Nation," *Chronicles*, March 1989, p. 23

7. *Nation*, as cited in *Cracker Culture*, Grady McWhiney (University of Alabama Press, Tuscaloosa, AL: 1988), p. 260

8. Niccolo Machiavelli, *The Prince and the Discourses* (Random House, Inc., New York, NY: 1950), p. 18

9. Ibid, pp. 182-83

10. Allen Nevins, as cited in *The Uncivil War*, Thomas B. Keys (The Beauvoir Press, Biloxi, MS: 1991), p. viii

11. *Official Records: War of the Rebellion* (hereinafter cited as O.R., Series I unless otherwise indicated), Ser. I, vol. II, p. 664

12. O.R., Ser. II, vol. I, p. 204

13. O.R., Ser, II, vol. IV, p. 533

14. O.R., vol. XV, p. 23

15. O.R., vol. XVII, pt. II, p. 35

16. Ibid

17. O.R., vol. XVIII, p. 541

18. Ibid, p. 182

19. O.R., vol. XXX, pt. III, p. 189

20. *Official Records: War of the Rebellion, Union and Confederate Navies* (hereinafter cited as O.R.N., unless otherwise indicated), Ser. I, vol. XXV, p. 701

21. O.R., vol. XXXIV, pt. IV, p. 188

22. O.R.N., vol. XXIII, p. 432

23. O.R., vol. XVII, pt. II, p. 16

24. Ibid, p. 390

25. Ibid, p. 556

26. Ibid, p. 81
27. O.R., vol. XXIV, pt. III, p. 574
28. O.R., vol. XXXII, pt. I, p. 176
29. O.R., vol. XLIV, p. 527
30. O.R., vol. XLVII, pt. II, p. 704
31. O.R., vol. VII, p. 551
32. O.R., vol. XXIV, pt. III, p. 92
33. O.R., vol. XLIII, pt. I, p. 57
34. O.R., vol. VIII, p. 507
35. O.R., vol. XVII, pt. II, p. 93
36. O.R., vol. X, pt. II, p. 204
37. O.R., Ser. III, vol. II, p. 53
38. O.R., Ser. I, vol. XXXIV, pt. IV, p. 270
39. Ibid, p. 315
40. O.R., vol. XLVIII, pt. II, p. 774
41. O.R., vol. III, p. 529
42. O.R., vol. VIII, p. 449
43. Ibid, p. 450
44. O.R., vol. XX, pt. II, p. 318
45. O.R., vol. XXXIII, p. 309
46. O.R., vol. XVI, pt. I, p. 640
47. Raphael Semmes, *Memoirs of Service Afloat* (The Blue and Gray Press, Secaucus, NJ: 1987), p. 236
48. O.R., vol. XXIV, pt. III, p. 157
49. Ibid, pp. 186-87
50. O.R., vol. XXXI, pt. III, p. 262
51. O.R., vol. XXXII, pt. II, pp. 280-81
52. O.R., vol. XXXIX, pt. II, p. 132
53. Ibid, p. 157
54. O.R., vol. XXXVII, pt. II, p. 366
55. John D. Winters, *The Civil War in Louisiana* (Louisiana State University Press, Baton Rouge, LA: 1963), p. 414
56. O.R., vol. XXXIX, pt. III, p. 162
57. O.R., vol. XLIII, pt. II, p. 340
58. O.R., vol. XLIII pt. I, p. 62
59. O.R., vol. XLIII, pt II, p. 553
60. O.R., vol. XLV, pt. II, p. 622

61. O.R., vol. XXX, pt. IV, p. 235

62. Janet S. Hermann, *Joseph E. Davis Pioneer Patriarch* (University Press of Mississippi, Jackson and London: 1990), p. 143

63. David A. Nichols, *Lincoln and the Indians* (University of Missouri Press, Columbia and London: 1978), p. 87

64. Ibid, p. 95

65. Ibid. p. 180

66. Lyon G. Tyler, *A Confederate Catechism* (Lyon G. Tyler, Holdcroft, VA: 1935), p. 14

67. Ludwell Johnson, "Furl That Banner?" *Southern Partisan*, vol. XII, First Quarter 1992, p. 20

68. Harriet Magruder, *A History of Louisiana* (D.C. Heath and Company, Boston, New York, Chicago: 1909), p. 291

69. Ibid, p. 295

70. Ibid

71. Dethloff and Begnaud, *Our Louisiana Legacy*, Second Edition, Teacher's Guide (Steck-Vaughn Company, Austin, TX: 1980), p. 208

72. Ibid, p. 221

73. Bryant Burroughs, "Legal Lynching," *Southern Partisan*, Third Quarter, 1991, p. 44

74. Andrew Nelson Lytle, *Southern Review*, Vol. I (Louisiana State University Press: 1935), p. 422

CHAPTER FOURTEEN

1. Raphael Semmes, *Memoirs of Service Afloat* (The Blue and Gray Press, Secaucus, NJ: 1987), p. 833

ADDENDA

1. James Madison, *Notes of Debates in the Federal Convention of 1787* (Ohio State University Press, Columbus, OH: 1966), p. 385

2. H. Storing, ed., *The Anti-Federalist*, "The Address and Reasons of Dissent of the Minority of the Convention of Pennsylvania to Their Constituents" (The University of Chicago, Chicago, IL: 1985), p. 205

3. *Jacobson v. Massachusetts*, 197 U.S. 11 (1905)

4. Patrick Henry, as cited in *The Anti-Federalist*, H. Storing, ed. (The University of Chicago, Chicago, IL: 1985) p. 297

5. James Madison, *The Federalist #39*, as cited in *Great Books of the Western World*, R. M. Hutchins, ed. (Encyclopaedia Britannica, Chicago, IL: 1952), vol. 43, p. 127

6. Confederate States Constitution, Article I, Section 2

7. Ibid, Article I, Section 3
8. Ibid, Article I, Section 2, Paragraph 5
9. Ibid
10. Sen. Thomas H. Benton, as cited in *Memoirs of Service Afloat*, Raphael Semmes (The Blue and Gray Press: Secaucus, NJ: 1987), pp. 57-59, 80
11. Raphael Semmes, *Memoirs of Service Afloat* (The Blue and Gray Press: Secaucus, NJ: 1987), p. 59
12. Confederate States Constitution, Article I, Section 8, Paragraph 1
13. Ibid, Article I, Section 8
14. Ibid, Article I, Section 9, Paragraph 9
15. Ibid, Article I, Section 9, Paragraph 10
16. Nicholson, *Comparative Analysis of the U.S. and Confederate Constitutions*, C.S. Bar Assn. J., March 1987, at 4, 14
17. Confederate States Constitution, Article II, Section 1
18. Ibid, Article V, Section 1

PHOTOGRAPHS AND ILLUSTRATIONS

1. *Pacific Marine Review*, "History of the Clipper Ship Nightingale," F. C. Matthews, October, pp. 557-60; W. E. B Dubois, *The Suppression of the African Slave Trade to the United States of America 1638-1870* (Russell and Russell Inc., New York, NY: 1965), pp. 162-63, 298
2. *The Untold Story of the Battle of Gatlinburg*, First Edition (Brannon Publishing Company Division of the Georgia Mint, Inc.: 1991), pp. 5, 7
3. John Ray Skates, *Mississippi's Old Capitol* (Mississippi Department of Archives and History, Jackson, MS: 1990), p. 106
4. *Alabama Historical Quarterly*, "The Forty-Sixth Alabama Regiment," Spring Issue, 1942, p. 155
5. *Official Records: War of the Rebellion, Union and Confederate Navies*, Ser. I, vol. 21, p. 594
6. Booth's Records, vol. III, book 1, p. 44,; Helen B. Wasson, *Our Kith & Kin* (Gateway Press, Inc., Baltimore, MD: 1986), pp. 39, 41
7. *The Southern Digest*, vol. 22, # 15, July 17, 1992 (Southern University, Baton Rouge, LA)
8. Arthur W. Bergeron, Jr., *Guide to Louisiana Confederate Military Units 1861-1865* (Louisiana State University Press, Baton Rouge, LA: 1989), p. 113
9. James Dinkins, *By an Old Johnnie* (Morningside Bookshop, Dayton, OH: 1975), pp. 25-26
10. James W. Nicholson, *Stories of Dixie* (Claitor's Bookstore Publishing Division, Baton Rouge, LA: 1966), p. 57

11. *Records of Louisiana Confederate Soldiers and Louisiana Confederate Commands*, Andrew B. Booth, ed. (The Reprint Company, Publishers, Spartanburg, SC: 1984), vol. III, book 2, p. 276 (hereinafter cited as "Booth's Records")

12. *Brand Family History*, National Archives records, Morgan L. Brand

13. William Couper, *The Virginia Military Institute at the Battle of New Market* (William Couper), p. 28

14. Booth's Records, vol. III, book 1, p. 348

Bibliography

BOOKS

Abrams, M. H., *The Nortons Anthology of English Literature*, Third Edition, W. W. Norton and Company, New York, New York, 1974.

Alford, Terry, *Prince Among Slaves*, Oxford University Press, New York, New York, 1986.

Bergeron, Arthur W. Jr., *Guide to Louisiana Confederate Military Units 1861-1865*, Louisiana State University Press, Baton Rouge, Louisiana, 1989.

Bowers, Claude G., *The Tragic Era*, The Riverside Press, Cambridge, Massachusetts, 1929.

Bronouski, J. and Mazlish, Bruce, *The Western Intellectual Tradition*, Harper and Row, New York, New York, l960.

Brutus, Junius, *Vindiciae Contra Tyrannos*, reprint of 1689 translation, Still Waters Revival Books, Edmonton, Canada, 1989.

Buchanan, George, *De Jure Regni Apud Scotos*, reprint of 1799 edition, Sprinkle Publications, Harrisonburg, Virginia, 1982.

Buckingham, J. S., *The Slave States of America*, Negro University Press, New York, New York, 1968.

Burnham, James, *Suicide of the West*, The John Day Company, New York, New York, 1964.

Calhoun, John C., *The Works of John C. Calhoun*, D. Appleton and Company, New York, New York, l844.

Carpenter, Jesse T., *The South as a Conscious Minority*, The New York University Press, New York, New York, 1930.

Catton, Bruce, *Picture History of the Civil War*, Bonanza Books, New York, New York, 1982.

Cannon, Devereaux D., *The Flags of the Confederacy*, Pelican Publishing Company, Gretna, Louisiana, 1988.

Carson, Taylor, and Wallband, *Civilization Past and Present*, Vol. II,

Sixth Edition. Scott Foresman and Company, Glenview, Illinois, 1969.

Chesnut, Mary B., *Mary Chesnut's Civil War*, Yale University Press, New Haven, Connecticut, 1981.

Coughtry, Jay, *The Notorious Triangle*, Temple University Press, Philadelphia, Pennsylvania, 1981.

Curry, J. L. M., *The Southern States of the American Union*, B. F. Johnson Publishing Company, Richmond, Virginia, 1895.

Curtis, George M. III and Thompson James J. Jr., Ed., *The Southern Essays of Richard M. Weaver*, Liberty Press, Indianapolis, Indiana, 1987.

Dabney, R. L., *A Defense of Virginia and the South*, Sprinkle Publications, Harrisonburg, Virginia, 1977.

DeRosa, Marshall L., *The Confederate Constitution of 1861*, University of Missouri Press, Columbia and London, 1991.

de Tocqueville, Alexis, *Democracy in America*, Mayer and Lerner, Ed., Harper and Row, New York, New York, 1966.

Dethloff and Begnaud, *Our Louisiana Legacy*, Second Edition, Steck-Vaughn Company, Austin, Texas, 1980.

Dinkins, James, *By an Old Johnnie*, Morningside Bookshop, Dayton, Ohio, 1975.

Dow, George F., *Slave Ships and Slaving*, Kennikat Press, Inc., Port Washington, New York, 1969.

DuBois, W. E. B., *The Suppression of the African Slave-Trade to the United States of America*, Russell and Russell Inc., New York, New York, 1965.

Eakin, Sue L. and Peoples, Morgan, *In Defense of My Country*, Corney Creek Festival, Bernice, Louisiana, 1983.

Edmonds, David C., Ed., *The Conduct of Federal Troops in Louisiana*, The Acadiana Press, Lafayette, Louisiana, 1988.

Edmonds, David C., *Yankee Autumn in Acadiana*, The Acadiana Press, Lafayette, Louisiana, 1979.

Ferguson and McHenry, *The American Federal Government*, Mc-Graw-Hill, New York, New York, 1969.

Fischer, Louis, *The Life of Mahatma Gandhi*, Harper and Row, New York, New York, 1983.

Fisher, David H., *Albion's Seed*, Oxford University Press, New York, New York, 1989.

Fleming, Walter L., *The Sequel of Appomattox*, Glasgow, Brook and Company, Toronto, Canada, 1970.

Fogel, R. W. and Engerman, S. L., *Time on the Cross*, Little, Brown and Company, Boston, Massachusetts, 1974.

Friedman, Milton, *Free to Choose*, Harcourt Brace Jovanovich, New York, New York, 1980.

Greene, Lorenzo J., *The Negro in Colonial New England 1620-1776*, Kennikat Press, Inc., Port Washington, New York, 1966.

Griffin, Edward G., *The Fearful Master*, Western Island Press, Boston, Massachusetts, 1964.

Grissom, Michael A., *Southern by the Grace of God*, Pelican Publishing Company, Gretna, Louisiana, 1988.

Grissom, Michael A., *The Last Rebel Yell*, The Rebel Press, Nashville, Tennessee, 1919.

Haley, John H., *The Rebel Yell and Yankee Hurrah*, Ruth L. Silliker, Ed., Down East Books, Camden, Maine, 1985.

Hampton, Charles W., *Bill Yopp: Narrative of a Slave*, DeKalb Litho and Advertising, Avondale Estates, Georgia, 1969.

Hatcher, William E., *John Jasper: The Unmatched Black Philosopher and Preacher*, Sprinkle Publications, Harrisonburg, Virginia, 1985.

Hermann, Janet S., *Joseph E. Davis Pioneer Patriarch*, University Press of Mississippi, Jackson, Mississippi, 1990.

Howe, W. D., *Political History of Secession*, Putman's Sons, New York, New York, 1927.

Hughes, Merritt, Ed., *John Milton Complete Poems and Major Prose*, The Odyssey Press, Indianapolis/New York, 1957.

Humphreys, Henry S., *Songs of the Confederacy*, The Willis Music Company, Cincinnati, Ohio, 1961.

Hutchins, Maynard, Ed., *Great Books of the Western World*, Vol. 43, Encyclopedia Britannica, Chicago, Illinois, 1952.

Jennings, Thelma, *The Nashville Convention*, Memphis State University Press, Memphis, Tennessee, 1980.

Jensen, Merrill, *The New Nation*, Northeastern University Press, Boston, Massachusetts, 1981.

Johannsen, R. W., Ed., *The Lincoln-Douglas Debates of 1858*, Oxford University Press, New York, New York, 1965.

Johnson, Thomas C., *The Life and Letters of Robert Lewis Dabney*, Banner of Truth Trust, Edinburgh, Scotland, 1977.

Jones, J. William, *Christ in the Camp*, Sprinkle Publications, Harrisonburg, Virginia, 1986.

Kent, James, *Commentaries on American Law*, Da Capo Press, New York, New York, 1971.

Keys, Thomas B., *The Uncivil War: Union Army and Navy Excesses in the Official Records*, The Beauvoir Press, Biloxi, Mississippi, 1991.

Kilpatrick, James J., *The Sovereign States*, Henry Regnery Company, Chicago, Illinois, 1957.

Kirk, Russell, *John Randolph of Roanoke*, Liberty Press, Indianapolis, Indiana, 1978.

Koger, Larry, *Black Slaveowners*, McGarland and Company, Jefferson, North Carolina, 1985.

Lawrence, T. E., *Seven Pillars of Wisdom*, Doubleday, Doran and Company, Inc., Garden City, New York, New York, 1938.

Lawton, Edward P., *The South and the Nation*, The Island Press, Fort Myers Beach, Florida, 1963.

Machiavelli, Niccolo, *The Prince and the Discourses*, The Modern Library, Random House Inc., New York, New York, 1950.

Magruder, Harriet, *A History of Louisiana*, D. C. Heath and Company, Boston, Massachusetts, 1909.

Mannix, Daniel P., *Black Cargoes*, The Viking Press, New York, New York, 1962.

Marshall-Cornwall, Sir James, *Grant as a Military Commander*, Van Nostrand Reinhold Company, New York, New York, 1970.

McGuire, Herman M. Mrs., *McGuire Papers*, The Louisiana Society, Daughters of the American Revolution, N S D A R, 1966.

McManus, Edgar J., *Black Bondage in the North*, Syracuse University Press, Syracuse, New York, 1973.

McWhiney, Grady, *Cracker Culture: Celtic Ways in the Old South*, The University of Alabama Press, Tuscaloosa, Alabama, 1988.

Minor, Charles L. C., *The Real Lincoln*, Sprinkle Publications, Harrisonburg, Virginia, 1992.

Moore, George H., *Notes on the History of Slavery in Massachusetts*, D. Appleton and Company, New York, New York, 1866.

Mumford, Beverly B., *Virginia's Attitude Toward Slavery and Secession*, L. H. Jenkins, Inc., Richmond, Virginia, 1915.

Nichols, David A., *Lincoln and the Indians*, University of Missouri Press, Columbia, Missouri, 1978.

Nicholson, James W., *Stories of Dixie*, Claitor's Book Store Publishing Division, Baton Rouge, Louisiana, 1966.

Omlor, Patrick Henry, *The Hundred Years Hoax*, Aladextra Press, Menlo Park, California, 1966.

Owsley, Frank, L., *Plain Folk of the Old South*, Louisiana State University Press, Baton Rouge, Louisiana, 1949.

Owsley, Frank, et al., *I'll Take My Stand*, Louisiana State University Press, Baton Rouge, Louisiana, 1983.

Paiewonsky, Isidor, *Eyewitness Accounts of Slavery in the Danish West Indies*, Fordham University Press, New York, New York, 1989.

Perkins, Howard C., Ed., *Northern Editorials on Secession*, Vol. II, The American Historical Association, Gloucester, Massachusetts, 1964.

Pole, J. R., Ed., *The American Constitution for and against The Federalist and Anti-Federalist Papers*, Hill and Wang, New York, New York, 1987.

Pollard, Edward A., *A Southern History of the War*, The Fairfax Press, New York, New York, 1978.

Rawle, William, *A View of the Constitution of the United States of America*, H. C. Carey and Lea, Philadelphia, Pennsylvania, 1825.

Rawley, James A., *The Transatlantic Slave Trade*, W. W. Norton and Company, New York, New York, 1981.

Rozwenc, E. C., Ed., *The Causes of the American Civil War*, D. C. Heath and Company, New York, New York, 1961.

Rutherford, Mildred L., *Truths of History*, M. L. Rutherford, Athens, Georgia, 1907.

Rutherford, Samuel, *Lex Rex*, reprint of 1644 edition, Sprinkle Publications, Harrisonburg, Virginia, 1982.

Sabine, G. H., *A History of Political Theory*, Rinehart and Winston, New York, New York, 1961.

Scott, Otto, *The Secret Six*, Times Books, New York, New York, 1979.

Semmes, Raphael, *Memoirs of Service Afloat*, The Blue and Gray Press, Secaucus, New Jersey, 1987.

Servan-Schreiber, Jean-Jacques, *The Radical Alternative*, W. W. Norton and Company, Inc., New York, New York, 1971.

Simkins, Francis B., *A History of the South*, Alfred A. Knopf, New York, New York, 1959.

Skates, John R., *Mississippi's Old Capitol: Biography of a Building*, Mississippi Department of Archives and History, Jackson, Mississippi, 1990.

Springer, Francis W., *War for What?*, Bill Coats Ltd., Nashville, Tennessee, 1990.

Stampp, Kenneth, *The Peculiar Institution: Slavery in the Antebellum South*, Alfred A. Knopf, New York, New York, 1956.

Steffgen, Kent H., *The Bondage of the Free*, Vanguard Books, Berkeley, California, 1966.

Storing, H., Ed., *The Anti-Federalist*, "The Address and Reasons of Dissent of the Minority of the Convention of Pennsylvania to Their Constituents," The University of Chicago, Chicago, Illinois, 1985.

Thompson, David, Ed., *Political Ideas*, Basic Books, New York, New York, 1966.

Thompson, W. Y., *E. M. Graham North Louisianian*, Southwestern University Press, Lafayette, Louisiana, 1984.

Tilley, John S., *Facts the Historians Leave Out*, Bill Coats, Ltd., Nashville, Tennessee, 1990.

Tourgee, Albion, *A Fool's Errand*, The Belknap Press of Harvard University Press, Cambridge, Massachusetts, 1971.

Trollope, Anthony, *North America*, Alfred A. Knopf, New York, New York, 1951.

Tyler, Lyon G., *A Confederate Catechism*, Lyon G. Tyler, Holdcroft, Virginia, 1935.

Upshur, Abel P., *The Federal Government: Its True Nature and Character*, 1840, St. Thomas Press, Houston, Texas, 1977.

Walvin, James, *Slavery and the Slave Trade*, University Press of Mississippi, Jackson, Mississippi, 1983.

Weaver, Richard M., *The Southern Tradition at Bay*, Arlington House, New Rochelle, New York, 1968.

Williams, T. Harry, *P. G. T. Beauregard: Napoleon in Gray*, Louisiana State University Press, Baton Rouge, Louisiana, 1954.

Wilkens, Steven J., *America: The First 350 Years*, Covenant Publications, Monroe, Louisiana, 1988.

Winters, John D., *The Civil War in Louisiana*, Louisiana State University Press, Baton Rouge, Louisiana, 1963.

Wright, Gavin, *Old South, New South*, Basic Books, Inc., New York, New York, 1986.

NEWSPAPERS

Charlotte Observer, Charlotte, North Carolina, April 25, 1982.

Daily Clarion Ledger, Jackson, Mississippi, February 23, 1890.

Evening Post, New York, New York, March 12, 1861.

The New York Times, New York, New York, March 23, 1861.

The New York Times, New York, New York, March 30, 1861.

The Shreveport Times, Shreveport, Louisiana, April 1990.

Times Democrat, Memphis, Tennessee, June 4, 1891.

Union Democrat, Manchester, New Hampshire, February 19, 1861.

Vicksburg Evening Post, Vicksburg, Mississippi, June 28, 1985.

Vicksburg Sunday Post, Vicksburg, Mississippi, September 23, 1984.

MAGAZINES AND JOURNALS

Chronicles, March 1989.

Civil War History, Kent State University Press, Vol. XXXII, No. 3, 1986.

Civil War Magazine, Berryville, Virginia, Vol. VIII, No. 3, Issue XXIII.

Civil War Quarterly, Vol. VIII.

Confederate Veteran, Houston, Texas, November-December 1989.

Confederate Veteran, Houston, Texas, November-December 1990.

Confederate Veteran, Vol. XXXII, No. 10, October 1924.

Georgia Historical Quarterly, Vol. LXVII, No. 2, Summer 1983.

Harper's Magazine, New York, New York, Vol. LXIX, No. CCCCXIII, October 1884.

Journal of Mississippi History, Jackson, Mississippi, Vol. XLII, May 1980.

Lagniappe, A Journal of the Old South, Oxford, Mississippi, Spring 1974.

North American Review, Boston, Massachusetts, Vol. XXII, April 1825.

Pacific Marine Review, October.

The Century Magazine, New York, New York, Vol. LXXVIII, 1909.

The Georgia Journal of Southern Legal History, Vol. I, No. 1, Atlanta, Georgia, Spring-Summer 1991.

Scribner's Magazine, Vol. XXVIII, No. 1, July 1900.

Southern Partisan, Columbia, South Carolina, Second Quarter, 1989.

Southern Partisan, Columbia, South Carolina, Third Quarter, 1991.

Stetson Law Review, Vol. XV, No. 2, St. Petersburg, Florida, Stetson University College of Law, 1986.

U.S. News and World Report, January 26, 1970.

GENERAL REFERENCE BOOKS

A Checklist of American Imprints for 1825, Richard H. Shoemaker, Ed., Metuchen, New Jersey, 1969.

Dictionary of American Biography, Vol. XV, Dumas Malone, Ed., Charles Scribner's Sons, New York, New York, 1935.

Journal of the House of Representatives, of the State of Mississippi, Regular Session Thereof, convened January 7, 1890, Jackson, Mississippi.

Messages and Papers of the Confederacy, Vol. I, James D. Richardson, Ed., United States Publishing Company, 1906, Nashville, Tennessee.

Records of Louisiana Confederate Soldiers and Louisiana Confederate Commands, Andrew B. Booth, Ed., Spartanburg, South Carolina, 1984.

The Centennial of the United States Military Academy at West Point, New York, Vol. I, Washington, D.C., 1904.

The National Cyclopaedia of American Biography, Vol. VII, James T. White and Company, 1897.

War of the Rebellion: Official Records of Union and Confederate Armies, Washington, D.C., 1884.

War of the Rebellion: Official Records of the Union and Confederate Navies, Washington, D.C., 1884.

FAMILY HISTORIES

Our Kith & Kin, Helen B. Wasson, Gateway Press, Baltimore, Maryland, 1986.

Stewart Family History, Stewart University Press, Centre, Alabama, 1976.

MISCELLANEOUS WORKS

The Gray Book, Jennings, Arthur H., Chairman, The Gray Book Committee, Sons of Confederate Veterans, Hattiesburg, Mississippi.

The Untold Story of the Battle of Gatlinburg, First Edition, Brannon Publishing Company, Division of the Georgia Mint, Inc., 1991.

Virginia Military Institute and the Battle of New Market, Col. William Couper.

Letter from Jim Holliman to Henry Holleman, November 17, 1929, in the possession of James K. Turner, Nashville, Tennessee.

The Unconstitutional Fourteenth Amendment, Kenneth S. Coe, Fredericksburg, Virginia (unpublished manuscript, copy in possession of the authors).

Index